1,107 Baby Names That Stand the Test *of* Time

JENNIFER GRIFFIN

WORKMAN PUBLISHING • NEW YORK

For CD, LVD, and JLD

Library of Congress Cataloging-in-Publication Data is available.

ISBN 978-0-7611-8016-6

Previously published as *Bring Back Beatrice!*

Cover design by Janet Vicario

Cover composite: Babies: HaywireMedia/fotolia and hartphotography/fotolia, Frame: Zakharov Evgeniy/fotolia.

Interior design by Jen Browning

Workman books are available at special discounts when purchased in bulk for premiums and sales promotions as well as for fund-raising or educational use. Special editions or book excerpts also can be created to specification. For details, contact the Special Sales Director at the address below or send an email to specialmarkets@workman.com.

Workman Publishing Company, Inc.
225 Varick Street
New York, NY 10014-4381
workman.com

WORKMAN is a registered trademark of
Workman Publishing Co., Inc.

Printed in the United States of America
First printing March 2014

10 9 8 7 6 5 4 3 2 1

Contents

Introduction

Name That Baby!

Congratulations! If you've picked up this book, you or someone you love is expecting a baby. There is a lot to do to prepare for your new family member's arrival, and one of the most important (and exciting) tasks is to choose your baby's name.

Shakespeare famously asked "What's in a name?" and suggested that names don't matter ("A rose by any other name would smell as sweet"). Most of us disagree with him. Names matter immensely. They tell the world in one stroke a lot about you and your family. They can reveal when or where you were born, your religion or culture, and your family's values and hopes for you. They can suggest your parents' education level, their passions, and whether they're traditional or free-spirited. They can help you blend in with the crowd or stand out. Names are powerful stuff.

And names, like so many other things in our lives, follow trends. Names become popular in waves and sometimes we can tell why—an actor or character inspires namesakes—and other times it just seems like many parents have had the same idea at the same time. Parents nowadays are more adventurous than ever with the names they give their children. It was only a few decades ago that John and Mary were the top picks, having held their positions for a century or more. Now, the names we choose range from the traditional (Emily; Michael) to the unorthodox (Madison; Logan) and include many trendy picks as well (Kayla; Jayden).

What's So Great About Timelessness?

This book's title is a nod to all the traditional but underutilized names out there. (It could just as easily have been called *Bring Back Barbara!, Where Have All the Ritas Gone?,* or *I Like Mike!*) And it's a clarion call to parents to break away from the pack when choosing a name for their child. Although you may find yourself suddenly loving the name Emma, for example, as if it came to you out of the blue, keep in mind that your ardor may be influenced by the name's recent surge in popularity. If you find a name you love but that's also outrageously popular, remember that you don't have to follow the crowd (unless you really want to).

In addition to traditional names that make excellent choices today, the book includes the most popular picks—with warnings if I think they may be *too* popular—as well as trendy choices, quirky ideas, and other clever, interesting names. Overall, the book's focus is on names that are *real*: names that will stand the test of time, reflect your values, and bring joy to your child. To that end, I do not hold back when I'm concerned that a name has become too widespread or sounds made up. I believe you should be informed when a name that seems traditional (such as Nevaeh, which many people believe related to the Irish name Niamh) is in fact a recent fabrication (Nevaeh is the word *Heaven* spelled backward). As always, knowledge is power.

Look Before You Leap

Take some time to think about what makes a name appealing to you. In the case of Emma, it might be its old-fashioned charm. So you might consider something similar like Lydia, Amelia, or Beatrice. (I call these the Colonial graveyard names. If you go to an old cemetery anywhere in New England, these are the ladies—along with Lucy, Abigail, Sophia, Isabelle, Olivia, and Hannah—you'll find there.) If the reason you like the name is the sound rather than the effect, then consider Alma, Tessa, or Zara. These have similarly feminine, comforting sounds. Any of these alternative options means that your child will still have a name steeped in tradition, but she will not be one of many in her class.

Some parents dislike traditional names and want to go with something really cool, really different. Like Madison. What a great idea for a girl! It's so unusual that nobody else will have it. Except that many parents are thinking the same thing. And many of them are going to choose Madison as well. In this case, I suggest

TAKE IT FROM A JENNIFER

Years ago, my friend Scott gave me a cartoon by Jack Ziegler that had appeared in *The New Yorker* in 1980. It was a drawing of a group of children having their nursery school class photo taken. Underneath the picture were the names of the children: Scott, Jennifer, Jennifer, Scott, Jennifer, Jennifer, Scott, and so on.

Maybe you have to be a Jennifer or a Scott to think it's funny. But let me tell you, there are a LOT of Jennifers and Scotts around to appreciate the joke. Why? Because Jennifer and Scott were the two most popular names for girls and boys from around 1970 to 1984. I could try to lie about my age, but my name will always give me away. And there are so many Jennifers around that I will never be anybody's only Jennifer. So *please* think long and hard before you give your child a name that is the most popular in the land.

you heed the Baby Naming Cardinal Rule: You can't go wrong with something traditional, no matter how popular the name becomes. My belief is that you are better off being one of a crowd of Emmas than one of many Madisons. Being one of many Madisons is more difficult because the name is so strong, so unorthodox, and has become so popular, that it is going to fall fast and hard. Trendy names tend to spike and then disappear. So if you learn that the name you love is in vogue, think before you commit to it. And if, after consideration, the name hasn't lost its luster, then proceed with confidence.

On Provenance

The call for a return to names like Beatrice is also a nod to provenance. We've become incredibly sophisticated consumers. We care about the origins of the things in our lives. We buy our organic food from local producers. We know where our T-shirts were made. We drink coffee from fair trade companies. We are very responsible about many of our choices nowadays because we know that they have consequences. We should care at least as much about what we name our children and should know as much about their names as we do about our groceries. You should be able to tell your child exactly why you named him as you did: why the name is special to you;

where it comes from; what it means; and what you hope it will bring him. The act should be conscious, deliberate, organic.

If you live green (or at least greener than your parents did), you should name green. The name Beatrice or any other traditional name is like a fine piece of china. I think of names like this—names with a past—as well-used, well-made, well-loved heirlooms that you can pass down to your child. Trendy, made-up names strike me as the equivalent of Styrofoam cups. They were whipped up recently, en masse—carelessly in some cases—and won't be around for very long.

How to Use This Book

It's clear that naming is serious business, but it is also fun. One of the great joys of being pregnant is wondering who will arrive and what the perfect

---

BRING IT BACK!

As you flip through the pages that follow, you'll see that some names are set off with a cute little $\wp$. These safety pin icons echo the intent of the book—they highlight the names that have fallen out of favor (or haven't yet received their due) and deserve to be discovered anew.

name for that new person will be. Many books offer suggestions for tens of thousands of names. This book is more discriminating, offering the *best* choices. It also gives you the tools you need to pick the ideal name for your baby. Together we'll look at rhyme scheme, tonal qualities, length, nicknames, family connections, and other factors that may help you make your decision. You will also find many boxes throughout the book that group names by category, help you work backward from the nickname, and make other informative observations about names.

When Michelangelo was asked how he carved the *David*, he is said to have replied that he just removed all of the marble that wasn't David. Naming should work similarly. You should do the research and then rule out everything that isn't your own, wonderful, unique baby. In short, this book provides everything you need to find the perfect name that your child was meant to have.

The Rules of the Name

There are no official rules for naming, but there should be. You need to consider sound, sense, your family's particular circumstances, monograms, nicknames, and more. Play by the rules and you are guaranteed to hit on the perfect name for your baby.

SCANSION

Scansion is the rhythm of the name. The word comes from the Latin for "to climb," the sense being that the meters of lines of poetry rise and fall like mountaintops. How does your choice of name scan? Ann Beck lands with two thuds. Anastasia Beck, on the other hand, is quite lovely. It skips flirtatiously off the tongue. The poetry of the name has been considered.

Behold the rules of rhythm:

1. Go for contrast. Jane Doe is boring. Ace Wright is wrong. Better to pair two or three syllables with a single-syllable last name (doesn't Madeline Doe sound better than Jane?) or a short first name with a long last name (Ace Thibodeau works well). Say the name out loud: If it sounds like it's from a nursery rhyme (like Jack Sprat or Simple Simon), keep looking.

2. Contrast matters less the more syllables you are dealing with. One syllable-one syllable (as in May Kent) is usually pretty clunky—it hits you over the head. Two syllables-two syllables (as in Sally Rodgers) is better. Three-three (Caroline Rodriguez) is better still.

The more syllables you have to work with, the more leeway there is. One reason for this is that the emphasis may fall on a different beat of the name. In the example above, Caroline Rodriguez sounds great despite the fact that both names contain three syllables. Why? In Caroline, the emphasis falls on the first syllable: CA-ro-line. In Rodriguez, it falls on the second: rod-RI-guez. This creates contrast between the names.

3. Sounds can compensate for syllables. Most likely, your last name isn't going to change. So look at the qualities of it and see if you can choose a first name that contrasts with the sounds. For instance, the last name Beck sounds like a peck or a jab. It has a sharp, abrupt sound, and Ann, in its own way, does, too. If the fictional Beck family really wanted a one-syllable first name, then softer sounding names might work: Faye Beck sounds better than Ann Beck because the dreamy, vowel-y sound of Faye (and visually, the *e* on the end) helps to create contrast between first and last names.

VOWEL SOUNDS, CONSONANT SOUNDS

Look for contrasting sounds in the names. Sharon Parrish was glad to take her husband's last name because she didn't like the flat *a* sound that occurred in both her first and last names. It was made worse by the fact that both *a*'s are followed by *r*'s and the fact that both names have two syllables. Similarly, Maisie Day is a great stage name or dog's name, but it's less successful for a little girl—the *a* sounds are just too strong. Even worse would be Daisy Day, where the vowels and the consonants repeat. Daisy Duke sounds much better: The initial consonants are the same, but the dissimilarity of the vowels makes the pairing pleasing to the ear.

LENGTH

Does the name pass the American Express card test? Lindsay Shyllon de Vaubicourt's name does not; it's way too long to put on plastic. Although Lindsay's problems are of her own making—she chose to incorporate her maiden name (Shyllon) into her married name (de Vaubicourt)—she was smart on her daughter's behalf: de Vaubicourt is a long and foreign

DOES IT TRANSLATE?

If you travel often, you might want to think about what happens when you take your child's name overseas. Little Hugh was two years old when he went to France. His parents arrived at passport control at Charles de Gaulle airport, submitted their paperwork, and waited. The inspector stamped it and then cheerfully said, "Bienvenue, Ugg!" The French, the Dutch, nearly everyone in Europe has a LOT of trouble with the name Hugh. No matter. When Hugh travels abroad, he introduces himself as Hugo, which is in the top ten in several European countries—very

name (unless you are in France), so her daughter is the simple but lovely (and increasingly popular) Ella de Vaubicourt.

FOREIGN AFFAIRS

Is your last name long and complicated? How about giving your child a break and making the first name short and easy. John Vanikiotis is a better name for an American boy (no matter how strong his ties to Greece) than Apostolios Vanikiotis. Not only will it simplify the child's life, but the contrast will be pleasing. Is your last name short and generic? Then consider a more ornate first name. If you are a Smith or a Jones, you can get away with a much more exotic

familiar. Jennifers don't fare much better. In France, Jen frequently becomes Jane, which seems easier for people. In Italy, I gave up altogether and started inviting people to call me Giovanna, which is about as close as it gets. Even if you are not a big traveler, it's smart to consider the common variants of your child's name. Louisiana-born food writer Paul Johnson found his name a bit bland, so he became Pableaux Johnson. Nothing bland about that. In fact, it's about as spicy as a bayou jambalaya. And you'll find that he can be Googled with no problem now.

first name than most other people, whereas simple names like John and Jane will be trickier for you.

BACKGROUND

Is there a family connection? It's grounding to name your child after a beloved family member. Your child will ask why you named him Vincent and you'll be able

---

THE FLAKY TEST

If you are considering an unorthodox name (or a name with an unorthodox spelling) for your child and are unsure about it, try these tests to determine if it works.

✦ Imagine your child saying, "Ladies and gentlemen, I'd like to welcome you aboard the aircraft. I'm your captain, [name] . . ."

✦ Imagine your doctor tells you that you need to see a specialist about your condition and hands you a business card. Imagine your child's name on that card with a medical specialty below it.

✦ Imagine a political advertisement with your child facing the camera saying, "I'm [name] and I endorse this message."

✦ Imagine a court bailiff announcing a trial and saying, "Court is in session, the honorable judge [name] presiding."

Your child may never find herself in any of these jobs, but wouldn't you like

to tell him that it was your grandfather's middle name. You'll give your child a tie to the past, and will be able to regale him with stories about all the wonderful, witty, wise things your grandfather did and said. If you want to cast a wider net for a meaningful name, ask your older relatives to help you make a family tree or point you to the family graveyard. You might be

to think that she could be anything she wants? Personally I'd rather be flown by Captain Amanda than Captain Aspen. I would think that Doctor Charles Someone would be more competent than Doctor Caden Someone. I'm unlikely to vote for Blossom or Blaze. And I would want my judge not to be named Jaxon or Journey.

What if you want your child to be a rock star? Should you give him or her a rock star name?

No. Give him a name that will work in any situation and if he wants a cooler name for show business, he'll change it himself. Kiss's Gene Simmons was born Chaim. Guns N' Roses front man Axl Rose was born William. Lady Gaga's real name is Stefani. The list of entertainers who have renamed themselves is long and distinguished. Remember: It's easier to create and adopt a quirky stage name than it is to legally change your name to something traditional.

astonished by the ancestors you find there and how cool their names were.

PLAY THE MIDDLE CARD

You *can* have it both ways: It is traditional to give a child a first name and a middle name. So if on the one hand you want your child to have a very traditional name but at the same time you wish you could really go crazy, then John Pilot Inspektor it is. (Pilot Inspektor is the real name of actor Jason Lee's son.) If he becomes a pop icon, he can sign his checks J. Pilot Inspektor Robinson; if he becomes a brain surgeon, he can be Dr. John P. I. Robinson. The middle name offers a great opportunity to include a family name that doesn't pass muster as a first name. (Say you hate the name Helen but your mother has her heart set on it. Throw the unwanted Helen in the middle and everybody wins.) Middle names can convey an attribute that you want your child to have but that perhaps doesn't seem appropriate for top billing. For example, you love the outdoors and want your daughter's name to include a nature reference, but you're worried about saddling her with something that sounds flighty or flaky. So instead of naming her Meadow or Rain, you might choose a more traditional first name and end up with something like Elizabeth Meadow Jones or Michelle Rain Cohen.

NICKNAMEPALOOZA

Nicknames offer an exciting loophole to tradition.
You can choose a weighty name and use a nickname
as a fun, playful workaround. So, instead of naming
your child, say, Coco, as actress Courteney Cox did,
why not name her Corinne, Colette, or Charlotte, and
shorten to Coco for her nickname? In fact, you could
name her just about anything you want and still call
her Coco. Then in the future, if she wants to run for
public office, she'll have a name that is seemly; and if
later she decides the senate isn't for her and she wants
to move to Hollywood and see her name in lights,
she'll have a zippy alternative ready to go.

If you want to ramp up your child's nickname
options, consider longer versions of shorter names,
for example, Susannah instead of Susan. Susan might
be nicknamed Suzy or Sue, but with Susannah, you get
Suzy, Sue, and Anna, too.

ETHNIC TRADITION

Is there something in your family customs that offers
a guideline? Traditionally, Catholics named their
children after saints. (It can be the middle name if you
want to go exotic for the first.) Many Jewish people
name their children after deceased relatives; never a
living one. And some Africans use names that describe
the circumstances surrounding a baby's birth (for
example, a name might indicate the day a girl is born,

or whether a boy is the second child). Every culture has its own traditions and many families have their own subtraditions. Think about following yours. It may help you to at least focus your search.

CULTURAL CONNECTIONS

Do you know why people don't name baby boys Adolf? Of course you do. It's a distinctive name with very negative associations. Ditto Ebenezer. Make sure you

ALL IN THE FAMILY

There are many family issues that arise when it comes to naming children. Here are some of the most common questions parents have about baby naming "etiquette":

Q: If the parents are from two different backgrounds, how do you find a name that works for both sides?

A: You negotiate. You'd be surprised how many names work for multiple cultures or at least travel well. The need

to please more than one culture can actually make your selection easier by limiting it.

Q: If you and your sister both love the same baby name, who gets to use it?

A: First come, first served. Don't wait or you may lose out on that great name you both love! But if someone more distant—say a cousin or close friend—uses the name you'd like to choose, it's polite to let that person

thoroughly investigate the names you like to ensure that your child doesn't end up Charles Manson Riley or something else inappropriate.

Similarly, you'll want to be mindful of last name agreement. Does your last name, when paired with the baby's first, create a combination that's unavoidably tease-able? For instance, if your last name were the perfectly lovely Lane, you might think twice before naming your child Penelope. Even if you never called

know in advance of your plans, saying something like, "We've always loved the name José and never more so than since we've come to know your adorable José. We'd like to name our baby after him and hope you'll be okay with that." If the cousin or friend has chosen a very distinctive, little-used name—such as Clementine—then think twice and see if there is any other name that will please you. It is a bit strange to have two in the family or in your circle of friends unless it's a name that comes down through your family.

Q: If your parents hate the name you've chosen, what should you do?

A: Ignore them. They'll probably come around when they meet the new addition to the family. And even if they continue to hate the name, they won't love the little one any less.

her Penny, others would. Walker is a nice last name, too, but if it were yours, you'd probably want to stay away from Luke as a first name (Skye would be even worse). And it goes without saying that you don't want to give your child a name that makes a silly sentence: Consider the unfortunate Ima Hogg and Curtis Strange (the real names of a philanthropist and a golfer on the PGA tour, respectively).

If your child wants to do something ridiculous with his name, let him do so himself—it could be a part of his teenage rebellion. There's no need to give him a head start.

REMEMBER THE MONOGRAM

When it comes to baby naming, a bit of foresight can work wonders. Katherine Iris Grant was going to be named Patricia until her parents realized that her initials would read "PIG." Needless to say, Katherine is relieved she didn't have to face endless taunts of "oink" on the playground.

HOW WILL IT PLAY OUT IN THE SCHOOLYARD?

Booker could be a very cool name. Just realize that for several years little Booker may be known as Booger. Simeon looks very current, too, but it sounds just like simian, which high school smart alecks may want to point out means "apelike." Silly playground jeers and misunderstandings may be no reason to nix a great name, but it's best to name baby with your eyes wide open.

Naming Trends

You now have some guidelines to help steer you clear of the most common baby naming pitfalls. But before you jump in with a splash, you may want to consider what's happening in the world of baby name trends.

1. Exotic letters are hot. If you want to pick a name that will be on-trend and irreproachably hip, get your Scrabble game and take out all the letters that have high point values. These are the exotic letters that don't occur often in speech and tend to have an edgy sound to them, especially: *X, Y, Z, J, K, V,* and *W.* (*Q, F,* and *H* are exceptions.) Any name that contains one or more of these letters is almost guaranteed to be fashionable. Examples include: Maddox, Jake, Vivienne, Elijah, Olivia, Ava, Alexis, Gavin, Zach, Kylie, Mackenzie, and Wyatt.

2. Colonial graveyard names are in fashion. Everything old is new again. As I mentioned on page ix, if you take a tour of an old graveyard in New England, you will see all the same names you hear in the sandbox: Lucy, Abigail, Emily, Sophia, Isabella, Hannah, et al. Even the boys are returning to tradition:

James, Noah, Owen, Benjamin, and Gabriel are there. (Or as Adam Gopnik hilariously notes in his book *Paris to the Moon*, kids these days are "the men your grandfather used to take a shvitz with": Sam, Max, Harry, Joe.)

3. People play it safe—and traditional—with boys; they are looser and more creative with girls. There are Haydens and Jaydens and Paxtons, to be sure, as well as Billy, Sam, and Joe (in addition to William, Samuel, and Joseph) but you'll find fewer flights of fancy overall with boys' names. Folks seem to think that girls can get away with creative names while boys are better served with more serious choices.

4. Pop culture has a strong pull on what we name our children. Movies and TV can have dramatic effects on naming patterns. Lara fell into heavy rotation as a girl's name in 1966 after the film *Doctor Zhivago* was released. The year 1966 also saw the boy's name Heath hit the charts. Modern parents think of actor Heath Ledger but it was Lee Majors's character in the TV series *Big Valley* that launched it. Logan as a girl's name was inspired by a character from the late 1980s soap *The Bold and the Beautiful*. Most of us do not run out and name our kids exactly what the celebrities are naming theirs, but film and

TV characters—and the actors who portray them—
have a powerful influence on our imaginations.

5. Unisex names are hot. Peyton, Jordan, Taylor.
Today's unisex names are not the nicknames of yore
(see "It's Pat," page 476); they are more likely to be
place-names, occupational names (see pages 316–317),
or last names turned first names.

**6. When a unisex name gets taken up by the
girls, the boys drop it.** Usually the boys start using
a unisex name, parents fall in love with it, it becomes
popular, and then the girls start claiming it as their own.
Once the girls start embracing a name in numbers, it
becomes thought of as a girl's name, and the boys' use
of it declines quickly.

7. Beware the Frankenname. What's a
frankenname? Take a part of one name and mash
it into another one, stitch it up, and you've got a
frankenname. Jayla is Jada meets Kayla. Ashlynn is
Ashley meets Lynn. Kyler is Kyle meets Tyler. *J* and
K names are the worst offenders in this category. And
the girls are usually bigger offenders than the boys.

8. Exotic spellings can look déclassé. There, I've
said it. You may not want to hear it but Kaitlynn doesn't
look as dignified as Caitlin. Kaydence doesn't look as

smart as Cadence. However, Erik looks just as good as Eric and Marc looks just as good as Mark, because both variations of the name exist legitimately. Erik is the Scandinavian version of Eric. Marc is the French version of Mark. So if you are using a newer, made-up (see "Beware the Frankenname," page xxvii), or exotic name, try at least to make the spelling normal.

9. Names look smart when they're trending upward, low-rent on the way down. Here is how naming trends work: People of influence choose a name that is unusual for their baby. Others of their set do the same, and then others follow suit until the name becomes popular. Then these same parents— who are always searching for the next, cool thing— move on to a new name, dropping the too-popular one that has been "discovered" by the masses. Meanwhile, the name darling of the trendsetter set catches on with the hoi polloi just as the name is starting to lose its luster and caché. The name then becomes known as something mainstream and even lowbrow, and gets a bad reputation. (There is a more detailed explanation of this phenomenon in the bestselling book *Freakonomics*, which contains a fascinating chapter on baby names.)

10. You can't go wrong with tradition. No matter how popular a name is, if it is a solid choice with a strong background, it will not risk sounding questionable. Classics never go out of style.

AN IMPORTANT NOTE ABOUT TRENDS

The popularity rankings referred to throughout this book come from the United States government's Social Security Administration (SSA), which has been keeping good records of baby names for more than a hundred years. The SSA posts the top 1,000 most popular boys' and girls' names each year, and also has a searchable database that allows you to assess the trendiness of your top picks; to do so, visit the website at www.ssa.gov/OACT/ babynames/. While naming trends in other English-speaking countries differ somewhat, the patterns are largely similar. If you are eager to find the official records from another country, try Googling terms like "baby names bureau of statistics Canada." (You can replace "Canada," of course, with the name of any country.)

The Names

Girls

A

Aaliyah An Arabic name, Aaliyah means "lofty" or "exalted." It reminds Americans of the late R&B singer of the same name. This ornate name complements many Muslim and African last names and offers great contrast to short, blunt surnames like Jones and Smith. Used almost exclusively by African American families, it is the female counterpart of the boy's name Ali.

Variations: *Aleah, Alea, Aliya, Alia, Aleeya, Aliyah, Allyiah*
Nicknames: *Liya, Ali*
Alternatives: *Malia, Aisha, Leila, Latifah, Bashira, Farrah, Salma*

Abigail Extremely popular in colonial times, Abigail fell out of favor in the early 1900s but has come roaring back. Now it's one of the most popular names out there (at the time of writing, it's in the top ten). It's a name that suggests reliability (Abigail Adams and Dear Abby) but is also pretty, feminine, and melodic (like the word *nightingale*). In the Old Testament,

Abigail is David's third wife. The name means
"a father's joy" or "giver of joy."

Variations: *Abagail, Abbigail, Abigayle*
Nicknames: *Abbey, Abbie, Abby, Abi, Gail, Gayle*
Alternatives: *Amelia, Lydia, Clara, Tabitha*

✒ **Ada** and its variations appear in many cultures
from Hebrew ("adornment") to German ("noble")
to African ("first daughter"). Ada is an old-fashioned
name that is on the rise. It sounds similar to the
überpopular Ava, but is distinct enough to make it an
excellent alternative. If you like Ada, consider using it
as a nickname and making her full name Adelaide.

Alternatives: *Lara, Enid, Mara*

Addison A last name turned first name, Addison
("son of Adam") was extremely rare until the 1990s.
It is climbing in popularity as it becomes fashionable
to give girls edgy, nontraditional names. (The popular
TV show *Private Practice* features a character called
Addison.) Addison offers the same benefits as Madison,
but since it is just a bit different, it's a smart pick for
parents who don't want the most popular name on the
playground. The name has a solid, patrician quality but
remains pretty, with hints of Allison and Adelaide.

Variations: *Addisyn, Addyson, Adyson, Adison*
Nickname: *Addy*
Alternatives: *Emerson, Darcy, Lacey, Cameron, Jordan, Kennedy*

✎ **Adelaide** We have King William IV of England to thank for the popularity in English of this German name. When the king married German princess Adelaide in 1818, interest in the name surged. The city of Adelaide in Australia was named for the queen in 1836, spreading the name even farther afield. Adelaide ("noble") is a name that had all but disappeared and is now being rediscovered. No wonder: it's lilting, feminine, and a clever alternative to more popular choices like Abigail and Amelia. And the name even has its own lullaby: You can serenade her with "Adelaide" from the musical *Guys and Dolls*.

Variations: *Adalaide, Adalayde, Adeline (also Adelyn), Adalyn (also Adalynn), Adele, Adela, Adelina*

Nicknames: *Ada, Addy (and variant spellings), Della, Delly, Laidey, Heidi*

Alternatives: *Clementine, Philippa, Imogen, Edwina, Beatrice, Lydia*

Adriana (and her more traditional cousin, Adrienne) means "from Hadria," or, as we know it, the Adriatic region, which borders the Adriatic Sea and includes Dalmatia and eastern Italy. The name can therefore be a salute to an Italian or Slavic heritage, a trip to the breathtaking beaches in the area (perhaps where the baby was conceived?), even a love of the ocean. Or it can be appreciated just for its beauty. Adriana is sweet and calming, with lots of vowels comfortably bobbing

Noble Names

The royals of Europe—past and present—offer a source of names that are regal (of course), feminine, and in many cases, unexpected.

- ADELA
- ADELAIDE
- AGNES
- ALICE
- BEATRICE
- BLANCHE
- ELEANOR
- ELENA

- EUGENIE
- GABRIELLA
- GRACE
- HENRIETTA
- ISABEAU
- ISABELLE
- JOAN
- MARGARET

- MARIE
- MARINA
- MATILDA
  (aka Maude)
- PHILIPPA
- SOPHIE
- VICTORIA
- ZARA

along on its many syllables. It's a great contrast to a plain last name or a complement to a complex one. Names starting and/or ending with *a* are in fashion now, and Adriana fits the bill with a bonus *a* in the middle. It doesn't get more feminine than this.

Variations: *Adrienne, Adrianna, Adria*
Alternatives: *Tatianna, Anabella, Juliana, Marianna, Gabriella, Natalia*

Agatha means "good." The name may sound British to our ears, thanks to prolific mystery writer Agatha Christie. If you prefer something that sounds Italian or Spanish, try Agata; there's also the elegant French version, Agathe (ah-GAT). Aggie is a cute alternative to the ubiquitous Abbie.

Variations: *Agata, Agathe*
Nickname: *Aggie*
Alternatives: *Matilda, Cornelia, Agnes, Hermione*

Agnes Old-fashioned and religious, Agnes means "holy." And it's so similar to the Latin word for "lamb" (*agnus*) that the name is strongly associated with it. Agnes is a traditional name in Catholic countries. Consider alternate pronunciations and variations on it: Inez (or Inès) is Spanish. The French pronounce

Isn't She Cute?

You can take any girl's name and make it cuter by adding a diminutive suffix that means "little one." Here are some of the top choices:

- ~ **ITA:** *Eva becomes Evita. Edite (Edith) becomes Edita. Mary becomes Marita.*

- ~ **ETTE:** *Georgia becomes Georgette. Paula becomes Paulette. Claude becomes Claudette.*

- ~ **EEN:** *Peg becomes Pegeen. Maura becomes Maureen. Dorothy becomes Doreen.*

- ~ **BELLE:** *Belle means "little pretty one." Mary becomes Maribelle. Anna becomes Annabelle. Sarah becomes Sarabelle.*

- ~ **SHKA:** *A Slavic favorite. Maria becomes Marishka. Natalie becomes Natashka. Anna becomes Anushka.*

Agnès a lovely way (ahn-YEHZ), as do the Italians, with Agnese (ahn-YAY-zay). The model Agyness Deyn and the French clothing chain Agnès B. may have paved the way for a comeback.

Variations: *Inez, Inès, Agnese, Agness, Agnetha (remember the ABBA singer?)*
Nickname: *Aggie*
Alternatives: *Harriet, Agatha, Anais, Frances, Eleanor*

Aida The heroine of one of Verdi's most beloved operas, Aida is an Ethiopian princess enslaved in Egypt and in love with one of the pharaoh's confidants, Radames. The name is Arabic in origin, meaning "visitor." It's often used by African American families to celebrate African roots as well as by Italian American families to pay tribute to Verdi. Arabic families who use the name or variations on it often pronounce it with two syllables (EYE-dah) rather than three (eye-EE-dah).

Variations: *Ayda, Aita, Aeeda*
Alternatives: *Ida, Candace, Iman, Aisha, Tosca*

Aileen You can think of Aileen as the English version of the very Irish Eileen, which is itself a version of Helen (meaning "sunshine" or "moonlight"). Or you can just think of it as an airy and light musical name in its own right. While many names ending in *een* have fallen from fashion (Kathleen, Colleen, Maureen),

Aileen's gentle start leavens the heavier ending of the name and makes it girlish and contemporary.

Variations: *Ailene, Ailyn, Alene, Aline, Eileen, Ileana, Ilene, Iliana, Leanne, Liana*
Nicknames: *Ailie, Lena, Lina*
Alternatives: *Alina, Elena, Hailey, Francine, Melody, Kathleen, Colleen, Maeve*

Aimée means "loved" or "beloved" in French. This version of Amy can be pronounced like the traditional Amy or like the French "EHM-ay." The risk here is that whatever pronunciation you choose, others may pick a different one. Adding the acute accent—like a little check of approval—to the first *e* will help people realize it should be pronounced in the French way.

Variation: *Amy*
Alternatives: *Carine, Jolie, Bella, Anais, Amélie, Aurelie, Noemi, Elodie*

Ainsley A last name turned first name, Ainsley is growing in popularity for girls and boys alike. It has a whiff of southern belle to it, in part because many Dixie girls can take a masculine name and make it ladylike faster than you can whistle "Dixie," and in part because the TV show *The West Wing* featured a character from the South called Ainsley. In the U.K., the first Ainsley that leaps to mind is the male cook and TV personality Ainsley Harriott.

Variation: *Ansley*
Alternatives: *Dabney, Kendall, Shelby, Aislinn, Ashley, Cora, Scarlett, Fleurine*

Aisha One of the most popular names in the Arab world, Aisha is climbing the charts in the United States. Aisha was the favorite wife of the prophet Mohammed; her name means "prosperous."
Variations: *Ayesha, Aeesha, Isha*
Alternatives: *Aaliya, Habiba, Leila, Yasmeen, Fatima, Leila, Aida*

Akira A Japanese name meaning "intelligent," Akira is traditionally a boy's name (think film director Akira Kurosawa) but is increasing in popularity for girls. It's an interesting alternative to Keira and Kyra, celebrity names, both.
Nicknames: *Kiki, Kira*
Alternatives: *Kiku, Keira, Malia, Ima, Miyu, Sakura, Ayaka, Saki, Asuka*

Alaina means "precious" and is closely related to Elaine, Alana, and ultimately, Helen. Alaina is a sweeter alternative to Elaine. It sounds more continental and less girl-next-door.
Variations: *Alayna, Alana, Alanna, Alannah, Alannis, Elaine*
Nicknames: *Lainey, Laina, Ali*
Alternatives: *Ilona, Elodie, Lacey, Idina*

Alexandra The female version of Alexander comes from the Greek and means "protector of mankind." Powerful yet feminine, this popular name has many distinctive nickname possibilities, and is traditional enough that it doesn't feel overly trendy. Alexandra evokes the royal families of several countries including Denmark, from which it migrated to England, Norway, Germany, and Russia. It sounds noble, hip (thanks to the exotic letter *x*), yet accessible. Most everyone nowadays knows an Alex.

Variations: *Alexis, Alexandria, Alessandra (Italian), Alejandra (Spanish), Alexa, Alexia*

Nicknames: *Alexa, Alex, Lexi, Lexa, Xan (pronounced Zan), Andra (AHN-dra), Zandra, Sandy, Sasha, Alé, Ally, Ali*

Alternatives: *Olympia, Simone, Matilda, Eugenia, Victoria, Sylvia*

Alexis From the Greek for "to defend," but with a whiff of Russia about it (Alexi is a popular boy's name there), Alexis popped onto the national radar because of the 1980s TV show *Dynasty*. Now it's wildly popular. (Thank you, Joan Collins.) If you want something similar but less well known, consider the variations Alexa and Alexia. The latter is becoming popular despite the fact that it's a medical term that means a loss of reading ability.

Variations: *Alexus, Alexia*

Nicknames: *Alex, Alix, Lexi, Ali*

Alternatives: *Zoe, Athena, Elektra, Kylie, Rowan, Violet*

It's a Mod, Mod, Mod, Mod World

Y ou don't have to look further than the success of
the Design Within Reach catalog to see that all
things from the mid-century period (around the 1950s)
are back in style. So why not the names? Here are
some classics from the time that will match your
Dunbar couch and Eames chairs.

~ BETTY	~ LAVERNE	~ NORMA
~ DARLENE	~ LORRAINE	~ PEGGY
~ FLORENCE	~ LUCILLE	~ PHYLLIS
~ GLADYS	~ MARILYN	~ SHIRLEY
~ JANET	~ MARION	~ TRIXIE
~ JOAN	~ MAVIS	~ WANDA

Alice is a Saxon name meaning "noble one." For many
of us, she will always be the little girl who fell down the
rabbit hole in Lewis Carroll's *Alice in Wonderland*. An
old-fashioned name, Alice gave way in popularity to
Allison years ago, but now is back on the rise.

Variations: *Alys, Allison, Adelaide, Adeline, Alyce*
Nicknames: *Al, Ali*
Alternatives: *Margaret, Beatrice, Elizabeth, Helena, Eleanor*

Alicia A very feminine sounding name, Alicia is
closely related to Alice. And you've really got two
names to choose from here: the three-syllable ah-

LEE-shah or the four-syllable ah-LEE-see-ah. The former is more down-to-earth, the latter is more ornate (and a bit more unusual).

Variations: *Alecia, Alethea, Alice, Alyssa*
Nicknames: *Ali, Leesie, Lisha*
Alternatives: *Laeticia, Lindsay, Patricia, Courtney, Erica, Bethany, Felicia, Allison*

🖋 **Alina** Related to Alaina, Elaine, and Helena, Alina is popular in the Slavic world. Aline is the Old English variation of it, which was in use during the Middle Ages. Alina and her variations mean "light" and "pretty," which they are. And the variation Alena can be short for names like Magdalena.

Variations: *Aleena, Aline, Elaine, Helena*
Alternatives: *Adela, Amalia, Aurelia, Cecilia, Edita, Ilona, Irena, Lydia, Matilda*

Alisha Take the classic Alicia, give it an Asian spin, and you might get Alisha. As a Hindu name, Alisha means "protected by God," and as an English name, it is a variant of Alice. Either way, it has a musical lilt to it. And unlike Alicia, there is only one way to pronounce it.

Alternatives: *Felicia, Annisa, Asha, Gita, Indira, Vandana*

Alivia is a creative way to spell Olivia, which in the *O* version is one of the hottest names out there now.

> ### *I'd love to call her . . .*
> **Ali**
>
> Always wanted an Ali but not all that fond of
> Allison? Make it a nickname for any name
> beginning with *Al*. These are some of the most popular:
>
> | | | |
> |---|---|---|
> | ~ **ALEAH** | ~ **ALICE** | ~ **ALIZA** |
> | ~ **ALEEZA** | ~ **ALICIA** | ~ **ALMA** |
> | ~ **ALEXANDRA** | ~ **ALINA** | ~ **ALTHEA** |
> | ~ **ALEXIS** | ~ **ALIYAH** | ~ **ALYSSA** |

With an *A*, the name evokes the word *alive*. (See Olivia
for more details.)

Variations: *Alyvia, Olivia*
Nicknames: *Ali, Liv, Livvy*
Alternatives: *Lydia, Lillian, Genevieve, Valeria*

𝒷 **Aliza** is a Hebrew name meaning "joy." The name
is vibrant and full of life—you can nearly hear the
word *alive* in it. Its similarity to Liza (Minelli) and
Eliza (Doolittle) add spunk to the name as well. The
wife of Israel's former prime minister Ehud Olmert
is Aliza Olmert. And a popular Israeli singer is Aliza
Kashi.

Variations: *Aleeza, Alizah, Alisa, Alyza*
Alternatives: *Galia, Allegra, Ayla, Aviva, Alma, Zelda, Zoe*

✐ **Allegra** Is there a cheerier name out there?
I don't know it. Allegra means "happy" in Italian.
In musical notation it means "light and quick; in
a happy way." And the word itself sounds bright
and optimistic, lacy without being overly frilly.
Why is Allegra not more popular than it is? Could
it be that the allergy drug of the same name is
deterring parents? It shouldn't. This name is ripe
for discovery—a unique gem.

Nickname: *Allie*
Alternatives: *Felicia, Chiara, Cosima, Domenica, Elena*

Allison is an American classic with Scottish roots.
It may have started as a nickname for Alice, but
through the ages it's become a popular and lovely
name in its own right. Alison (or Alyson) is the name
of Chaucer's Wife of Bath, who argues—at notorious
length—for women's sovereignty. It's also the subject
of many songs, perhaps most famously one by Elvis
Costello (who, like the name Allison, is a British expat
who makes a home stateside). In Allison, you get an
attractive but serious name that's as comfortable
in the boardroom as its nickname, Allie, is in the
schoolyard.

Variations: *Alison, Alyson, Alisson*
Nicknames: *Allie, Ally, Ali*
Alternatives: *Lauren, Caitlin, Vivian, Lillian, Sydney, Morgan*

✒ **Alma** If your block is overrun by Emmas and Annas, consider Alma, a similarly feminine name that's a bit more grown-up. Alma is an erudite old soul—the name means "soul" in Latin and Spanish and "learned" in Arabic. (She's also a nurturer: Alma mater is, after all, your "nourishing mother" or school.) Lest you worry that Alma is too much of a good girl, remember vivacious Alma Mahler, the Viennese composer who charmed the likes of composer Gustav Mahler, artists Gustav Klimt and Oscar Kokoschka, Bauhaus architect Walter Gropius, and novelist Franz Werfel.

Alternatives: *Ada, Andra, Esme, Inès, Katja, Lena*

Alondra is a pretty and unusual name with many angles to it. The word is "lark" in Spanish. *Londres* (pronounced LON-dra) is London in French. And the name evokes Alexandra and Ilona. It's hard to come by rich, meaningful, lyrical names that are not overused. This is one of them.

Alternatives: *Ilona, Eloise, Ramona, Paloma*

Alyssa is believed to come from alyssum, a hardy plant with colorful, fragrant flowers that grows all over the world. Alyssa can also be considered a derivation of Alice, though it also calls to mind Elizabeth and her variations: Lisa, Liza, and so on. Elissa was the Greek name for the Phoenician queen Dido, who founded the city of Carthage, now in Tunisia. (For more, see Elissa.) If you're feeling cheeky, name your daughter Alyssa and use Dido as a pet name.

Variations: *Alisa, Alissa*
Nickname: *Lyssie, Dido*
Alternatives: *Clarissa, Marina, Selena, Elyse*

Amanda means "to be loved" in Latin. The name is of relatively recent origin, becoming a popular name in seventeenth-century English literature, poetry, and drama. "Farewell Amanda" is a cute Cole Porter song from the Hepburn-Tracy movie *Adam's Rib*. And of course, Barry Manilow's "Mandy" is a cheesy classic we all love to hate or hate to love.

Nicknames: *Mandy, Manny (for the tomboy)*
Alternatives: *Amandine, Amata, Miranda, Samantha, Aimée, Tamara*

Amani means "trust" in Arabic, and is a name increasing in popularity for boys and girls. The similarity to "Armani" may give it a luxurious "Tiffany" touch to some parents. Amani is popular with African American families.

Alternatives: *Amala, Farrah, Imani, Salma*

✏ **Amara** means something different to everyone: What's "immortal" in Greek and Sanskrit is "graceful"

in Africa and "bitter" in Latin (though it's close
enough to *amare*—the Latin verb "to love"—to suggest
adoration, as well). With notes of Mary and of *mare*,
Italian for "sea," Amara has pleasing associations;
it's a refreshing choice.

Variations: *Amari, Amaris*
Nicknames: *Ama, Mara*
Alternatives: *Tamara, Damaris, Marianna, Irina, Lara,
Adora, Zoe*

Amber is fossilized tree resin that is prized as a
gem. The name was barely on the map until the 1944
publication of the bodice-ripper *Forever Amber*. Then
it shot up in popularity, peaking in the 1980s, and it
has been in decline in the United States ever since.
(In the U.K., however, the name is in the top fifty.)
These days, Amber feels almost as fresh as the
petrified resin it's made from. It's stuck in time.

Alternatives: *Ruby, Beryl, Crystal, Gemma, Jade, Opal, Pearl,
Jewel*

Amelia is a classic name found on colonial
gravestones in the American South. It was extremely
popular in the 1800s and then declined in the
middle of the twentieth century, only to experience
a renaissance—like Abigail and Lucy, Amelia is
very much back in style. The French version of the
name, Amélie, was given a boost by the 2001 movie

of the same name. The Eastern European version, Amalia, is pretty, too. The name means "industrious" and evokes such hard workers as aviatrix Amelia Earhart, American suffragette Amelia Bloomer, even the fictional wacky housekeeper Amelia Bedelia. Amelia is a strong alternative (and forerunner) to the enduringly popular Emily.

Variations: *Amélie, Amalia*
Alternatives: *Cornelia, Lydia, Sarabeth, Eliza, Emily, Susannah, Louisa, Clara, May, Tabitha*

America At first glance, America seems like a trendy, made-up name (albeit a patriotic one). Not so. It was popular in the nineteenth century, all but disappeared in the twentieth, and is now experiencing a rousing revival. When you think about it, America, the country, was named for Amerigo Vespucci, so the feminization—and Americanization—of his name really is not outlandish. Actress America Ferrera has helped keep the proud, patriotic name in the spotlight.

Nicknames: *Erica, Rica*
Alternatives: *Justice, Honor, Liberty, Veronica*

Amy could be Jennifer's sister. And in many cases, she probably is. It's a name whose heyday can be charted with near carbon-dating precision. Amy was one of *the* names of the 1970s and has since fallen precipitously in usage. The name is still a good, solid

> *I'd love to call her . . .*
> ## Amy
>
> Adore little Amy but think it feels a bit flighty as a proper name? Make it a nickname for one of these:
>
> - **AMABEL**
> - **AMALIA**
> - **AMANDA**
> - **AMARA**
> - **AMELIA**
> - **AMERICA**
> - **AMITY**
> - **MAY** (everyone loves a good anagram!)

one, meaning "beloved," from the Latin *amare*. If you like the idea of Amy but think it is too dated, consider an alternate spelling: Aimée or Aimie. Or consider a similar but much less common alternative like Esme.

Variations: *Aimee, Aimie*
Alternatives: *Esme, Ada, Inez, Fanny, Daisy, Lacy, Ginny*

Anahi Persian for "immaculate," Anahi is a short form for Anahita, goddess of the water. Lyrical, with a whiff of the Middle East, but not easy to pinpoint, Anahi offers mystery and beauty. An ideal choice for girls with very basic last names: Brown, Smith, and the like.

Nicknames: *Ana, Anya*
Alternatives: *Amira, Aleah, Lila, Imani, Hannah, Ana*

Anastasia A Russian classic meaning "resurrection," Anastasia is an old-world, romantic name. It evokes

19

> ## *I'd love it if she sounded . . .*
> ### Russian
>
> | | | |
> |---|---|---|
> | ~ ANASTASIA | ~ LUDMILLA | ~ OLGA |
> | ~ EKATERINA | ~ NATALIA | ~ SOPHIA |
> | ~ IRINA | ~ ODESSA | ~ SVETLANA |
> | ~ KATYA | ~ OKSANA | ~ TATIANA |

the daughter of the last Russian czar, who may or may not have survived her family's execution. The name is elegant and ornate, so it goes well with short, plain last names that don't compete for attention (or demand lingual dexterity). Choose from one of several ways to pronounce it: Anna-STAY-zsah, Anna-STAH-zsah, or Anna-stah-ZEE-ah. This name is on the longer side, but you'll find no shortage of nicknames to choose from.

Nicknames: *Ana, Stacy, Anya, Natasha, Tasha, Tacey, Stasha, Zsa Zsa*

Alternatives: *Natasha, Katerina, Irina, Natalia, Larissa, Miroslava, Tatiana, Zofia, Yelena*

Andrea You may have known an Andrea growing up—it was a popular name in the '70s and '80s, and has been a classic choice for girls since the seventeenth century. This feminization of Andrew (meaning "strong," "virile") has a few pronunciation choices:

Will she be Ahn-DRAY-ah or ANN-dree-ah or AHN-dree-ah? Either way, a word of caution for frequent fliers to Europe: Andrea (and Andreas) is a boy's name in many countries. For an alternative, consider Ondina (or Ondine or Undine), which means "little wave" in Latin, and has a similar tone.

Nicknames: *Andie, Drea, Andra*
Alternatives: *Ondina, Kendra, April, Danielle, Laura, Rebecca*

Angela comes from Angel, meaning "messenger of God." The name may sound commonplace, but there are interesting variations of this lovely classic in every country, including Aingeal (Ireland) and Angèle (France). Choose from one of several forms: Angelina, Angeline, Angelica, Angelique. You can shorten any of them to Angel, and you can call her Angie if you like. There are lots of famous Angelas: actresses Angela Lansbury, Angela Bassett, Angie Dickinson, Angie Harmon, Angelina Jolie, Angelica Houston, and the German chancellor Angela Merkel.

Variations: *Angel, Angelina, Angelique, Angelica, Aingeal, Angèle*
Nickname: *Angie*
Alternatives: *Antonia, Aurelia, Celestine, Stella, Teresa, Veronica, Victoria*

Anne has been one of the most popular names throughout the ages. The English equivalent of the Hebrew name Hannah ("God has graced me with a child"), St. Anne is believed to have been the mother of the Virgin Mary, and is the patron saint of mothers. There have been many a Queen Anne across Europe, giving the name a regal air. Although Anne may seem too vanilla to some, the name is surprisingly versatile. It goes well with complicated last names and is often used as a middle name—it sandwiches easily between more ornate words. Place it after any traditional first name and you'll end up with a name that sounds like it's straight out of the 1950s or the American South. As with so many old-school names, nicknames and variations abound.

Variations: *Ann, Anna, Anabel, Anabelle, Annabelle, Annabella, Annick, Annika, Anika, Anouk, Anita, Annette, Annetta, Annalise, Anya, Ayn, Anissa*

Nicknames: *Annie, Nan, Nancy, Nanette, Nanny, Nettie, Anita, Nina*

Alternatives: *Mary, Margaret, Sarah, Jane, Catherine, Joan, Bette, Nell*

Anya A Russian take on the traditional Anna, Anya is also a Sanskrit name meaning "inexhaustible." Anya is a prime choice for parents who are considering Anna or Emma but want something just a bit more unusual. The twisting sound the *y* makes offers intrigue.

Variation: *Aniyah*

Alternatives: *Anna, Alexis, Asha, Natalia, Anastasia, Ilona, Edita, Elena, Irina, Saskia*

Anne's Infinite Varieties

Anne is a favorite part of some names as well as a classic stand-alone. Adding it to a name, either by elision or as a separate name, creates something new, with a wholesome, country feel to it. Here are some of Anne's most popular iterations:

~ ANNABELLE	~ ANNEMARIE	~ MARIANNE
~ ANNABETH	~ ANN LOUISE	~ MARYANN
~ ANNALEIGH	~ BARBARA ANN	~ ROSANNE
~ ANNALISE	~ GEORGIANNE	~ ROXANNE
~ ANNALYNNE	~ JOANNE	~ RUTHANN
~ ANNAMARIA	~ LILIANNE	~ SUZANNE

April The month of April was named for Aphrodite, the Greek goddess of love. To Americans and Europeans, the name evokes springtime. April is pretty in other languages, too (see below).

Variations: *Abril (Spanish), Avril (French), Aprile (Ah-preel-ay; Italian)*

Alternatives: *Averill, Aubrey, Avery, January, June, May, Venus, Summer*

Arabella A centuries-old name, Arabella probably started life as a variation of Annabelle. Some people speculate that the name instead could have come from the Latin word *orabilis,* or "prayerful." Arabella is a classic example of a name that was popular in the 1800s, disappeared in the twentieth century, and is being rediscovered. Arabella Donn is the antiheroine in Thomas Hardy's *Jude the Obscure,* and Arabella Fermor was immortalized as Belinda in Alexander Pope's poem "The Rape of the Lock." Arabella makes an excellent alternative to the blockbuster popularity of Isabella. Call her Ara, Ari, Bella, or Belle. Or consider similar yet even more exotic names like Mirabel or Araminta.

Nicknames: *Ara, Ari, Bella, Belle*
Alternatives: *Mirabel, Araminta, Belinda, Annika, Sabina, Alina, Wilhelmina*

Araceli A Spanish name that means "altar of heaven," it's an unexpected, unusual name that steals the spotlight from more common Emily and Natalie.

Variations: *Aracely, Arely*
Alternatives: *Jenna, Arabella, Celestina, Cecilia, Melody*

Aria As a name, Aria has a harmonious, tuneful, airy quality—after all, an aria is a song or melody. In Hebrew, the word *aria* means "lioness," so there is an undercurrent of strength to the name. Will she be a diva, always in the limelight? Between the meaning of the name and the proximity to Maria (think Callas), you could be sealing her fate as a star.

Alternatives: *Daria, Harmony, Allegra, Philomela, Jacinta*

Ariana derives from the Greek name Ariadne, which means "most holy." Ariadne of Greek mythology was the daughter of King Minos of Crete. She betrayed her father by helping Theseus slay the Minotaur with a thread that he used to find his way out of the labyrinth. (Because of that thread, spiders and spiders' webs are named for her in several languages, including French and Spanish.) Aryana (with a *y*) is to Persia what Colleen is to Ireland and Nina is to Spain, which is to say, it means "pretty girl." Ariana is gaining in popularity, along with the other -*a* names. It's a graceful, pleasing option with some kicky nicknames.

Variations: *Arianna, Aryana, Aryanna, Arianne*
Nicknames: *Aria, Ari, Anna, Anya, Ree*
Alternatives: *Aurora, Rihanna, Athena, Andromeda, Calliope, Penelope, Alana, Zoe, Cassandra, Alexandra*

Ariel was the sprite in Shakespeare's *The Tempest* and the mermaid in Disney's *The Little Mermaid*. Ariel is also another word for the city of Jerusalem in the book of Isaiah in the Bible. The name itself sounds, well, airy, and the associations of the name Ariel are undeniably mystical and romantic. In Hebrew, the name means "lion of God," and the name is used for both girls and boys. To feminize it completely, tweak the spelling to Arielle.

Variations: *Ariella, Arielle*
Alternatives: *Stella, Astrid, Nahla, Leona, Ilianna, Brielle*

Ashanti The Ashanti ethnic group was a powerful kingdom of Ghana in the seventeenth century. The name evokes an African heritage with a whisper of Hindu and Buddhist traditions, calling to mind as it does the famous yoga mantra *Om Shanti*. (*Om* is the sound of the universe, *shanti* means "peace.") The name has become more visible lately thanks to the singer and actress Ashanti.

Alternatives: *Aaliyah, Ayanna, Imani, Nahla*

Ashley is a fashion victim if ever there was one. It's the Jennifer of the early 1990s—roaring from oblivion to number one and now on the wane. The name comes from the ash tree and was originally a last name. From there, it became a boy's first name (think Ashley Wilkes in *Gone with the Wind*), and then a girl's name. Its transition from last name to masculine name to feminine name was likely helped by the Laura Ashley brand, whose sweet, floral patterns were the epitome of girlishness for 1980s consumers. This very English-sounding name is now popular with Hispanic families. For an Irish take on the name, consider Aislinn (pronounced Ashlynn).

Variations: *Ashly, Ashleigh, Ashlyn, Ashtyn, Ashton, Aislinn*
Alternatives: *Bailey, Dabney, Shelby, Macy*

Aspen An aspen is a type of poplar, a willowy tree known for leaves that tremble in the wind. It is also a

> ### *I'd love it if she sounded . . .*
> ## Scandinavian
>
> | | | |
> |---|---|---|
> | ~ ANNIKA | ~ ELSA | ~ SIGRID |
> | ~ ASTRID | ~ FREYA | ~ SOLVEIG |
> | ~ BIRGIT | ~ HEDDA | ~ SONJA |
> | ~ BRITT | ~ INGRID | ~ ULLA |
> | ~ DAGMAR | ~ LIV | ~ ULRIKA |

chic Colorado ski resort. As a girl's name, Aspen has an outdoorsy quality to it. Picture someone lithe and stylish with windblown hair and ruddy cheeks.

Alternatives: *Rowan, Willow, Meadow, Sierra, Sage*

Astrid Scandinavian for "beautiful goddess," Astrid has a celestial ring to it. It would make a nice alternative to the increasingly popular Stella. The most famous Astrid in recent times is Brazilian bossa nova singer Astrud Gilberto.

Nicknames: *Asta, Asa*
Alternatives: *Stella, Annick, Dagmar, Greta, Inga, Sigrid, Nora, Elke*

Athena The Greek goddess of the hunt, wisdom, and war, Athena is often depicted wearing a helmet, dressed in armor, and accompanied by an owl. The city of Athens is named for her. This name is a powerful yet traditional and pretty one that bestows strength, smarts, and independence.

Alternatives: *Calliope, Dimitra, Cleo, Agatha, Eleni, Rhea, Echo, Artemis, Aglaia, Minerva (Athena's Roman counterpart), Theodora*

Audrey Thank you, Audrey Hepburn. You have ensured that this name will forever be associated with your swanlike, old-Hollywood elegance. Audrey has existed for decades—she was a clown in Shakespeare's *As You Like It* and a saint (also called Ethelreda) from the 600s whose name inspired the word *tawdry*. But to the modern ear, Audrey evokes Ms. Hepburn. Other forms of the name are becoming popular, especially Audrina. Or, for a variation on the theme, try Aubrey, one of the last name turned boy's name turned girl's names that gives you the elegance of Audrey with an edgy, unexpected twist.

Variation: *Audrina*
Alternatives: *Sabrina, Eliza, Holly, Avery*

✐ **Augusta** August means "dignified," "eminent," even "majestic." Augusta is a proud, noble name, which automatically gives the chin a little lift. (Note that a brisk wind whips through the name as a "gust.") Augusta relates to Augustus Caesar, also known as Octavian, who was one of the best of the Roman emporers, launching an era of tranquility, the Pax

Romana. (Bonus: When teenager Augusta is going
through a phase or starting a rock band, she can
legitimately rename herself Octavia.) Geography buffs
will also recognize Augusta as the capital of Maine.
And literary types will recall that the formidable Lady
Bracknell in Oscar Wilde's *The Importance of Being
Earnest* was named Augusta.

Nicknames: *Asta, Gus, Gussy*
Alternatives: *Georgia, Julia, Eudora, Dixie, Louisa, Daisy,
Octavia*

Aurelia, which means "golden," was the name of
Julius Caesar's mother. It's a fitting name for someone
sure to shine.

Variations: *Aurelie, Oralie, Aurelina, Auriel*
Alternatives: *Gilda, Marigold, Sabina, Sylvia*

Aurora was the Roman goddess of the dawn (the sky
reference is fitting—think aurora borealis) and the
name of the main character in the film *Sleeping Beauty*.
You can call her Aura or Rory or Zora. She can rename
herself Dawn or Eos (the Greek goddess of the dawn).

Nicknames: *Aura, Rory, Zora*
Alternatives: *Dawn, Eos, Sunny, Roxana, Zaria, Danica*

Autumn is, of course, the time of the harvest, of
plenty, of giving thanks and retreating to the warm
hearth before the arrival of winter. The word also

suggests maturity (as in the autumn of your life). As a name, it's lovely and lyrical, but it can carry a whiff of melancholia. After all, autumn is the season just before the winter, when the world is becoming darker and colder and the year is winding down.

Alternatives: *Auburn, Dawn, Summer, Dimitra (from Demeter, Greek harvest goddess), Fallon, Daphne, Diana*

Ava Now one of the ten most popular names, Ava was not even in the top 1,000 just thirty years ago. What happened? Perhaps people noticed the appeal of a name that is short on letters but long on meaning. Simple but pretty, sweet (like Eve) but sophisticated (like Ava Gardner), Ava is related to Eva, which is its phonetic twin. In Hebrew, Eve or Eva is Chava, a name that means life, and, of course, evokes the first woman on Earth, the biblical mother of everyone. Ava also seems close to the Latin *ave,* which means "hail" (think "Ave Maria"). There's no doubt it's a worthy name, but these days little Ava can expect to be one of many.

Variations: *Avah, Aviana, Ave, Aven, Avia, Aveline, Avelyn, Hava, Eva, Eve*
Alternatives: *Viva, Ella, Zoe, Lara, Vera, Lilah, Kyra, Nina, Zara*

Avery Stemming from the word *elf,* Avery is related to the masculine name Alfred. The name sounds more modern than the more obvious (and clunky) Alfreda,

The Golden Era of Film

There is nothing like a name from Hollywood's heyday to inject glamour into your little girl's life from the get-go. Here are some of the top picks from the 1930s through 1950s.

- **AUDREY** *(Hepburn)*
- **AVA** *(Gardner)*
- **BETTE** *(Davis)*
- **CLAUDETTE** *(Colbert)*
- **ELSA** *(Lanchester)*
- **ESTELLE** *(Parsons)*
- **EVA MARIE** *(Saint)*
- **GINGER** *(Rogers)*
- **GLORIA**
  (Swanson and Grahame)

- **GREER** *(Garson)*
- **GRETA** *(Garbo)*
- **HATTIE** *(McDaniel)*
- **HELEN** *(Hayes)*
- **NORMA** *(Shearer)*
- **RITA** *(Hayworth)*
- **SHIRLEY**
  (Temple and Booth)
- **TALULLAH** *(Bankhead)*
- **VIVIEN** *(Leigh)*

and is more pleasing to the modern ear. Avery also evokes images of birds, as it's close to "aviary." And it contains the word *aver,* which means "to assert" and gives the name a quality of strength and purpose. It also contains the word *very,* which gives it amplitude. Once a boy's name, Avery is now much more popular for girls.

Variations: *Averi, Averie, Averill*
Alternatives: *Waverly, Dove, Phoebe, Starling, Freya*

Ayla Rising quickly in popularity, Ayla means "oak tree" in Hebrew and "aura" in Turkish. The similar sounding Ayala means "doe" in Hebrew and is related to Ayelet.
Alternatives: *Galia, Ada, Eden, Aspen, Kyla, Asha*

Azul, meaning "blue" in Spanish, first appeared on the radar in America in 2007. It's still rare, but rising.
Alternatives: *Marina, Iris, Slate, Skye, Neela, Beryl*

Bailey is a last name turned boy's name turned girl's name that's inspired by a work name: A bailey or bailiff is a keeper of the castle. The position was one of high rank, so a bailey had to be reliable and honest. Television has been good to Bailey: The character Bailey Quarters on the TV series *WKRP in Cincinnati* gave the name a boost in the late 1970s. And in 2005, another bump came from the character Miranda Bailey on *Grey's Anatomy*. Bailey is always a strong, self-sufficient sort of girl.
Variations: *Bailee, Baylee*
Alternatives: *Piper, Taylor, Reeve, Jagger, Molly, Kayley*

✒ **Barbara** When you hear the Beach Boys' upbeat anthem to girl-next-door Barbara Ann, it's hard to imagine that the name Barbara, which is Latin in origin, shares roots with the word "barbarian" and means "strange" or "foreign." But maybe it's that hint of the exotic that once made Barbara synonymous with glamour: Think Barbara Stanwyk, Barbara Hutton, and even Barbra Streisand (she was born Barbara). Barbara can be sophisticated or sweet, but she's always ladylike and strong. (In the Roman Catholic tradition, St. Barbara protects against fire and lightning, and is the patron saint of fortifications, architects, and stonemasons.)

Nicknames: *Bar, Barb, Babs, Babette, Basia (the Polish version, pronounced Basha), Bunny*

Alternatives: *Patricia, Helen, Virginia, Joan, Frances, Diane, Evelyn, Joanne, Roberta, Corinne*

✏ **Beatrice** was the subject of Italian poet Dante's adoration. She was also a queen (Beatriz of the Netherlands), princess (one of Queen Victoria's daughters), beloved illustrator (Beatrix Potter), comedienne (Bea Arthur), dramatic heroine (in Shakespeare's *Much Ado about Nothing*), beleaguered older sister (Beezus, from Beverly Cleary's *Ramona* books), and enterprising girl detective (fictional Trixie Belden). Beatrice ("one who brings joy") and her sisters Beatrix and Beatriz are equal parts refined gentlewoman and tough cookie—they are classical beauties poised for a comeback.

Variations: *Beatrice, Beatrix, Beatriz*

Nicknames: *Bea/Bee, Bibi, Beah, Trish, Trixie, Bice (bee-chay)*

Alternatives: *Eugenia, Martha, Sonya, Victoria, Elena, Georgiana*

Belen A popular name in Spanish, Belen means "Bethlehem." It's a snazzier alternative to Ellen, Helen, and the increasingly popular Eleanor—and one that's equally traditional.

Alternatives: *Bevan, Inès, Selene, Pilar, Carmen*

✐ **Belinda** is pretty times two: Belle means "pretty" and Linda does as well. Belinda has an upbeat, sugar-pop sound to it, in part thanks to Belinda Carlisle, lead singer of the 1980s girl band the Go-Go's. But the name reaches back into history: Belinda is the heroine of Alexander Pope's 1712 poem "The Rape of the Lock."

Nicknames: *Belle, Bella, Linda, Lindy, Linnie*
Alternatives: *Amanda, Bedelia, Melinda, Samantha, Matilda, Arabella, Carissa, Helena*

Bella Once a nickname, many parents are cutting to the chase and just naming their daughter Bella. If you want to call her Bella but prefer to start with a longer, more traditional name, consider Annabella, Arabella, or one of the other options below. Bella as a stand-alone name is already on the rise, thanks to Stephanie Meyer's astronomically popular *Twilight* series (first books, then movies), in which curious high schooler Bella falls in love with lusty vampire Edward.

Alternatives: *Annabelle, Isabelle, Arabella, Clarabelle, Maribel, Belinda*

Bernadette When you picture little Bernadette, is she wearing a plaid kilt? There are few names that more succinctly say "Catholic school girl" than this one. The feminization of Bernard ("strong," "bearlike") is closely connected to the nineteenth-century French saint who is celebrated at Lourdes. The hit 1940s movie *The Song of Bernadette,* a biopic of the saint, strengthened the connection.

Variations: *Bernadine, Bernice*
Nicknames: *Bernie, Bern*
Alternatives: *Emmanuelle, Chantal, Odette, Teresa, Monica, Claudette, Brigid*

Bethany sounds like just one of the gals hanging out at the mall with Ashley and Heather, but the roots of the name run deep: It has biblical beginnings. According to the New Testament, it's the name of the village outside Jerusalem where Lazarus and Simon the Leper lived. And according to the book of Luke, Jesus ascended into heaven near Bethany. The name—wistful but of-a-time (the 1980s)—is believed to come from the town's Old Testament name, Ananiah ("the poor"), plus the prefix Beth ("house of").

Nicknames: *Beth, Betty, Betsy*
Alternatives: *Melanie, Simone, Dominique, Stacy, Rachel*

🖋 **Bettina** Overlooked in the United States, appreciated in countries like Germany and Italy,

Bettina is a cuter and sassier cousin of Elizabeth (closest, in fact, to its diminutive nickname Betty). Bettina is lively and sweet, and a name that sounds unusual despite its traditional roots.

Nicknames: *Betty, Betsy, Tina, Teenie, Bette*
Alternatives: *Gisele, Annelise, Tabitha, Nellie, Alina*

Bianca means "white" in Italian and therefore suggests purity. Bianca was the sister in Shakespeare's *The Taming of the Shrew*. Blanche, Bianca's French form, was the aging diva in Tennessee Williams's

Northern Lights

If you are looking for a goddess name but don't want to pull from Ancient Greece or Rome, consider Norse mythology. Note that these names have an earthy, New Agey bent to them.

~ **BRUNHILDE:** *the most beautiful of the Valkyries*

~ **EIR:** *goddess of medicine and healing*

~ **FREYA:** *goddess of love, beauty, and fertility*

~ **FRIGG:** *Odin's wife and the Queen of Asgard; inspiration for the modern name Frigga*

~ **GERSEMI:** *goddess of treasures and riches*

~ **NOTT** (*call her Notta*)*: the night personified*

~ **OSTARA:** *goddess of spring and fertility; also known as Oestre. (You can probably guess which spring holiday is named after her.)*

~ **SAGA:** *goddess of poetry*

~ **SKADI:** *giant goddess of skiing and winter*

A Streetcar Named Desire. Blanca is the Spanish form of the name.

Variations: *Blanca, Blanche*
Nickname: *Bibi*
Alternatives: *Alina, Chiara, Elsa, Kyrie*

Brenda is believed to come from the word "sword" in Old Norse and seems to be related to the word "brand" in English. That's a big name for a little girl. But Brenda has been popular, indeed. In the 1940s, Brenda Starr was a young (fictional) reporter and her popularity caused the name to surge in the late forties and early fifties. The unrelated but similar sounding boy's name Brendan has kept interest in Brenda alive. But for many of us, the name sounds as tough as actress Brenda Vaccaro's gravelly voice.

Nickname: *Bren*
Alternatives: *Sandra, Lori, Deborah, Denise, Tammy, Rhonda*

Brenna A classic with fairly recent origins (it didn't come into use until the 1950s), Brenna is the feminized form of the Irish surname Brennan. Brennan itself comes from two different names, one meaning "tear" or "droplet," the other meaning "raven" or "black." The name is similar to the enormously popular Brianna, but different enough that you'll likely have the only Brenna on the block.

Alternatives: *Fiona, Fionna, Tara, Nina, Maeve, Makena, Raven*

Brianna This female form of Brian, which means "strength" and was the name of an Irish king, went from unknown in the 1960s to the top one hundred in the 1990s. The name is not traditional in Ireland and seems like a modern American invention, though it did appear as a woman's name in Edmund Spenser's sixteenth-century epic poem *The Faerie Queene*. Some parents, finding Brianna too popular, are tweaking the ending of the name to get Brielle.

Variations: *Breanna, Briana, Bryanna, Bria*
Alternatives: *Finola, Nora, Bridget, Moira, Tessa, Brielle*

✐ **Bridget** Speaking of Ireland, Bridget was until very recently an ethnic name. Saint Brigid is one of Ireland's patron saints. The name has very strong sounds, no lilting vowels here, so it's best paired with a softer-sounding last name. Famous Bridgets include actresses Brigitte Bardot and Bridget Fonda, fictional chick lit heroine Bridget Jones, and Brigitta von Trapp of *The Sound of Music*.

Variations: *Birgitta (Sweden), Brigitta (Germany), Brigitte (France), Birgit, Birkita, Britt, Britta*
Nicknames: *Birdie, Bridie, Gidget, Gita*
Alternatives: *Oona, Nora, Maeve, Enya, Bevan*

Briony is a climbing plant that boasts tender berries and small flowers. The fashion for the name began in England, where floral names have always

Celtic Goddesses

I f you want to assert your Celtic heritage, look to the strong and unusual names of the goddesses, some from the myths of the Gauls and some from Gaelic tradition.

- **ANDARTA:** *goddess of war (Gaul)*

- **BELISAMA:** *goddess of lakes (Gaul)*

- **BRIGIT:** *goddess of healing and poetry, but also of martial arts (Gaelic)*

- **CARLDWEN:** *goddess of corn and protector of poets (Gaelic)*

- **DAMARA:** *goddess of fertility (Gaul)*

- **DANU:** *goddess of wind, wisdom, and fertility, who birthed the original inhabitants of Ireland (Gaelic)*

- **MORRIGAN:** *shape-changing mother goddess (Gaelic)*

- **SIRONA:** *goddess of healing (Gaul)*

been popular. Used famously by Ian McEwan in his acclaimed novel *Atonement,* Briony is the prying little sister whose rash action alters the course of a family's history. The name conjures poetry (sounds a bit like Byron), mischief (there's irony in there, too, and maybe a briar patch), and tradition (it's a good alternative to Brianna as a feminine response to Brian). Make sure the pronunciation is BRY-oh-knee, not brie-OH-knee like the men's suit manufacturer.

Variation: *Bryony*

Alternatives: *Flora, Maisie, Bronwyn, Diana, Violet, Hyacinth*

Big Apple Babies

Brooklyn and Bronx may seem overdone (thanks to the Beckhams and the Simpson-Wentzes), but there are plenty of New York place-names to go around:

- **ASTOR** *(Place)*
- **CHELSEA** *(neighborhood)*
- **CHERRY** *(Lane)*
- **CHRYSTIE** *(Street)*
- **CORNELIA** *(Street)*
- **ELIZABETH** *(Street)*
- **LIBERTY** *(Place)*
- **MERCER** *(Street)*
- **MINETTA** *(Lane)*
- **PERRY** *(Street)*
- **SUTTON** *(Place)*
- **WAVERLY** *(Place)*

Bristol A town in England whose name means "by the bridge," Bristol shot to national recognition during the 2008 presidential campaign as the name of Sarah Palin's pregnant teenage daughter. Sounds like Crystal, but cooler. Look for it to increase in popularity in the coming years.

Alternatives: *Piper, Scout, Brooke, Chelsea, Madison, Sutton*

Brittany A windswept region on the Atlantic coast of France, Brittany (or *Bretagne,* in French) is an old Celtic land with strong ties to Ireland and England, as the name suggests. These days you can't think about the name without pulling up a picture of tabloid train-wreck Britney Spears. Brittany has had her moment of fame and is quickly retreating from the top of the popularity charts.

Variation: *Britney*
Alternatives: *Norma, Victoria, Bethany, Paris, Britta, Stephanie*

Bronwyn is Welsh and means "white breast." It's one of the fair lady names like Guineviere that evokes the pastoral rambles of Olde England. Bronwyn is the heroine of the classic Welsh novel *How Green Was My Valley*. If you like Gwyneth but worry it's too Hollywood, Bronwyn might be a better fit.

Variations: *Bronwen, Bronya*
Alternatives: *Gwyneth, Gwendolyn, Fiona, Winifred, Brynn*

Brooke A stream of water, Brooke is a name that once sounded trendy and maybe even a little flaky but has established itself as a popular, legitimate name. Socialite Brooke Astor lent the name credibility and stature, while model Brooke Shields gave it sex appeal. If yours is chatty, she'll be called a babbling Brooke.

Alternatives: *Bristol, Claire, Sage, Hope, Blair, Quinn, Sloane*

Brynn A *brynn* is a hill in Welsh. (The Pennsylvania college Bryn Mawr means "big hill.") The name is usually spelled with one *n* and assigned to boys, but because it looks like Lynn, it has been used for girls—these days with increasing frequency.

Alternatives: *Briana, Brielle, Bronwyn, Gwendolyn*

Cadence is the rising and falling inflection of music or poetry. It has become a name only recently, appearing on charts in the United States in the 2000s, and quickly leaping to the top 200. It looks traditional like Candace but with musicality and a free, vaguely hippie, spirit.

Variations: *Kaydence, Kadence*
Nicknames: *Kay, Cate*
Alternatives: *Aria, Allegra, Harmony, Reed, Lyric, Prudence*

Caitlin Pert and friendly, Caitlin is related to the classic, timeless Katherine, and the old-fashioned Irish name Kathleen. Caitlin is a young girl with an air of Ireland about her. In its Irish form, the name is pronounced KAT-leen, which became Kathleen. (More Kathleens were born in the United States in 1949 than at any other time; Caitlin had her heyday in the 1990s.) In its Anglo and American form, it is pronounced KATE-lynn. In all forms, it means "pure" and, as a group, the *Cat-* and *Kat-* names are enormously popular. Parents sometimes try to make their kittens distinctive by playing with spelling and form.

Variations: *Caitlyn, Kaitlin, Kaitlyn, Catelyn, Cailyn, Kaylin, Caylee, Colleen, Kathlynn*
Nicknames: *Cate, Kate, Cait, Lynn, Cat, Kit, Kitty*
Alternatives: *Carey, Bridget, Peyton, Keeley, Arcadia, Casey, Mamie*

Cali (pronounced Callie) started appearing in numbers on American birth certificates in the late 1990s. It is typically short for Calista, which is a Greek name meaning "beautiful cup" (the cup refers to the Eucharist, so there's a religious tinge there). Actress Calista Flockhart gave the name notice when her show *Ally McBeal* aired in 1997. Note that Kali (KAH-lee) with a *K* is a name of Hindu origin meaning "black." Kali was the destructive wife of the god Shiva (more on that on page 142).

Variation: *Callie*
Alternatives: *Millie, Dahlia, Hallie, Mila, Lacey*

Cameron A Scottish clan name, Cameron means "crooked nose." This surname turned first name is a popular choice for both boys (director Cameron Crowe) and girls (actress Cameron Diaz).

Variations: *Camryn, Kamryn*
Nicknames: *Cammie, Ronnie*
Alternatives: *Brodie, Lindsay, Paisley, Ferguson, Campbell, Mackenzie*

Camilla is strong and pure—she was the warrior maiden in Virgil's *Aeneid*. In French, Camilla becomes Camille, which was the name of the heroine of Alexandre Dumas's play *La Dame aux Camélias,* the basis for Verdi's opera *La Traviata.* If Camilla reminds you of British Prince Charles's longtime love

> *I'd love it if she sounded . . .*
> **British**
>
> | | | |
> |---|---|---|
> | ~ ANNA | ~ GEMMA | ~ PIPPA |
> | ~ BEATRIX | ~ IMOGEN | ~ POPPY |
> | ~ CAMILLA | ~ JEMIMA | ~ SIBYL |
> | ~ FELICITY | ~ LUCY | ~ TAMSIN |

turned second wife, Camilla Parker Bowles, consider Camellia. It has a similar ring to it, and though it's not really in use as a girl's name, it has all the hallmarks of working well as one. It sounds like the beloved Amelia and it is the name of a flowering shrub with luscious blossoms.

Variations: *Kamila, Camille, Camila*
Nicknames: *Cammie, Milla, Millie*
Alternatives: *Rose, Lilah, Alice, Edith, Violet, Maude*

Campbell An ancient Scottish clan name, Campbell's origins are disputed. Is the name Celtic from the words for "bent mouth" (*carn-beul*) or is it Norman for "beautiful fields" (*campo bello*)? Who knows. The name works for boys (actor Campbell Scott) and girls (journalist Campbell Brown). Would Campbell Brown be regarded as a tough reporter if she had stuck with her given first name, Alma? There's no question that Campbell is the stronger name. If you want to soften

it, you can call her Belle or Cammie. But then ask
yourself why you named her Campbell in the
first place.

Nicknames: *Cammie, Belle*
Alternatives: *Kendall, Cameron, Brodie, Paisley, Lindsay*

Candace was the hereditary title of Ethiopian queens
during biblical times (it was akin to the honorific "Your
Highness"). One Candace is mentioned in the Bible
in the book of Acts, another was recorded by Roman
writer Pliny the Younger. Candace is therefore a strong,
regal, classical name with ties to northern Africa.
Famous Candaces include actress Candice Bergen and
writer Candice Bushnell. Candy is a possible nickname
but is too sweet for many parents' tastes.

Variation: *Candice*
Nicknames: *Candy, Dizzy*
Alternatives: *Cadence, Amber, Cleo, Aida, Cynthia, Delphine*

Cara means "dear" in Italian. There are many
variations for this short and sweet name, all of which
can also start with a *k*.

Variations: *Carina, Carissa, Carissima, Carita*
Nicknames: *Carrie, Cari*
Alternatives: *Lara, Mara, Alma, Tara, Aria, Tacey, Selah, Clarissa*

Carla derives from Charles, which means "free man."
Charles and its variations and feminizations are regal

and venerable (they date back to after the fall of the Roman Empire). Carla is one of the sassier, more approachable derivations. If you want to go in a more formal direction, choose Charlotte (or even Caroline) and use Carla as a nickname. Carla lost its luster in recent decades—perhaps not helped by the brassy Carla Tortelli character on the TV series *Cheers*—but it got a big boost in profile in 2008, when French President Nicolas Sarkozy married sexy singer/model Carla Bruni.

Variations: *Charlotte, Caroline, Carlotta*
Nickname: *Carlita*
Alternatives: *Chiara, Angela, Donna, Gemma, Paola, Sylvia, Maria*

Carly A diminutive form of Carla, which is itself a short form of Charlotte and Caroline, sweet, girly Carly became popular in the 1970s and 1980s, aided

---

I'd love it if she sounded . . .
Spanish

~ ALEJANDRA	~ ESPERANZA	~ MARITZA
~ CARMEN	~ INEZ	~ MERCEDES
~ DOLORES	~ JIMENA	~ PALOMA
~ ELIANA	~ LUCIA	~ VALERIA
~ ESMERELDA	~ MARISOL	~ YESENIA

perhaps by singer Carly Simon. The name was starting to wane when the Nickelodeon children's show *iCarly* launched in 2007, giving it another boost.

Variations: *Carlee, Carleigh, Carley, Carlie, Karly, Karley*
Alternatives: *Carrie, Fanny, Millie, Miranda, Lilly, Pippa, Cara*

Carmen Popular with Spanish-speakers, Carmen means "song" in Latin-based languages. The name has a dash of exoticism and a femme fatale quality thanks to composer Georges Bizet's opera *Carmen,* about a gypsy siren. Although the name may bring fruited hat–wearing singer Carmen Miranda to mind, it's an intriguing choice, one that's playful without being frivolous.

Alternatives: *Lucia, Lina, Paloma, Anita, Belen, Pilar*

Carol and sister Caroline are among the most popular feminizations of the name Charles; Charles means "free man" and is one of the stateliest names in history. A carol, or song (think Christmas carol), may lend the name a sense of musicality. Carol, Carole, and Carolyn were very popular in the 1930s, '40s, and '50s. Caroline followed the opposite trend: it was most popular after the mid-twentieth century. There is no shortage of famous Carols and Carolines to admire: comic actresses Carol Burnett and Channing and Kane; actresses Carole Lombard and Bouquet; singer/songwriter Carole King; fictional TV mom Carol Brady; Caroline Kennedy (Neil

47

Diamond's song "Sweet Caroline" was inspired by her); and fashion designer Carolina Herrera.

Variations: *Karol, Carole, Caroline, Carolina, Carolyn*
Nicknames: *Caro, Lina, Lynn*
Alternatives: *Marilyn, Beverly, Frances, Dorothy, Joyce, Linda, Norma, Marjorie, Gail, Glenda, Lucille*

Casey is an Irish last name that has turned into a unisex first name. Casey became famous in the United States in 1888, through the publication of the baseball poem "Casey at the Bat." It was bolstered again at the turn of the century, with the story of folk hero Jonathan "Casey" Jones. Jones, nicknamed for his hometown of Cayce, Kentucky, was a railroad engineer who died saving the lives of his passengers in 1900. Songs were written about his heroism, and little boys were named for him. Casey projects an all-American, no-nonsense air. It's a fine choice for girls and boys alike, and a cute nickname for a girl with the initials "K. C." Spelling Kasey with a *K* makes it more feminine.

Variation: *Kasey*
Nickname: *Cate*
Alternatives: *Macy, Mallory, Stacy, Lacey, Chelsea*

Cassandra is a tragic heroine from Greek mythology. She was the daughter of King Priam of Troy on whom Apollo bestowed the gift of prophecy. When she

Patron Saints

For every ailment, profession, state of being, there is a patron saint who's got your back. Here are some samples of the wide-ranging interests these ladies have and the people they are looking out for. Note that some of the faithful believe in choosing a patron saint for themselves personally and praying to him or her on every topic.

- **ST. AGATHA:** *nurses*
- **ST. ANNE:** *mothers*
- **ST. BARBARA:** *architecture*
- **ST. BRIDGET:** *blacksmiths*
- **ST. CATHERINE:** *libraries and lawyers*
- **ST. CECILIA:** *music*
- **ST. CLARE:** *embroidery*
- **ST. EDITH:** *children*

- **ST. ELIZABETH:** *brides*
- **ST. GENEVIEVE:** *fevers*
- **ST. JOAN:** *soldiers*
- **ST. LUCY:** *eyesight*
- **ST. MARTHA:** *cooks*
- **ST. MONICA:** *housewives*
- **ST. RITA:** *lost causes*
- **ST. THERESA:** *illness*
- **ST. VERONICA:** *photography*

spurned his affections, he cursed her, ensuring that nobody would believe her predictions. Despite her inauspicious history, her name has been beloved. It projects wisdom and womanly strength, and has a number of lively, girlish nicknames.

Variation: *Kassandra*

Nicknames: *Cassie, Sandra, Casey, Andra, Cass*

Alternatives: *Diana, Anastasia, Salome, Delilah, Susannah*

Catherine Saint Catherine has given her name
to many a little girl—it has been one of the most
historically popular names for centuries. It is believed
to come from the Greek for "pure." Many royal and
influential women were named Catherine, including
Catherine of Aragon (Henry VIII's first wife),
Catherine de Medici (who married King Henry II of
France), and Catherines I and II (Russian empresses).
Actresses include Catherine Deneuve, Catherine Zeta-
Jones, and Catherine "Cate" Blanchett. The name is
wildly versatile and appears in multiple forms in most
languages.

Variations: *Katherine, Kathryn, Katrina, Ekaterina, Carine,
Catarina, Catalina, Kathleen, Caitlin, Catalina*
Nicknames: *Katie, Kate/Cate, Kat, Cathy/Kathy, Katya, Kitty,
Kay*
Alternatives: *Eleanor, Caroline, Margaret, Charlotte, Alice,
Virginia, Patricia, Pamela, Rebecca*

🖉 **Cecilia** Cecile is an old-fashioned name that has
fallen out of favor since the early part of the twentieth
century. Cecilia, on the other hand, is an old-fashioned
name that is being rediscovered à la Lucy, Abigail,
and Amelia. But unlike Lucy, which means "light,"
Cecilia is believed to derive from the Latin root for
the word "blind." Still, Cecilia has much to offer in the
way of lyricism: St. Cecilia, one of the most important
Catholic saints, is the patroness of music. The name

is a meaningful choice for parents passionate about music or hopeful for a child with musical chops.

Variations: *Cecile, Cecily, Celia*

Nicknames: *Sissy, Cece, Lia, Ceci (pronounced chay-chi which is Italian for "chickpea." How cute is that?)*

Alternatives: *Bettina, Lucia, Lydia, Clara, Emilia, Amelia, Beatrice*

Celeste means "heavenly" (think "celestial"). In an orchestra, the celeste is a percussion instrument that makes ethereal sounds. The fictional elephant Babar's wife is Celeste. The name is a great alternative to the name Stella, which has a similarly astral meaning but which has become too much of a star for some parents' taste.

Variations: *Celestia, Celia, Celine, Selin, Selena, Celestine (Alert: This may be too close to the '90s new-age bestseller* The Celestine Prophecy! *Too soon? Your call.)*

Alternatives: *Estella, Eden, Aria, Vanessa, Astrid, Cleo*

Chana This Hebrew variation of the increasingly popular Hannah is pronounced much the same way (the initial *Ha* sound is a bit throatier). It's also seen as Shana and Chanya. Hannah was the mother of Samuel, and she was unable to conceive for many years until she became pregnant with him. (See Hannah, pages 111–112, for more.)

Alternatives: *Hava, Shoshanna, Ayala*

Chantal was the last name of a French saint, Sainte Jeanne-Françoise de Chantal. Chantal has been a beloved girl's name in francophone countries since then. It experienced a surge in the United States in the 1990s, but interest has waned since then. The name has the word "chant" in it, which gives it some music and spirituality. And while it has an international flavor, it is easy for Americans to pronounce.

Alternatives: *Celine, Talia, Dahlia, Tamara, Camille, Daphne, Claudine*

Charity comes from the same root as cherish, meaning "dear." The word itself has come to mean benevolence, generosity, and selfless love. It is a virtue name (see "The Value of a Name," page 214), so it goes well with other names like Grace and Hope. An old-fashioned choice, it got a bump in the 1970s, perhaps in response to the musical *Sweet Charity* of 1966 (Shirley MacLaine starred in the movie version) and perhaps because it has a hippie, love-child appeal that's in keeping with the Age of Aquarius.

Alternatives: *Grace, Patience, Faith, Honor, Mercy, Hope*

Charlie A casual, feminine variation on the regal name Charles (see page 331, and also Carla, Charlotte, and Carol), this is best used as a nickname for Charlotte. Charlie and her sisters are approachable, happy, tomboy names. Charlize feels hip and modern (thanks, actress Charlize Theron). Prince Albert of Monaco's marriage to a Charlene may spark the rise of that variation. Charlie all but disappeared during the mid-twentieth century and has only just come back. It's a creative choice for music lovers, especially for fans of bebop saxophonist and composer Charlie Parker (in which case you could nickname her Birdie, riffing on Parker's nickname Bird).

Variations: *Charlee, Charlize, Charlene, Charly*
Alternatives: *Birdie (from Roberta), Jamie, Correy (from Cornelia), Billie (from Wilhelmina)*

Charlotte A feminization of Charles, which means "free man," Charlotte is a good, solid, traditional name making a comeback along with Isabelle, Hannah, and Emma, and others you see in American colonial-era graveyards. Charlotte has royal ties and literary flavor as well: There's the famous Victorian writer Charlotte Brontë, author of *Jane Eyre,* and also the enterprising spider star of E. B. White's beloved children's novel *Charlotte's Web*. In France, rocker Charlotte Gainsbourg gives the name a cool factor. In the United States, it's a bit more prim— think of the buttoned-up TV character from *Sex and the City*.

Nicknames: *Charlie, Carlotta, Carla, Chaz, Charla, Lottie*
Alternatives: *Beatrice, Eugenie, Victoria, Adelaide, Louise, Alice, Maude, Helena, Augusta*

Chastity In company with other character-based names like Faith, Hope, and Charity, Chastity is the quality of being chaste, pure, or virginal. The name has a religious ring to it. You can call her Chaz if she thinks Chastity is too saccharine. (See "The Value of a Name," page 214 for more virtuous names.)
Alternatives: *Patience, Hope, Mercy, Honor, Faith*

Chaya Pronounced HAI-ah, Chaya means "life" in Hebrew. Think of the famous drinking toast *L'Chayim,* which means "to life." The name is similar to the girl's name Hava (both are related to Eve) and the boy's name Chaim.
Alternatives: *Eden, Eve, Hava, Aliza, Amaya, Mara*

Chelsea Formerly a place-name—it's a neighborhood in London and New York—Chelsea has been used for girls since the late part of the twentieth century. (The word is Old English and literally means "chalk place.") Former President Bill Clinton's daughter is Chelsea. She was named for the Joni Mitchell song made famous by Judy Collins, "Chelsea Morning," which was about the New York City neighborhood.
Alternatives: *Kelsey, Phoebe, Bristol, Hailey*

Cheyenne sounds softer than, say, Dakota, which is similar because of its origins. North American

Plains Indians, the Cheyenne were historically known for their horsemanship. They migrated west into the Dakotas and Rocky Mountains. Thanks to the Indian nation, as well as the capital of Wyoming, also Cheyenne, the name has a rugged, equestrian sound to it. The name is a good choice for families who like the freedom and untamed quality of the American West.

Variations: *Cheyanne, Shyann*
Alternatives: *Dakota, Sierra, Sage, Shiloh, Scout, Savannah*

I've Got a Right to Sing the Blues

It isn't easy being a girl in a man's world. The ladies who sing blues, jazz, and pop standards are originals. No wonder at their top ranks they boast names of great interest. If you are looking for Jane and Mary, go elsewhere. These girls have names full of personality and verve.

- **ALBERTA** *(Hunter)*
- **ANITA** *(O'Day)*
- **BILLIE** *(Holiday)*
- **BLOSSOM** *(Dearie)*
- **ELLA** *(Fitzgerald)*
- **ETTA** *(James)*
- **DIANA** *(Krall)*
- **DINAH** *(Washington)*
- **LENA** *(Horn)*
- **NINA** *(Simone; use first or last name)*
- **PEGGY** *(Lee)*
- **ROSEMARY** *(Clooney)*
- **SHIRLEY** *(Horn)*
- **VAUGHAN** *(Sarah; call her Vaughan for distinction)*

Chiara The Italian word for "light," the name Chiara, like the similar Ciara, discussed opposite, can offer pronunciation challenges. Although it is pronounced kee-AH-rah, some people may want to say chee-AH-rah. Its recent burst of popularity in the mid-2000s (it was in the top ten briefly) has helped with that problem, and now that it's better known, it feels more mainstream and less resolutely ethnic.

Variations: *Claire, Clara*
Alternatives: *Lucia (loo-CHEE-ah), Francesca, Ariana, Donata*

Chloe A Greek name meaning "blooming," Chloe was the heroine of the ancient Greek story *Daphnis and Chloe*. Once considered exotic, Chloe is now

---

BERYL, CHERYL, MERYL

Beryl is a gemstone (emeralds are beryls) and was the name of a daring aviatrix flying in Africa, Beryl Markham. That name, popular in the 1940s and 1950s, sparked variations, the most notable of which was Cheryl. Cheryl is a mash-up of Beryl and Cherry or Cher (French for "dear"). Cheryl Tiegs and Cheryl Ladd are emblems of the name, now rarely used. Meryl is inextricably linked to actress Meryl Streep, who was born Mary Louise and nicknamed Meryl.

common. It was wildly popular in France and England in the 1990s and 2000s and it migrated overseas. It's now near the top of the list. Reality TV star Khloe Kardashian has also put the *K* variation on the map.

Variations: *Cloe, Khloe*
Alternatives: *Daphne, Phoebe, Zoe, Cleo, Lois*

Christine and its variations come from the word *Christ,* which means "Messiah." The names were very popular in the 1960s and 1970s, and are much less so now. Christine is a likely sister for other classics like Katherine and Susan, and as with those names, most of us have at least one Christine in our lives. Christine, despite its sober religious roots, is light and lively on the tongue. For something similar but even more winsome, try Christina or the less common Christiana (pronounced either christi-anna or christi-ahna).

Variations: *Christina, Cristina, Christiane, Christiana, Kristina, Krestyna*
Nicknames: *Chris, Chrissy, Christy, Christa, Christie, Crissa, Tina, Teeny, Trista*
Alternatives: *Katherine, Laura, Cynthia, Pamela, Stephanie, Angela, Carolyn, Kristen*

Ciara This Irish name is the feminine form of Ciaran (aka Kieran) and means "black." As with Chiara, discussed opposite, you might run into pronunciation troubles. Some say kee-AH-rah; others KEIR-ah. The name has been a popular choice since the 1980s.

Variations: *Keira, Kira, Chiara*
Alternatives: *Lucia, Enya, Maria, Oona, Cara*

Claire comes from the Latin for "bright," suggesting clarity and light. The related Clara was popular in the 1800s and then fell into disuse, only to experience a revival recently. Both versions of the name are appealing in the way that Charlotte, Abigail, Lucy, and Hannah are: They are feminine and traditional. No surprise that Claire in all its forms is being revived. Clara was the number one name in France in 2008.

Variations: *Clare, Clara, Clarissa, Clarice*
Alternatives: *Alice, Charlotte, Lydia, Lucy, Julia, Adair*

Claudia and her relatives are feminizations of the Latin name Claudius, which means, unfortunately, "lame." Claudia Schiffer, the famous model, suggests fame and glamour, as did Hollywood it-girl Claudette Colbert. Claudine, another variation, was made popular by writer Colette, whose Claudine series launched in France in 1900. In Germany, where the name is popular, the pronunciation sounds less like CLAW-dee-ah and more like CLOUD-ee-ah, which makes the name dreamy and airy.

Variations: *Claudine, Claudette, Claude*
Alternatives: *Nadine, Nadia, Miranda, Leonora, Augusta, Paula*

Music and Lyrics

Every girl deserves to be serenaded. Choose a name that appears in song, and you practically guarantee your little one will be.

- **ALISON:** *"Alison"* by Elvis Costello
- **CAROLINE:** *"Sweet Caroline"* by Neil Diamond
- **CATHY:** *"Cathy's Clown"* by the Everly Brothers
- **CECILIA:** *"Cecilia"* by Simon & Garfunkel
- **CLARABELLA:** *"Clarabella"* by the Beatles
- **CLEMENTINE:** *"My Darling Clementine"* (folk song)
- **DAISY:** *"A Bicycle Built for Two"* (folk song)
- **DOLLY:** *"Hello, Dolly!"* from the Jerry Herman musical of the same name
- **DONNA:** *"Donna"* by Ritchie Valens
- **EILEEN:** *"Come On Eileen"* by Dexy's Midnight Runners
- **ENID:** *"Enid"* by the Barenaked Ladies
- **GIGI:** title song from the Lerner & Loewe musical
- **GLORIA:** *"Gloria"* by Van Morrison
- **JANE:** *"Sweet Jane"* by the Velvet Underground
- **JOLENE:** *"Jolene"* by Dolly Parton
- **LAYLA:** *"Layla"* by Derek and the Dominoes
- **LULU:** *"Lulu's Back in Town"* by Fats Waller
- **MARIA:** from West Side Story by Leonard Bernstein
- **MICHELLE:** *"Michelle"* by the Beatles
- **ROXANNE:** *"Roxanne"* by the Police
- **RUBY:** *"Ruby, Don't Take Your Love to Town"* by Kenny Rogers
- **SADIE:** *"Sexy Sadie"* by the Beatles
- **SALLY:** *"Mustang Sally"* by Wilson Pickett
- **SUSANNAH:** *"Oh, Susannah"* (folk song)
- **VERONICA:** *"Veronica"* by Elvis Costello

✐ **Clementine** Oh, my darlin', Oh my darlin' . . . ! Get used to this refrain from the folk song "My Darling Clementine," because if you choose this adorable variation on the boy's name Clement, you're going to be hearing it a lot. If you can overcome—or embrace—that, then you'll have a sweet name to enjoy. The name means "merciful" (think *clemency*), and also is the name of the juicy winter fruit related to the orange. The name has a darling, diminutive, almost Southern cast to it. It's a great choice for a traditional name that has not been rediscovered yet. It was popular in the 1880s and early 1900s but is rarely seen today.

Alternatives: *Mercy, Evangeline, Philippa, Marigold, Joanna, Matilda, Gertie, Perdita*

Colette is an untraditional name that seems like it's been around for ages—in a good way. It was the last name of the French writer Sidonie-Gabrielle Colette (most famously, creator of *Gigi*). It is also the name of a trend-setting department store in Paris. Thus the name evokes France and all things Paris chic. It can also be a diminutive variation of Nicole (as in Nicolette). Coco is an adorable nickname, as is the more demure Letty. If you name her for the writer Colette, then you can reasonably call her Sido (pronounced SEE-doe), the nickname of Colette's real first name. Grab this one while it's hot: Colette is not on the mainstream radar screen yet (she is not in the top 1,000 names), but given the upswing in Ellas and Ettas, she may catch on quick.

Alternatives: *Sidonie, Gabrielle, Gigi, Nicolette, Delphine, Elodie, Chanel*

Cora A simple, old-fashioned choice. Cora appeared in James Fennimore Cooper's *The Last of the Mohicans* in 1826, which gave it a boost. And Cora was another name for Persephone, the Greek goddess of fertility as well as the underworld. The name was popular in the late 1800s, then sank into disuse; it's just starting to come back. Cora is short and sweet, but if it's *too* short and sweet, consider Coretta (as in Coretta Scott King, Martin Luther King Jr.'s wife), Corinna (an ancient Greek poet, and also the name of Roman poet Ovid's muse), or Corinne. And for nature lovers, there is also Coral.

Variations: *Corinna, Corinne*
Nickname: *Cory*
Alternatives: *Eleanor, Georgia, Zora, Ilona, Delia*

Cornelia is a sleeper. This Roman name means "horn" and sounds like Delia or Amelia but is less trendy. The nicknames are charming and varied. If you are looking for something that's unique but that has solid backing, Cornelia might be it.

Nicknames: *Corry, Neely, Nelia, Celia*
Alternatives: *Theodora, Matilda, Edwina, Adelaide, Josephine, Ursula*

> ### *I'd love to call her . . .*
> ## Coco
> ---
> Coco can come from any name that begins with a hard *C*, or it can be a mash-up of first and last names that begin with *C*, as a J-Lo effect. Favorite names to begin with:
>
> - CHARLOTTE
> - COLETTE
> - COLLEEN
> - CORA
> - CORALIE
> - COREY
> - CORINNE
> - GABRIELLE
>   *(Coco Chanel's birth name)*

Courtney You can target the age of a Courtney with almost the accuracy of a torpedo. The name became huge in the 1980s and 1990s, only to practically disappear again. (Actress Courteney Cox, born in the mid-'60s, was ahead of the trend.) It is a last name turned first name that comes from a place-name in France (Courtenay). Perhaps it owes its erstwhile popularity to Brittany and other Francophilic names. While its presence has waned in the United States, it's still quite popular in the U.K.

Alternatives: *Heather, Danielle, Nicole, Kelsey*

Cynthia comes from the Greek Mount Kynthos, which was believed to be the birthplace of the goddess Artemis, patron of the hunt. Because Artemis was also a goddess of the moon, some people think of Cynthia as meaning "moon." It was very popular in the United States in the 1940s through 1960s. Although Cynthia is often called Cindy, which for some of us brings to mind the treacly daughter of TV's *Brady Bunch,* there is a fresh nickname option in Thea. Maybe this moon should be on the rise again.

Nicknames: *Cindy, Cinda, Thea, Cinny*
Alternatives: *Selena, Lucinda, Daphne, Pamela, Patricia*

Dabney A last name turned boy's name turned first name, Dabney comes from the French *d'Aubigné,* meaning "from the town of Aubigné." It is a very southern name in the United States, thanks to two brothers, John and Cornelius d'Aubigné, who emigrated from France, via Wales, to Virginia in the early 1700s. If Dabney isn't to your taste (or reminds you of comic actor Dabney Coleman), consider Darcy, from *d'Arcy,* which means "from Arcy." It has a literary air and is sure to please fans of Jane Austen (Mr. Darcy is the cad turned catch in her novel *Pride and Prejudice*). Dacey is in use now as well. It's a way of getting the Dabney or Darcy effect with a more feminine frill (sounds like Lacey and Stacy).

Alternatives: *Darcy, Dagmar, Shelby, Addison, Riley, Sutton*

Dahlia is a colorful summer flower, which was named for Swedish botanist Anders Dahl in the 1700s. Dahlia is feminine and, of course, floral. It just started gaining popularity in the United States within the last few years. It means "valley."

Nickname: *Dillie*
Alternatives: *Delia, Talia, Dale, Camellia, Lily, Rose*

Daisy A perennial favorite in the United States for more than a century, Daisy is derived from the perennial plant of the same name. The word *daisy* comes from "day's eye," a nod to the flower's sunny appearance. Daisy is the cute, cheerful girl next door. She's Fitzgerald's heroine in *The Great Gatsby* and Henry James's leading lady in the novella *Daisy Miller*. She is the girl on the bicycle built for two in the old song. And she is the attractive good ole girl on TV's *The Dukes of Hazard* (thanks to the show, cutoff shorts are now called "Daisy Dukes"). Daisy is also a pet name for girls named Margaret, maybe because *marguerite* is the French name for "daisy." Warning: Daisy is one of the most popular names for dogs. Given that, it might be best as a nickname.

Alternatives: *Margaret, Poppy, Hazel, Lily, Holly, Rose, Maisie*

Dakota means "friend" in the Sioux language. The Dakota are an American Indian nation for whom North and South Dakota were named. The Dakota is the historic New York City building that John Lennon lived in (and died in front of). It was so-named because at the time it was built (the 1880s) it was considered to be so far away from the action of midtown and downtown New York that it might as well have been on the frontier. Dakota was barely known before the 1980s, when it started appearing on name charts. The young actress Dakota Fanning has raised the profile of the name.

Alternatives: *Cheyenne, Sierra, Sage, Savannah*

Damaris is a woman from Greece in the New Testament who converted to Christianity and was believed to have been of high rank. The origins of the name are disputed. Is it a corruption of *damalis,*

Three Names to Shout from the Rooftops

~ **ADRIENNE:** *Remember the scene in Rocky where Rocky shouts "Adrienne!" from the top of the steps of the Philadelphia Museum of Art? You can shout Adrienne from anywhere.*

~ **MARIA:** *The famous* West Side Story *song begs to be belted out for your little Maria.*

~ **STELLA:** *Nobody yells "Stella!" like Marlon Brando as Stanley Kowalski in* A Streetcar Named Desire. *Picture yourself on the playground when it's time to go home and channel that energy.*

meaning "calf," or does it relate somehow to Damara, the Celtic goddess of fertility?

Alternatives: *Maris, Tamara, Candace, Phyllis, Gladys, Demetra, Anitra*

Dania is a variation both of Dana ("from Denmark") and Danielle (Hebrew, feminine for Daniel). It's a good alternative to Dana, which is used for both girls and boys, because it removes the gender ambiguity. If you are thinking of it as a version of Danielle, why not name her Danielle and just use Dania as a nickname? Another option is Danica, a variation of Dana—and a good choice for fans of car racing (think Danica Patrick, the race car driver).

Variations: *Dana, Danica*
Nickname: *Dani*
Alternatives: *Rania, Nadia, Diana, Dina, Daria, Annika, Rory, Jordana, Edita*

Danielle is the female version of Daniel, meaning "judgment of God." Daniel was an Israelite who worked for the court of Babylon and whose talent for interpreting dreams led him to achieve high rank as a prophet. Daniel famously spent the night in a lion's den and emerged unscathed, proof of God's love.

Variations: *Danelle, Daniela, Daniella*
Nicknames: *Danya, Danica, Danny, Dani, Danna*
Alternatives: *Gabrielle, Adrienne, Gisele, Anabelle, Mariana*

Daphne is from Greek mythology. She was a nymph whom Gaia, the earth goddess, turned into a laurel tree to save her from the amorous advances of Apollo. Daphne du Maurier was a British suspense writer. In entertainment, Daphnes include actress Daphne Zuniga; Daphne Moon, a character on the 1990s TV show *Frasier;* and cute girl detective Daphne Blake on the TV show *Scooby-Doo! Where Are You?*

Nickname: *Daffy (if you think she'll forgive you)*
Alternatives: *Chloe, Zoe, Dabney, Delphine, Philippa, Tabitha*

Dara In Hebrew, Dara means "wisdom." In Gaelic, it means "oak tree." In Arabic, "halo." The name sounds like a variation of Daria or a feminization of Darren. Dara Torres won a silver medal in swimming at the Beijing Olympics when she was forty-one years old.

Variation: *Darra*
Alternatives: *Darla, Dora, Tamara, Farrah*

Daria is a Greek name, a female form of Darius, the ancient Persian king. Saint Daria lived in the third century. The name is popular in Russia and Slavic countries as well as Arabic countries, where it means "learned." Note that in the 1990s, *Daria* was an animated series on MTV about a smart, disaffected high schooler named Daria Morgendorffer.

Nickname: *Dasha*
Alternatives: *Amalia, Basia, Maria, Irena*

✏ **Deborah** A strong biblical name, Deborah was a prophet and judge who led the Jews to victory over the Canaanite army. The name means "bee" in Hebrew, and it is believed to have become popular with Puritans and other Christians because the bee is a symbol of hard work. It's a name with a strong foundation and deep meaning but declining popularity. Deborah was in the top ten in the 1950s and '60s but now is in the 800s. Famous Deborahs: actresses Deborah Kerr, Debbie Reynolds, Debra Winger, and Debra Messing.

Variations: *Deborah, Debora, Debra, Deberah, Devorah*
Nicknames: *Deb, Debbie, Decca*
Alternatives: *Delilah, Sarah, Martha, Judith, Rebecca, Esther, Dinah*

Deirdre An Irish name, Deirdre comes from a legend in which a king kills Deirdre's lover and forces her to marry him instead. Irish writers Yeats and Synge each featured Deirdre in plays. Tragic ties aside, the name sounds like "dear" and is strongly Irish, so it appeals to families interested in reclaiming their roots. Deirdre hasn't hit the top 1,000 since 1990.

Nicknames: *Didi, Dee*
Alternatives: *Fiona, Maude, Deandra, Dido, Dinah*

Delaney is an Irish surname meaning "of the dark one" that has become a girl's first name. It sounds like it could have roots in the American South, where last names for girls have been common for decades.

Alternatives: *Kendall, Dabney, Ainsley, Shelby, Mackenzie*

Delia means "from Delos." The island of Delos was the birthplace of the Greek goddess of the hunt, Artemis. Artemis's Roman equivalent is Diana, which creates a connection between Delia and Diana. Delia Ephron is a well-known screenwriter. Food personality and cookbook author Delia Smith is the Martha Stewart of England. Cute and swingy, Delia has ancient chops and contemporary zing.

Alternatives: *Cordelia, Dahlia, Ophelia, Cornelia, Celia*

Delilah Though she is the lover and betrayer of Samson in the Bible's book of Judges, Delilah is a euphonious word, sounding like delightful and lilacs. So maybe you can overlook the seduction and treachery of the biblical character. Lots of cuddlier nickname possibilities warm this up.

Nicknames: *Delia, Della, Lilah, Lily, Layla, Lia*
Alternatives: *Jezebel, Sheba, Lillian, Malia, Deva, Esther*

Delphine This name, very popular in France, is so pretty it deserves a look. It means "from Delphi," the location on Mount Parnassus (of the famous Delphic oracle), which was dedicated to Apollo. Delphi was believed by the ancient Greeks to be the center of the

> *I'd love it if she sounded . . .*
> ## French
>
> | | | |
> |---|---|---|
> | ~ AMÉLIE | ~ FLAVIE | ~ MARTINE |
> | ~ AURELIE | ~ LYDIE | ~ PASCALE |
> | ~ CLOTILDE | ~ MANON | ~ SIDONIE |
> | ~ DELPHINE | ~ MARIANNE | ~ SYLVIE |

universe and comes from the word for "womb." The word dolphin is related: Apollo was believed to have arrived at Delphi in the shape of a dolphin. And the delphinium plant (aka larkspur) also shares a common root and gives the name a floral touch; its blossoms look like dolphins when they unfold.

Variations: *Delphina, Delfina, Delphinia*
Alternatives: *Aurelie, Sandrine, Eloise, Elodie, Anais, Clara, Veronique, Annick*

Denise is the feminine of the French boy's name Denis, which comes from Dionysus, the Greek god of wine. Saint Denis is the patron saint and former bishop of Paris. Denise was at her most popular during the 1950s and '60s. She's a girl next door like Nancy, Susan, and Carol, but she's slightly more sophisticated, with a vaguely continental air. Be warned: There is an old joke that says that an uncle had to name his sister's newborn twins, so he named the girl Denise, which the family liked. Then he named the boy Denephew.

Variation: *Denisse*
Alternatives: *Aurelie, Claudine, Gabrielle, Natalie, Camille, Juliette, Clarisse*

Desiree From the French meaning "desired," Desiree is a popular name in the African American community. The name wasn't seen much in the United States before the 1950s and peaked in popularity in 1983. Desiree Rogers was President Barack Obama's first social secretary.

Variation: *Desirae*
Nicknames: *Desi, Rae*
Alternatives: *Renée, Dixie, Melody, Cadence*

Diana is the Roman goddess of hunting and the moon. Her Greek counterpart is Artemis. The Diana of myth was beautiful and chaste, thus Elizabethan poets wrote verses in honor of Queen Elizabeth, the virgin queen, using Diana as an allegory. She is often depicted with a deer, and also associated with oak groves, both nods to her strength. Fictional superhero Wonder Woman's name is Diana. The most famous Diana that leaps to mind is, of course, Diana, Princess of Wales, who was known for her beauty and compassion, as well as for being hunted by paparazzi. The name in all its forms peaked in popularity in the 1950s.

Variations: *Diane, Dionne, Deanna, Diandra, Dayana, Dayanara*
Nicknames: *Dee, Dina, Didi, Dinah*

Alternatives: *Artemis (Greek version), Luna (the moon goddess she supplanted), Minerva (another Roman goddess), Cynthia (named for the mountain on which Diana was born), Apollonia (Apollo was Diana's twin brother), Delphine (the site of her twin, Apollo's, oracle)*

Dixie comes from the word *ten* in French, which is *dix* (pronounced deece). It also has a clear connection to the American South: That region is called Dixie. Experts surmise that it may take its name from the Mason-Dixon line that separates north and south, or from the ten-dollar bills issued by the Citizens Bank of Louisiana before the Civil War, which were called

---

Maids of Mount Olympus

Where better to look for a strong name than the peak of Mount Olympus? The goddesses of Greek mythology (and their Roman counterparts) offer some great inspiration.

- **APHRODITE/VENUS:**
  goddess of love

- **ARTEMIS/DIANA:**
  goddess of the moon and the hunt

- **ATHENA/MINERVA:**
  goddess of war and reason

- **DEMETER/CERES:**
  goddess of the harvest

- **EOS/AURORA:**
  goddess of dawn

- **HERA/JUNO:**
  goddess of marriage and childbirth

- **HESTIA/VESTA:**
  goddess of the hearth and home

"dixies." The name has a pert, sassy ring to it. It was popular in the 1930s and '40s, and later, actress Dixie Carter helped boost its profile. A lively moniker for a little girl with moxie (who you wouldn't dream of naming Moxie).

Alternatives: *Pixie, Patricia (call her Trixie), Louisa, Scarlett, Carolina, Georgia, Clara, Lucy (call her Lulu)*

Djuna A name created just for writer Djuna Barnes by her father. Her whole life fans asked her what the origins of her name were and were disappointed by the lack of a good story. The name has a slightly foreign air. The combination of the *d* and the *j* make it look African or Indian, but the similarity to June gives it a familiarity. And the connection to Barnes lends the name a tomboyish, bohemian, Greenwich Village–in-its-heyday feel (Barnes was famous for her lesbian-themed fiction). Woody Allen used the name for one of the characters in his film *Everybody Says I Love You* and nicknamed her DJ.

Nicknames: *Juna, DJ*
Alternatives: *Luna, June, Diana, Juno*

Doe The name for a female deer has such a gentle, pastoral sound and meaning, it's a wonder more people don't choose it. If it's too crunchy-granola for you, then name her Dorothy and nickname her Doe. This pick is ideal for parents considering other names that suggest tranquility. You don't often find a one-syllable name for girls that is so distinctive.

Alternatives: *Paloma, Olive, Dolores, Brooke, Willow*

Dominique means "Lord" (think *anno domini*), and is the feminine form of Dominic. Saint Dominic is the patron saint of astronomers and founded the Dominican order of monks. The word means "Sunday" in other languages (in Spanish it's *domingo*). This sophisticated sounding name has less of a resoundingly religious ring to it than other names of Catholic origin, such as Bernadette.

Variations: *Domenica (Italy), Dominika (Eastern Europe), Domeniga (Spanish)*
Nicknames: *Mika, Mima, Nikki, Nikka, Meeka, Mina, Mini, Nico*
Alternatives: *Bernadette, Genevieve, Veronica, Emmanuelle*

Donna means "lady" in Italian and is a respectful way of addressing a woman of rank. (It's the female version of Don, as in Don Giovanni or "a mafia don.") It can also be a feminine version of Donald. Donna was in the top ten most popular baby names in the 1960s. Ritchie Valens's hit ballad "Donna," which was released in 1958, surely helped its rise. Madonna is a variation, as is Mona (Mona Lisa is a contraction of Ma [*my*] and Donna). If Donna doesn't do it for you, consider Donatella and Donata—which are not related, and come from the word "given"—but sound similar.

Variations: *Madonna, Mona*
Alternatives: *Donatella, Donata, Gina, Angela*

Doris means "a Dorian woman," referring to the tribe of ancient Greeks that founded Sparta. Doris was also a goddess, the daughter of sea god Oceanus. The name was popular in the early twentieth century (Hi there, Doris Day!) but has not yet made a comeback, unlike many other old-fashioned names. If you like the sound of Doris but worry that it lands with a thud, try Iris, Maris, or Ellis.

Alternatives: *Maris, Mavis, Agnes, Daria, Athena, Iris, Dorie (Dorothy)*

Dorothy is an old-fashioned name that hasn't yet roared back to life alongside Amelia and Emma. Perhaps it's because it has a grandmotherly ring to it; most Dorothys were born in the 1920s and '30s, so it might take another generation for the name to come back. Still, Dorothy has a lot going for it—it suggests a woman who's sassy, strong, and unafraid to speak her mind. Think Dorothy Zbornak, the lead character (played by Bea Arthur) on *The Golden Girls,* Dorothy of *The Wizard of Oz,* and Dorothy Parker, the witty Depression-era writer. *Sesame Street* keeps the name alive for a younger crowd: Dorothy is Elmo's pet fish. The name Dorothy comes from the Greek and means "gift of God." It is the inverse of Theodora—a good option if you like the message but aren't wild about the name.

Variations: *Dorothea, Dorota (Eastern Europe), Dasha*
Nicknames: *Dottie, Dot, Dort, Dolly, Dodie, Dorie*
Alternatives: *Theodora, Marjorie, Helen, Frances, Evelyn, Josephine*

Dulcie (pronounced DULL-sea) comes from Dulce (pronounced DOOL-seh), Spanish for "sweet." Many families anglicize the spelling by adding the *i* to ensure that the pronunciation will be on the mark. This cute name earns points with the sweetness of its meaning and diminutive "sea" sound at the end, but its "dull" start might turn some people off.

Alternatives: *Lourdes, Carmen, Pilar, Lacey, Dulcinea*

Dylan is a unisex last name meaning "great sea" in Welsh. The Welsh poet Dylan Thomas may have sparked the use of the name, which started in the 1960s shortly after his death, or maybe we should hold accountable folk rocker Bob Dylan, who rose to fame in the '60s. Dylan is favored by parents seeking gender-neutral names, but as a result it's a bit overused.

Variation: *Dillon*
Alternatives: *Fallon, Ellen, Marion, Sloane, Kennedy, Lauren, Harley*

E

Eden In the Bible, Eden is the paradise inhabited by Adam and Eve; the word in Hebrew means "palace of pleasure." The name became popular in the 1980s and is in ever more use. Eden is hopeful and outdoorsy and maybe even a little bit hippie around the edges. Parents are starting to use it for boys, too.

Alternatives: *Eve, Jenna (same meaning in Arabic), Summer, Skye, Selah, Emi, Elza, Alia*

 Edith was hot in the 1800s and early 1900s and has fallen way down in popularity. But why? It's a pretty, old-fashioned name that deserves to be revived by the same kinds of parents who put Olivia, Lucy, and Emma at the top of the charts. The name comes from the Old English and means, oddly, "spoils of war." It is a variation on the male name Edgar; Edgar the Peaceful, an Old English king, was the father of the first Edith (then called Eadgyth). If Edith suggests a little old lady in a housecoat, consider calling her the younger, sassier Edie (incidentally, the name of Andy Warhol's muse).

Variations: *Edita/Edyta (Eastern Europe), Edite (Germany and France), Editta (Italy)*
Nicknames: *Ditta, Dita, Edie*
Alternatives: *Enid, Lillith, Gwyneth, Martha, Pearl, Nellie, May, Grace, Rose*

Eileen A Gaelic name that comes from the French Aveline, Eileen is related to Evelyn and Helen. It likely means "bright." Eileen has been popular in the United States since the mid to late 1800s and peaked in the 1940s. The traditional Irish spelling is Eibhlin or Aoibheann, but that'll be a mouthful for your daughter's teachers—and everyone else. Expect to hear a few bars of the 1980s hit "Come on Eileen" every now and then.

Variations: *Aileen, Aline, Aveline, Evelyn, Ilene, Ileanna, Lena, Lina*

Alternatives: *Colleen, Maureen, Kathleen, Aislinn*

Let's Get Political

Do you want to bestow a legacy of leadership on your little girl? Consider naming her after one of history's great stateswomen.

- **BENAZIR** (Bhutto)
- **CONDOLEEZZA** (Rice)
- **DIANA** (Princess of Wales)
- **ELEANOR** (Roosevelt)
- **GERALDINE** (Ferraro)
- **GOLDA** (Meir)
- **HILLARY** (Rodham Clinton)
- **INDIRA** (Gandhi)
- **MADELEINE** (Albright)
- **MARGARET** (Thatcher)
- **MICHELLE** (Obama)
- **OVETA** (Culp Hobby)
- **SANDRA** (Day O'Connor)
- **REAGAN** (Ronald): Sure, this is a man's name, but presidential last names can make snappy (and meaningful) girl's names. Just don't choose Hoover. Some other options: Carter, Cleveland, Harrison (nickname her Hettie), Kennedy, Madison, McKinley, Quincy, Truman (Tru).

Elaine, like Eileen, is a variation of Helen, meaning "bright, shining." The name has an Arthurian slant to it: Elaine of Astolat was celebrated by Thomas Malory in *Le Morte d'Arthur* in 1485 and in the 1800s by Tennyson in *Idylls of the King* and *The Lady of Shalott*. She was known for dying of her love of Lancelot. Another Elaine (of Carbonek) was Sir Galahad's mother. Because many names in Arthurian legend have Celtic roots, there is suspicion that Elaine may come from the Welsh for "fawn." Elaine was most popular in the United States in the 1940s. Nowadays it suggests a smiling, quirky girl next door, thanks to Jerry Seinfeld's fictional TV sitcom pal Elaine Benes.

Variations: *Elaina, Elena*
Nicknames: *Lainey, Laina, Ella, Ellie, Elle, Laila, Lena*
Alternatives: *Mallory, Morgan, Evelyn, Shirley, Peggy, Linda, Marlene*

Eleanor is a leader. She is Eleanor of Aquitaine, the powerful queen of England and France from the twelfth century. She is Eleanor Roosevelt, first lady, civil rights crusader, U.N. cofounder, and overall force of nature. Call her Eleanor and you bestow a legacy of willfulness and success onto your girl. The origins of the name are murky: Eleanor of Aquitaine, one of the first recorded Eleanors, is believed to have been named for her mother, Aenor, with the prefix *ali* added to mean "other Aenor." Some people suspect that the name is ultimately related to Helen. Other famous Eleanors include Elinor Dashwood, heroine of *Sense and Sensibility,* actress Eleanor Parker, and the Beatles' lonely lady Eleanor Rigby. You can name her the stately Eleanor and call her the playful Ellie.

Variations: *Alienor, Elinor, Eleanora, Leonora, Leona, Lenore*
Nicknames: *Nell, Nelly, Ellen, Ellie, Nora, Norie*
Alternatives: *Theodora, Margaret, Victoria, Frances, Josephine, Beatrix, Marion*

Elena The Italian and Spanish version of Helen. Lilting and feminine. (See Helen, page 117, for more.)

Variations: *Eleni, Yelena, Elenka, Ilona, Ellen*
Alternatives: *Imelda, Eliza, Amira, Estella, Edita, Helene, Aviva*

℘ **Eliana** In Hebrew, Eliana is "God has answered." The name may also be a form of Helen ("bright"). It's similar in sound to Ariana but less well known, and a more ornate, slightly exotic-sounding alternative to the überpopular Ella.

Variations: *Iliana, Ileanna, Elianna, Elliana, Liana, Allana, Eliane, Liane*
Nicknames: *Lia, Elia, Eli, Lina, Lana, Ana*
Alternatives: *Adriana, Leonora, Anastasia, Natasha*

Elizabeth is one of the most popular names in modern history. Elizabeth has always been in the top twenty-five names in the last 130 years (since the United States government has kept good records), and it is usually in the top ten. It means "God is my oath." Elizabeth was the mother of the biblical John the Baptist, so there is a strong Christian component. There is also an equally compelling royal angle. Queen Elizabeth I was the patroness of Shakespeare, under whom English arts and poetry flourished. Elizabeth Bowes-Lyon, aka the Queen Mum, became a heroine to the British when she refused to leave London during the blitz of World War II, when the city was under siege. Her daughter, Queen Elizabeth II, is one of England's longest-ruling monarchs in history. And there is an elegance and glamour connection. Actress Elizabeth Taylor has represented beauty and sophistication for more than sixty years, and others like Liz Hurley and Elizabeth Banks have followed suit. Within Elizabeth—and her many variations and nicknames—there is every kind of girl.

Variations: *Elisabeth (French, German, Spanish), Elisabetta (Italian), Erzebet (Hungarian), Elspeth (Scottish), Elisabet (Scandinavian)*

Nicknames: *There are the folksy: Betty, Betsy, Elsie, Libby; the girl next door: Liz, Lizzie, Lisa, or Beth; a showstopper: Liza; the funky: Biz, Litzy; the exotic: Elsa; the continental: Babette, Bettina, Elisa, Elise, Elyse, Eliza, Lizbeth; and the veddy, veddy British: Lilibet (QE II's nickname).*

Alternatives: *Margaret, Victoria, Anne, Matilda, Isabelle, Marguerite, Catherine, Mary*

Ella started life as a prefix. *Al* or *el* means "other" in Old German. Alienor (aka Eleanor) meant "the other Aenor," which referred to the fact that Alienor was named after her mother. That was then; this is now. Ella (and her French-ish variation, Elle) have become stand-alone names as well as shortened forms of all kinds of other names, including Eleanor, Elizabeth, Ellen, Helen, Isabella, Belle, Marielle, Joelle, Adella, Annabella, Arabella, Carmella, Christabel, Daniella, Emmanuelle, Gabrielle, Jezebelle, Maribelle, Mirabella, Philomela, Raphaella, Sybella, and many more. Bottom line: You can take almost any girl's name, lop off the end, add *elle* or *ella,* and end up with a pretty good name whose ideal nickname would be Elle or Ella.

Variation: *Elle*
Alternatives: *Anna, Selah, Mira, Asta, Isla, Elsa*

Ellen started out as a variation of Helen, which means "bright." The Helen of Greek myth was the beauty for whom the Trojan War was fought. Nowadays, Ellen exists on her own and in numerous related forms. For many, the name lands with a thud; for others it has the virtue of vanilla ice cream: It is a basic staple easily passed over as too plain but fervently appreciated by connoisseurs of subtlety.

Variations: *Helene, Eleni, Elaine, Elin, Elena*
Nicknames: *Nell, Nelly, Ellie*

Alternatives: *Kay, Carrie, Annie, Jenny, Fanny, Maggie, Maude, Olive, Ruth*

⌇ **Elodie** The meaning of the name Elodie is disputed. What's clear is that the name combines the French flair of Eloise and Amélie with the musicality of a melody. It sounds like it should be a bird's name, maybe a type of lark, singing to the heavens. A basic, stolid last name would be greatly improved by the frills of a name like this.

Variation: *Elodia*
Alternatives: *Amélie, Emilie, Eloise, Louisa, Dodie*

⌇ **Eloise** is the French version of Louise, which relates to Louis and Ludwig and means "fighter." There are two famous Eloises: Heloise, the nun who fell in love with her tutor, Abelard; she became an abbess, and he an abbot, and they wrote love letters to one another their whole lives long; and Eloise, the frisky little girl from Kay Thompson and Hilary Knight's children's books, who wreaks havoc in New York's Plaza Hotel where she lives. So perhaps we can say that Eloise is a little bit naughty and a little bit nice. You could call her Lou or Lulu or Lola, but then why name her something as special and different as Eloise if you aren't planning to use it?

Nicknames: *Lois, Lulu, Lou*
Alternatives: *Eliza, Kay, Amélie, Esme, Valentina, Margareta*

Elsa A variation of Elizabeth, Elsa was made famous by Joy Adamson in her 1960 memoir and the film based on it, *Born Free*. Adamson and her husband raised Elsa, an orphan lion cub, in Kenya and then returned her to her pride. A darling, slightly Germanic-sounding alternative to Ella.

Variation: *Ilsa*
Nickname: *Elsie*
Alternatives: *Elke, Inez, Selma, Selah*

Elyse A variation, with Elisé, of Elisabeth (see page 81). Elyse has a bit of continental glamour to it, thanks to the long eeeese sound. She is no Liz or Betsy.

Variations: *Elise, Ilyse*
Alternatives: *Simone, Celine, Audrey, Aimee*

Emily is a variation of Amelia. Like Amelia, it was popular in the 1800s, but Emily is in a class by herself: The name was number one throughout the late nineties and early 2000s, and has a timeless, utterly untrendy quality like Elizabeth and Anne. But Emily is a more romantic, less regal name. It has a whiff of moodiness and poetry about it, thanks to Emily Brontë and Emily Dickinson.

Variations: *Amelia, Amalia, Emilie, Emilia, Emmalee, Emely, Emmeline*
Nicknames: *Emmy, Emma, Millie*
Alternatives: *Aurelie, Camilla, Anabelle, Elodie, Agnes, Annalise*

Emma Warm, romantic, and (thanks to Jane Austen) wildly popular, Emma started off life as . . . Ermintrude. It's an Old German name meaning "entirely beloved" that migrated to England with the Normans. That name lands with a thud, while Emma envelops in a maternal embrace (you can hear a baby's first word of mum-mum-mamma in it). Although Emma does not come from Emily, some people use it as Emily's nickname. Emma is in a class with Olivia and Lucy and Abigail and Charlotte: It's an old-fashioned name that has been revived with enthusiasm.

Variations: *Emmeline, Emmy*

Alternatives: *Anna, Lucy, Aria, Mamie, Gemma, Jenna, Alma, Ebba*

🖊 **Enid** A name from Arthurian legend, Enid was the patient wife of Geraint who was celebrated in Tennyson's *The Idylls of the King,* published in 1859. It's a solid name, with strong Celtic ties. But it is out of fashion with the lacey, girly, vowelly names so popular now (Sophia, Isabella, Amelia, Emma). But the tides of fashion shift, and Enid is ripe for rediscovery. Enid was the best friend of Elizabeth Wakefield in the *Sweet Valley High* book series started in the 1980s. And it was the title of a hit song for the Barenaked Ladies in the 1990s.

Alternatives: *Inez (or Inès), Esme, Edith, Astrid, Adele, Eleanor, Anya*

Erica is the feminine form of Eric, which means "eternal ruler." It's a Scandinavian name that migrated over to England before the eleventh century. (Eric the Red was a Norwegian explorer who went to Greenland via Iceland in the 900s.) Erica also happens to be the Latin word for "heather." Erika is the preferred spelling in Scandinavia and Eastern Europe.

Variation: *Erika*
Alternatives: *Annika, Veronica, America, Heather, Freya, Ingrid, Ulrika*

Erin means "Ireland." It wasn't until the 1950s that many Americans started using the name for girls; before then it was a name that stuck close to its roots, with use primarily limited to Americans of Irish descent. Erin peaked in the top twenty in 1983 and remains in the top 200. Her ethnic cast has rubbed off over the years, and she has become much more mainstream.

Alternatives: *Kelly, Shannon, Tara, Chiara, Aileen, Ann, Kathleen, Caitlin*

✐ **Esmée** (or Esmé) comes from the French *estimer* ("to esteem"), which is also related to *aimer* ("to love"). So Esmé is a closer relation to Amy than she is to Esmerelda, though it may not sound like it. Esmé isn't cracking the popularity charts in the United States yet, but she's got some of the markers for success. The

Fictional Females

The characters of literature can inspire us as much as the stories they inhabit. Some of these play lesser roles than others, but all have names that capture the imagination.

- **AFFERY** *(Little Dorrit by Charles Dickens)*
- **ANNA** *(Anna Karenina by Leo Tolstoy)*
- **ANTONIA** *(My Antonia by Willa Cather)*
- **ARWEN** *(The Lord of the Rings by J.R.R. Tolkien)*
- **AYLA** *(Clan of the Cave Bear by Jean M. Auel)*
- **CELIE** *(The Color Purple by Alice Walker)*
- **DAISY** *(Daisy Miller by Henry James)*
- **EMMA** *(Emma by Jane Austen)*
- **ESMÉ** *("For Esmé—with Love and Squalor" by J. D. Salinger)*
- **ESTELLA** *(Great Expectations by Charles Dickens)*
- **FRANNY** *(Franny and Zooey by J. D. Salinger)*
- **GWENDOLEN** *(The Importance of Being Earnest by Oscar Wilde)*
- **MAISIE** *(What Maisie Knew by Henry James)*
- **NORA** *(A Doll's House by Henrik Ibsen)*
- **OLIVE** *(Olive Kitteredge by Elizabeth Strout)*
- **SONIA** *(Uncle Vanya by Anton Chekhov)*
- **TESS** *(Tess of the d'Urbervilles by Thomas Hardy)*

name is in the top one hundred in the U.K. It scans like Emma but is more exotic. And it sounds like it might include the star-maker letter *z*. The cherry on top: It was the name of a character in the *Twilight* series.

Alternatives: *Inez, Estelle, Irma, Zoe, Alma*

> ## She's a Star
>
> These celestial baby names will evoke the stars for your little sparkler:
>
> - ASTA
> - ASTRID
> - CELESTE
> - CELINE
> - ESTELLE
> - ESTHER
> - ESTRELLA
> - ISHTAR
> - MARIS
> - STELLA
> - TARA

Estella After a long dormancy, Stella has made a big comeback. She's Lucy's cousin. She's Hannah's BFF. You can find Stellas in kindergartens and nursing homes around the country but barely anywhere in between. It's great that she's back: Stella has star appeal (literally—the name means "star"). Estella, on the other hand, still has a frowsy feel to it and is not picking up steam. Estelle Getty, actress from the TV sitcom *The Golden Girls,* leaps to mind. As does Pip's cruel love from Dickens's *Great Expectations*. Estrella, on the other hand, is a variation that is suddenly hitting the charts. Go figure.

Alternatives: *Hannah, Lucy, Amelia, Asta, Ilona, Erica*

Esther Queen Esther is one of the heroines of the Old Testament. She was a Jewish captive who married Xerxes, the king of Persia, and at the risk of her own life, saved the Jewish people of the kingdom from a massacre. Her Hebrew name is Hadassah, which means "myrtle." Esther is either a translation of Hadassah or it is the Hebrew form of the Persian name Ishtar. Ishtar was the goddess of love, equivalent to Venus, and meaning "star." Hester is a variation of Esther, but sounds colonial-dour (Hester Prynne was the wearer of Hawthorne's scarlet letter)—probably best to stick with the original.

Variations: *Hester, Hadassah, Ishtar*
Nicknames: *Essa, Estée (as in Lauder), Estelle, Etty, Etta, Asta, Nettie*
Alternatives: *Stella, Rachel, Rebecca, Naomi, Miriam, Ruth, Iris, Viola*

ℓ **Eugenia** While Eugene has been looked down on in recent years as a nerd's name, Eugenia is a name for a princess. There have been several Eugenias throughout royal history, but the most recent and currently famous is British Prince Andrew and Fergie's daughter, Eugenie. Eugenia is a popular name in Spain. It deserves a look by parents who are considering unabashedly frilly, feminine names like Anastasia, Josephine, and Theodora.

Nicknames: *Gina, Genie, Euna, Nia, Gigi*
Alternatives: *Victoria, Beatrice, Adelaide, Matilda*

Eva is from Eve and means "life." A short and sweet
classic that has trendy appeal (ends with an ah sound
and contains an exotic letter *v*), it can be pronounced
EH-vah, AY-vah, or EE-vah. It may be the ambiguous
pronunciation that propelled its phonetic sister Ava,
which has only one pronunciation, to the head of the
pack. Eva is a name that suggests serenity and balance
(even) and eternity (ever).

Variations: *Eva, Eve, Evie, Evangeline, Evangelina, Evita,
Ava, Evita, Ewa (Poland), Aoife (popular in Ireland), and
Hava (Hebrew)*
Alternatives: *Ada, Isla, Alma, Lexi, Zoe, Elsa, Elke, Arden*

✐ **Evelyn** Though Evelyn evokes universal mother
Eve, it's more closely related to Ava. Ava comes from
Aveline, an old Norman name. Evelyn is its anglicized
Irish form. Evelyn was among the top ten in 1915,
which is why it sounds like a grandmother's name—
it is. But if you wait long enough, anything comes
back into style. And Evelyn is on the move. She's
edging her way up the popularity scale now, and
when today's Evelyn starts her own rock band in
a few years, the name might be cool again.

Variation: *Evelin*
Alternatives: *Frances, Lilian, Flora, Louise, Virginia, Marion,
Hazel, Rory*

F

Faith is one of the seven virtues of Christianity, including Hope, Charity (or Love), Prudence, Justice, Temperance, and Fortitude (or Courage). The latter four are cardinal virtues (these can be achieved through human effort); the first three are theological virtues (divinely bestowed by God); Faith means having belief in God. It, along with the other virtues, was a very popular name with Puritans. The name declined for a while, and is now in the top one hundred. It has a pretty sound with a light touch. If you like the sound of it but find the religious connotations a bit heavy-handed, consider Fay, which sounds like Faith and means fairy.

Nicknames: *Fay, Faye*
Alternatives: *Hope, Charity, Prudence, May, Heather, Hailey*

Fanny A nickname for Frances, Fanny is very popular in France. Writer Marcel Pagnol gave the name a boost when he made Fanny the lead character in his 1932 play of the same name and the movies that resulted from it. There are numerous well-known Fannies, including Fanny Ardent (French actress), Fannie Flagg (American novelist), and Fannie Farmer (of eponymous cookbook fame). A word of caution: Fanny has a vulgar meaning in England, and in the United States it is slang for rear end.

Alternatives: *Frances, Francoise, Honoria, Manon, Pascale, Allie*

> ### I'd love it if she sounded . . .
> ## Islamic
>
> ~ **AISHA** *("woman")*   ~ **SANAA** *("brilliance")*
>
> ~ **AZIZA** *("beloved")*   ~ **SHAKIRA** *("grateful")*
>
> ~ **FARRAH** *("joy")*   ~ **SURAYA** *("stars")*
>
> ~ **IKRAM** *("glory")*   ~ **YASMEEN** *("jasmine flower")*
>
> ~ **IZAZ** *("esteem")*   ~ **ZARA** *("bright," "blossom")*
>
> ~ **JENNA** *("heaven")*   ~ **ZARIA** *("rose")*
>
> ~ **LEILA** *("night")*   ~ **ZIA** *("light")*
>
> ~ **NAHLA** *("drink")*

Farrah means "fair" to English speakers; "joy" to Arabic ones. Farrah is a place-name in Asia and the Middle East—it's a town in India and a town and river in Afghanistan. To most Americans, however, Farrah evokes the actress Farrah Fawcett. The *Charlie's Angels* actress epitomized the easy, sunny glamour of California in the 1970s.

Variations: *Farah, Farra*
Alternatives: *Darra, Lara, Leila, Zahra*

Fatima An Arabic name, Fatima was the favorite daughter of the prophet Mohammed and the only one of his children to carry on the line. She was one of the four perfect women according to the Koran (with

Khadijah, Mary, and Aisha). She is a woman of virtue and purity; what Mary is to Christians, Fatima is also to Muslims. Fatima is also a location in Portugal where three children were said to have seen the Virgin Mary in 1917, so the name is also celebrated by Christians.

Variations: *Fatimah, Fatma (Turkey), Fadma, Fatma*
Nickname: *Fati (pronounced Fahti)*
Alternatives: *Aisha, Zahra, Leila, Selma, Salima*

Faye means "fairy" and could be the perfect name for your lively little sprite. The root of the word comes from the Latin for "fate." The name is dreamy and magical, and gets an Arthurian element from Morgan le Fay, Arthur's sorceress half-sister.

Variation: *Fay*
Alternatives: *Destiny, Faith, Sylvia, May, Freya*

Felicia means "happiness" and "good luck," from the Latin *felix,* and the name extends its cheerfulness to the natural world as well: Felicia is a type of sunflower. Felicia was a popular character on the TV soap opera *General Hospital* during the 1980s, but in the 2000s the hot pop culture version of the name (thanks to an eponymous TV show) was Felicity. Either one bestows blessings of joy.

Variaions: *Phyllicia (Phyllis meets Felicia), Felicity*
Nicknames: *Flip, Lici, Licia, Lecia*
Alternatives: *Allegra, Joy, Alicia*

Fern A fern is a plant that thrives in shady, moist conditions. The name is associated with rural areas and hasn't been used much since the 1960s. Fern was the farm girl in E. B. White's *Charlotte's Web*. It might call to mind *Where the Red Fern Grows,* a children's book set in the Ozarks. Fern is a name that people either seem to love or hate. Some parents think it's got the retro appeal of Ivy and Ruby, while others think it's a name for a hayseed.

Alternatives: *Hazel, Willow, Aspen, Olive*

Fernanda The feminine version of Fernando and Ferdinand, the name means "brave traveler" from the Old German. Ferdinand was popular in the Spanish royal family, and migrated to England when Queen Mary I married a Spaniard in 1554. Still mostly used by Spanish-speaking families, it's a vivacious, assertive name for a girl with a short or plain last name.

Nicknames: *Fern, Ann, Nanda, Randa*
Alternatives: *Alejandra, Marcella, Lucia, Valentina*

Fidelia means "loyal." It's a Spanish name that is pretty as well as meaningful. Note that it's the feminine of Fidel, which makes Cuban dictator Castro leap to mind.

Variation: *Fidelma*
Nickname: *Delia*
Alternatives: *Delia, Felicia, Adele, Esperanza*

Finley A boy's name in Ireland and the British Isles and more often spelled Finlay there, Finley has appeared in the top 1,000 for girls in the United States since 2005. The name means "fair haired" in Gaelic. Finn has become increasingly popular for boys in the United States, giving a nickname for Finley a tomboyish air—this could be a good or bad thing, depending on your preferences.

Alternatives: *Riley, Darcy, Casey, Campbell, Avery*

Fiona comes from Fionn mac Cumhail (aka Finn), a hero of old Irish legend. Stories of Finn's band of warrior poets have existed since the third century. The eighteenth-century poet James Macpherson wrote an epic poem about Finn, furthering interest. Like Finn, Fiona means "fair." It is from Finn that we get Sinn Fein, the Irish nationalist organization. Fiona became mainstream in the United States in the 1990s. For Fiona lovers who want something a bit off the beaten trail, there's Finola (Irish, "white shoulders") and Fenella (an anglicization of Finola).

Nickname: *Fi (pronounced Fee)*
Alternatives: *Siobhan (pronounced shuh-VAUN), Niamh (pronounced neeve), Darina, Deirdre, Maeve, Mairead (pronounced mah-RAID), Nola*

Flora was the Roman goddess of flowers. The name came into use in the 1700s. One Flora Macdonald helped Prince Charles II escape from England to France via her native Scotland in 1746. To put a French spin on Flora, call her Fleur ("flower" in French).

Nickname: *Flo*
Alternatives: *Rose, Poppy, Zara, Lily, Dahlia*

Florence means "blooming, flourishing" and came into being in the Middle Ages, first as a boy's name. Florence Nightingale's heroism as a nurse during the Crimean War in the late 1800s caused the name to spike in popularity. She was named for the city of her birth, Florence, Italy. To contemporary ears, the name seems dated, evoking actress Florence Henderson (aka Carol Brady from *The Brady Bunch*) and the housekeeper on the sitcom *The Jeffersons*. And the nicknames sound like diner waitresses (Flo from Mel's Diner on the sitcom *Alice*) and cows (Flossie). But it's a solid name and it only takes one cool Florence to turn things around. The U.K. is realizing this: Florence is in the top one hundred there. Florentia is the Latin name for the city and the way the moniker first appeared. Maybe cooler as a boy's name: Florent or Florian.

Variations: *Florida (Esther Rolle's character on '70s sitcom* Good Times*), Fleur, Flora*
Nicknames: *Florrie, Flossie*
Alternatives: *Venetia, America, Frances, Rosemary, Poppy*

✏ **Frances** means "from France" and came to English via the Italian name Francesco. Saint Francis of Assisi was born Giovanni (John) in the eleventh century in Italy, but was nicknamed Francesco because of his father's extensive business dealings in France. Saint Francis is associated with caring for the poor and a love of and respect for nature, especially birds. Francis migrated to England in the sixteenth century. In the seventeenth century, Francis with an *i* became associated with boys; Frances with an *e* for girls. Frances was in the top ten around 1915. She'd go well with Sadie and Lucy. It's time for a comeback.

Variations: *Francesca (popular in Italy), Françoise (France), Francine*
Nicknames: *Fanny, Fran, Francie, Franny, Frankie*
Alternatives: *Evelyn, Margaret, Virginia, Catherine, Josephine, Martha, Ruby*

Frida means "peaceful lady" in Old German. The name is found mostly in German and Scandinavian countries. Famous Fridas include painter Frida Kahlo (her father was German) and ABBA singer Frida Lyngstad. Freya, a variation on the name, was the Norse goddess of love. Freya has a flower girl sway to it, which could explain its big popularity in the U.K., where floral names are all the rage.

Alternatives: *Freya, Enid, Ingrid, Wilhelmina (Mina for short), Dagmar*

The Artist's Way

Visual artists have often used muses to inspire them. Turn the tables on the art world and let these masters be your naming muses:

- **ANNIE** *(Leibovitz)*: visionary American portrait photographer

- **ARTEMESIA** *(Gentileschi)*: acclaimed Italian Baroque painter

- **BERENICE** *(Abbott)*: photographer in Paris and New York best known for her work in the 1920s

- **BERTHE** *(Morisot)*: Impressionist painter whose primary subject was women

- **CATARINA** *(van Hemessen)*: believed to be the earliest female Flemish painter

- **CINDY** *(Sherman)*: groundbreaking conceptual photographer and filmmaker

- **CLARICIA**: thirteenth-century convent student and manuscript illuminator

- **DOROTHEA** *(Lange)*: noted photographer of the Great Depression

- **ELISABETH** *(Vigée-Le Brun)*: French, recognized as the most famous female painter of the eighteenth century

- **FRIDA** *(Kahlo)*: Mexican painter known for her vibrant, surreal self-portraits

- **GEORGIA** *(O'Keeffe)*: American twentieth-century painter who drew inspiration from nature

- **KARA** *(Walker)*: contemporary American artist best known for her politically charged life-size paper silhouettes

- **KIKI** *(Smith)*: contemporary American multimedia artist

- **MAYKEN** *(Verhulst)*: sixteenth-century Flemish painter

- **OROVIDA** *(Pissarro)*: granddaughter of Impressionist painter Camille Pissarro, and artist in her own right

- **SÉRAPHINE** *(Louis)*: self-taught French painter of the early twentieth century

- **VICTORINE** *(Meurent)*: artist and muse for Parisian artists of the late nineteenth century

G

Gabriella comes from the boy's name Gabriel. Gabriel was one of the archangels, with Michael, Uriel, and Raphael. To Jews, he is the messenger of God; to Christians, he made the annunciation to Mary; to Muslims, he revealed the Koran to Mohammed. It is believed that Gabriel will blow his horn to reveal Judgment Day. Gabriella means "God's heroine" and became very popular in the 1980s; today it is in the top ten in the United States for African American and Hispanic babies. Gabriella's more demure sister, Gabrielle, arrived on the scene in the 1950s but today lags behind in popularity.

Variations: *Gabrielle, Gabriela*
Nicknames: *Gabby, Elle, Ella, Brie, Brielle*
Alternatives: *Giselle, Camille, Clementine, Josephine, Raphaella*

✐ **Gaia** is the ancient Greek goddess of the earth. Gaia has a hippie, back-to-nature vibe, which is in sync with today's interest in all things green. The name is a great alternative to Maya.

Alternatives: *Rhea (Gaia's daughter, Zeus's mother, who also is known as "earth mother"), Cybele (Greek goddess known as "mountain mother"), Maia, Kaia*

Gemma means "gem" or "jewel." Popular in the U.K., it has just hit the top 1,000 in the United States. Look for it to rise as an alternative to Jenna and other jewel names like Ruby and Jade.

Variation: *Jemma*
Alternatives: *Jemima, Imogen, Jenna, Ruby, Emma, Alma*

Genesis The first book of the Bible, Genesis tells of the creation of the world and the lives of the patriarchs. In Hebrew, it is *Bereshith* ("in the beginning"). The name sounds like a new made-up name, but it dates to the early fourth century. Saint Genesius of Rome is the patron saint of actors. There was also a St. Genesius of Arles. A heads-up: Genesis is also used for boys.

Nicknames: *Jenny, Jen*
Alternatives: *Destiny, Maris, Dolores, Charity, Eden, Isis*

 Genevieve is the patron saint of Paris who lived around the year 500. The name is Celtic with French influences. Geneviève (je-ne-VY-EHVE) is the French pronounciation; Genevieve (JEN-eh-veeve), the English. This elegant lady was not popular in the United States until 2000, when she started climbing the charts. The name is at home in the city and the country, evoking both cosmopolitan sophistication and fresh-faced purity. Guinevere, which sounds similar, is the name of King Arthur's unfaithful wife and spawned the popular English name Jennifer. You can use Jen or Jenny as nicknames for either.

Nicknames: *Gigi, Viva, Jen, Jenny, Gina, Jenna*
Alternatives: *Guinevere, Jennifer, Geneva (means "juniper"),*
Ginevra (Spanish), Adelaide, Veronique, Vivienne

Georgia is a feminization of George, which means
"farm work." Ironic, considering George is one of the
most regal names around. Many kings (and, of course,
presidents), have been named George, and St. George
slayed the dragon in legend and became the patron
saint of England in the 1300s. The feminine Georgia
is a wonderful way to honor a grandpa, uncle, or other
important George, and offers an adorable tomboyish
nickname in Georgie. Last popular in the 1920s, the
name is now coming back.

Variations: *Georgina, Georgiana, Georgette, Jorja*
Nickname: *Georgie*
Alternatives: *Virginia, Savannah, Augusta, Caroline, Dakota*

I'd love to call her . . .
Gigi

Although irresistibly charming and oh-so-French,
you may think Gigi is *too* adorable to use as
a first name in its own right. Here are some other
options that will grow with her:

~ ANGELINA	~ GEORGIA	~ GISELLE
~ EUGENIA	~ GEORGINA	~ REGINA
~ GABRIELLE	~ GENEVIEVE	~ VIRGINIA

Gertrude was among the top twenty-five most
popular names in the late 1800s, and declined slowly
but surely until it fell off the chart in 1965. The name
is Germanic, meaning "strength of the spear," and it
migrated to England from the continent sometime
between the eleventh and thirteenth centuries. The
name is so out of fashion that it could become a cool
pick. It goes well with German last names and would
offer a nice counterpart to more ornate last names
filled with vowels. If it's just too dusty to consider,
then have a look at Greta (page 108), which might fit
the bill.

Nicknames: *Gert, Gertie, Trudi, Trudle*
Alternatives: *Greta, Gretchen, Clementine, Harriet, Amandine,
Evangeline, Joan, Gwendolyn, Josephine*

Giacinta is pronounced ja-SIN-tah and means
"hyacinth" in Italian. As floral names become more
popular in the United States and the U.K., names
like this one, which are poetic and ornate, are worth
another look.

Variations: *Hyacinth, Jacinta (Spanish)*
Nicknames: *Gia, Cindy*
Alternatives: *Giovanna, Francesca, Cynthia, Araminta*

Giada means "jade" in Italian. It's in a class with
Amber, Gemma, Ruby, Diamond, Crystal, and the other
jewelry names, but—perhaps because of its European

Baubles, Bangles, and Beads

Many parents want an ornamental name for their girls. You can't get much flashier than jewelry, so they name their daughters after precious stones, or general jewelry terms. These are the favorites:

- **AMBER**
  (once hot, now déclassé)

- **BERYL** *(a shiny mineral; emeralds are beryls)*

- **BIJOU** *(French, "jewelry")*

- **CORAL**

- **CRYSTAL** *(Beware: TV's Dynasty casts a long shadow)*

- **DIAMOND**

- **ESMERELDA**
  ("emerald" in Spanish)

- **GEMMA** *(Italian, "jewel")*

- **GIADA** *(Italian, "jade")*

- **JADE**

- **JEWEL**

- **OPAL**

- **PEARL**

- **RUBY**

- **SAPPHIRE**

- **TIARA**

- **TIFFANY**

lineage—it feels smarter and more cultured than its flashier sisters. The name has been popularized by the ever-grinning TV chef Giada De Laurentiis.

Nickname: *Gia*

Alternatives: *Ana, Gianna, Rana, Marta, Jade, Joanna*

Gianna hit the top 1,000 in 1989 and has since surged to the top one hundred. The name is the feminization of Gianni, which is John in Italian. So think of it as the

Italian Jane. The longer form, Giovanna, is not nearly as popular as the shorter Gianna.

Nicknames: *Gia, Gina*
Variations: *Giana, Gianina, Giovanna*
Alternatives: *Giovanna, Kianna, Tiana, Jenna, Raina*

✎ **Gillian** A feminization of Julian, Gillian didn't split off into a different name until the sixteenth century. Julian came from Julius, which was the name of two popes as well as Roman emperor Gaius Julius Caesar. Gillian is a pretty, lilting name, one that's evocative of a lush English garden (maybe because it shares syllables with Lilian and thus lilies). It's a lovely choice for a little girl, and one she will surely grow into as she gets older.

Variation: *Jillian*
Nicknames: *Jill, Gigi*
Alternatives: *Lilian, Megan, Julianne, Mallory, Giselle*

Gina was not a popular name until the 1940s. The success of Italian actress Gina Lollobrigida in the mid-twentieth century must have been what put it on the map. Or was it Italian Americans embracing their roots? No matter, it's a great name, one that's full of spunk—and that makes an even better nickname. You can start with a longer form like Georgina, Regina, or even Virginia, and call her Gina for short.

Alternatives: *Gigi, Nina, Rita, Lina, Lola, Kiki*

Giovanna is like Joanna in Italian. It's a derivative of John, which means it's related to Joan and Jane as well. Lately the shorter form Gianna is more popular in the United States, maybe because of its simplicity and its reminiscence of names like Maya, Emma, and Chiara. Giovanna, being longer and more complicated, has more nickname possibilities.

Nicknames: *Giova, Vanna, Giogio, Anna, Gia, Gina*
Alternatives: *Joanna, Valerie, Lucianna, Vivianna, Angelina*

Giselle Though it evokes a graceful, long-legged animal, Giselle actually comes from the Germanic word for "pledge" or, less kindly, "hostage." In ancient and medieval Europe, noble children were sometimes sent to a neighboring country to be brought up. This was done to create or strengthen an alliance. The names Giselle (for girls) and Gilbert (for boys) came from this practice. The ballet *Giselle* (1841) popularized the name. (The 1958 movie *Gigi* gave it staying power.) It's poised for a big comeback: It has cute nickname possibilities (Gigi, Elle, Ella); the heroine of the 2007 Disney movie *Enchanted* is named Giselle; and model Gisele Bundchen has given it an air of effortless beauty.

Variations: *Gisele, Gisella, Gisselle*
Nicknames: *Gigi, Elle, Ella*
Alternatives: *Clara, Delphine, Gabrielle, Aurora, Ariel, Jasmine, Bella, Graziella*

Revolutionary Names

The Revolutionary War, that is. Visit any colonial graveyard in New England and take a look at the headstones. You'll note that the ladies buried there sport names that are the same as those in the local playground down the road. If you wait long enough—sometimes 200 years—anything comes back into fashion. Here are some favorites from colonial America, a few of which are sleepers, and others that top the charts:

~ ABIGAIL	~ ESTHER	~ LYDIA
~ ALICE	~ FRANCES	~ MARGARET
~ AMELIA	~ GRACE	~ MARIA
~ ANNE	~ HANNAH	~ MARTHA
~ CHARLOTTE	~ HELEN	~ MARY
~ CLARA	~ ISABELLA	~ MERCY
~ DEBORAH	~ JANE	~ OLIVIA
~ DOLLEY	~ JOANNA	~ PRISCILLA
~ EDITH	~ JOSEPHINE	~ RACHEL
~ ELEANOR	~ KATHERINE	~ REBECCA
~ ELIZABETH	~ LOUISA	~ SARAH
~ EMILY	~ LUCRETIA	~ SOPHIA
~ EMMA	~ LUCY	~ SUSANNAH

✏ **Gloria** is an old-fashioned favorite that deserves a revival. It means, no surprise, "glory," and so is a celebration of joy, honor, and praise. The name barely existed before 1900—George Bernard Shaw is credited with coining it for his play *You Never Can Tell* (1898). It hit the top twenty in the 1920s and remained popular through the 1950s, though now it lingers low on the list. Alternative picks include Gloriana, which was used in reference to Queen Elizabeth I; or Glory, which sounds very contemporary and patriotic.

Nickname: *Glo*
Variations: *Gloriana, Glory*
Alternatives: *Joyce, Felicia, Barbara, Shirley, Glenda*

Grace From the Latin (*gratia*), Grace is one of the virtue names (see "The Value of a Name," page 214) and was enormously popular with Puritans, along with similar names like Mercy and Patience. Considered frowsy and old-fashioned in the 1970s, Grace is now as beloved as it was in the late 1800s. The Graces of Greek and Roman mythology were goddesses of beauty and charm. Also called the Charities, Greek writer Hesiod gave them names: Thalia ("blooming"), Aglaia ("splendor"), and Euphrosyne ("joy"). The name Grace got a boost in 1838 when Grace Darling, the daughter of a lighthouse keeper in England, helped her father rescue nine people from a shipwreck in a raging storm. Grace Kelly livened up the name in the 1950s and 1960s. And singer Grace Jones gave it a cool, strong edge in the 1980s. In the 1990s and 2000s, sitcom *Will and Grace* coincided with the name's revival.

Variations: *Gracelyn, Graciela (Spanish), Grazia (Italian)*
Nickname: *Gracie*
Alternatives: *Faith, Patience, Charity, Hannah, Abigail, Emma*

🖋 **Greer** comes from the name Gregory. It evokes Hollywood's heyday as it calls to mind star Greer Garson. (Her first name at birth was Eileen; Greer was a family name.) Brooke Shields named her younger daughter Grier, perpetuating the Hollywood legacy. The name has the distinct ring of Scotland and Ireland to it and a pleasing, not-too-girly but not-too-last-namey sound. A contemporary choice that is on-trend.

Variation: *Grier*
Alternatives: *Reed, Keira, Brett, Lane, Flannery*

🖋 **Greta** Short for Margareta, which, along with all other derivations of Margaret, means "pearl," Greta brings to mind Germany and Scandinavia. Think *Hansel and Gretel* (1812). Think reclusive Swedish actress Greta Garbo. The peak of Garbo's career, the 1930s, coincides with the hightest popularity of the name. It's a great choice for families with Scandinavian or Germanic origins, and it has the pleasures of Ava and Emma but with more of an edge.

Variations: *Gretchen, Gretel*
Alternatives: *Nora, Magda, Lena, Leonie, Vanessa, Tessa*

¡Hola Maria!

Catholics in Spain and Latin American countries have a special relationship with the Virgin Mary. She is revered above all other saints, and she is referred to by many other names besides Maria. Here are some favorites:

~ **ASUNCION:** *"assumption"*

~ **CARMELA:** *Our Lady of Mount Carmel*

~ **CONSUELO:** *"comfort"*

~ **DOLORES:** *"sorrows"*

~ **GUADALUPE:** *name of the Virgin as she appeared in Mexican legend*

~ **LOURDES:** *a French town where an apparition of Mary appeared*

~ **LUZ:** *"light"*

~ **MERCEDES:** *"mercies"*

~ **MILAGROS:** *"miracles"*

~ **MONSERRAT:** *a peak in Spain associated with Mary*

~ **PAZ:** *"peace"*

~ **ROSARIO:** *"rosary"*

✏ **Gwendolyn** is a Welsh name meaning "white ring" or "white bow." According to Arthurian legend, Gwendolyn was Merlin's wife. Parents started naming their daughters Gwendolyn in the late 1800s, perhaps inspired by two characters from literature: Gwendolen in George Eliot's novel *Daniel Deronda* (published 1874–1876) and Gwendolyn in Oscar Wilde's play *The Importance of Being Earnest* (first staged in 1895). More recently, Gwendolyn Brooks was an acclaimed poet and the first African American to win a Pulitzer Prize for poetry.

Variation: *Gwendolen*
Nicknames: *Gwen, Lynn, Wendy*
Alternatives: *Gwyneth, Guinevere, Elaine, Isolde, Evelyn*

Gwyneth Originally spelled Gwynedd, Gwyneth was a region of medieval Wales. Actress Gwyneth Paltrow is probably the first (and perhaps only) Gwyneth who comes to mind, but this lithe lass has literary connections: Gwyneth Vaughan was a novelist in the early twentieth century, and Gwyneth Lewis was Wales's first national poet from 2005 to 2006. The name has an ethereal and feminine quality; it evokes a young maiden gamboling through misty, heath-covered hills.

Nicknames: *Wynne, Gwen*
Alternatives: *Delyth, Cheryth, Bronwyn, Gwendolyn, Winifred, Meredith, Glynnis*

H

Hadley (also Hedley) means "heather field" in Old English. This name is a last name turned first name. It's a welcome respite from Heather, which can seem too girly and of a time (it was very popular around the time Jennifer and Amy were—in the 1970s). It's a nice alternative to Hailey as well, which has also been overused of late. Hadley is a creative way to give your daughter a nature name that also has an edge. People started realizing this in the late 1990s; Hadley's popularity is on the rise.

Variations: *Hadleigh, Hedley*
Nicknames: *Leigh, Lee, Leah, Lea*
Alternatives: *Kylie, Riley, Hayden, Shelby, Dabney, Hallie*

Hailey means "hay meadow" in Old English and is the name of a town in Oxfordshire. It sprang into wide use in the United States in the 1970s. Hayley Mills, who worked as a child actor in the 1960s, sparked interest in the name. Hailey's cometlike rise has sparked many variations in spelling and pronunciation. Actress Halle Berry has helped along the one with the flat *a*, also seen as Hallie.

Variations: *Hailee, Haley, Hailie, Haleigh, Haley, Halle, Hallie, Haylee, Hayley, Haylie*
Nicknames: *Lee, Leigh, Leah, Lea*
Alternatives: *Riley, Bailey, Paisley, Cameron*

Hannah is from the Hebrew for "God has graced me with a child." Hannah is the prophet Samuel's mother in the Old Testament. She had trouble conceiving and promised God that if he graced her with a child, she would dedicate him to God's service. Hannah has always been popular with Jewish families; Puritans adopted it in the seventeenth century. It's

Come On, Get Happy

We all want the best for our children, and for some parents that includes giving their daughters a name that bestows happiness. Some of the best names suggesting happiness include:

- ALLEGRA
- BEATRICE
- BLITHE
- FARRAH
- FELICIA
- FELICITY
- GLADYS
- GLORIA
- GOLDIE
- HAPPY
- HARMONY
- HILLARY
- JOY
- LAETITIA
- MERRY
  (short for Meredith)
- SUNNY

experiencing a major revival now. It was number two in the late 1990s. Miley Cyrus's TV show *Hannah Montana* (first aired in 2006) reflected the trend.

Variations: *Hana, Hanna, Hanne, Chana*
Nicknames: *Nan, Nanni*
Alternatives: *Susannah, Josie, Emma, Annabelle, Eve, Hallie, Anne*

Harley Do you really want to name your baby girl after a motorcycle? Yes, Harley is a place-name from England that became a last name and then a first name. Yes, it has a meaning: "rock field." But let's face it, the reference that leaps to mind first is the motorcycle company Harley-Davidson. The

name is used for boys, too, and seems to work better
for them.

Nicknames: *Lee, Leigh, Leah, Lea*
Alternatives: *Harlow, Hadley, Darla, Avery, Harlem, Vespa,*
Mercedes

Harmony means "agreement, unity." Harmonia was
the Greek goddess of order and concord. She oversaw
marital relations, ensuring that they were untroubled.
In music, harmony is the joining together of sounds
into chords. Harmony has come to mean happiness
and peace, as well. The name came into vogue in the
mid-seventies, disappeared for most of the 1980s,
and reappeared in the late 1990s. It's climbing in
popularity.

Variation: *Harmonia*
Alternatives: *Hermione, Cadence, Melody, Allegra, Aria*

Harper is lyrical in almost the literal sense: A harper
is someone who plays the harp. The term became a
last name long ago and has become a first name. In
use since 2004, it is more popular for girls but is also
given to boys. Harper has a southern air, partially
because it is a last name turned first name, and also
due to its ties to reclusive author Harper Lee from
Alabama, who is famous for her 1960 classic, *To Kill a*
Mockingbird.

Alternatives: *Dabney, Harlow, Taylor, Jagger, Carter*

Harriet is an old-fashioned name that has been dusted by Lucy, Sadie, Emma, and others. Unlike her contemporaries, Harriet shows few signs of a revival, which is a bit of a surprise given the enormous resurgence of Harry (both names come from Henry, which means "powerful ruler") and its increasing trendiness in England. To some parents, the name may sound too much like harried ("hassled") or harridan ("nagging old woman"); if that's the case,

African American Icons

These names not only have history and meaning, they're very fashion forward, yet also evergreen.

- **ALBERTA** *(Hunter)*
- **ALTHEA** *(Gibson)*
- **ANGELA** *(Davis)*
- **AUDRE** *(Lorde)*
- **BASIE** *(as in Count Basie; a darling girl's name)*
- **BESSIE** *(Smith and Delaney)*
- **BUTTERFLY** *(McQueen)*
- **FAYE** *(Wattleton)*
- **GWENDOLYN** *(Brooks)*
- **HARRIET** *(Tubman)*
- **HATTIE** *(McDaniel)*

- **JOSEPHINE** *(Baker)*
- **LENA** *(Horne)*
- **LEONTYNE** *(Price)*
- **LIL** *(Hardin)*
- **MARIAN** *(Anderson)*
- **NELLA** *(Larsen)*
- **NINA** *(Simone)*
- **OPRAH** *(Winfrey)*
- **SADIE** *(Delaney)*
- **WILLA** *(Brown)*
- **ZORA** *(Neale Hurston; Neale or Nealie would be great, too)*

a better bet might be Henriette or Henrietta. Hattie is an adorable nickname, and one that would be in good company—but unique—among Maddies and Ellas.

Variations: *Harrietta, Harriette*
Nicknames: *Hattie, Etta, Harry, Hatsy, Henny*
Alternatives: *Frances, Georgia, Augusta, Matilda, Hazel, Lucy*

Haven A haven is a safe place, a refuge, making this a calming, serene name for your baby. It sounds like the boy's name Aiden as well as the girl's name Eden, and it contains the exotic letter *v*. Though not traditional, this name is perfectly on target for popularity and meaningfulness.

Alternatives: *Eden, Raven, Serena, Halcyon*

Hayden is an English last name turned first name meaning "hay valley." It's a meaningful choice for music lovers—though pronounced differently, it's reminiscent of the surname of Austrian composer Franz Joseph Haydn.

Alternatives: *Jada, Caden, Hailey, Hadley*

Hazel is a tree and the nut that comes from it. The branches of the tree were traditionally used in England as divining rods, giving the name a mystical edge. And there's poetry in it, too: Shakespeare used hazel in *Romeo and Juliet* to describe the color of Benvolio's eyes. The name was in the top twenty-five in the late 1800s, declined steeply, and then reappeared in the late 1990s (Julia Roberts named one of her twins Hazel, which might be giving the name a lift). It's a name with warmth, one that would work especially well for a little girl with golden brown hair. The name has the uncommon but trendy letter *z* at its center, which gives it just enough sass to keep it from feeling old-ladyish. Although Hazel doesn't have many organic nicknames, go ahead and call her Hazelnut or Filbert—adorable.

Alternatives: *Willow, Rowan, Aspen, Hannah, Rose, Julia*

Heather is a hardy, short, purple-flowered plant common to the Scottish and English countrysides, especially Yorkshire. It evokes the rugged beauty of the region and the romanticism of Yorkshire's native Brontë sisters. The name has become so common—it was big in the 1970s and '80s, hitting number three in 1975—that much of that romanticism has been lost. The cult movie *Heathers* featured a clique of cruel girls known as "the Heathers," further sullying Heather's sweet-and-sentimental reputation.

Variations: *Erica (Heather in Latin), Jennifer, Amanda, Melissa, Nicole, Michelle*

Heidi A name with strong ethnic ties, Heidi was traditionally a choice for families with German backgrounds. It comes from Adelheid, which is

Adelaide ("noble") in German, and is likely to remind anyone of that plucky little girl with braided pigtails (if not the supermodel Heidi Klum).

Alternatives: *Adelaide, Greta, Luisa, Sadie, Paige, Holly*

Helen was the face that launched a thousand ships. According to Greek myth, she was the beautiful wife of Menelaus; she caused the Trojan War when she ran off with Paris. The name could have a number of meanings: Some say it comes from the Greek word for "sunshine" (*helios*), others believe it is "moonlight" (relating to *selene*). The name became popular in Christian circles thanks to Emperor Constantine's mother, Helena. She supposedly traveled to Jerusalem and brought home a piece of the true cross.

Variations: *Helena, Helene, Ellen, Elaine, Eleanor, Eleanora, Elena, Eleni, Aileen, Eileen, Elenka, Eliana, Elin, Ilona, Ileana, Lenore, Olena, Yelena, Galina, Alana, Aline*
Nicknames: *Nell, Nelly, Ellen, Elena, Leni, Laney, Laina*
Alternatives: *Alexandra, Selena, Cassandra, Alice, Haven, Charlotte, Caroline*

Henrietta The feminine of Henry, meaning powerful ruler, Henrietta has hit the skids while Henry is making a comeback. Henrietta is an excellent alternative to Charlotte, Lydia, Amelia, and co., but may be too froufrou for some families. The *etta* suffix is not as popular now as it used to be, which could be

Girls Will Be Boys

Boys' nicknames have a rough-and-tumble cuteness when used for girls. Pick a nickname you like and work backward:

- **BILLIE** *(Wilhelmina, Elizabeth)*
- **BOBBIE** *(Roberta)*
- **CHARLIE** *(Charlotte)*
- **FRANKIE** *(Frances)*
- **FREDDIE** *(Frederica, Winifred)*
- **GEORGIE** *(Georgiana, Georgia)*
- **HENRY** *(Henrietta)*
- **JO** *(Joanne, Joanna, Josephine)*
- **NICKIE** *(Nicole)*
- **RONNIE** *(Veronica)*
- **SAM** *(Samantha)*
- **STEVIE** *(Stephanie)*
- **TEDDIE** *(Theodora, Edwina)*

holding her back. She is big in England, though, so there may still be hope for Henrietta across the pond.

Nicknames: *Henny, Hen, Hettie, Rita, Etta, Hatsy, Harriet, Harry*

Alternatives: *Josephine, Emmeline, Philippa, Joanna, Margaret, Theodora*

Hermione was a daughter of Helen and Menelaus, according to Greek mythology. The name may come from Hermes, the Greek messenger god, which suggests travel, but thanks to the *Harry Potter* novels, it might evoke mysticism and benign witchcraft nowadays. Hermione is a character in Shakespeare's *The Winter's Tale* who is presumed dead but then seems to come back to life. Two real-life Hermiones played witches: Hermione Gingold in *Bell, Book, and Candle,* and Hermione Baddeley in TV's *Bewitched*. So Hermione appears to be a name that casts spells.

Nicknames: *Iona, Miya, Hero*
Alternatives: *Samantha, Morgan, Cressida, Imogen, Tamsin, Miranda, Portia, Titania, Violet*

Hillary is funny. No, really, the name comes from the same root as the word "hilarious." It started being widely used in the United States in the 1960s, peaked in the early 1990s, declined, and then came back a bit. Hillary Clinton leaps immediately to mind. As do actress Hilary Swank and Sir Edmund Hillary, conquerer of Everest. The name used to be a boy's name and spelled with one *l*. Now it is rarely used for boys.

Variations: *Hilary, Hillery*
Nicknames: *Hills, Hill, Hillie*
Alternatives: *Marjorie, Ashley, Mallory, Lindsay*

Holly is an evergreen shrub with dark green, pointy leaves and bright red berries. It's a symbol of Christmas and brought indoors for decoration, a merry reminder of life during the cold, dark winter. Holly sounds cheerful—it's one letter away from being "Jolly," and the beloved song "Have a Holly, Jolly Christmas" reinforces that connection. Holly has been used since the 1930s, peaking in the 1970s. It's in the top twenty-five in the U.K., along with other trendy floral names. Holly Golightly, the heroine of *Breakfast at Tiffany's,* gives the name a classy Audrey Hepburn touch. Actress Holly Hunter leaps to mind, too.

Variation: *Hollie*

Alternatives: *Molly, Polly, Poppy, Lily, Rose, Hollis, Camilla, Hallie*

𝒫 **Honor** A virtue name, Honor has been out of fashion, lacking a big vowelly finish. But she's the perfect antidote to frilly names. Honor is serious and grown-up and noble sounding. This is a name for her to grow into with pride. Actress Jessica Alba recently named her daughter Honor.

Variations: *Honour, Honoria (warning: sounds like a certain venereal disease!), Honora*

Alternatives: *Faith, Hope, Constance, Valerie, Augusta*

Hope According to the Bible, Faith, Hope, and Charity are the three theological virtues, meaning they are bestowed by God. Virtue names (see page 214) are coming back, and this is one that never left. Hope means "expectation," and it has a timeless quality. It is demure, understated, and elegant—expect it to be around for a long time.

Alternatives: *Faith, Charity, Constance, Honor, Patience, Joy, Peace*

I

Iliana probably comes from the Greek word *helios,* meaning "sun," which would make it a close relative of Helen, Elaine, and Liane. Iliana certainly sounds like a glittering, sunny name—many parents have taken a shine to it. The name is especially popular with Hispanic and Greek families.

Variations: *Iliana, Aliana, Illeana, Ileana*
Nicknames: *Illy, Ili, Ana*
Alternatives: *Ariana, Cassandra, Mariana, Ilsa, Eloisa, Lilia, Ilana*

Ilona is the Helen of Hungary. Helen's meaning is "sunny" and "beautiful." Ilona adds a note of strength as well as individuality.

Alternatives: *Alondra, Ilsa, Ramona, Dora, Astrid*

✐ **Ilsa** She'll always have Paris. Ingrid Bergman's Ilsa was the love of Humphrey Bogart's Rick in the movie *Casablanca*. It's a variation of Elizabeth ("God is my oath") but sounds more exotic since it comes from Scandinavia. An edgier version of Elsa, it's a name that's not widely used—though it should be. It's a unique alternative to other ubiquitous *a*-ending names like Ella.

Alternatives: *Elsa, Ingrid, Sylvia, Selah*

121

Drama Queens

Naming your child after an iconic actress can lend a sense of glamour to her life.

- **ANNETTE** (*Bening*)
- **AUDREY** (*Hepburn*)
- **BARBARA** (*Stanwyck*)
- **BETTE** (*Davis*)
- **CATHERINE** (*Deneuve*)
- **CYBILL** (*Shepherd*)
- **DEMI** (*Moore*)
- **GRACE** (*Kelly*)
- **HALLE** (*Berry*)
- **INGRID** (*Bergman*)

- **JUDY** (*Garland*)
- **JULIA** (*Roberts*)
- **KATHARINE** (*Hepburn*)
- **LAUREN** (*Bacall*)
- **MERYL** (*Streep*)
- **MIRA** (*Sorvino*)
- **NATALIE** (*Wood*)
- **RITA** (*Hayworth*)
- **SIGOURNEY** (*Weaver*)
- **TÉA** (*Leoni*)

Imani means "faith" in Arabic and is a variation of the word *iman*. (Iman is the name of David Bowie's supermodel wife.) The name is quite lyrical and may appeal to families with Mediterranean (sounds a bit Italian, like Armani), African, or Arabic ties.

Variations: *Iman, Amani*
Alternatives: *Aaliyah, Zara, Farrah, Aisha, Amaya*

India To most Westerners, the name India calls forth the Asian country and a colorful imagined tapestry of rajahs and elephants, saffron and saris, yoga and curries. India has a long history of colonial rule, becoming independent from England in 1948, so it is more familiar to Westerners than some other Asian nations. The word itself is beautiful—and comes from the Indus River—but it can be tough to pull off without a connection to the country.

Alternatives: *Indira, Asia, Diana, Ruby*

Inez is in the top ten in France, but hasn't been used in the United States much since the 1970s. The name is primed for comeback since parents now are in love with exotic consonants like *z*. Inez, and the softer Inès, is Agnes in Spanish. Agnes means "holy" and is related to the lamb of God (*agneau* is "lamb" in French). While Agnes sounds old-fashioned (but maybe so old it's new), Inez sounds cool.

Variations: *Inès, Agnes*
Alternatives: *Esme, Cosima, Fanny, Manon, Anais*

Ingrid Ing is the fertility god of Norse myth, and Ingrid means "beautiful Ing." The name is strongly associated with Scandinavia and evokes the actress Ingrid Bergman. The name became popular in the United States only in the 1940s, when Bergman's career was taking off. To some ears, it sounds glamorous and exotic; to others, severe. It's an easy pick for families with Scandinavian roots; a daring one for others.

Variations: *Inga, Inge*
Alternatives: *Sigrid, Meryl, Greta, Astrid*

Ireland The Emerald Isle, Ireland is the lush, green land that evokes shamrocks, leprechauns, U2, and Aran Island fisherman's sweaters. It was a major source of immigrants to America from the time of the potato famine in 1847 through the early twentieth century. As many people turn back to their roots, the name Ireland seems like a great way to celebrate one's heritage. Two generations ago, parents named their lasses Kathleen, one generation ago they named them Erin. Now people are going hardcore—Siobhan, Niamh, Sorcha, and so on. For something easier on the ear (and tongue) but still edgy, go for Ireland.

Variations: *Erin, Kelly, Shannon, Tara, Cashel, Eire, Innisfree*

Irene means "peace" in Greek. The name was used by a goddess of peace, a wife of Constantine, and a Byzantine empress, so it goes way back. It used to be pronounced with three syllables (eye-REEN-ee) but now it's just two (eye-REEN). The French pronunciation is nice, too (ee-WREN). And the Russian version is popular: Irina.

Variations: *Irena, Irina, Irène*
Nicknames: *Iri, Rena, Reenie*
Alternatives: *Natalie, Angeline, Maxima, Justine, Ravenna, Selene*

Iris is "rainbow" in Greek. Iris was a messenger of the gods, an arc connecting heaven and earth. The name was given to a flower and a part of the eye, both of which display many different colors. Irises are found

in ancient Egyptian art. The fleur-de-lis, the symbol
of France, is a stylized iris. The name is popular in the
Netherlands.

Variations: *Eris, Irisa*
Alternatives: *Isis, Lily, Enid, Edith, Phyllis, Ione*

Isabella is a variation of Elizabeth. It's a name that
fell out of use after the 1940s, then appeared in the
top 1,000 in 1990, and less than twenty years later hit

The Ella Effect

Ella has been a popular suffix for girls' names for
centuries, and now is used in its own right. Add
ella to the end of any name and it instantly becomes
more feminine, and often more playful, too. These days,
it appears most often in the nearly ubiquitous Isabella,
but if you want an "ella," you don't have to follow the
pack. There's plenty of girly goodness to go around.

- ARABELLA
- ARIELLA
- CARMELLA
- CHRISTABELLA
- DANIELLA
- EMMANUELLA
- ESTELLA
- GABRIELLA
- GISELLA
- GRAZIELLA
- JANELLA
- LOUELLA
- MARCELLA
- MARIBELLA
- MARISELLA
- RAPHAELLA

number two. The name is becoming the Jennifer of its time. Look for it to sink just as quickly; popularity like this usually isn't sustained for very long. That said, the name itself is beautiful and more lyrical than Elizabeth and certainly more traditional than Jennifer. The queen who sponsored Christopher Columbus's journey was Isabella, as were many other royals.

Variations: *Isabelle, Isobel, Isabela, Isabell, Izabella, Izabelle*
Nicknames: *Izzy, Isa, Belle, Bella*
Alternatives: *Arabella, Mirabella, Sarahbelle, Cornelia, Marcella*

Isis The ancient Egyptian goddess of motherhood and fertility, Isis was a major, powerful deity whose name means "of the throne." She was renowned throughout the Mediterranean for centuries, and temples were built to her in the Middle East, Greece, and Italy as well as throughout Egypt. Isis was to the ancient Egyptians what Juno was to Romans, Hera was to Greeks, and Mary is to Christians—the most important female of the religion and a mother figure. The name first came into the mainstream in the mid-1990s and remains popular.

Alternatives: *Giza (a temple location), Nefertiti, Cleopatra, Hathor (another goddess), Ishtar (Persian for Esther), Zoe*

Itzel (eat-ZELL) was the name of a Mayan goddess, also seen as Ixchel. She was the goddess of childbirth and medicine. Her unusual, beguiling name is most

Ancient Egypt, Cool Names

For families looking for a connection to the past and/or to Africa, Ancient Egypt may be just the place to look. Consider these choices.

- **ANUKET:** *Nile River goddess*

- **BASTET:** *feline goddess depicted as a woman with the head of a cat*

- **CLEOPATRA** *(call her Cleo): legendary ruler of Egypt and lover of Caesar*

- **DENDERA** *(Dera for short): site of one of the great ancient temple complexes*

- **HATHOR:** *cow goddess*

- **HATSHEPSUT:** *one of the most powerful, successful pharaohs, male or female*

- **ISIS:** *the quintessential Egyptian fertility goddess*

- **NEFERTITI** *(Neffi is cute): the Audrey Hepburn of ancient Egypt (that swan's neck!)*

- **SESHAT:** *goddess of writing*

often used by Hispanic families; perhaps the inclusion of the *z* will give it a wider reach.

Alternatives: *Hazel, Maritza, Isla, Zelda*

Ivy is creeping back into fashion. The name of a hardy evergreen plant, Ivy suggests endurance and steadfastness, as well as smarts—think about the Ivy League. As nature and flower names bloom again in the baby name garden, Ivy seems another option just ripe for the picking.

Alternatives: *Hazel, Holly, Olive, Fern, Livvy, Piper, Penny, Laurel, Ruby*

J

Jacqueline is a feminization of the French boy's name Jacques, which comes from the English name James, which comes from the Hebrew name Jacob. Whew! Jacqueline will forever be associated with Jacqueline Bouvier Kennedy Onassis, the American first lady beloved for her style and dignity.

Variations: *Jacquelyn, Jaqueline, Jacklyn, Jacquetta*
Nicknames: *Jackie, Jacqui*
Alternatives: *Josephine, Patricia, Violette, Camilla, Genevieve*

Jade is the precious green stone from Asia. In China, the word for jade means "treasure," because it is one of the most beloved, prized substances in the world. The Chinese call it "the stone of heaven" and believe it symbolizes everything good, from loyalty and wisdom to beauty and immortality. In the Western world, associations are less favorable: The word *jade* comes from the Spanish for "stone of the flank," as jade was believed to cure intestinal distress. The word in English means a broken-down horse or a nagging woman, or to become hardened and weary (jaded). However, shortly after Mick Jagger named his daughter Jade in the 1970s, the name took off. Now even more popular than Jade are its variations: Jada and, mostly for boys, Jayden. Jaeda is an unrelated Arabic name whose merits will sadly go

Frankennames Starting with J

There are more funky, mashed-up (read: made up) names starting with *J* than with any other letter. I call them Frankennames. Here are some picks from the top 1,000:

- **JACEY** *(or Jaycee):* Jay + Lacey or Tracy
- **JAELYN** *(or Jaelynn):* Jay + Lynn
- **JAKAYLA:** Jay + Mikayla or Kayla
- **JALIYAH:** Jay + Aaliyah
- **JAMIYA** *(or Jamya):* Jamie + Aaliyah
- **JANAE:** Jane + Faye
- **JANESSA:** Jay + Vanessa

- **JANIAH** *(also Janiya and Janiyah):* Jan + Aaliyah
- **JASLENE** *(or Jaslyn):* Jasmine + Lynn
- **JAYDEN** *(or Jada):* variation of Jade (see opposite)
- **JAYLA** *(or Jaylah):* Jay + Kayla
- **JAYLEE** *(also Jayleen, Jaylen, and so on):* Jay + Lee or Lynn
- **JAZLYN:** Jasmine + Lynn
- **JULISSA:** Julie + Melissa *(or Alissa)*

unappreciated in a world filled with Jadas, Jaydas, and Jadens.

Variations: *Jada, Jaida, Jayda, Jayden, Jadyn, Jaiden, Jaidyn, Jaden*

Alternatives: *Ruby, Pearl, Gemma, Jagger, Asia, Esme, Giada*

Jamie is a feminization of James. It is a boy's nickname so it has a casual, tomboy spirit to it. Think actresses Jamie Lee Curtis and Jami Gertz.

You can also spell it Jaime, which is "I love" in French (*J'aime*), but you may run into trouble with pronunciation. Jamie was in spotty use until the 1930s, when it became a mainstay of American names. It rose to the top twenty in the late 1970s and has slid since then.

Alternatives: *Aimee, Jackie, Casey, Amanda*

✏ **Jane** Plain Jane. See Jane Run. Jane Doe. Poor Jane gets a bum rap. She was the everygirl of the 1920s through '50s—never the most popular, never the most pretty, but well liked, dependable, and solid. When the swinging sixties came along, Jane's popularity started to ebb. Now Jane is in the middle of the pack— still there, always hanging around, neither beloved nor forgotten. The name, a feminization of John ("God's grace"), is a great one and should be in the current vogue along with Abigail, Lydia, Lucy, et al. Jane is for lovers of literature (Jane Eyre, Jane Austen), Jane is for Anglophiles (Lady Jane Grey, Jane Seymour), Jane can even be for bombshells (Jane Russell, Jayne Mansfield). Jane is a strong, independent girl who can take care of herself without compromising her femininity. For a country effect, make Jane her middle name: Mary Jane, Sarah Jane, Emily Jane.

Variations: *(see box, opposite)*
Nicknames: *Janey, Jana, Jenny*
Alternatives: *Anne, Mary, Claire, Emily, Suzie, Maggie*

Jane's World

Jane is a name with seemingly endless variations, making it easy to honor a Jane without going the plain route.

~ **GIANNA** (Italian)
~ **GIOVANNA** (Italian)
~ **IVANA** (Eastern Europe)
~ **JAN**
~ **JANELLE**
~ **JANET**
~ **JANICE**
~ **JAYNE**
~ **JEAN**
~ **JEANNE**
~ **JEANNETTE**
~ **JOAN**
~ **JOANNA**
~ **JUANITA** (Spanish)
~ **SHANE** (England)
~ **SHEENA** (Scotland)
~ **SINÉAD** (Ireland)
~ **VANNA**

Jasmine is the rose of the Middle East: a beloved, fragrant flower that has lent its name to many girls. Jasmine and its variations got a boost from the 1992 Disney movie *Aladdin,* in which Jasmine was the princess. If the *j* sound gives this blossom a hard edge to your ear, try the softer (and even more exotic sounding) Yasmeen or Yasmina.

Variations: *Jessamine, Yasmin, Yasmeen, Yazmin, Yasmine, Jazzmine, Jazlyn, Yasminia*
Nicknames: *Jessie, Jazzy, Jazz, Yaz, Meena*
Alternatives: *Farrah, Leila, Selma, Rose, Lily, Willow, Ruby*

Jayden is a variation of Jade (see page 128). Jade became Jada, which became Jaden, which split into many variations. The name is becoming wildly popular. It is much more popular for boys than girls, and is particularly trendy among African American and Hispanic families. Britney Spears was part of the Jayden zeitgeist, naming her second son Jayden in 2006. And Will Smith was on the front lines with his son Jaden, born in 1998. If you want to clarify that your child is a girl, you are better off with Jada.

Variations: *Jadyn, Jaiden, Jaidyn, Jaden*
Alternatives: *Jada, Jade, Hayden, Kayla, Cadence, Hailey*

🖊 **Jemima** means "dove" in Hebrew, and thus suggests peace, purity, and love. The name is popular in England (socialite Jemima Goldsmith; Beatrix Potter's character Jemima Puddle-Duck) but never caught on in the United States—perhaps because of pancake icon Aunt Jemima. But breakfast syrup or not, the name is sweet; it has beauty and music in it and a peaceful meaning. It's an ideal pick for a traditional, pretty, but not overused name.

Nicknames: *Jemma, Mimi*
Alternatives: *Dove, Imogen, Tamsin, Antonia, Piper, Ursula*

Jenna In Arabic, Jenna means "heaven." It's a smart alternative to the overused Jennifer and a softer name than Jean. Several Jennas have cropped up lately, boosting the name's profile: former first daughter Jenna Bush, actress Jenna Elfman, and *30 Rock* character Jenna Maroney.

Alternatives: *Jemima, Farrah, Zara, Leila, Sonya, Selma*

Jennifer The epitome of trendiness, Jennifer was the number one name in the early 1970s. It is an unusual variation of Guinevere (meaning "soft and white"), and George Bernard Shaw is credited with the twentieth-century boom of the name. The heroine of his play *The Doctor's Dilemma* is a Jennifer. Before that appearance, the name was little known outside of Cornwall, England. The name got another bump from actress Jennifer Jones, who was popular in the 1940s. Now everybody knows a Jennifer.

Variations: *Jenifer, Ginnifer, Gennifer*
Nicknames: *Jenny, Jen, Jenn, Jenna*
Alternatives: *Geneva, Juniper, Ginevra, Guinevere, Jenna, Meredith, Heather*

Jessica Shakespeare invented Jessica for the daughter of Shylock in *The Merchant of Venice*. It sounded like a Jewish name to him, perhaps because there is a Jesca in the Bible who was said to have been Abraham's niece. Or maybe it was his feminization of the Hebrew boy's name Jesse. Jessica is taken to mean "foresight," and some think it shares common roots with Sarah, who was a prophet. The name was number one in the late 1980s and early 1990s and is now much less fashionable, though no less pretty.

Nicknames: *Jess, Jessie*
Alternatives: *Rebecca, Miranda, Samantha*

Jill This variation of Jillian (and Gillian) has stood on its own since the 1400s. Jillian is a feminization of Julian, which comes from Julius, the name of two popes as well as Roman emperor Gaius Julius Caesar. While the feminine Juliana is a serious name, Jill is short, girlish, and swingy. Jill, like Jane, is a kind of everygirl name.

Variations: *Jillian, Gillian*
Alternatives: *Lilian, Julianne, Jane, May, Carrie, Suzanne*

Jimena (pronounced hee-MEHY-nah) or Ximena is believed to be a Spanish-language variation of Simone, which means "hearing." The name appeared in the top 1,000 American names in 2001, and its popularity climbs every year.

Alternatives: *Simone, Deja, Melania, Natalia*

Joanna, John for girls, is more ornate than her sibling Jane (page 130), which also comes from John, and slightly more popular these days. With the success of Hannah and Ava, you would expect Joanna to be

She Will, She Will Rock You

Want her to sound like she can jam with the best of them? Try one of these rock-inspired names:

- ALANIS
- BLONDIE
- BOWIE
- CHRISSIE
- DUSTY
- DYLAN
- HENDRIX
- HOLIDAY (or Billie)
- JAGGER
- JETT
- JONI
- JOPLIN (or Janis)
- LENNON

- MACY
- MADONNA
- MARLEY
- NICO
- PRESLEY
- RAMONA (in honor of the Ramones)
- REED (as in Lou)
- SIMONE (or Nina)
- SINÉAD
- TORI
- ZAPPA

climbing fast, but instead she holds steady in the middle of the pack. She's spunkier than her quiet, thoughtful sister Joanne, who is less popular (as names go, at least).

Variations: *Johanna, Joanne*
Nicknames: *Jo, Joey, Jojo, Anna*
Alternatives: *Susannah, Rowena, Samantha, Rosemary, Juliana*

Jocelyn An Old German name meaning "member of the Gauts tribe." The name was a last name, then a boy's first name, and now is a girl's first name. It's pretty, ornate, and evocative of the upper crust—a classy name that sounds fresher and more youthful than the similar Joyce.

Variations: *Jocelynn, Joslyn, Josceline, Yoselin*
Nicknames: *Joss, Lynn*
Alternatives: *Roselyn, Rosalind, Joyce, Evelyn*

Jolie If you don't want to name her Angelina but are looking for glamour, choose Jolie instead. That's the conclusion that many parents have been coming to since 2000, when Jolie became trendy thanks in no small part to actress Angelina Jolie. The name means "pretty" in French, has a whiff of merriment to it as well (you can hear "jolly" in there), and is a creative alternative to more ordinary choices like Julie. For a similar choice warmed by a breeze from the American South, try Jolene.

Nickname: *Jo*
Alternatives: *Aimee, Sadie, Ada, Angelina, Holly, Juliana*

Jordan is a modern tomboy name with religious roots: Christ was baptized in the river Jordan, which is one of Christianity's holiest spots. Jordan was first a last name, then a boy's name, and then (since 1978) a girl's name. Basketball superstar Michael Jordan helped its modern rise. The unisex name is more common for boys, but until recently was widely used for girls. In case your tomboy grows up to be a lilies-and lace-loving girlie girl, you might consider the feminine and unusual Jorie as a nickname.

Variations: *Jordin, Jordyn, Jorden, Jordana*
Nicknames: *Jo, Jorie*
Alternatives: *Morgan, Shiloh, Bethany, Eden, Kendall*

Josephine is the feminine equivalent of Joseph, meaning "God adds." Josephines tend to be strong women who have no problem bucking trends: Empress Josephine was Napoleon Bonaparte's beloved wife. Josephine Baker was the African American dancer who delighted Paris in the 1920s. Josephine (Jo) March is the heroine of Louisa May Alcott's *Little Women*.

Variations: *Josiane, Josefina*
Nicknames: *Jo, Josie, Fifi, Jojo, Fina, Pina (from the Italian Giuseppina)*
Alternatives: *Theodora, Antonia, Alexandra, Jacqueline, Marianne, Eleanor, Marguerite, Beatrix*

Journey Americans have been naming their girls Journey since 1999. A journey can be a quest, a mission, a voyage, a pilgrimage. It can also be a tribute to the 1980s rock band whose anthem "Don't Stop Believing" is back in vogue. The name recalls abolitionist Sojourner Truth, and also has a love-child, airy, hippie feeling to it.

Alternatives: *Destiny, Summer, Justice, Marley, Dylan, Karma*

Joy to the world! Joy is a name of expansive happiness, glee, exaltation. In the old days, Joy was a religious name, at home alongside Faith, Hope, and Charity. Now it has cast off that mantle and is simply a celebration of life and happiness.

Alternatives: *Faith, Hope, Allegra, Bliss, Felicity, Aglaia, Hillary*

Joyce was in the top fifteen in the 1930s. Now it sounds old-fashioned, and parents who might have chosen Joyce go with Joy instead. The name, meaning "Lord," was originally for boys and was used in the Middle Ages. Joyce doesn't look like she's going to make a comeback anytime soon.

Nickname: *Joy*

Alternatives: *Gloria, Nancy, Marilyn, Lois, June, Donna*

Judith A strong name for a strong girl. Judith ("Jewess") was the biblical heroine from the apocryphal book of Judith, who saves her people from the Assyrians by decapitating their leader, Holofernes. The name used to be considered very Jewish, but that has changed over the years. Judith is the warrior. Judy is the girl next door. For an edgier variation, call her Jude.

Nicknames: *Judy, Jude, Jodie*
Alternatives: *Lillith, Esther, Rachel, Miriam, Deborah*

Julia is from the Roman family name Julius. It evokes the glory days of Rome, including powerful Julius Caesar, and now, the power of Hollywood. Julia and all her variations have been made popular by several famous actresses, including Julie Andrews, Julie Christie, Julie Walters, Julia Roberts, Julia Stiles, Julianne Moore, and Juliette Binoche. Culinary pioneer Julia Child was not necessarily glamorous, but beloved, and may have helped as well. And Romeo's Juliet is one of the most famously adored women in theater. The names are considered sweet and girly (Julie sounds like *jolie,* which is French for "pretty"), and they have many variations.

Variations: *Julie, Julianna, Juliana, Julianne, Juliet, Juliette, Yulia, Yuliana*
Nickname: *Jools*
Alternatives: *Georgia, Angela, Joelle, Melissa, Evangeline, Simone*

❦ **June** is the warm summer month named for the Roman queen of the gods, Juno. The summer is considered the year's prime time, and metaphorically it's the prime of our lives as well. June was popular in the mid-twentieth century (think actress June Allyson) but is barely used anymore. Look for the

variation Juno to take off in the wake of the hit movie
about a spunky pregnant teenager. And Junia is
another variation that you might consider. (Will you
pronounce it JOON-ya or joon-EE-ah?)

Nickname: *Junie*
Alternatives: *Juno, Summer, May, Lucille, April, January,
Rose*

Justice is a quality name in the mold of Prudence
and Chastity. Unlike those, which can sound frowsy,
Justice sounds strong and righteous. It has been
popular since the early 1990s and is used nearly
equally for boys and girls. It goes well with many
last names except extremely long, ornate ones.
It is a name that promises fairness and good
treatment.

Alternatives: *Prudence, Charity, Faith, Justine*

Justine means "just" or "fair." It is the feminine
version of Justin. There have been saints (Justina)
and emperors (Byzantine ruler Justinian) with related
names. More recently Justine was popularized by
the novel of the same name from Lawrence Durrell's
Alexandria Quartet, published in the 1950s, and 1980s
actress Justine Bateman.

Variation: *Justina*
Alternatives: *Augustine, Valentina, Jenna, Lauren*

Preppy Nicknames

Preppies love their nicknames. Usually these monikers are cute as can be—and have nothing to do with a person's real name. If you want your child to fit in with the country club set, try on one of these names/nicknames for size.

- **BABE**
  (socialite Paley, née Barbara)

- **BINKY**
  (literary agent Urban, née Amanda)

- **BITSY**
  (for a girl; use for Elizabeth)

- **BOOTSIE** *(for a girl)*

- **BUNNY**
  (heiress Mellon, née Rachel)

- **KICK**
  (Kennedy, née Kathleen)

- **KIKI**
  (for a girl; use for Kristen or Katherine)

- **MUFFY** *(for a girl)*

- **SLIM**
  (socialite Keith, née Nancy)

- **SUNNY**
  (heiress Von Bulow, née Martha)

- **TINSLEY**
  (socialite Mortimer; Tinsley is her real name)

- **BIFF** *(for a boy)*

- **CASS**
  (book editor Canfield, first name Augustus)

- **CHIP**
  (for a boy; usually short for Charles)

- **FLIP**
  (short for Philip or Philippa)

- **JOCK**
  (Whitney, né John)

- **SKIP**
  (academic Gates, né Henry)

- **TAD**
  (writer Friend, né Theodore)

- **TOPPER**
  (Mortimer, né Robert)

- **TREY**
  (meaning three, for a boy who is a "third")

- **TRIP** *(for a boy)*

Kaitlin is derived from Katherine. In its Irish form, it is pronounced Kat-LEEN, which became Kathleen. In its Anglo and American form, it is pronounced Kate-lynn. In all forms it means "pure," and, as a group, the *Cat-* and *Kat-* names are enormously popular. Parents sometimes try to make their kittens distinctive by playing with spelling.

Variations: *Caitlyn, Kaitlin, Kaitlyn, Catelyn, Cailyn, Kaylin, Colleen, Kathlynn*
Nicknames: *Cate (Kate and Cait), Lynn, Cat, Kitty*
Alternatives: *Kasey, Hayden, Peyton, Callie, Hadley*

Kali The fierce Hindu goddess of time and change (others say "destruction"), Kali means "black" in Sanskrit. That's powerful stuff for a little girl. Forgetting the background, the word *Kali* itself is pretty and more exotic than similar names like Kelly and Carrie. Note that Cali with a *C* is usually short for the Greek name Calista (see page 43).

Variations: *Kallie, Cali*
Alternatives: *Aparna, Tara, Padma, Alisha*

Kara Cara means "dear" in Italian. Swapping the *K* for the *C* gives the name a bit more of an edge as well as a more Germanic, Russian, or Scandinavian quality.

Variations: *Karina, Karine, Karissa, Karissima, Karita, Karrie, Kari*
Alternatives: *Mara, Lara, Katrina*

Karen The Danish form of Katherine became common in the United States in the 1920s, and was one of the top five most popular names through most of the 1960s. The Danish writer known as Isak Dinesen was really Karen Blixen. The name sounds utterly ordinary to contemporary ears because it was so popular a generation ago. It's in company with Susan, Lisa, and Laura. Think Karen Carpenter. Its consonant ending is out of fashion now—only names that are truly edgy or tomboyish end in consonants these days. But other *-en* names, like Jayden and Caden, are extremely popular, so

IS THAT *K* OKAY?

K is the place where some *C* names kome to look kool. Before you name your daughter Kaitlin or Karla, ask yourself if the *K* really does look okay. If you have a Scandinavian, Russian, or German last name (or roots), your *K* girl will probably be just fine. If you are a Kardashian stretching to keep the family monogram intact, it may not be. It can look affected on some names (like Khloe) if there is no real reason for the choice.

maybe Karen is a more traditional way of joining
the pack?

Variations: *Karin, Karina, Karyn, Carin*
Nickname: *Karrie*
Alternatives: *Lauren, Susan, Maren*

Karla derives from Karl, which derives from Charles,
which means "free man." Charles and its variations
and feminizations are ancient and regal. Carla with
a *C* got a big boost in profile when French President
Nicolas Sarkozy married sexy Italian pop singer
Carla Bruni in 2008. Karla with a *K* has a northern
Europeanness to it.

Variations: *Karleen, Karolina, Karley*
Alternatives: *Marlena, Carmen, Kayla, Greta*

Karma What goes around, comes around. And since
2005, one thing that has come around as a name is
Karma. An alternative to Destiny, Karma has a New-
Agey Zen feel as well as a girlie sound to it. The sitcom
Dharma and Greg may have helped pave the way for
love-child names like this one.

Alternatives: *Carmen, Destiny, Journey, Echo, Eden*

Kassandra Cassandra is a tragic heroine from Greek
mythology. She was the daughter of King Priam of
Troy on whom Apollo bestowed the gift of prophecy.
When she spurned his affections, he cursed her,

ensuring that nobody would believe her predictions. Despite her inauspicious history, her name—spelled with either a *C* or a *K*—has been beloved.

Variation: *Cassandra*
Nicknames: *Kassie, Sandra, Kasey, Andra, Kass*
Alternatives: *Elisha, Micah, Deandra, Delilah, Bathsheba, Jessica*

Birds of a Feather

M any parents take names or nicknames from the animal kingdom. If you are looking for a name that suggests grace and levity, turn your gaze skyward and consider birds' names. They usually suggest freedom, elegance, peace, and wisdom.

~ CRANE	~ LARK	~ SPARROW
~ DOVE	~ MAVIS	~ STARLING
~ EGRET	~ PETREL	~ SWIFT
~ EIDER	~ PHOEBE	~ TEAL
~ HERON	~ RAVEN	~ WILLET
~ IBIS	~ ROBIN	~ WREN

There are lovely bird names and there are lousy bird names. Here are just a few bird names that should be off the table for your little chick: Albatross, Booby, Bushtit, Chicken, Coot, Cowbird, Creeper, Cuckoo, Goose, Grackle, Noddy, Nuthatch, Sapsucker, Tattler, Titmouse, Turkey.

Kassidy Cassidy is used for boys and girls, but starting the name with a *K* gives it a feminine twist. Kassidy means "curly haired" in Gaelic. It's a name with happy hippie connotations, one that's sure to bring fond memories to erstwhile Deadheads (who likely twirled joyously to the song "Cassidy," which features the lyric "born to me, Cassidy"). It may also remind some Americans of '70s teen idol Shaun Cassidy, and Kathy Lee Gifford's daughter, about whom she spoke *often* on her morning talk show with Regis Philbin in the 1990s.

Variation: *Cassidy*
Nicknames: *Kass, Kassie, Kat*
Alternatives: *Casey, Cressida, Chastity, Verity, Penelope, Sidonie, Phoebe*

I'd love to call her . . .
Kate

Always loved this sweet, fresh-faced nickname but not crazy about Katherine—or the possibility of Kathy? Try one of these:

~ CADENCE	~ CARYS	~ KATHLEEN
~ CAITLIN	~ CATALINA	~ KATRINA
~ CALISTA	~ CATRIONA	~ KATYA
~ CALLA	~ CECILIA	~ KAYLYNNE
~ CAROLINE	~ KADY	

Katherine One of the most versatile, beloved, and traditional of all names, Katherine means "pure" in Greek. The name is perennially popular, maybe because it offers something for everyone. It has belonged to saints (four of them), Hollywood royalty (Katharine Hepburn, Catherine Deneuve, Catherine Zeta-Jones, and Cate Blanchett), and *actual* royalty (Catherine of Aragon, Catherine de Medici, Catherine the Great). For the Irish, Katherine becomes Kathleen; for the German, Katarina; and for the Russian, Ekaterina or Katya. For the girl next door, there's Kate and Katie. And for the edgy girl next door, there's Kat.

Variations: *Katharine, Kathryn, Catherine, Katrina (Trina), Ekaterina, Carine, Catarina, Catalina (Lina), Kathleen, Kaitlin, Katelynn, Katelyn, Katya*
Nicknames: *Kate, Katie, Kat, Kathy, Kitty, Kit, Kay, Kick*
Alternatives: *Margaret, Elizabeth, Mary, Jane, Anne*

Kayla A name since 1959, Kayla, which combines Kay and Ella or Michaela, snowballed in the 1980s and 1990s. There was an extremely popular love story on the soap opera *Days of Our Lives* in the late 1980s involving a Kayla, which rocketed this pretty name to recognition.

Variations: *Kaila, Kaylah, Keyla*
Alternatives: *Camilla, Kenya, Carina, Leila, Freya, Kylie, Lara, Shayla*

Frankennames Starting with *K*

I n the realm of made-up, patched-together names, *k* rivals *j*. Here are the most popular iterations and where they come from:

~ **KAELYN** (also Kaylen, Kaylin, Kaylyn, Kaylynn): Kay + Lynn

~ **KAILEY** (also Kailee, Kaley, Kaleigh, Kaylee): Hailey with a K or Kay + Lee

~ **KALIYAH:** Aaliyah with a K

~ **KAMARI:** Camaro with a K meets Ferrari

~ **KAMILA:** Jamila with a K (Jamila was popular in the 1970s and '80s; it means "lovely" in Arabic. Now Kamila is in.)

~ **KARLEE** (also Karley, Karly): Karla + Lee (variation of Caroline)

~ **KAYA** (also Kaia, Kaiya): Maya with a K

~ **KAYDEN:** Jaden meets Kadence

~ **KAYDENCE:** Cadence with a K

~ **KAYLA:** Kay meets Ella or Michaela (see page 147 for more)

🖊 **Keely** A Gaelic name meaning "slender," Keely is an excellent alternative to the more popular Kelly. It still communicates youth and Irish heritage, but it does it with a twist.

Variations: *Keeley, Kayley*
Alternatives: *Grier, Kylie, Neely, Sheila, Mila*

Keira The female version of Kieran comes from the Gaelic Ciaran. It means "black." Kyra, which is pronounced the same as Keira, comes from the Greek, meaning "lady." All of these names evoke the Greek *kyrie,* which means "lord." "Kyrie Eleison" is a liturgical phrase meaning "Lord have mercy," which was brought to pop culture attention in a 1980s song. And more recently, actresses Kyra Sedgwick and Keira Knightly have brought the name into the public consciousness. Opera singer Kiri Te Kanawa has a similar name but is of Maori ancestry; her name means "skin" or "bark" in Maori.

Variations: *Kiera, Kierra, Kira, Kiara, Kyra*
Nickname: *Kiki*
Alternatives: *Kayla, Krista, Rika (from Ulrika or Veronika), Raina, Katinka*

Kelly as a girl's name came into being in the 1940s. The 1940s and '50s were a time when Irish immigrants were well settled into the United States and their children and grandchildren were starting to feel a nostalgia for the old country. Kelly is the second most common surname in Ireland (Murphy is number one), and the name quickly migrated from last name to boy's name to girl's name. Kelly green, the color, was coined for the bright hue of green seen frequently in Ireland and the popular name.

Variation: *Kelli*
Alternatives: *Keely, Kerry, Tara, Kennedy, Shannon, Cashel, Sela, Maggie*

Kelsey is a last name turned first name. It used to be used for boys (think actor Kelsey Grammer) but is now more popular for girls thanks to the darling ring at the end that evokes Elsie and Chelsea. The name itself means "ship of victory" in Old English.

Variation: *Kelsie*
Alternatives: *Chelsea, Casey, Elsie, Macy, Callie*

Kendall A last name turned first name, Kendall usually refers to the Kent region in England. The name has a British air to it as well as a ring of the American South, where last names are popular for girls. Picture Kendall going with Dabney, Ainsley, and Reese to a Junior League meeting. For a softer way to honor a Ken in the family, try Kenley (which may mean "meadow in Kent").

Variation: *Kendal*
Alternatives: *Cameron, Campbell, Shelby, Reese, Ainsley, Courtney, Ashley*

Kendra turned up as a girl's name in the 1940s. It comes from the Scottish last name MacKendrick. Kendra is a strong name—MacKendrick seems to mean something like "royal power."

Alternatives: *Kennedy, Kendall, Audra, Audrey, Andra, Krissa*

Kenna is a bit of a hash. Is it the feminine for Kenneth ("born of fire") or is it a more feminine version of

Kennedy or is it a tweak of Jenna? It's unclear, but families have been using it happily since 1999.

Alternatives: *Jenna, Gemma, Kendall, Karla, Brenna*

Kennedy has a lyrical quality in English and evokes Ireland as handily as Erin, Kelly, and Kerry do. The name has a whiff of dynastic nobility to it thanks to JFK and family. Although a pretty name in English, the Gaelic meaning is unattractive: "ugly head." But the meaning, it seems, isn't stopping anyone: Kennedy has almost cracked the top one hundred most popular names.

Variation: *Kennedi*

Alternatives: *Murphy, Griffin, Sullivan, Quinn, Clancy*

Kenya is a country in east Africa famous for safaris and colonial plantations. It is where Isak Dinesen lived and was inspired to write *Out of Africa,* and where Ernest Hemingway went to shoot game. It was known as British East Africa until liberation in 1920. President Barack Obama's father was Kenyan. The word itself is pretty, so it has been picked up as a name, most often used to celebrate an African heritage.

Alternatives: *Candace, Malika, Sheba, Dafina*

✐ **Kezia** is an uncommon but traditional name that's a clever alternative to the increasingly popular Kenzie (short for Mackenzie). Kezia, along with

Jemima and Keren, was one of the biblical Job's late-born daughters. Kezia was born after Job's troubles had abated. That coupled with the name's meaning, "cassia," which is a tree with yellow flowers, suggests only good things.

Variations: *Mackenzie, Kezie, Keziah*
Alternatives: *Cassia, Jemima, Keren, Maisie, Kennedy*

Kiana A made-up name of recent vintage, Kiana is popular in Hawaii, where the word *keanu* means "breeze." Actor Keanu Reeves brought the name to light, and Kiana seems to be a feminization of it.

Variation: *Kianna*
Alternatives: *Tiara, Leilani, Akela, Oliana*

Kiara Chiara is Italian for "light" and Ciara is Irish for "black." The related name Kiara rose from obscurity in the 1960s, but she and her siblings have remained somewhat under the radar. Kiara is a variation on the more traditional *C* name. *K* is an edgier letter than *C* and it ensures proper pronunciation. (Many people want to start "Chiara" with a *Ch* like "church" instead of a hard *C* like "car.") *K* also adds some other possible dimensions to the name. It could be a variation on the sparkly Tiara in this arrangement.

Variation: *Chiara*
Alternatives: *Aoife, Niamh, Molly, Clara, Corinna, Cosima, Vincenza*

I'd Love to Call Her . . .
Kiki

Kiki is a cute nickname, but your child should have a more solid proper name—she'll need it when she interviews for college. Start with one of these:

- AKIRA
- ERIKA
- KATHERINE
- KIARA
- KIERA
- KIMBERLY
- KIRSTEN
- KRISTEN
- ULRIKA

Kimberly You'll find Kimberly hanging out at the playground with Jennifer and Amy. Look on the benches; she's one of the moms now. Kimberly, often called Kim, was number two in 1966 and '67. Although the name, which means "royal meadow," has had more staying power than that of her friends, it is definitely of a time. The name originated as an English place-name. Kimberley (with different spelling) later came to attention during the Boer War (it was a town in South Africa that saw action) and was first given to little boys.

Variations: *Kimberley, Kimberlee, Kimberleigh*
Nicknames: *Kim, Kimi, Kimber, Kimba*
Alternatives: *Michelle, Heather, Aimee, Kimball, Cecilie, Amberly*

Kimora has become quite popular since 2004, thanks to fashion and television personality Kimora

Lee Simmons. It has some Kimberly in it and a little Tamara with a twist.

Variation: *Kamora*
Alternatives: *Ramona, Tamara, Amani*

Kinsley It's a little bit Ainsley; it's a little bit Delaney. Add some Kenley and you have a name that is short on tradition but long on fashion. A few things to consider: Kinsley is a bit of a mouthful. It would go best with a very simple last name. And it's similar to Kinsey, which is the name of a famous researcher of sexual behavior. Kinley is less trendy and easier to say.

Variation: *Kinley*
Alternatives: *Kenley, Ainsley, Delaney, Coralee, Lorelei, Tenley*

Kristen and her many variations come from Christina, which means "Christian." In the 1980s, Kristen was in the top fifty, a nice, traditional name. (Who doesn't know a Kristen?) Nowadays, it's rare to hear her name called on the playground. But the name is versatile, with lots of variations and nicknames (including those with a *C*, see page 57). Kirsten is one, which can be pronounced "CUR-sten" or "KIER-sten"; some families that prefer the latter change the spelling to Kiersten to ensure proper pronunciation.

Variations: *Kristen, Kristin, Kristan, Krista, Kristina, Kirsten, Kiersten, Kristian, Kristiana*
Nicknames: *Kris, Krissa, Krissy, Kristy, Kirsty, Tina, Trista, Trixie*

Alternatives: *Freya, Astrid, Marit, Malena, Petra, Ellen, Ingrid, Dagmar*

Kylie The feminine form of Kyle is Gaelic for "narrow" or "sound" as in a channel of water. Kyle is Scottish. Kylie sounds like it was influenced by the Irish name Kelly as well. The name is very popular in Australia, where it means "boomerang" in the native Nyungar language. Kylie has been on the rise in the United States since 1978, and gained exposure in the late '80s from Australian pop singer Kylie Minogue.

Variations: *Kiley, Kylee, Kyleigh, Kyle*
Alternatives: *Mila, Riley, Keely, Kyla, Micah, Skylar*

A Spring in Her Step

Look to the world of dancing if you want to give your daughter a name with grace, swing, and movement. Here are some unconventional and traditional choices:

~ **AILEY:** *(choreographer Alvin)*

~ **ANNA:** *(ballerina Pavlova)*

~ **GINGER:** *(actress Rogers; Ginger is short for Virginia)*

~ **GRAHAM:** *(choreographer Martha)*

~ **ISADORA:** *(dancer Duncan)*

~ **JOSEPHINE:** *(dancer Baker)*

~ **LINDY:** *(the swinging Lindy Hop)*

~ **MARGOT:** *(ballerina Fonteyn)*

~ **MARIA:** *(ballerina Tallchief)*

~ **MERCE:** *(choreographer Cunningham)*

~ **SAVION:** *(tapper Glover)*

~ **TWYLA:** *(choreographer Tharp)*

L

Lacey is an Irish last name that has been popular as a girl's name since the 1970s. The name, which evokes the delicate ornamental fabric, suggests union and intertwining. The sensational 1984 miniseries *Lace* may have had an influence on the name's rise.

Variations: *Laci, Lacy*
Alternatives: *Tracy, Stacy, Macy, Darcy, Lucy, Casey*

Laila or Leila is a beloved Arabic name that means "night." Lord Byron is credited with popularizing the name in the nineteenth century by including an exotic Leila in two poems. The name and all its variations are on the rise. Today it has a whiff of foreign romanticism but is also easily pronounced and accessible. It's *la-la* sound gives it musicality and all the vowels are poetic. The name is a great alternative to the over-popular Lily, unless you live in the Arab world where it is already very common.

Variations: *Leila, Lailah, Layla, Laylah, Leyla, Lila, Lyla*
Alternatives: *Zara, Leilani, Luna, Selena, Leia, Lelia*

Lana immediately evokes sultry screen bombshell Lana Turner, who brought the name into the spotlight. Its origins are murky. Does it come from the Latin word for wool (*lana*)? Is it short for Alana? Is it a scramble (and feminization) of Alan? Does it relate to Elaine and thus Helen? The name is vague enough in origin that nearly any meaning can be applied to it. It will always have a mysterious, ethereal, Hollywood quality to it. And no nicknames here.

Alternatives: *Marilyn, Salome, Rita, Luna, Mara, Lola*

✒ **Laney** is Lacey's slightly tomboyish sister. The name is usually short for the classic Elaine or trendy Delaney, but it could be a name in its own right. The word *lane* is in there, which suggests a journey. And Lane as a name also has echoes of Lois Lane, Superman's spunky girlfriend.

Variation: *Lainey*
Nicknames: *Laina, Lane*
Alternatives: *Raina, Lara, Keely, Nahla, Kylie*

Lara Americans started naming their daughters Lara exactly one year after the release of the blockbuster film *Dr. Zhivago*. The year was 1965 and the heroine of the movie, played by gorgeous Julie Christie, was Lara. The

MAY THE FORCE BE WITH YOU!

Leia, as in Princess Leia, was used a couple of decades after the initial release in 1977 of the film *Star Wars*. The name disappeared and is now coming back as a variation of Laila. Obi-Wan has yet to hit the list.

haunting music was called "Lara's Theme." The name is traditionally related to the name Larissa, which comes from a Greek town. These days, swapping out the *L* for a *Z* to make Zara is the hip way of getting similar glamour and exoticism into your daughter's name.

Variation: *Larissa*
Alternatives: *Clara, Zara, Rita, Mira*

Laura, Laurel, and Lauren descend from the laurel plant, which commonly grows in the Mediterranean region. Laurel is a symbol of victory, distinction, and peace: Wreaths of it decorated the heads of Roman emperors and Olympic athletes. It represents accomplishment in academia as well (think poet laureate). The name also suggests the air ("aura") and might have an ethereal quality to it if it weren't so common. Laura evokes everyone's favorite fresh-faced half-pint from the TV series *Little House on the Prairie* (and to soap fans of a certain age, it recalls an iconic character on *General Hospital*). Laurel is outdoorsy, strongly evoking the plant, while Lauren brings to mind Lauren Bacall, who popularized the name. Singer Lauryn Hill reinforced an unorthodox spelling and added a cool factor.

Variations: *Laura, Laurel, Lauren, Lauryn, Loren, Laurence, Laure, Lorena, Loretta*
Nicknames: *Laurie, Lori*
Alternatives: *Daphne, Beatrice, Lilah, Maria, Anna*

Tradition, Tradition!

The Old Testament in the Bible is an invaluable source of strong and lovely girls' names. Here are some favorites:

~ **ABIGAIL:**
(Hebrew, "father's joy")

~ **DEBORAH:** *(Hebrew, "bee")*

~ **DELILAH:**
(Hebrew, "languishing")

~ **DINAH:** *(Hebrew, "judged")*

~ **ESTHER:** *(Persian, "star")*

~ **EVE:** *(Hebrew, "life")*

~ **HANNAH:** *(Hebrew, "grace")*

~ **JEMIMAH:** *(Hebrew, "dove")*

~ **JUDITH:**
(Hebrew, "woman of Judea")

~ **LEAH:** *(Hebrew, "weary")*

~ **MICHAL:**
(Hebrew, "who is like God?")

~ **MIRIAM:** *(Hebrew, possibly "bitter" or "rebellion")*

~ **NAOMI:**
(Hebrew, "joy" or "pleasantness")

~ **RACHEL** *(Hebrew, "ewe")*

~ **REBEKAH:**
(Hebrew, a "noose" or a "snare")

~ **RUTH:**
(Hebrew; literally "sorrow," figuratively "loyal friend")

~ **SARAH:** *(Hebrew, "princess")*

~ **TAMAR:** *(Hebrew, "date palm")*

📖 **Leah** In the Bible's book of Genesis, Jacob is promised that he can marry beautiful Rachel if he labors for seven years. The night after his wedding, he realizes he's been tricked into marrying Rachel's older, tired sister Leah. He finally marries Rachel, too, but has to work another seven years afterward. An ugly story for a beautiful name. Others are nicer: In England a "lea" is a meadow, and many names end

159

on that sound. In Hawaii, Lea is the native goddess of
canoe making. Some parents, who want to make sure
the name is pronounced with two syllables instead of
one, go with the alternate spelling of Lia.

Variations: *Lea, Lia*
Alternatives: *Lee, Leia, Leila, Lilah, Liana, Hava, Alma*

𝓔 **Leda** was the Queen of Sparta and the mother of
several children, including Clytemnestra, twins Castor
and Pollux, and Helen, aka "Helen of Troy." The name
suggests swanlike elegance, for Leda is famous for
having succumbed to Zeus while he was in the form of
a swan. With classical roots but a simple spelling and
a popular -*a* ending, Leda has all the hallmarks of a
fashionable name.

Variations: *Leta, Lida*
Alternatives: *Lina, Mina, Delia, Selma*

Leilani In Hawaii, a *lei* is a "flower" and *lani* is
"heaven," so Leilani is "blossom of heaven." What
could be more feminine and poetic? The name also
evokes meadows (leas) and night (Leila is in there),
and it is filled with mellifluous-sounding vowels. As
pretty as it is, it's very ornate, so it may not go with
long, complicated last names. And it says "Aloha, I'm
from Hawaii" as strongly as Fiona says "Kiss me, I'm
Irish." Leilani is a rare name that doesn't rise and fall
in popularity predictably. There has been spotty use

160

of the name since 1937, which can be good for parents looking to avoid trendiness.

Nicknames: *Leia, Lani, Leila, Laney*
Alternatives: *Kiana, Tiara, Akela, Oliana, Mirabella*

✎ **Lena** started life as a nickname for Marlena, Helena, Magdalena, and others. Singer Lena Horne brought it to prominence. Lina is an alternative spelling and a diminutive of names like Carolina and Evangelina, but it's also a name in its own right. In Arabic, *lina* is a young palm tree, representing peace and tenderness, and the name is popular in North Africa and the Middle East.

Variations: *Lina, Leena*
Alternatives: *Lana, Rita, Carla, Zara, Nina, Delilah*

Leslie An ancient and prominent Scottish place-name that became a boy's name (think of the late actor Leslie Nielsen of *Airplane!* and the *Naked Gun* movies). Robert Burns used Lesley as a girl's name in a poem in 1792. Now it is almost exclusively a girl's name. Pixie-like dancer Leslie Caron is one of the most elegant examples of the name.

Variations: *Lesley, Lesly*
Alternatives: *Nancy, Kelly, Kelsey, Lelia*

Leticia Laetitia was a Roman goddess of good humor. In medieval England, the name was seen as Lettice.

Leticia sounds like a name that was popular with grandmothers, but it didn't really hit in the United States until the 1950s. It's on the slide now and hasn't made a comeback along with other old-fashioned names. It's similar in sound to the name Latisha, which was once trendy with African American families, but some of its variants, such as Laetizia (lay-TEE-zee-ah) and Laetitia (lay-TISH-ah) change both the spelling and the pronunciation.

Variations: *Laetitia, Lettice, Letizia, Laetizia*
Nicknames: *Letty, Leta, Lita*
Alternatives: *Rosemary, Willa, Alicia, Lula*

✐ **Liana** is related to Elaine, which comes from Helen. The name has been used since the 1970s with middling popularity. It can also be a short form of names like Liliana and Juliana. And the alternate spelling Leanna suggests a mash-up of Lee and Anna. If the origins are

---

I'd love to call her . . .
Libby

If you adore Libby but want to give your daughter a formal name with more substance and keep Libby a nickname, try one of these:

- ELIZABETH
- LINNET
- LYRIC
- LIBERTY
- LYDIA
- OLIVIA

---

murky, the sound is lovely. It sounds vaguely Hawaiian (Leilani), a little bit Arabian (Leila, Lina), a little old Hollywood (Lana), and contemporary (Lilly meets Hannah). There's something here for everyone.

Variations: *Lianne, Liane, Leanne, Lianna, Leanna*
Alternatives: *Mariana, Karina, Alaina, Anissa, Georgiana*

Libby Since 2002, people have been naming their daughters Libby. Why? Probably as an alternative to the wildly popular Lily. Lily is a stand-alone name; Libby is not. It's a nickname, short for Elizabeth. If you like Libby, great. But consider giving her a name she can use on her resume—and then calling her Libby for short.

Alternatives: *Nellie, Katie, May, Fanny, Carrie*

Liberty has been on record as a girl's name in the United States since 2001. Could the recent surge in patriotism have sparked this choice? Liberty means "freedom." And it starts the formal name of the Statue of Liberty: Liberty Enlightening the World. It's a new spin on a name taken from a value, and uniquely American.

Nicknames: *Libby, Bertie*
Alternatives: *America, Justice, Destiny, Honor, True*

✐ **Lilah** is a variation of Delilah (Hebrew for "languishing"). Delilah is the woman in the book of Judges in the Bible who enraptured Samson and

163

sapped his strength by cutting off his hair. It can also be a variation of Leila ("night"), especially when it appears as Lila. The name (especially in its *h*-free form) has been on the rise.

Variations: *Lila, Lyla*
Alternatives: *Dahlia, Lily, Zara, Salome*

🖊 **Lillian** is believed to have started life in Elizabethan times as a pet name for Elizabeth. (Remember that Queen Elizabeth II was called Lilibet by her family.) The name appears closely related to Lily as well. Take Lily, add Anne, and you end up with Lillian. Lillian is the more formal, sophisticated name; Lily is the swingy, cool version. The lily is a symbol of purity, and in Christianity it is associated with the Virgin Mary. Lily was considered too old-fashioned a few decades ago, but now it is all the rage. Lillian is a more understated, less trendy choice.

Variations: *Lilian, Lilia, Lilias, Liliana, Lilliana, Lillianna, Lillie, Lilly, Lily*
Alternatives: *Lilah, Neela, Lauren, Carmen, Camilla, Shoshana* (shoshan *is "lily" or "rose" in Hebrew)*

Linda means "pretty" in Spanish; the word has been used as a name since the 1800s. The name may have split off from longer names like Belinda, Rosalinda, and Lucinda. It may also relate to the linden tree, which comes from *linde* meaning "flexible." Linda was

A Rose by Any Other Name . . .

F lowers have been a source of girls' names since ancient days. They have a pleasing scent, they come in gorgeous colors, they represent the promise of spring, fertility, and renewal. What's not to love? Here are some of my favorites:

~ AMARYLLIS	~ HYACINTH	~ MYRTLE
~ BLOSSOM	~ IRIS	~ PANSY
~ BRIONY	~ JACARANDA	~ PETUNIA
~ CAMELLIA	~ JESSAMINE	~ POPPY
~ DAHLIA	~ LAUREL	~ POPPY
~ DAISY	~ LILAC	~ TANSY
~ HONEYSUCKLE	~ LILY	~ VIOLET

the number one name for girls in the late 1940s to the early 1950s and was in the top ten until 1966. Now it sounds a bit of an antique . . . and unlike other dated names like Ruby and Pearl, not necessarily in a good way. The nickname Lindy is a swingier choice.

Variations: *Belinda, Melinda*

Nicknames: *Lindy, Linnie*

Alternatives: *Nancy, Carolyn, Shirley, Betty, Barbara, Patricia, Liana*

Lindsay means "the wetlands of Lincoln." It is a place-name in English that was taken to Scotland in the twelfth century. The name used to be used for boys (Lindsey Buckingham was the guitarist in Fleetwood Mac), but is almost always a girls' name now (actress Lindsay Lohan leaps to mind). The name sounds like a cool twist on Linda, which could be why it became popular in the 1970s, around the same time Linda started to wane.

Variation: *Lindsey*
Alternatives: *Cameron, Paisley, Robin, Leslie, Hillary*

Lisa was originally a nickname for Elizabeth ("God is my oath"). Until the 1930s, Lisa was rarely chosen as a name itself. In 1937, it hit the charts and rapidly gained speed. Lisa was the number one most popular name for most of the 1960s, and didn't drop out of the top ten until 1977. It is much less popular now, sharing a similar trajectory with Amy, Kim, and Jennifer. Almost everyone knows a Lisa: actresses Lisa Kudrow, Bonet, and Rinna; talk show host Leeza Gibbons; and child prodigy Lisa Simpson of the animated series *The Simpsons* come to mind.

Variations: *Lyssa, Lisi, Litzy*
Alternatives: *Jennifer, Heather, Melissa, Kimberly*

Livia is short for the immensely fashionable name Olivia (see page 207). Some parents are choosing this cropped variation to separate their Livs from the pack. In ancient times, the name came from the

Roman last name Livius. The modern version of the name suggests liveliness, with the clear "liv" being out front, and extends a branch of peace with the olive connection. One of the characters in James Joyce's novel *Finnegan's Wake* was Livia. And the name does have a whiff of Ireland to it: It's evocative of the River Liffey, which runs through Dublin.

Nicknames: *Livvy, Liv*
Alternatives: *Vivian, Lilia, Sylvie, Viola, Leta, Linnea*

Logan is a Scottish last name. In the U.K., a logan stone is a boulder that is balanced in such a way that it can be moved with very little effort. In the United States, a logan is a small inlet or area of boggy water. Logan has also been used as a boy's first name. The use for girls in 1988 was inspired by a character on the soap opera *The Bold and the Beautiful*. The name suggests the rugged Scottish highlands, making it an outdoorsy name with a fresh-air feel.

Alternatives: *Brooke, Regan, Arden, Cameron, Maren*

Lola "Whatever Lola Wants, Lola Gets." That's the title of a song from the musical *Damn Yankees,* and it sums up Lola pretty well. She's a temptress. Lola has been used as a nickname for Dolores, and for Lourdes (as in the case of singer Madonna's daughter). With a dimunitive ending, the name turns into Lolita, evoking Nabokov's provocative novel—but you probably don't

---

I'd love to call her . . .
Lola

Lola's a spitfire—maybe too much so to be used as a first name. Try making her a nickname for one of these tamer options:

- ~ CAROLINE
- ~ DOLORES
- ~ ELOISE
- ~ ENOLA
- ~ FINOLA
- ~ LORELEI
- ~ LOUELLA
- ~ LOURDES
- ~ PENELOPE

---

want to go there. It's a cute, sassy name, though one that's best used judiciously.

Nickname: *Lolita*
Alternatives: *Coco, Gigi, Kiki, Mira, Nora, Nola*

London is the capital city of England. The name has been widely used for girls since 1999, and in the last handful of years, it has increased enormously in popularity. There is an heiress named London on the Disney TV series *The Suite Life of Zack and Cody,* on air since 2005, which may be reinforcing its popularity. If you like the idea of a British place-name but London's too cosmopolitan, try Albion, a poetic name for England.

Variation: *Londyn*
Alternatives: *Bristol, Paris, Hadley, Spenser, Henley, Cornwall*

Lorelei is a rocky peak jutting over a narrow point of the Rhine River in Germany. Legend held that Lorelei was a siren, luring sailors to their doom. Lorelei Lee, the bombshell from the movie *Gentlemen Prefer Blondes,* played by Marilyn Monroe, was another kind of siren altogether. Lorelai was the main character on the TV series *Gilmore Girls,* and it was she we have to thank for the name's current popularity. (Lorelai named her daughter after herself and called her Rory.)

Variation: *Lorelai*
Nicknames: *Lori, Rory*
Alternatives: *Marilyn, Salome, Delilah, Sabrina, Leilani*

Lorna is a name that was made up by novelist R. D. Blackmore for his 1869 novel *Lorna Doone,* a sprawling romance about forbidden love and mistaken identity in seventeenth-century England. (You may also recognize the bonnie lass from your supermarket—her name adorns a brand of shortbread cookies.) Lorna is the female equivalent of Lorne, an area in Scotland that the name may come from. (Lorne became a Canadian name for boys; think of actor Lorne Greene and producer Lorne Michaels.) Lorna sounds like a more grown-up sibling to Lola, though for a sweet nickname, you could take your cues from the shortbread and call her Cookie.

Alternatives: *Norma, Lauren, Nora, Bonnie*

✏ **Louise** Where is Louise? And what about Louisa? These traditional lovelies are hardly being used anymore. (Neither is their cousin, Lois.) Both names come from Louis, which means "famous warrior" and was the name of many French kings. In a world increasingly filled with Lucys and Amelias, it's shocking that Louisa and Louise are being overlooked. These are classic names—ones that, later on, won't suggest you hopped on the trend-wagon.

Variations: *Louisa, Luisa, Lois, Louella*
Nicknames: *Lou, Lola, Weezie, Lulu*
Alternatives: *May, Beatrice, Victoria, Matilda, Elizabeth, Arabella, Clarissa*

Lucy means "light." The name is also associated with insight and eyesight. Lucy was a spinster name thirty years ago, dusty and forgotten amid the Melissas and Heathers. Now it's the hottest thing on the playground, in a class with Abigail, Stella, and Emma. There are many variations, all of which have their pleasures. The Italian is Lucia (loo-CHEE-ah), French is Lucie, Spanish and Scandinavian is Lucia (loo-SEE-ah), and Luciana is a mash-up of Lucia and Anna used in Italy. Lucinda is a name Cervantes made up for *Don Quixote* in 1609, a combo of Lucia and Linda. Lucille is a retro take on the name, one that evokes Lucille Ball. Beware: Lucy is also a very popular name for dogs. There will be other Lucys, two- and four-legged.

Variations: *Lucia, Luciana, Lucinda, Lucille, Lucie*
Nicknames: *Lulu, Lou*
Alternatives: *Daisy, Maisie, Suzy, Ruthie, Lydia*

Luna means "moon" in Italian. The French version, also used, is Lune. The moon was believed to represent changeability as well as the life cycle—each month it starts small, grows full, and eventually withers away again. It represents mystery and shadows. So the name is alluring and suggests that the girl will have hidden depths. FYI, there is a crazy aspect to the moon as well, and "Lunatic" and "Loony" might be unwelcome nicknames. (And think twice before nicknaming her Lunette, which suggests "eyeglasses" in French.)
Variation: *Lune*
Alternatives: *Diana, Artemis, Stella, Skye, Selena, Leila, Lupa*

I'd love to call her . . .
Lulu

If you like the nickname Lulu and are looking for a more proper name to give her, try one of these:

~ JULIA	~ LUANNE	~ LUCY
~ LAUREN	~ LUCIA	~ LUNA
~ LOUISA	~ LUCILLE	~ LUZ
~ LOUISE	~ LUCINDA	~ TALLULAH

Luz In Spanish, *luz* is another word for "light," making the name Luz similar to Lucia. It is an homage not to St. Lucia but to the Virgin Mary, who is also known as Our Lady of Light. Luz is also a Hebrew word meaning "almond wood," and is the name of a town in the Old Testament. It was where Jacob had his dream about a ladder; when he woke he renamed the city Bethel. Luz is used almost exclusively by Hispanic families, but shares an ineffable quality with other potential crossovers like Isla and Inès.

Alternatives: *Pilar, Azul, Luna, Monserrat, Lucia, Paz*

✎ **Lydia** is an area of Anatolia (modern Turkey) named for an ancient King Lydus. The Lydians were famous for their wealth; their last king, before defeat by the Persians, was Croesus. There is a Lydia mentioned in the New Testament, and the name was picked up by Protestants in the 1600s and widely used then. Go to any colonial graveyard in New England and you can be assured to find a Lydia amid the Hannahs, Marys, and Abigails.

Variations: *Lydie, Lidie*
Alternatives: *Leda, Lina, Amelia, Justine, Alina, Diana, Pearl*

Lynn was an incredibly popular name throughout the twentieth century. In 1996, it finally fell out of use, and it's no longer in the top 1,000. It started life as either a variation of Linda or a lopping off of longer names like

Carolyn, Evelyn, and Marilyn. You'll find fresher takes on the name in Lynna or Lynnie.

Variations: *Lynne, Lynna, Lynnie*
Alternatives: *Lillian, Maryann, Terry, Jill, Quinn*

Lyric is a celebration of music, poetry, and meaningful feelings. People have been using the word as a girl's name since 1995. It sounds a little like Lydia, a little like Kyra. And it has a quality that is one part Greek mythology (makes you think of Erato, muse of lyric poetry) and one part rock 'n' roll.

Nickname: *Lyra*
Alternatives: *Harmony, Kyrie, Cadence, Aria, Lina*

Mabel comes from the word "amiable," suggesting a friendly and open nature. Desperately out of fashion, the name is so out in a world of trendy Emmas and Amelias, it might just come back in. It carries a whiff of spring with it (May), the beauty of Belle, and more gravitas than similar-sounding Maisie.

Nicknames: *May, Belle, Bella*
Alternatives: *Hazel, Myrtle, Marion, Ellen, Madge*

Mackenzie is a Scottish last name that means "attractive." Actress Mackenzie Phillips sparked the craze for the name when TV sitcom *One Day at a Time*

McDon't

Unless McSomething is your family name and you'd like to pass it on intact, think long and hard before you name your child McSomething. It's nicer to have a name that is spelled phonetically: Mackenzie, Mickenzie, and so on. Otherwise you are setting your child up for a lifetime of misspelled mail. Some popular (and unfortunate) McDon'ts:

- ~ MCKAYLA
- ~ MCKENNA
- ~ MCKENZIE
- ~ MCKINLEY
- ~ MCNUGGET
  (just kidding)

aired in 1975. One year later, the name was being widely used. It hit the top fifty in 1990, but is starting to wane.

Variations: *McKenzie, Makenzie*
Alternatives: *Philippa, Cameron, Kendra, Zelda, Mackay, Findlay*

Macy is a place-name that is believed to have migrated to the U.K. from northern France. It has been used as a girl's name since 1990, one year after a Macy appeared on the soap opera *The Bold and the Beautiful*. The name appeals to families who like Lacey but want more edge (though be aware it conjures images of a certain department store).

Variations: *Maci, Macie, Macey*
Alternatives: *Lacy, Tracy, Stacy, Maisie, Marcy*

Madeline comes from Magdalene, as in Mary
Magdalene. Magdalene means "from Magdala,"
a town on the Sea of Galilee. *Magdala* means
"towering, great" in Aramaic. Mary Magdalene
was a sinner who was redeemed by Christ and
became one of his most ardent followers. Madeline
is beloved as the frisky French schoolgirl from the
children's books by Ludwig Bemelmans. And a
madeleine is a small French sponge cake that
famously sparked Proust's deluge of childhood
memories in *Remembrance of Things Past*.

Variations: *Madalyn, Madalynn, Madeleine, Madelyn,
Madelynn, Madilyn, Madilynn, Madelaine*
Nicknames: *Maddie, Lina, Manon*
Alternatives: *Adeline, Clementine, Magalie, Marianne,
Virginia*

Madison You can look up the provenance of this
name and find that it means "mighty warrior" and
"son of Mad" and that it might be related to Madeleine
and Magdalene. Don't kid yourself. This name means
"Manhattan mermaid." Madison was the name of
Darryl Hannah's mermaid character in the 1984 hit
movie *Splash*. She didn't speak English well and she
named herself after Madison Avenue. Tom Hanks's
character was surprised because the name was so
ridiculous, especially for a girl. But he smiled and went
along with it. So did America. Before the movie was

released, Madison was unheard of. Now, twenty-some years later, it's one of the most popular girls' names.

Variations: *Maddison, Madisyn, Madyson*
Alternatives: *Addison, Truman, Jefferson, Monroe, Buchanan, Kennedy, Reagan*

Maeve is the name of the Queen of Connacht, a powerful warrior in an ancient Irish epic (and who is mentioned in passing in *Romeo and Juliet*). In Gaelic, the name appears as Meadhbh and means "intoxicating"—note the similarity between the name and the honey beverage "mead." Maeve is a strong, proud Irish name in use in the United States since 1997. The most famous Maeve is bestselling author Maeve Binchy. It's a sophisticated alternative to Ava.

Variations: *Medb, Meadhbh*
Alternatives: *Maude, Siobhan, Niamh, Maisie, Raven*

Magdalena is named for Mary Magadalene, one of Christ's most devoted followers. Mary was "from Magdala," a town on the Sea of Galilee that means "towering" in Aramaic. Magdalena is popular in Spanish-speaking and Eastern European countries like Poland. The English-language form is Madeline (see page 175).

Variations: *Magdalene, Magalie*
Nicknames: *Magda, Lena, Alena, Alene*
Alternatives: *Marlena, Dahlia, Maris, Makena, Margaret, Tallulah, Jordan*

Maisie A nickname for Margaret that came from its Gaelic variation, Mairead (rhymes with parade). The name is still somewhat obscure, although it has appeared in popular fiction more than once: in the Henry James novel *What Maisie Knew;* in the contemporary mystery series set in 1920s England, *Maisie Dobbs;* and in the bestselling kids' books about a little mouse named . . . you guessed it (note that this little mouse spells her name with a *y*). Maisie would be in perfect company with Stella, Sadie, and Lucy, but why not name her Margaret and call her Maisie for short?

Variations: *Maisy, Margaret*
Alternatives: *Macy, Sadie, Flora, Lucy, Maeve, Hazel, Emmy, Mabel*

Makena suggests abundance—it is a Hawaiian word meaning "many gathered." The name is a new addition to the charts, and its uptick may be attributed to parents who visited Makena Beach in Maui. Others may have been looking for an alternative to the widely used Mackenzie, and stumbled upon this name, which has similar letters and tone. McKenna would be an alternative for someone who likes the name but wants to honor Irish lineage (however, keep in mind that "Mc" is usually used as a prefix for a surname).

Variation: *Makenna*
Alternatives: *Kiana, Leilani, Marlena, Mari, Lilo, Oliana*

Malia was made famous in 2008 when Barack Obama won the presidency. All eyes turned to his family, especially his daughters, Malia and Sasha. Malia means "still water" in Hawaiian. It is also what the name Mary (Maria) becomes when translated into Hawaiian. It has the felicitous sound of many vowels, reminiscent of names like Aria and Aaliyah. (A warning: words beginning with *mal-* are a turn-off to some ears since *mal* suggests something bad, like malignant, maladroit, and so on.) The name has been in spotty use since the 1970s but has lately caught on and become quite trendy.

Variations: *Maleah, Mailyah*
Alternatives: *Aaliyah, Aria, Lea, Amelia, Maria, Melanie*

Mallory In 1982, the sitcom *Family Ties* debuted. In 1983, families started naming their girls Mallory, for the beautiful, ditzy daughter on the show, played by Justine Bateman. Mallory was previously a last name, as in Renaissance poet Sir Thomas Malory, author of *Le Morte d'Arthur.*

Alternatives: *Hillary, Lindsay, Marlow, Valerie, Molly*

Mara means "bitter" in Hebrew. In the book of Ruth in the Bible, Naomi, after a tragic turn of events, announces that she should be called Mara for all of the bitter fortune God has brought her. It may be nicer to name your little one something more auspicious

like Tamara ("date palm," pages 253–254), Dagmar
("Dane's joy," page 63), or Mairead ("pearl," page 177),
and just call her Mara.

Alternatives: *Tamara, Damaris, Maria, Tara, Sarah, Farrah,
Cara*

Maren is an Irish name, a variation of the Gaelic
Muireann, which means "fair lady of the sea." It's also
a Gaelic form of Mary (see pages 183–184). The name
is all waves and blue water—it evokes "marine." And
it brings to mind the naturally stunning area north of
San Francisco, Marin County.

Variations: *Marion, Martine, Marianne, Marina, Marin, Maris*
Alternatives: *Lauren, Karen, London, Tamryn*

🖋 **Margaret** It's hard to find a more versatile name
than Margaret, which means "pearl" in Greek. The
name has been in wide use since the Middle Ages. There
have been saints, royals, writers (Atwood, Drabble),
scientists (Mead), and stateswomen (Thatcher) all
bearing the name. Margaret may have more nicknames
than any other traditional name, making it incredibly
useful and fun to play with. Marguerite is the source of
many colorful pet names: Daisy (*marguerite* is "daisy"
in French), Greta, Gretchen, Rita, Gita, and Tita. In
Ireland, Margaret is Mairead (rhymes with parade).
The retro nicknames are coming back as names on
their own: shortcuts like Maisie, Mamie, and Maggie.

Variations: *Margot, Margit, Marguerite, Mairead, Mared, Marjorie, Margery, Marietta, Magali, Meghan, Megan, Mette*
Nicknames: *Maggie, Meg, Peg, Peggy, Meggie, Mamie, Maisie, Marg, May, Margie, Daisy, Greta, Madge, Marge, Mags, Gretchen, Rita, Gita, Tita, Midge*
Alternatives: *Elizabeth, Valerie, Simone, Magdalena, Antonia, Pearl*

✎ **Maria** is the Mediterranean version of Mary. In Shakespeare's day, the name was pronounced mah-RYE-ah, whereas now it is more commonly pronounced mah-REE-ah. Maria is a deeply traditional and religious name but it sounds utterly modern. The name exists in Islam, too: Maria was a wife of Muhammad. It trips poetically off the tongue, reminding us of *The Sound of Music* (How do you solve a problem like her?), *West Side Story* (Tony's love, the subject of the song "Maria"), opera diva Maria Callas, and the soaring hymn "Ave Maria." Singer Mariah Carey brought the old-fashioned pronunciation back into the mainstream. Variations Marie (the French standard) and Marion are considered dated. But Marion—the heroine of *Robin Hood* and *Raiders of the Lost Ark* as well as one of Sarah Jessica Parker's twins—may make a comeback.

Variations: *Mary (see pages 183–184), Mariah, Moriah, Mariana, Marie, Mariyah, Marion, Marianne*
Alternatives: *Malia, Scheyla, Rihanna, Nina, Martha*

Marley immediately evokes Bob Marley, the beloved reggae musician; Jacob Marley, Ebenezer Scrooge's spectral business partner; and the dog made famous in the bestselling memoir *Marley & Me*. Marley can claim a couple of origins. It is an English last name meaning "lakeside meadow" that has become a first name. And it is a nickname for Marlene, which comes from Mary Magdalene. A more feminine spelling is Marlee.

Variations: *Marlee, Marlie*
Alternatives: *Marlena, Marlow, Harley, Karla, Darcey*

MARCIA, MARCIA, MARCIA!

For those of us who grew up watching *The Brady Bunch*, Marcia was a symbol of the perfect girl. She was pretty, smart, popular, well-adjusted. In fact, some of us thought she was too perfect (especially her sister Jan). Did Marcia Brady kill interest in the name or was it always destined to fade away? Marcia, Marsha, and Marcy are no longer in the top 1,000 most popular girls names in the United States. Marcy sounds like the most likely candidate for revival. She shares a lot in common with Macy and Lacy and Darcy. We look to her, or to Marcella, an Italian name, to keep the Marcia flag flying.

Around the World

Some place-names are so handsome and memorable that they are irresistible, particularly to parents who are just as likely to have a suitcase as a stroller in hand. Here are some ideas, both well loved and brand new, for girls and boys. If you choose a place-name, make sure it sounds at least a little bit like a real name—your little one won't thank you for naming her Butte.

- **UNITED STATES:** *America, Arizona, Augusta, Austin, Boston, Bronx, Brooklyn, California, Carolina, Carson (City), Cheyenne, Dakota, Dallas, Helena, Jackson, Juneau, Kauai, Montana, Philadelphia (Jane Austen had an Aunt named this)*

- **EUROPE:** *Albi, Albion (ancient name for England), Arles, Bari, Calais, Cashel (Ireland; one of Daniel Day Lewis's kids), Dax, Dover, Florence, Forli, Galway, Georgia, Kilkenny, Lazia, Lisbon, London, Nancy, Odessa, Palma, Paris, Ravello, Ravenna, Riga, Roma, Sevilla, Shannon, Sicily*

(or Sicilia in Italian), Siena, Sintra, Taormina (Italy; call her Mina), Valence, Venezia or Venetia (for Venice, Italy), Verona

- **ASIA AND OCEANIA:** *Asia, Burma, China, Everest, India, Kathmandu (call her Kat), Kerala, Laos, Madras, Nepal, Simla (once the summer seat of the British Raj)*

- **AFRICA:** *Alexandria, Algeria, Dakar, Ivory, Kenya, Khartoum, Mali, Mauritania, Nairobi, Nigeria, Sahara (or in Angelina Jolie's child's case, Zahara), Saqqara, Senegal, Seychelles, Somalia, Zambia, Zanzibar*

Martha is the perfect name for happy homemaker Martha Stewart. The name has always been associated with domestic service since biblical times. When Jesus visited the house of Mary and Martha, it was Martha who did all the work serving him. The name was considered a good, demure choice for a dutiful wife. Colonial graveyards in the United States are filled with Marthas (most notably Martha Washington, Martha Jefferson). The name continued to be popular from the 1800s through the early twentieth century, but it began a slow decline in the 1960s that has picked up speed since the 1990s.

Variations: *Marta, Marthe*
Alternatives: *Martina, Marcella, Thalia, Dahlia, Anne*

Mary is the mother of all girls' names. You would be hard pressed to find another name that has been so enduringly popular and so resistant to trends as Mary. It was number one or two in the United States until 1965. Its popularity has slid, but it remains in the top one hundred today. Mary in French is Marie; in Spanish and Italian, Maria; in Hebrew and Arabic, Maryam or Miriam. Mary means "drop of the sea," which was later tweaked to "star of the sea" (*stella maris* in Latin). There were a number of Marys in the Bible, but one outshines them all: Jesus's mother, the Virgin Mary. Mary shows up in all kinds of forms and in every Christian country, with nicknames ad infinitum. If you're not comfortable with Mary straight up, consider it with a twist, in a first name–middle name combination such as Mary Kate, Mary

Frances, or Mary Elizabeth. There's also the reverse: Annamarie, Rosemary.

Variations: *Maria, Marie, Mariah, Mariel, Mariela, Marilyn, Marina, Marisa, Marissa, Maritza, Marisol, Maris, Maribel, Marion, Marin, Maura, Moira, Muriel, Moriah*
Nicknames: *Mitzi, Mamie, Mia, Marika*
Alternatives: *Elizabeth, Margaret, Jane, Miriam, Rose*

Matilda A German name meaning "strength in battle," Matilda is the name of several medieval queens, including the wife of William the Conquerer. The name was anglicized to Maud or Maude in England. Matilda was in wide use from the 1800s to the 1950s and then dropped off. In Europe, especially Scandinavia, the name is quite popular. Matilda just started hitting the United States charts again, and with good reason. It's charming and of a kind with other popular names from its heyday. The name has been popular with Australians, whose unofficial national anthem is "Waltzing Matilda." (Matilda is slang for "backpack.") The late Australian actor Heath Ledger named his daughter Matilda, which renewed interest in the name. (Incidentally, Aussie actress Rachel Griffiths named her son Banjo for Banjo Paterson, the lyricist for the aforementioned folk song.) The name also offers itself up for adorable truncations like Mattie, Tilda, and Tillie.

Variation: *Mathilde*

Nicknames: *Mattie, Tilda, Tilly*
Alternatives: *Theodora, Justine, Emmeline, Arabella*

Maude And then there's Maude. *Maude* is familiar
to most Americans of a certain age as the *All in
the Family* spinoff. The 1970s sitcom was liberal
and feminist and calls to mind star Bea Arthur, as
Maude, wearing a large muumuu. To fans of Irish
literature, Maud calls to mind Maud Gonne, who was
poet Yeats's unrequited love and the muse of many
of his poems. Maude is the anglicized version of
Matilda (see opposite) and the name of some ancient
British royalty, including Empress Maud, who was
the last rightful heir of William the Conqueror, her
grandfather.

Alternatives: *Maeve, Matilda, Claude, Paulina, Audrey,
Mavis*

✐ **Mavis** It isn't just for nursing home residents
anymore! Okay, most Mavises you know or have
heard of are elderly, but the name has some of the
hallmarks of popularity, so think seriously about it.
It's a bird name meaning "song thrush." It sounds like
Maeve, the increasingly trendy Irish name, as well as
like "maven," a word full of enthusiasm, and the name
has retro-cool appeal. It's so out it could be in. Mavis
deserves to come back alongside picks like Evelyn.

Alternatives: *Evelyn, Lucille, Maris, Ellis*

Maya is a celebration of May and the Roman goddess Maia for whom the month was named. May itself sounds old-fashioned now, but Maya is all the rage, arriving in the United States in 1970 and quickly rising to the top one hundred. The name brings with it a sense of freshness and hope, the youthful bloom one associates with spring. It also evokes the Mayans, who thrived in Mexico's Yucatan peninsula around the time of Jesus, and who still live there today. Maya is even more popular in Israel than the United States, and is welcomed by Indians as well—Maya is the Hindu goddess of illusion.

Variations: *Mya, Maia, Mayra, Myah*
Alternatives: *Gaia, Mae, Mia, Amaya, Flora, Mila, Leia*

Meadow If a hardened mobster can name his daughter Meadow, then I can, too. That's what parents said in 2001, two years after Tony Soprano and his family hit the TV screen. A meadow, of course, is a field, often left wild, maybe filled with flowers, sometimes used for pasturing animals. The name is romantic, bohemian, a free-spirited salute to nature.

Alternatives: *Summer, River, Lark, Willow, Lake*

Megan is a variation of Margaret (page 179). Some prefer Megan (MEE-ghan), others Meghan (MEH-ghan). Both names have a strongly Irish bent to them.

Megan appeared in the United States in 1952 and hit the top ten in 1985. Meghan has followed a similar trajectory, but has always been less popular than her sister.

Variation: *Margaret*
Alternatives: *Regan, Morgan, Parker, Maureen, Maria, Tegan*

Hindu Goddesses

The Greeks and Romans aren't the only ones with a pantheon of great gods and goddesses. Check out these Hindu favorites, the inspiration for a number of great Indian names.

~ **ADITI:** *a benevolent mother goddess; a protector*

~ **ANNAPURNA:** *the goddess of food and cooking, a symbol of nourishment*

~ **DURGA:** *a fiercer, demon-fighting form of Parvati*

~ **KALI:** *the complex goddess of time and change, but also of fairly violent annihilation*

~ **LAKSHMI:** *goddess of almost all things good—grace, charm, wealth, fertility, courage, and wisdom*

~ **MAYA:** *the goddess of illusion, who creates the sense of an individual self*

~ **PARVATI:** *a mother goddess*

~ **RADHA:** *a goddess associated with love—she was Lord Krishna's romantic interest*

~ **SARASWATI:** *goddess of wisdom; if you're not Hindu, you might consider calling her Sara for short*

~ **SHAKTI:** *the divine feminine force of the universe, the name means "to be able"*

Melanie means "dark." Think of her as your dark beauty. The name worked its way from Greece, where Melanie was an important saint in the fifth century for her selfless works with the poor, into France, where it became Melania, and to England. It was rarely used in the United States until the blockbuster novel *Gone with the Wind,* published in 1936, introduced the world to Melanie Wilkes, and by 1938, the name was on the rise. Famous modern Melanies include actress Melanie Griffith and Donald Trump's wife, Melania.

Variations: *Melania, Melany, Melina*
Nicknames: *Lainey, Mel, Melly, Lina*
Alternatives: *Belinda, Laney, Maryellen, Chiara, Raven, Melody*

𝓔 **Melissa** means "honeybee" in Greek. According to mythology, a nymph named Melissa discovered honey and brought it to the world; the bees were named in her honor. The Melissae were nymphs who nursed the baby Zeus, so the name is associated with soothing as well. Later, Melissa was a powerful prophet in the epic sixteenth-century poem "Orlando Furioso."

Variation: *Melita*
Alternatives: *Melisande, Alyssa, Elizabeth, Amanda, Samantha*

Melody The melody is the principal tune that carries a song. The word itself has the felicitous rise and fall of music, but sounds enough like the more traditional

I Could Just Eat You Up

There are several established names that come from the food world. And there are others that parents choose that are more creative: Gwyneth Paltrow shocked the world by naming her daughter Apple. Here are some of the top picks from the pantry. Notice that most of them are sweet.

- **AMANDINE** (*French name relating to almonds*)
- **APPLE**
- **CANDY**
- **CHERRY**
- **CLEMENTINE**
- **COOKIE** (*best as a nickname*)
- **GINGER** (*short for Virginia*)
- **LETTICE** (*variation of Letitia but sounds just like lettuce*)
- **MELISSA** (*honey*)
- **OLIVE**
- **PEPPER**
- **PIPPIN** (*a small apple*)
- **PUMPKIN** (*best as a nickname*)
- **ROSEMARY**
- **SAFFRON**
- **SAGE**
- **SUGAR**

names Melissa, Melinda, and Melanie that it's less hippie-dippy than other tuneful names.

Variation: *Melodie*

Nicknames: *Lola, Mel, Melly, Dodie*

Alternatives: *Elodie, Lyric, Cadence, Harmony, Allegra*

Mercedes means "mercy" in Spanish. It is a name like Dolores or Guadalupe in that it refers to the Virgin

My One and Only

Some names (for both gals and guys), are totally distinctive. They make a statement. You can look at any one of them and immediately fill in the last name, because there's really only one person who leaps to mind.

~ ARETHA	~ DEEPAK	~ MERYL
~ AYN	~ EARTHA	~ OPRAH
~ BARACK	~ EBENEZER	~ SAVION
~ BENEDICT	~ KERMIT	~ SIGMUND
~ BEYONCÉ	~ KIMORA	~ TWYLA

Mary—in this case, Mary of Mercies. The name is mostly used by two groups: devout Catholics or people who believe that the name has a luxury sound thanks to its connection to expensive car brand Mercedes-Benz.

Nickname: *Sadie*
Alternatives: *Monserrat, Dolores, Guadalupe, Luz, Tiffany, Marcy, Portia*

Meredith is a Welsh surname, the meaning of which is believed to be "great lord." It migrated over to the United States and became a girl's first name in the late 1800s; it was popular by 1910. The name is associated with mirth because so many Merediths become

Merrys. And it has a whiff of the sea (the French *mer*) as well as horses (Mer, one of her nicknames, sounds like "mare").

Nicknames: *Merry, Mer*
Alternatives: *Gwyneth, Edith, Jennifer, Miranda, Tabitha, Evelyn*

Mia Thank Mia Farrow for the popularity of this nickname for Maria. (Farrow's own real first name is Maria.) Mia has been in use on its own since 1964, right around the time the pixie actress's film career took off, and it has value in its own right—the word *mia* means "mine" in Italian. The name has skyrocketed and is now in the top twenty.

Variations: *Miah, Miya, Maria, Amelia*
Alternatives: *Maya, Myra, Mina, Mila, Aimee, Aria, May*

Micah A biblical name that is a variation of Michael ("who is like God?"), Micah was a prophet and the author of the Book of Micah. Although the name is traditionally for boys, girls have been using it since the 1970s, probably because of the lilting, feminine *-ah* sound at the end.

Alternatives: *Camille, Gabriella, Domenica, Mira*

Michaela Strong and mighty Michaela takes her name from Michael, one of the great names of the Bible. In Christianity, Michael is the warrior archangel, the commander of the army of the Lord, winged, clad in armor, sword in hand, ready for battle. He is the patron saint of soldiers. In Jewish tradition, Michael is the defender of Israel. He is an angel at the left hand of God in Islamic tradition. Michaela is edgier than the more traditional Michelle. It has been used in the United States since 1967 and became quite popular in the 1990s, when the TV series *Dr. Quinn, Medicine Woman* was airing (the lead character was Michaela).

Variations: *Mikaela, Mikayla, Makaila, Makayla*
Nicknames: *Kayla, Micky*
Alternatives: *Michelle, Nyla, Micah, Caitlin, Ella, Mackenzie*

✒ **Michelle** "Michelle, my belle." Pretty and sweet as a dusty pink rose, Michelle is a traditional feminization of Michel, the French version of Michael (for more, see Michaela, above). Fashionable in America since the 1930s, Michelle was climbing the pop charts when the Beatles's song hit the airwaves in 1966. That rocketed it to the top ten, where it remained until 1980. It's been undergoing a correction since then, but may be worth a second look—it has a variety of compelling nicknames.

Variations: *Micheline, Michaeline*
Nicknames: *Shelly, Misha, Elle, Mia, Midge, Micky*
Alternatives: *Miranda, Lisa, Karen, Jennifer, Christine, Pamela*

Milagros means "miracles" in Spanish. It is similar to Mercedes, Dolores, and Guadalupe, in that it ultimately points back to the Virgin Mary, aka Our Lady of Miracles. Many families are realizing that the -*gros* on the end of the name lacks appeal (and begs teasing) in English, so they are lopping it off and just calling her Mila.

Nickname: *Mila*
Alternatives: *Miranda, Luz, Mercedes, Mira, Pilar*

Miley Thanks, Miley Cyrus, aka Hannah Montana. Your childhood nickname (short for Smiley) has hit the top 1,000 names. Cyrus legally changed her name to Miley in 2008. Let's keep this one a nickname, folks.

Variations: *Mylee, Mylie*
Alternatives: *Hannah, Kylie, Keely, Destiny (Cyrus's name at birth), Marley, Riley*

✐ **Millicent** America has been on the outs with Millicent since the 1960s. The name comes from the Old French moniker Melisende, which means "strength." Queen Melisende ruled Jerusalem in the 1100s. The name was anglicized to Millicent, which has a super-cute nickname, Millie. The word *mille* means "one thousand" in Latin-derived languages, which gives the name a kind of power beyond its meaning. I vote for its vibrant return.

> *I'd love to call her . . .*
> **Millie**
>
> ---
>
> I f you like the nickname Millie, consider these
> formal names as starting points:
>
> - AMELIA   - LUDMILLA   - MILDRED
> - CAMILLA   - MELINDA   - MILLICENT
> - EMILY   - MILAGROS   - MIREILLE

Variation: *Melisende*
Nickname: *Millie*
Alternatives: *Melissa, Vincenza, Geraldine, Mathilda,
Martha, Agnes*

Mina is a nickname turned real name. Short for a
variety of names—Wilhelmina, Yazmina, Anna Maria,
and others—Mina is so cute and so *now* (it's like Mia
with a twist) that people are not bothering to find a
long form. The name works in most languages—around
the world it can mean anything from "gem" to "fine."
Alternatives: *Mira, Mila, Micah, Gemma, Pia*

Mira can be all things to all people. It's from the Latin
root that gives us words like "miracle" and "mirage," all
of which mean to "look upon something with wonder."
So it is closely related to names like Mirabel and
Miranda. It's also an Indian name (think film director

Mira Nair) that means "prosperous" in Sanskrit. In Eastern Europe, Mira can be short for Miroslava, which means "worship peace." (Roger Federer's wife is Mirka, short for Miroslava.)

Variations: *Meera, Miranda, Mirabel, Mirabella, Miroslava*
Nickname: *Mirka*
Alternatives: *Kyra, Pia, Mina, Rita, Nina*

Miracle The rising popularity of this name is concurrent with the number of babies born through IVF (in vitro fertilization). Coincidence? Maybe. Or maybe not. This name has been climbing in popularity since 1995 and is now in the top 500. You can communicate the same sense of gratitude and awe with more traditional (and subtle) names like Mirabel and Miranda, and even just Mira (see opposite).

Alternatives: *Mila, Destiny, Hope, Joy, Faith*

✎ **Miranda** is a wonderful name. It means "wondrous" and "admirable," from the Latin word *mirandus*. Miranda has literary origins—her name was created by Shakespeare for a character in *The Tempest*—and was fashionable in the 1800s and again in the 1950s. It's a name with beauty and poetry, one that would go especially well with Germanic last names that could use some softening.

Nicknames: *Mira, Randy, Randa*
Alternatives: *Amanda, Mirabel, Mireille, Ariel*

Mireya Mireille is the Provençal version of Miranda, which, like all *mira-* names, suggests amazement and admiration. However, Mireille (meer-AY) is ripe for roll-call mispronunciation, while Mireya, a Spanish variation, is easy to say. There is a hint of sunlight in the name with the sound of *ray* at the end.

Variations: *Mireille, Miranda*
Alternatives: *Freya, Mirabella, Joy, Marjorie, Margareta*

🖉 **Miriam** One of the great names from the Bible, Miriam was Moses's older sister who watched as the Pharaoh's daughter discovered her baby brother. The name is very popular among observant Jews and Muslims. It is similar to Mary—Mary becomes

Wonder Women

Some names are awe inspiring. They suggest power and competence. These are some of the most compelling heroic girl's names from comics, mythology, history, and elsewhere:

~ ANDROMEDA	~ ELEKTRA	~ NATASHA
~ ATHENA	~ GODIVA	~ OLYMPIA
~ BARBARELLA	~ ISIS	~ PROMETHIA
~ CLEOPATRA	~ JEANNE	~ TITANIA
~ DELILAH	~ JEZEBEL	~ VICTORIA
~ DIANA	~ LARA	~ XENA

Maryam in Arabic and Miriam in Hebrew. Nobody is sure what the origins of the name are. Because Moses and Aaron (the names of Miriam's brothers) are Egyptian names, Miriam probably is, too. To bring Miriam into the twenty-first century, you could call her Miri, which is graceful and cute, or Miro, which has an artistic bent.

Variations: *Mariam, Maryam*
Alternatives: *Sonia, Mariah, Hava, Esther*

Moira Take the Gaelic Maire (Mary), anglicize it, and you have Moira or Maura. Ballerinas at heart will remember Moira Shearer from the film *The Red Shoes*.

Variations: *Maura, Moyra*
Alternatives: *Mairead (rhymes with parade), Maureen, Fiona, Niamh (pronounced neeve)*

Molly Once an Irish nickname, lately Molly gets top billing and is popular way beyond the land of Eire. Molly has a carefree, jolly sound to it. Still, why not name her something else—Margaret or Mary are the traditional starting points—and just call her Molly?

Variations: *Mollie, Polly*
Alternatives: *Holly, Sally, Maggie*

Mona is a name that crosses boundaries easily. In Gaelic, it means "noble." In Greek, "singular." In Arabic, "wish." It's a nickname for names as diverse as Madonna

197

(as is Mona Lisa), Ramona, and Monica. Mona sounds seductive rather than perky. Bonus: Her name will probably never be mispronounced or misspelled.

Alternatives: *Madonna, Ramona, Romola, Monica, Sonia, Monet*

Bookish Girls

What we read in childhood affects us strongly. The heroines of our favorite children's books can make excellent sources for naming. Consider:

- **ANNABEL** (Freaky Friday)
- **ANNE** (Anne of Green Gables)
- **CADDIE** (Caddie Woodlawn)
- **CLAUDIA** (from The Mixed-Up Files of Mrs. Basil E. Frankweiler)
- **DOROTHY** (The Wizard of Oz)
- **ELOISE** (of the Plaza Hotel)
- **FERN** (Charlotte's Web)
- **HARRIET** (the spy)
- **LAURA** (Ingalls Wilder, Little House on the Prairie)
- **MADELINE** (from the Bemelmans series)
- **MAISY** (the mouse)

- **MATILDA** (Matilda by Roald Dahl)
- **MEG** (A Wrinkle in Time)
- **NANCY** (Drew, teen sleuth)
- **OLIVIA** (the pig)
- **PIPPI** (Longstocking, short for Pillipotta. Call yours Philippa)
- **SARA** (Crewe, A Little Princess)
- **SCOUT** (To Kill a Mockingbird)
- **TACY** (from the Betsy-Tacy books by M. H. Lovelace; short for Anastacia)
- **TIB** (from the Betsy-Tacy books by M. H. Lovelace; short for Thelma)
- **WENDY** (Peter Pan)

Monica was the mother of St. Augustine, and it was she who led her son to convert to Christianity. As a result, her name is thought to mean "advisor." The name is pretty and familiar—maybe too familiar to viewers of the sitcom *Friends*. To some, it has a windswept, beachy feel, thanks to Santa Monica, the city on the sea next to Los Angeles. If you go with the widely known French version of the name, Monique, you have a name with some mystery to it.

Variations: *Monika, Monique*
Nicknames: *Mona, Nica, Nickie*
Alternatives: *Teresa, Veronica, Erica, Cecilia*

Monserrat The name means "jagged peaks" in Spanish (*serrat* is related to the word *serrated*). Monserrat is another way of naming a girl for the Virgin Mary. The Virgin of Monserrat is an icon located in a monastery on the mountain Monserrat, in the Spanish region of Catalonia (it's also the name of one of the Leeward Islands in the Caribbean). The statue is one of the "black Madonnas," the wood used to carve it having darkened over the several hundred years of its existence. Monserrat is used mostly by Spanish-speaking families.

Alternatives: *Mercedes, Dolores, Luz, Milagros*

Morgan Less ankle bracelets and flowy fabrics than Rhiannon, but more mystical than similar-sounding

199

Arthurian Legends

For romantic names that evoke the mists of time, you can't do much better than Arthurian legend. While Morgan has hit it big, most others are sleepers.

~ **CAELIA:** *Not a major character, but a very cool name—a fairy queen*

~ **GUINEVERE:** *A cloud goddess by nature, Guinevere took mortal form to become Arthur's wife (and Lancelot's lover)*

~ **IGRAINE:** *Though she mothered Arthur, with her first husband she birthed the three evil daughters who eventually gave Arthur a m-Igraine*

~ **MORGAN LE FAY:** *An enchantress who toes the line between healer and witch*

~ **NIMUE:** *Sorceress, lover, and eventual enslaver of Merlin, Nimue may also be the Lady of the Lake who, as Monty Python put it, "lobbed a scimitar" at Arthur*

Logan, Morgan has magical associations thanks to King Arthur's sorceress sister, Morgan le Fay. The name originally comes from Wales and means "culmination." It also has a patrician, old-money whiff to it thanks to industrialist J. P. Morgan. Morgan wasn't often used for girls until 1976, when actress Morgan Fairchild came to prominence. Now it is in the top fifty.

Variations: *Morgane, Morgana*
Alternatives: *Fay, Jordan, Logan, London, Regan*

Myla A mash-up of popular names Maya and Miley, with a little Mia thrown in for good measure, Myla has been in use since 2005 and is growing in popularity. It is unlikely to be related to the boy's name Miles, which means "soldier" and is sometimes linked to Michael.

Alternatives: *Kyra, Ayla, Mila, Myra*

Nadia A French variation on the Russian name Nadya, which means "hope." Russian names became popular in France after the Ballet Russe, Diaghilev's company, was created in Paris in the early 1900s. Nadia remains popular in Francophone countries, as well as in Arab countries where it means "tender." The name has been used in the United States since 1976, and suggests a little girl who's peppy and indomitable. Thank you, Olympic gymnast Nadia Comaneci.

Variations: *Nadya, Nadine*
Alternatives: *Viola, Clara, Katia, Danica*

Naima An Arabic name meaning "peaceful" and "bliss," it's also the title of a rich and seductive John Coltrane love ballad.

Alternatives: *Nahla, Salima, Minu*

Nancy used to be a nickname for Ann. (Ann gets turned around and becomes Nan, Nan turns into Nancy.) But for more than a century, it's been a name in its own right. Nancy was in the top ten from 1935 to 1955 and has been in decline since then. It's a great girl-next-door name. Nancy seems open and cheerful. Maybe the name will rise again in the wake of the popular children's series of books *Fancy Nancy*.

Variations: *Nancie, Nanci*
Nickname: *Nan*
Alternatives: *Linda, Sandra, Sharon, Janet, Barbara, Maggie*

🖊 **Naomi** A timeless classic that will never go out of style, Naomi comes from the Old Testament (she was Ruth's mother-in-law). The name means "pleasant" in Hebrew. Australian actress Naomi Watts ups the name's Hollywood quotient.

Variation: *Noemi (pronounced no-AY-me)*
Alternatives: *Mara, Ruth, Orpah (biblical Naomi's other daughter-in-law), Omani*

Natalie has slowly and steadily inched into the top twenty names for girls. The name comes from the Russian Natalya, which became popular in France in the early twentieth century as Natalie. The word relates to *natal,* meaning "birth," and refers to Christ's birth. Actress Natalie Wood boosted the name's popularity in the United States in the 1960s, and now actress Natalie Portman is keeping the glamour flame alive.

Variations: *Natalee, Natalya, Natalia, Nataly, Nathalie, Nathalia, Nathaly*
Alternatives: *Nadia, Justine, Noelle, Emmanuelle, Christina*

Natasha isn't just for Russians anymore. This nickname for Natalya has become a popular name in itself for many Americans since 1965. Both names refer to Christ's birth. Natasha hit the top one hundred in the mid-1980s. Actress Natasha Richardson helped raise the profile of the name for non-Russians. Sasha Obama, President Obama's younger daughter, is a Natasha.

Nicknames: *Tasha, Sasha*
Alternatives: *Noel, Katrina, Irina, Mariska, Krista*

Nevaeh It looks like Niamh, the name from Irish mythology meaning "bright." But it's not. It's actually "heaven" spelled backward. It hit the charts in 2001 after Christian singer Sonny Sandoval introduced his daughter Nevaeh to audiences on MTV the year before. The name has skyrocketed to the top fifty—but it lacks serious roots. If you like the sound of it but want something with tradition, go for Neve, which is the English spelling of the Irish name Niamh.

Variation: *Neveah*
Alternatives: *Neve, Eden, Heaven, Miracle, Destiny*

Nia is the Welsh equivalent of the Irish name Niamh (pronounced neeve), which means "bright." It's an unusual alternative to very mainstream Mia (though when you call for her in the playground, all those Mias may come running). It can be used on its own, or as a nickname for names like Tania, Virginia, and Melania, which contain the three-letter combo. And there are more options: Actress Nia Long's real name is Nitara; Nia Vardalos's name is Antonia.

Alternatives: *Antonia, Virgina, Melania, Mia, Maria, Natina*

Nicole is a serene and elegant name, the feminine form of Nicholas, which means "victory" in Greek. Saint Nicholas was a fourth-century saint who is the patron of a vast number of groups—sailors, merchants, and others—as well as the jolly old soul who brings presents to children on Christmas Day. Nicky brings out her frisky side.

Variations: *Nicola, Nikola, Nicolette*
Nicknames: *Nico, Nicky*
Alternatives: *Corinne, Kimberly, Gillian, Muriel*

✐ **Nina** Niña means "girl" in Spanish. As a name it started life as a shortened version of Antonina and as a nickname for Ann. Nina has been consistently popular for the last hundred years. She is never the most popular girl on the block, but always solid. This spunky moniker is an out-of-the-ordinary pick for today's parents who favor Anna, Ella, Mia, and other short, sweet names ending with *a*.

Alternatives: *Mona, Mira, Nora, Elsa*

Noelle Noel is French for "Christmas." Noelle is a feminine form of the word. The name is a good choice for babies due in late December. It offers all the cozy imagery of Christmas—pine trees, holly berries, snowdrifts, carolers, and twinkling lights.

Alternatives: *Natalie, Christine, Natasha*

Nola is a short form of the traditional Irish name Fionnuala, which means "white shoulders." It's a unique choice for a world filled with Lolas and Cocos and Annas and Emmas. There's also music and soul in it—it can be a nod to New Orleans, for which it is a nickname (N.O., LA). Although the name disappeared from 1965 through 2007, Nola is back. Look for her popularity to grow.

Alternatives: *Nora, Mona, Lola, Lana*

Nora An Irish name, Nora may have started life as a nickname for old-fashioned picks like Leonora and Honor. Nora was in the top one hundred in the late

---

I'd love it if she sounded . . .
Irish

~ CLAIRE	~ KATHLEEN	~ NIAMH
~ COLLEEN	~ KERRY	~ NORA
~ DEIRDRE	~ MAEVE	~ OONA
~ FINOLA	~ MAIREAD	~ SINÉAD
~ FIONA	~ MOIRA	~ SIOBHAN

1900s. The name has been coming back, slowly but surely. It's a good way to honor Irish roots—James Joyce's wife was Nora. More recent well-known Noras include writer Nora Ephron and musician Norah Jones.

Variation: *Norah*

Alternatives: *Greta, Sasha, Cora, Anya*

🖊 **Norma** is the tragic druid sorceress from Bellini's 1832 opera *Norma*. The name is believed to have been coined for the opera. Of course, it evokes "normal" and sounds like "Norman." Marilyn Monroe was born Norma Jeane—so maybe prim Norma has a glamorous streak. Although the name was in the top twenty-five in the early 1930s, now she's about to fall out of the top 1,000. Goodbye, Norma Jeane. Let's hope not.

Alternatives: *Marilyn, Mona, Carla, Ramona, Nora*

Nyla is a very popular name with murky origins. Does it relate to the River Nile and mean "blue" in Sanskrit? Does it come from the Irish boy's name Niall (which is believed to mean "winner")? No one really knows. It certainly has the earmarks of a successful name: Exotic letter? Check. Ends with an *ah* sound? Check. Two syllables, and scans like Maya? Check. Similar to a celebrity baby name? Check. (Halle Berry's daughter, Nahla.) Look for this one to rise even higher.

Variation: *Nylah*

Alternatives: *Nahla, Kenya, Zara, Lana, Aaliyah*

Octavia comes from *octavus* or "eighth" in Latin. In the nineteenth century, this name or its male counterpart, Octavian, was used for the eighth child in a family. Octavia is related to Augusta: Both names evoke Augustus Caesar, who was also referred to as Octavian and whose sister was Octavia. The name also connotes musicality (octave).

Nicknames: *Ava, Vivi*
Alternatives: *Augusta, Justine, Julia, Theodora, Priscilla*

Olive represents peace, harmony, and life: Olive branches are extended as signs of peace. The dove Noah sent from the ark returned with an olive branch in its beak, indicating that life had returned to earth. The name Olive is similar to Olivia but nowhere near as trendy. It has a simpler sound that harkens to another time—you can just picture someone's aproned grandma canning the summer tomatoes. It also evokes a shade of green that is, well, olive drab, which may be holding it back. Still, the word itself and its meaning are lovely.

Nicknames: *Liv, Ollie*
Alternatives: *Hazel, Fern, Aspen, Athena*

Olivia This name's origins are in dispute. Its popularity is not. Olivia roared from the middle of the pack in

1960 to the top of the charts today. The name could come from olive, suggesting peace and vitality. (You can hear the word *live* in it.) Or it could come from the Old Norse as a feminization of Oliver, meaning "heirloom." Olivia is the heroine of Shakespeare's

THE RISE AND FALL OF GREAT NAMES

Did you feel that you were the first one of your friends to choose the name Olivia? So why then does it seem like everywhere you turn, people are copying you? Why does everyone else have the same idea at the same time? Although some names become popular immediately upon discovery—widespread use of Miley, for example, coincides with the rise of singer Miley Cyrus's career—others are from moments in our childhood that we savor, store, and use later. One reason that Olivia may be so fashionable today is that many of the girls who grew up admiring Olivia Newton-John are now having children of their own. They think about what names they like, and when they come to Olivia, they think it sounds terrific. They may not connect it precisely to a love of the *Grease* good girl, but positive associations in childhood may appear years later. Thus the girls who loved *Grease* and the boys who loved *Star Wars* start naming their kids Olivia and Luke.

Twelfth Night, and that play gave her a boost. Olivia Newton-John paved the way for the name's resurgence, and the pig from the children's series *Olivia* is keeping up interest.

Variations: *Alivia, Livia*
Nicknames: *Liv, Livia, Olia, Viva, Ollie*
Alternatives: *Amelia, Lydia, Jemima, Arabella*

Olympia A fabulous alternative to the wildfire-like Olivia, this is also a terrific name in its own right. Olympia comes from Mount Olympus, which was the home of the ancient Greek gods, their seat of power. The name, evocative of the mountain, suggests strength, power, a connection to the spiritual world (after all, that was some mountain), and makes a respectful nod to Greece (it is most common in Greek communities). It has wonderful classical roots.

Nicknames: *Pia, Olia*
Alternatives: *Penelope, Cassandra, Ariadne, Leta, Minerva, Ariana*

Oona is an Irish name meaning "lamb." There is a handful of model Oonas in history, including the mother of the ancient Irish hero Conn Cetchathach; the wife of seventeenth-century Irish poet Tomás Costello, whose Oona died for love of him after her parents separated them; and Charlie Chaplin's wife, the daughter of Eugene O'Neill. Some families like the

209

A Girl for All Seasons

A number of seasonal names are in the top 1,000: April, May, June. But don't be a fair-weather friend—you have a whole year to choose from.

~ **JANUARY:** *from Janus, the god of beginnings and endings—an interesting way to give a nod to the past or the future*

~ **FEBRUARY:** *named for Februa, Roman festival of purification*

~ **MARCH:** *for boys, consider Mars (the Roman war god), for whom the month is named*

~ **APRIL:** *for Aphrodite, goddess of love*

~ **MAY:** *for Maia, goddess of spring. A cheery name*

~ **JUNE:** *Juno's month. A lovely old-fashioned name*

~ **JULY:** *named for Roman Julius Caesar*

~ **AUGUST:** *for Augustus Caesar. August works for boys; Augusta is the commanding feminine version*

~ **SEPTEMBER:** *named for the number of the month; September was the seventh month of the Roman calendar and could be used for a seventh child*

~ **OCTOBER:** *for the number eight, consider Octavio (page 471) for boys, Octavia (page 207) for girls*

~ **NOVEMBER:** *based on the number nine*

~ **DECEMBER:** *based on the number ten. Dixie, also based on ten, may be a better choice.*

~ **AUTUMN** *and* **SUMMER** *are in the top 1,000, but not* **WINTER** *and* **SPRING***.*

fact that Oona seems to say "one" (the Latin for "one" is *una*), suggesting that Oona is tops.

Variation: *Una*

Alternatives: *Nora, Fiona, Niamh, Bridie*

Opal has a mysterious quality: The Romans called the stone the "queen of gems" because it is iridescent and contains every color. Shakespeare likened the opal to the changeability of a woman's nature. Now that Ruby is the toast of the town, and other old-fashioned picks like Fern and Ivy are stepping into the limelight, it's time to give Opal a second look.

Alternatives: *Matilda (opal is the Australian national gem), Hope, Amber, Pearl, Ruby, Naomi*

P

Paige Now-forgotten actress Janis Paige put this name on the map in the 1950s. Before then, the name as it is currently spelled did not exist. A page was a medieval servant and the job title became a last name, which then became a first name, usually for people with the name in the family and typically for boys. It's certainly a good choice if you want to avoid nicknames.

Variation: *Page*
Alternatives: *Sage, Blake, Laney, Faye*

Paisley You might name your child Paisley if you have the last name Paisley in your family and want to honor it. Or you might like the swirly patterned fabric that is made in Paisley, Scotland. Maybe you are a fan of the singer Prince and his song "Paisley Park."

If you just like the sound of it, realize that there are many associations that end up giving the name a New Agey feel. If you favor the name because it sounds a bit southern, you might want to go with an alternative that is less loaded: Ainsley or Daisy.

Alternatives: *Lindsay, Hillary, Mackenzie, Cameron, Patsy, Ainsley*

Paloma means "dove" in Spanish. The dove is a symbol of peace and hope and good tidings. A dove carried the olive branch back to Noah after the flood. And doves, which are a type of pigeon, have been messengers since antiquity. Paloma scans beautifully and would go well with last names that are vowelly (particularly Spanish and Italian names) and would lend softness and poetry to harder, Germanic names.

Alternatives: *Dove, Olive, Paola, Jemima, Selena*

Pamela was invented by Elizabethan poet Sir Philip Sidney for his prose poem "Arcadia." The name was further promoted by Samuel Richardson, whose novel *Pamela* (1740) starred a beguiling and virtuous servant. Nowadays we emphasize the Pam in the name. Centuries ago, the emphasis was on the second syllable. People speculate that the name has something to do with honey, as *mela* is "honey" in several languages. The name cracked the top ten in

1953 and remained popular through the early 1980s. It's been waning since then, but it might be worth another look—especially if a "no Pam" rule is strictly enforced.

Nicknames: *Pam, Ella*
Alternatives: *Lucinda, Patricia, Amanda, Carmela*

Paris Fans of classical mythology think of Paris as a man's name. Paris was the Trojan who lured Helen away from Sparta, sparking the Trojan War. Celebrity heiress Paris Hilton has changed all that. Now she's the first Paris most Americans think of (for better or worse), with the second being Michael Jackson's daughter. The name evokes, of course, the sensual, glamorous capital city of France. If that's the legacy you hope to pass on to your daughter, perhaps choose another Gallic name like Delphine or Simone.

Alternatives: *London, Helen, Marianne, Genevieve*

Parker In the Middle Ages, the gamekeeper of a park was called a "parker." Like so many other job descriptions, it became a last name—and then the last name became a first name. It's only in the past decade that the name—a bit tomboyish, but with something of a crisp, British air—has been used widely for girls. It is still much more popular for boys. But for parents looking for an edgy choice for

The Value of a Name

For centuries, parents have given their children names of virtues that they hope their offspring will embody. Value names were once strongly associated with the Puritans. Nowadays, everyone uses them. Note that most but not all are girls' names, and some are more religious-sounding than others. But even a name like Faith, if you hear it enough, loses its church-y vibe.

- **CHARITY**
- **CHASTITY**
- **CONSTANCE**
- **FAITH**
- **FELICITY**
- **FIDELITY**
  (Fidel or Fidelia)
- **GRACE**
- **HARMONY**
- **HONOR**

- **HOPE**
- **JOY**
- **JUSTICE**
- **LIBERTY**
- **MERCY**
- **PATIENCE**
- **PEACE**
- **PROVIDENCE**
- **PRUDENCE**
- **PURITY**

- **REVEREND**
  (Reverence)
- **SERENITY**
- **SINCERE**
  (Sincerity)
- **TEMPERANCE**
- **TRUTH**
- **UNITY**
- **VERITY**
- **VICTORY**

daughters, Parker, like compatriots Harper and Bailey, may do nicely. Actress Parker Posey (who was named for model/actress Suzy Parker) proves that feminine girls can have strong, masculine names.

Alternatives: *Piper, Sawyer, Taylor, Bailey*

Patience is a virtue and back in style. The name all but disappeared after the 1800s until a comeback in 1994. Now it is inching its way up the chart. It's nowhere near Grace and Hope and some others, but in an age of Tweeting and texting and channel surfing, Patience is a nice quality to remember. And if you want to avoid nicknames, it's a good choice.

Alternatives: *Faith, Hope, Charity, Grace*

∅ **Patricia** is ready for her comeback. This feminine counterpart of Patrick (page 475) was big in the 1930s through the '50s, but has been on a slide since then. The name is feminine, subtly Irish, and aristocratic (it means "patrician"—appropriate when you consider it was the name of a Kennedy). The name can be anything to anyone, thanks to a wide selection of nicknames: Patsy and Trixie for fun, Patty for the girl next door, Pat for the tomboy, Trish for easygoing down-to-earthness.

Nicknames: *Pat, Patty, Patsy, Trish, Tricia, Trixie*
Alternatives: *Barbara, Pamela, Alicia, Carolyn, Dorothy*

Paula, the basic feminine of Paul (which means "small"), was in the top one hundred during the 1950s through the early 1970s. Now it's not even in the top 500. Paola, on the other hand, the Italian version of the name, is in the top 300. Not bad for a name that just came to the United States in 1983. Paola is much more in keeping with the times—that nice round *o* sound is more alluring and exotic than the lowing *aw* sound of Paula. Paulina has been in use since 1988, which was the peak of model Paulina Porizkova's career.

Variations: *Paola, Paulina, Paulette, Paule*
Nickname: *Polly*
Alternatives: *Claudine, Gloria, Beverly, Jane, Sharon, Laura*

🖋 **Penelope** was Odysseus's patient wife. She waited for his return for twenty years. In Odysseus's absence, she promised her suitors she would choose a new husband from among them when her weaving was finished. Every day she wove, and every night she would undo her work. The name comes from a Greek word for "duck." But Penelope is known as an ideal of faithfulness, cleverness, and fortitude. Actress Penelope Cruz has given the name sex appeal.

Nickname: *Penny*
Alternatives: *Cassandra, Olympia, Annabelle, Cornelia, Phoebe*

Perla Pearl was a popular name in the 1800s, a celebration of the milky jewel that is born of an oyster's grit and suffering. That name evokes singer Pearl Bailey and author Pearl S. Buck—talented ladies both, but not va-va-voom. Perla is an attempt to make the name zippier and more modern; it has been used since 1979.

Variations: *Pearl, Perle (Yiddish)*
Alternatives: *Margaret ("pearl" via Greek), Peninnah ("coral" in Hebrew), Ruby, Opal*

Perry is short for peregrine, which means "wanderer" or "traveler," and is also associated with pear trees. The name is most famously associated with men: clothing designer Perry Ellis, singer Perry Como. But more and more, families are realizing it makes a melodious girl's name, similar to Merry or Sheri, but unusual enough to sound a bit hipper. Actress Peri Gilpin and author/ journalist Perri Klass are the best-known users.

Variations: *Perri, Peri*
Alternatives: *Marie, Merry, Penelope, Sally*

Petra means "rock" in Latin, and the name is a feminization of Peter, the "rock" upon which Christ built his church. Peter is considered one of the founders of Christianity. Petra is also an ancient city in Jordan with classical architectural façades intricately carved into giant sandstone cliffs. There are not many of these little female Peters running around, which makes it a good choice for an unusual name with traditional roots.

Variations: *Peternelle, Pietra, Petrova, Pet, Perri*
Nicknames: *Peta (warning: this may be confused with PETA, the animal rights organization), Pet, Perri*
Alternatives: *Becca (from Rebecca), Katya, Mirka (from Miroslava), Ilsa, Rochelle*

Peyton is a place-name that has skyrocketed
in popularity as a girl's name. It first showed up
in 1992 and it's now in the top one hundred, as is
the alternative spelling Payton. *Peyton Place* was
a bestselling novel of 1956 that chronicled the
scandalous lives of the residents of a small New
Hampshire town. Peyton Manning is the celebrated
quarterback for the Indianapolis Colts.

Variations: *Payton, Paityn, Payten*
Alternatives: *Shelby, Paisley, Delaney, Harper, Paxton*

✏ **Philippa** This feminine version of Philip is not
in the top 1,000 names in the United States, but it's
popular in the U.K. and it's a cute one. It means
"lover of horses" and the nicknames are adorable
and full of energy: Phil, Flip, and Pippa.

Nicknames: *Phil, Flip, Pip, Pippa, Pina*
Alternatives: *Edwina, Lavinia, Imogen, Helena, Jemima,
Charlotte*

Phoebe has a sweet, spritely sound (FEE-bee) and a
perennially fresh, contemporary feel, although it's a
classical name. The name means "bright" and comes
from a Greek goddess associated with the moon.
Phoebe, also the name of a small bird, was fashionable
in the early part of the twentieth century, but in the
1960s it flitted off the radar. It only made a comeback
in 1989, and was later helped along by Lisa Kudrow's

character Phoebe in the sitcom *Friends,* which
debuted in 1994.

Alternatives: *Chloe, Zoe, Penelope, Bebe*

Phoenix is invincible. This gorgeous bird of
mythology dies in flames and rises from the ashes
to live again. It symbolizes hope, perseverance, and
rebirth. In Greek mythology, Phoenix was the founder

Greek Deities and Spirits

You know the greats: Athena, Aphrodite, and Hera.
Meet some other players in the Greek pantheon.

- **ALETHEIA:** *the
personification of truth*

- **AMPHITRITE:** *the mother
of seals and dolphins*

- **ANANKE:** *you're bound to
name your girl Ananke, goddess
of destiny and inevitability*

- **ARETHUSA:** *a nymph who
became a cloud, a stream, and
then a fountain on the island
of Ortygia*

- **CHLORIS:** *a very flowery
spring nymph who married
the west wind*

- **DEMETER:** *goddess of the
harvest*

- **ECHO:** *a mountain nymph*

- **EIRENE:** *the goddess of peace*

- **GAIA:** *mother earth*

- **HESTIA:** *goddess of the
hearth*

- **NYX:** *goddess of night and
hiding*

- **PERSEPHONE:** *queen of
the underworld during one season
a year—winter*

- **RHEA:** *a great mother and
queen of the mountain winds*

- **THALIA:** *goddess of banquets
and muse of comic poetry*

of the Phoenician civilization. And the word means "violet-red" in Greek. The name calls to mind actors River and Joaquin Phoenix, as well as the city in Arizona. There are more boys named Phoenix than girls, but that may be changing.

Nickname: *Fi*

Alternatives: *Griffin, River, Raven, Lark, Skye*

Phyllis means "foliage" in Greek. It also means "I was born before 1958." Okay, there have been some Phyllises since then, but not many since 1984. Phyllis was Mary Richards's annoying neighbor played by Cloris Leachman on *The Mary Tyler Moore Show*. And she might also be your mom's bridge partner.

Alternatives: *Shirley, Lydia, Patricia, Pamela*

Piper has a cute-with-an-edge quality that many last name turned first name and occupational names do (a piper is someone who plays the bagpipes). Sarah Palin's daughter Piper boosted the profile of the name during Palin's vice-presidential campaign in 2008. Despite her worker roots, Piper seems sunny and cheerful, like a girl who'd enjoy a day at the beach. Perhaps that's because a sandpiper is a jaunty little bird that skitters around on the sand.

Alternatives: *Parker, Bailey, Harper*

Presley Elvis may have left the building, but his legacy lives on. Presley has been used for a girl's name since 1998 and its popularity is growing. The name means "priest's meadow" and it is a place-name in England.

Variations: *Preslee, Preslea, Preslie*
Alternatives: *Marley, Harley, Bailey, Paisley*

Princess A name since 1979, Princess is better suited to a title (if she can swing it) or a nickname. If she wants to be a doctor or run for the Senate, this froufrou name won't do her any favors. Better to choose a name that hints at royalty (say, Diana or Grace) instead of shouting it.

Alternatives: *Jewel, Heaven, Dulce, Sarah, Cherish, Carissa*

Priscilla is a solid name that seems nearly trend averse. It's surprising that folks aren't shying away from a name that sounds, well, prissy. The name means "ancient." Priscilla appeared in the Bible as a woman who hosted St. Paul. Priscilla Presley, Elvis's widow, leaps to mind, as does the wacky Australian movie about drag queens *Priscilla, Queen of the Desert*.

Nicknames: *Prissy, Cilla*
Alternatives: *Penelope, Katherine, Margaret, Philippa, Sabrina*

Q

Quinn Used for boys since the 1960s, Quinn has been gaining ground as a girl's name since 1995. It's from the Gaelic, a last name turned first name meaning "leader." The Latinate prefix *quin* means "fifth," so the name can also be used to denote a fifth child. Quinn may also be short for Quincy, which is a patriotic American name (think John Quincy Adams) and a unique choice for music lovers (think Quincy Jones).

Alternatives: *Finlay, Peyton, Nina, Gwen, Maeve, Brynn*

R

Rachel In the Bible, Rachel is the beloved wife of Jacob and the mother of Joseph. The name suggests softness and comfort in its meaning, which is "ewe." If Rachel is too girl-next-door for your liking (and reminds you of Jennifer Aniston's character on *Friends*—and her ubiquitous shag haircut), you might want to consider Raquel. It's less innocent and more hot-to-trot à la Raquel Welch.

Variations: *Rachael, Rachelle, Raquel*
Nicknames: *Ray, Rach, Shelly, Kelly, Roxie (for Raquel)*
Alternatives: *Rochelle (means "little rock"), Rebecca, Esther, Hazel, Shayla, Amanda*

✐ **Raina** is a way of naming your child for the rain without sounding too New Agey. And it makes a good nickname for traditional names like Lorraine. Adding an *a* to the end of Rain gives the name a feminine lilt. An alternate spelling, Reina, evokes royalty: both in its aural similarity to "reign" and in its meaning, "queen." Rania, the name of the queen of Jordan, is similar enough that it helps keep Raina on her throne.

Variations: *Rayna, Rayne, Reina, Reyna*
Alternatives: *Regina, Kayla, Shayna, Meadow, Rena, Elaina*

Raven That's so Raven. If you give your baby bird this moniker, get used to hearing that. The phrase was the title of a hit Disney TV show that ran from 2003 to 2007, starred actress Raven-Symoné, and is still on in reruns. Curiously, the show did not boost the name's popularity; it's actually been sliding from its heyday in the mid-1990s, which is when Raven-Symoné was playing Bill Cosby's granddaughter Olivia on *The Cosby Show*. A raven is a highly intelligent black crow, famously celebrated in Edgar Allan Poe's poem of the same name. The bird is a symbol of wisdom in Nordic mythology. Ravens have long been associated with gods and royalty. And "raven" is a poetic way of saying "dark," as in Byron's poem "She Walks in Beauty" in which he writes of his love's "raven tresses."

Alternatives: *Lark, Dove, Paloma, Riva*

Rebecca is the Aramaic wife of Isaac, and the mother of Jacob and Esau in the Old Testament. She was credited with being kind and beautiful. Daphne du Maurier's haunting novel *Rebecca* was published in 1938 with the Hitchcock film following in 1940, and these may have nudged the name along. Like Rachel, Rebecca was once most common in Jewish families, and now it's used by everyone, hitting the top ten in the early 1970s.

Variation: *Rebekah (Hebrew)*
Nicknames: *Becca, Becky, Reba*
Alternatives: *Rachel, Erica, Susannah, Daphne, Rowena*

Reese Thanks, Reese Witherspoon. The name's popularity arc parallels film actress Reese Witherspoon's career. *Election* and *Cruel Intentions* had just been released the year before the name hit the top 1,000 in 2000. Smash hit *Legally Blonde* (2001) sealed the deal. Reese is a last name turned first name. (Reese is Witherspoon's mother's maiden name and one of the actress's middle names.) It may come from the Welsh boy's name Rhys, which means "love."

Alternatives: *Penelope, Julia, Elle, Darcy, Parker*

Regan Some people believe the name Regan is related to the Celtic word for "queen." Modern parents may like that it sounds like traditional Megan—with some edge. Regan was the name of one of King Lear's daughters. She wasn't exactly Daddy's little girl (she

turned him out into a storm after getting half of his
property), but that doesn't mean your Regan won't be
sweet. Reagan, a surname turned first name, is another
variation—but be aware that for many, President
Reagan leaps to mind.

Variations: *Raegan, Reagan*
Alternatives: *Teagan, Morgan, Peggy, Harlow*

Regina means "queen" in Latin. The name is usually
given as a reference to the Virgin Mary, aka "the
queen of heaven." Regina also evokes Queen Victoria,
whose initials were VR, Victoria Regina, and for whom
Regina, the capital of Saskatchewan, was named.

Nicknames: *Reggie, Gina, Geenie*
Alternatives: *Cosima, Melinda, Sabrina, Georgina*

Renée is born again! Truly: *re* means "again" and *née*
is French for "birth." Renée is an affirmation of one's
Christianity. Famous Renées include opera singer
Renée Fleming and actresses Rene Russo and Renée
Zellweger. Renée's heyday was in the late 1960s, early
1970s. She has been on the slide since then.

Variation: *Renata*
Alternatives: *Natalie, Celine, Tatiana*

Rhea In Greek mythology, Rhea (REE-ah) was the
mother of the gods and goddesses. (Her Phrygian
counterpart is the gracefully named Cybele.) In

Roman mythology, Rhea Silvia (aka Ilia) was Romulus and Remus's mother. According to legend, her twins were nursed by a wolf and went on to found the city of Rome. Rhea is also a Hindu name meaning "singer." Phonetically, it can also evoke "river" in Spanish, traditionally spelled *río*. Rhea was popular until the 1960s, but it is rarely used now.

Variation: *Riya*

Alternatives: *Ilia, Silvia, Cybele, Gaia (another earth mother), Alethea*

R.I.P. RHODA AND RHONDA

For people of a certain age, Rhoda will always pull up an image of Valerie Harper decked in bell-bottoms and a head scarf. Rhoda was Mary Richards's neighbor and BFF on *The Mary Tyler Moore Show*. The character then got a spin-off of her own. Schlumpy Rhoda Morgenstern killed this name. It dropped right off the charts after 1975. (See Phyllis, page 220.)

The Beach Boys are likely partially to blame for Rhonda's disappearance. "Help Me, Rhonda" was a major hit of 1965, when the name Rhonda was at the peak of its popularity. Can you imagine naming your child this and not having that tune stuck in your head All. The. Time? Neither can most other parents. Rhonda was gone by 1995.

Rihanna The pop singer Rihanna is the inspiration
for the sudden burst of interest in this pretty name.
An alternate spelling, Rhianna, was in intermittent
use earlier. It's thought to be related to Rhiannon, the
Welsh goddess made famous by a Fleetwood Mac song
in 1976. Rihanna sounds like an offbeat variation of
the trendier Brianna. It could also be a ladylike take
on Ryan.

Variation: *Rhianna*
Nicknames: *Riri, Ree, Ria, Hanna*
Alternatives: *Briana, Ryanne, Johanna, Ariana*

Riley Meaning "field of rye," Riley is a place-name in
England and an anglicization of the Irish last name
Reilly. Riley has become enormously popular since
1990. It's now in the top fifty names for girls. Like
Miley and Kylie but with an Irish twist, it has a breezy,
happy-go-lucky air, maybe because when you've got it
good, you're living "the life of Riley." Note: This unisex
name is very popular down under. For boys it is in the
top ten.

Variations: *Rylie, Ryleigh, Briley, Brylee*
Alternatives: *Hayley, Keely, Kylie, Miley, Kennedy*

✐ **Rita** sounds like a lot of fun. She brings to
mind sultry actress Rita Hayworth and spirited
performer Rita Moreno. Rita began life as a nickname
for Margarita, which means "daisy," but she has

connections to other flowers as well: St. Rita is the patron saint of impossible causes, and is associated with roses. Despite Rita's many charms, the name fell out of the top 1,000 in 2003. This flower should bloom again.

Alternatives: *Gina, Mia, Mina, Tina, Rica*

✒ **Roberta** The feminine version of Robert means "famous." The name was associated with early Norman as well as Scottish royalty. Roberta's heyday was the 1930s and 1940s. It would be an unusual choice for today (it fell out of the top 1,000 in 1992), but a dignified one with several hip nickname possibilities, including Bertie and Birdie.

Nicknames: *Bobbi, Robbie, Bertie, Birdie, Robin*
Alternatives: *Patricia, Barbara, Jacqueline, Martina, Petra*

I'd love to call her . . .
Rosie

Rosie is all pink cheeks and chubby legs—which may not be the image your daughter wants to project when she reaches adulthood. Here are some more mature options to work from:

~ MARYROSE	~ ROSALIE	~ ROSARIO
~ MAYROSE	~ ROSALIND	~ ROSE
~ MELROSE	~ ROSALINE	~ ROSEANNE
~ ROSALIA	~ ROSAMUND	~ ROSEMARY

Robin is a common songbird, a harbinger of spring's arrival. The birds are famed for their red breasts and for their blue eggs (as in "robin's egg blue"). As a name, Robin started life as a nickname for Robert, then as a boy's name of its own (mostly in the U.K.), and finally as a girl's name in honor of the bird. American parents first flocked to it in the 1930s, and they hatched many little Robins in the mid-twentieth century. But Robin grew up and left the nest—the name hasn't been in regular use since 2004. Alas, the United States is not rockin' Robin anymore.

Alternatives: *Hillary, Leslie, Diane, Cheryl, Denise, Janet, Rowan, Lark*

Rose, the queen of the garden, was the first flower to become a name, probably because of its association with the Virgin Mary, who is often symbolized by roses. Mary is said to have kissed a white rose on her entrance to heaven, causing the flower to turn red. Roses represent purity and were used to ward off disease and evil in the Middle Ages. The name was most popular around the 1910s. But time has done little to fade its beauty—today it seems to be *the* middle name of choice.

Nickname: *Rosie*
Variations: *Rosa, Rosita, Rosario, Rosalie, Roselyn, Rosalind, Rosamund, Roseanne, Maryrose, Rosemarie*

British Blossoms

Floral names are blooming abundantly in Britain. All of the following pop up repeatedly in the flower patch (that is, they're in the top one hundred).

- **DAISY**

- **FLORENCE**

- **HOLLY** (and Hollie)

- **JASMINE**

- **LILY** (and Lilly)

- **POPPY**

- **ROSIE**

Rosemary This old-fashioned name may be a conjoining of Rose and Mary (which is sort of like Mary times two—see Rose, page 229). Or it may relate to the herb, which is hearty, evergreen, and symbolizes remembrance and fidelity, and whose name means "dew of the sea."

Nickname: *Rosie*
Alternatives: *Mary, Elizabeth, Jane, Lily, Dahlia, Daisy*

Rowan A rowan is a kind of tree that sports bright red berries. The name, not surprisingly, means "red." The tree was believed to protect against magic and spells. Rowan Atkinson, a British (male) comic who plays the hapless buffoon Mr. Bean in the TV series of the same name, helped boost the unisex name's prominence.

Alternatives: *Scarlett, Willow, Norma*

Rowena A Saxon name that might mean "joyous fame," Rowena was popularized by writer Sir Walter Scott, whose heroine in *Ivanhoe* (1819) was Rowena. The name has not been widely used since 1964, but it has great potential. It's long with a soft, lilting cadence, an unusual alternative to similarly syllable-dense names like Madeline and Abigail. Rowena's ornateness would add a nice flourish to common last names (like Jones, Smith, and Johnson) or Germanic ones (such as Gerber, Schem, and Unger).

Alternatives: *Rebecca, Penelope, Anastasia, Priscilla, Alina*

Roxanne If you are looking for drama, your search is over. Roxanne delivers it in spades. Roxanea was the wife of Alexander the Great and the title character of Daniel Defoe's 1724 novel, *Roxana;* Roxanne, the heroine of Edmond Rostand's play *Cyrano de Bergerac* (1897), the subject of a famous song by the Police ("Roxanne," 1978), and the heroine of the musical *Chicago* (as Roxie). Names with *x*'s in them are hot these days, yet Roxanne was popular from the 1930s through 2000. If you can take the heat (and the annoying first two notes of the Police song, which you will hear *over and over*), then this a great choice.

Variations: *Roxane, Roxanna, Roxana*
Nicknames: *Roxy, Anne/Anna (if she wants to play it safe)*
Alternatives: *Joanne, Rowena, Axelle, Roseanne, Shoshana*

Ruby A precious jewel of a rich red color, the ruby represents passion, vitality, and power. Ruby was all the rage in the 1910s, epitomized by showgirl Ruby Keeler. By the 1970s, Ruby was more likely to be the waitress in your local diner. Now she's staging a comeback; in the U.K. in 2008, Ruby was the number two name after Olivia. Stand back, colonial Emma and Isabella, flapper Ruby is on her way to a playground near you.

Variation: *Rubi*
Alternatives: *Opal, Pearl, Poppy, Evie, Violet*

Ruth In the Bible, Ruth is the loyal daughter-in-law of Naomi; after Ruth's husband dies, she accompanies her mother-in-law back to her native land. She says to Naomi, "Wherever you go, I will go . . . your people shall be my people and your God, my God." The name suggests loyalty and constancy as well as sorrow and mercy (from "rue"). Ruth was in the top five at the turn of the twentieth century, but now the name is much less common. Although Ruth hasn't been snatched up with the other antiques, it may be an overlooked treasure. In Ruthie, it has a nickname that softens its edges and makes it sweetly appealing.

Alternatives: *Esther, Naomi, Miriam, Sarah, Beth*

Ryan Celtic for "king," Ryan was a last name, and then a boy's first name that surged to popularity thanks to Ryan O'Neal's star turn in the 1970 movie *Love Story*.

Parents of girls quickly followed suit, painting Ryan pink in 1974. The name has been in the top twenty for boys since 1976. If the girls keep using it, look for the popularity for boys to slump quickly. (Girls are often given boy's names; not so the other way around.) Some parents add a feminine twist to the name by adding another *n* to the end, which changes the pronunciation from RYE-un to rye-ANNE. The name may also be related to Rhiannon (see Rihanna, page 227).

Variations: *Ryann, Ryanna*
Alternatives: *Bryna, Rihanna, Chiara, Sharon, Diane*

S

Sabrina is the Latin name for the river Severn, located in western England near Wales. The river gave its name to a myth about a maiden who was drowned in it by her king-father's wicked queen and turned into a nymph of the river. The water goddess connection was strengthened by Milton's 1634 poem/song "Sabrina Fair." The play *Sabrina Fair,* which opened in 1953, caused Sabrina to hit the top 1,000 in the United States for the first time. The Audrey Hepburn–Humphrey Bogart spin-off movie the following year caused a huge surge in usage. The name is elegant and poetic even without the afterglow of Audrey Hepburn's aura.

Nicknames: *Brina, Bree*
Alternatives: *Serena, Audrey, Morgan, Juliette*

Sadie Out of the rocking chair, into the spotlight!
A turn-of-the-twentieth-century favorite, Sadie
was written off in the late 1960s and early 1970s as
impossibly grandmotherly. Now she's coming back
to join friends Violet, Olivia, and Rose. Traditionally,
Sadie was a nickname for Sarah. The name has a
few pop-culture associations: Sadie Hawkins was
an unattractive spinster from the Al Capp *Li'l Abner*
comic strip in the 1930s, whose father was desperate
to get rid of her, and who spawned "Sadie Hawkins
Day," a day (February 29, every four years) on which
girls may ask boys to dance (or marry!). "Sadie, Sadie,
Married Lady" is a song from the musical *Funny Girl*
(1964). And "Sexy Sadie" was a Beatles song from 1968.
Sadie is sweet but sassy—a little bit ragtime, a little bit
rock 'n' roll.

Variations: *Sarah, Zadie*
Alternatives: *Lucy, Ellie, Esme, Fanny, Maisie*

Sage is brimming with meaning: "wise," "prophet,"
"green." The herb itself is a symbol of immortality.
Sagebrush, the scrubby shrub that grows in dry areas,
evokes the rugged expansiveness of the American
West. The name is used for boys as well as girls.
Many parents stick an *i* in the name to make it
girlier, akin to Paige.

Variation: *Saige*
Alternatives: *Paige, Paisley, Rosemary, Sierra*

From the Herb Garden

Herbs have healing and soothing qualities. No wonder they have been a source of inspiration for names throughout the ages.

~ ANGELICA   ~ ROSEMARY   ~ TANSY

~ CHAMOMILE   ~ SAFFRON   ~ THYME

~ PEPPER   ~ SAGE   ~ VERBENA

Salma A popular Arabic name meaning "peace," the name has taken off in the United States alongside actress Salma Hayek's career. (Hayek's father has a Lebanese background.) The name is easy to pronounce and pretty. It has a bit of onomatopoeia to it: Salma sounds peaceful—the word "calm" is nearly in the name. Alma (see page 15) is in there, too, evoking "nurture." The name's similarity to Selma gives it strong crossover potential.

Alternatives: *Salima, Selma, Alma, Salome*

Samantha is believed to be a feminization of Samuel, with the suffix coming from the antiquated name Anthea. Samuel means "to be listened to" and Anthea means "flower." Samantha sounds poetic, like Amanda, but with more allure. (Is there a panther to be heard purring in there?) The name fell out of use in the early twentieth century, and was revived in the

1960s by the sitcom *Bewitched,* whose lead character, played by the lovable Elizabeth Montgomery, was the appealing nose-twitching witch Samantha.

Nicknames: *Sam, Sami*
Alternatives: *Amanda, Tabitha, Anthea, Anabella*

Samara Samarra is an ancient city located in present-day Iraq that is famed for its ninth-century spiral minaret. The name Samara means "evening conversation" in Arabic. In Hebrew, it means "protected by God." Samara is a city in Russia on the Volga River. And it is the botanical name for seeds that come in helicopter cases, like those from elms and maples. A feminine choice with multiple meanings, Samara sounds exotic without being too unfamiliar (it shares similarities with Samantha and Tamara); as a result, it has been eagerly taken up since the late 1990s.

Nicknames: *Sam, Sami, Mara*
Alternatives: *Tamara, Damaris, Marisa, Lara, Samantha*

Sanaa This graceful, ethereal name means "brilliant" or "sublime" in Arabic. In the United States, it is used most often by African American families. The name feels exotic, possibly because it's less well known than similarly lilting names like Aaliyah, which may make it a strong alternate choice.

Variations: *Sanai, Saniya*
Alternatives: *Rana, Zahra, Layla*

Sandra used to be a nickname for Alexandra (which is Alessandra in Italian). It became common as a name itself in the late 1880s, inspired by a now-forgotten novel (*Sandra Belloni*). The name was big in the 1940s through 1960s; actresses Sandra Dee and Sandra Bullock were born during its heyday. Supreme Court justice Sandra Day O'Connor (b. 1930) was ahead of the curve. The *Grease* song "Look at Me, I'm Sandra Dee," certainly hasn't done the name any favors. But there's life in it yet—Sandrine, the French take on the name, is cool and beguiling, and may influence the name's shape in the future.

Variations: *Sondra, Sandrine, Saundra*
Nickname: *Sandy*
Alternatives: *Alexandra, Cassandra, Selina, Amanda, Miranda*

Sarah is the little black dress of girl's names. It never goes out of style. Sarai was the stunningly beautiful wife of Abraham, whom God renamed Sarah in the Bible's book of Genesis. Just as well. Sarai is believed to mean "argumentative," while Sarah means "princess." Sarah gave birth to Isaac when she was an older woman, and he came to be one of the patriarchs of Judaism. Enduringly popular, Sarah is trend-proof, meaningful, and brimming with variations and nicknames.

Variations: *Sara, Sarahi, Sarai, Sariah, Zara, Soraya*
Nicknames: *Sally, Sadie, Shari*
Alternatives: *Rachel, Jane, Hannah, Princess, Raina*

Sasha Familiarity dims exoticism. That's what has happened to Sasha. Once a nickname for Alexandra or Natasha that smacked of orientalism, Sasha has been a name on its own since 1972. Still winsome and lively with its whispers of "sashaying," Sasha, while no Madison, is a pretty common name. President Obama's younger daughter, Sasha, may give it a boost in years to come. The name is also used for boys, though not so much in the United States.

Variations: *Natasha, Alexandra*
Alternatives: *Dasha (see Dorothy), Charla, Shayla, Alexis, Zoe, Saskia*

✑ **Saskia** An uncommon name, Saskia deserves a look. If you are searching for a name with honest origins, one that's easy to pronounce, edgy, but still feminine, this could be it. It's an interesting selection for a family with artistic leanings—Saskia was the wife of the Dutch master painter Rembrandt. The name means "Saxon," and was popular in the Middle Ages in Europe.

Alternatives: *Katrina, Mirka (Miroslava), Esme, Tosca, Anya*

Savannah The Savannah River in the American South gave its name to two cities, one in Georgia and one in South Carolina. A savanna is a wide-open plain. The word sounds like other girl's names—there's some Samantha in there, some Susannah, some Hannah—so

Funny Girls

If you want to name your daughter something that imparts a legacy of humor, consider taking cues from a comedian or comedic actress:

- **AMY** (Poehler)
- **CAROL** (Burnett)
- **DIANE** (Keaton)
- **DORIS** (Day)
- **ELAINE** (May)
- **ERMA** (Bombeck)
- **FALLON** (for Jimmy Fallon)
- **GILDA** (Radner)
- **GINGER** (Rogers)
- **GOLDIE** (Hawn)
- **JOAN** (Rivers)

- **LILY** (Tomlin)
- **LIZA** (Minelli)
- **LUCILLE** (Ball)
- **MAE** (West)
- **MEG** (Ryan)
- **PHYLLIS** (Diller)
- **ROSEANNE** (Barr)
- **TINA** (Fey)
- **TRACEY** (Ullman)
- **WENDY** (Wasserstein)
- **WHOOPI** (Goldberg)

it made a good choice for a tweak on some classics. (Nowadays the seldom-used Susannah would be the edgier pick.) The name was popular in the nineteenth century, then disappeared for a while, and was revived by the now-obscure movie *Savannah Smiles* in 1982. These days, there are many Savannahs running around the schoolyard.

Variations: *Savanna, Savanah*
Alternatives: *Georgiana, Susannah, Valentina, Carolina, Sierra*

Scarlett used to be a vamp—or worse. Think Scarlett O'Hara and Miss Scarlet from the board game Clue. Think *The Scarlet Letter* or a "scarlet woman." Traditionally there was such a taint of passionate abandon attached to the name that it was barely in use before 1992. (Scarlett O'Hara may be the one famous film character who did *not* inspire legions of parents to name their girls after her.) Times are changing and many parents are choosing the name, perhaps helped along by sultry (and talented) actress Scarlett Johansson.

Variation: *Scarlet*
Alternatives: *Ruby, Violet, Delilah, Tallulah, Arden, Opal*

BEWARE THE NOVA

Remember the Chevy Nova? It was a disaster of a car. Why? *No va* in Spanish means "doesn't go." No Spanish speaker wanted to buy a car that might as well have been called the Chevy Clunker. If you plan to make up a name, be sure you vet it thoroughly. If it sounds like it might be a word in another language, you should always make sure you know the definition. For example, if you combine Rhea (Greek earth mother) and Diana (Roman goddess of the moon) you might end up with Rheadiana . . . or Diarrhea. Which actually sounds lovely—if you don't know what it means.

🖉 **Selah** is a mysterious word that appears in the
Bible's book of Psalms. Scholars argue about what
it means and theories abound: "connect," "forever,"
"reflect." The word appears to be an ancient musical
notation whose meaning has been lost. Scholars
hypothesize it represents an instruction to the reader
or singer of the psalm to pause before proceeding to
the next section of the text. Whatever its meaning,
its sound (either see-LAH or say-LAH) is perfectly
on-trend: feminine, ending in an *ah* sound (like
Lilah, Delia, Hannah, Lola, and so on). And there is a
beautiful Selah role model in actress Sela Ward.

Alternatives: *Mira, Helena, Selena, Maria*

Selena comes from Selene, an ancient Greek moon
goddess. The name suggests serenity, being one
consonant away from Serena. It was put on the map
in the United States by the young Tejano singer
Selena, whose promising career was cut short at its
peak in 1995, and more recently, by the rising star
Selena Gomez, who was named after her.

Variation: *Selina*
Alternatives: *Celestia, Luna, Skylar, Valentina, Serena*

Serena means "calm," "peaceful." The name feels like
a modern twist on an old-fashioned value name like
Patience, but in fact, it has been used for centuries.
The recent variation in wide use (since 1997) is

Serenity. Tennis player Serena Williams and TV series
Gossip Girl character Serena van der Woodsen keep
the name in the pop culture news.
Variation: *Serenity*
Alternatives: *Patience, Amani, Irena, Salome, Placida*

Shania Canadian country singer Shania Twain is
responsible for moving this name up the pop charts.
Born Eileen, she later took Shania to honor her
stepfather's Ojibwa ancestry. The name, pronounced
shuh-NYE-uh, means "I'm on my way" in Ojibwa.
It's sort of like a softer, whispered take on Mariah.
Variation: *Shaniya*
Alternatives: *Shane, Malia, Mariah, Cheyenne*

Shannon is the longest river in western Ireland
(and an airport). Irish Americans in the 1970s *really*
liked this name. Shannon is friends with Erin and
Kerry, other names that have a hint of American
blarney to them.
Variation: *Shanna*
Alternatives: *Tara, Kerry, Erin, Maureen, Fiona, Caitlin*

Sharon "I am the rose of Sharon, and the lily of the
valleys." This famous line from the Old Testament's
Song of Solomon refers to the Plain of Sharon, which
was a fertile stretch of land in ancient Israel. The
name Sharon evokes roses and lilies and, to Christians,

She's a Little Bit Country . . .

Country singers are down to earth, no nonsense, and they speak to matters of the heart. They are a rich source of naming inspiration.

- **CRYSTAL** *(Gayle)*
- **DOLLY** *(Parton)*
- **EMMYLOU** *(Harris)*
- **FAITH** *(Hill)*
- **GILLIAN** *(Welch)*
- **LeANN** *(Rimes)*
- **LORETTA** *(Lynn)*
- **LUCINDA** *(Williams)*
- **MARTINA** *(McBride)*

- **MELBA** *(Montgomery)*
- **MELISSA** *(Etheridge)*
- **PATSY** *(Cline)*
- **REBA** *(McEntire)*
- **SHANIA** *(Twain)*
- **TAMMY** *(Wynette)*
- **TANYA** *(Tucker)*
- **TRISHA** *(Yearwood)*
- **WYNONNA** *(Judd)*

Jesus, who is considered by some to be "the rose of Sharon." To others, the Song of Solomon is all about love and pleasure and is the most joyful of verses. Sharon can evoke that exuberant ardor as well. The name was at its peak in the 1940s through 1960s.

Alternatives: *Shiloh, Jordan, Rose, Shannon*

Shayla Believe it or not, Shayla comes from Cecilia. It can be traced back like this: Shayla comes from Sheila, which comes from Celia, which comes from Cecilia. (Sheila used to be a popular Irish name that

in Australia was slang for "girl." Cecilia is the patron
saint of music, though her name comes from a Roman
last name that meant "blind.") Shayla is a superior
alternative to the ubiquitous Kayla and Makayla.
When spelled with an *i*, as Shaila, it becomes a Muslim
name meaning "candlelight."

Variations: *Shaylee, Scheyla, Shyla*
Alternatives: *Sheila, Hailey, Celia, Charla, Sara*

Shayna This name has two faces: in Yiddish it means
"beautiful" (from the German *schöne*); it can also be
a feminization of Shane, which comes from the name
John (see Jane, page 130). Shayna sounds a bit like
Shania, a bit like Shayla. It's light and pretty but has
a modern twang. Shayna is steady and dependable—
she's been in circulation since the 1970s but hasn't
been overused like other similar sounding names.

Variations: *Shana, Shaina*
Alternatives: *Raina, Shane, Bella, Shea*

Shea An Irish last name meaning "hawklike," Shea
has been used for boys and girls since the 1970s.
(For boys, it can be a nickname for Seamus, the Irish
James.) The name is falling fast in popularity, which
means it will either be a great choice—no one else
will have it—or it will seem unfashionable in a few
years. The name may be best used by families that
have a connection to the name (or who really love

the New York Mets—Shea is the name of the ball team's old stadium).

Alternatives: *Shayla, Mairead (see Margaret), Siobhan, Skye, Leah*

Shelby Thank Barbara Stanwyk and Julia Roberts for the popularity of this name. Stanwyk played Shelby Barret in the 1935 movie *The Woman in Red*. Roberts played Shelby Latcherie in 1989's *Steel Magnolias*. The name leaped enormously after each movie's release. Shelby sounds like she was born and raised in the American South. Thanks in large part to Isaac Shelby, a Revolutionary War hero and the first governor of Kentucky, many places in the South take the name. Picture your Shelby drinking mint juleps on the front porch with Harper, Dabney, and Tallulah.

Alternatives: *Ainsley, Reese, Darcy, Chelsea*

Shiloh appeared on the United States baby name charts in 2007 soon after Shiloh Jolie-Pitt was born, in 2006. It was the name Angelina Jolie's parents had chosen for their first child before her mother had a miscarriage. Shiloh was an ancient city in Israel that housed the Ark of the Convenant. It is also an American Civil War battle site in Tennessee. The word means "peaceful" in Hebrew.

Alternatives: *Jordan, Sharon, Bethany, Ariel, Dove, Shayla*

Shirley is still doing the jitterbug. This name, used for boys in the nineteenth century, became a girl's name thanks to Charlotte Brontë, who single-handedly changed the sex of the name with her 1849 novel *Shirley*. But the name really took off in the 1930s, following in the toe-tapping footsteps of child star Shirley Temple. The name means "country meadow." Shirley has a lot to overcome—its treacly girlishness, its old-fashioned associations, and the joke popularized by the movie *Airplane!*:

"Surely you can't be serious."

"I am serious. And don't call me Shirley."

Alternatives: *Betty, Patricia, Florence, Dinah, Charlene*

Sierra The Old West meets the New Age in Sierra. The name evokes the jagged peaks of the Sierra Nevada Mountains of California (*sierra* means "saw" in Spanish). As a girl's name, Sierra promises expansiveness, freedom, and fresh air (think Sierra Club). It's a nature name that sounds like a traditional name.

Variation: *Cierra*

Alternatives: *Siena, Savannah, Sage, Cheyenne, Sedona, Chiara*

Simone The feminine of Simon emigrated from France in 1960, the year after French actress Simone Signoret won the Academy Award for best actress for *Room at the Top*. Jazz musician Nina Simone, who named herself after Signoret, also boosted the profile of the name. Her first album, *Little Girl Blue,* was released in 1958, her second, *Nina Simone and Her Friends,* in 1959. In addition to sensuality and musicality, the name can also suggest feminism thanks to *The Second Sex* (1949) author Simone de Beauvoir.

Alternatives: *Danielle, Nina, Aurelie, Inès, Sabine, Manon, Louise*

Skye can either be a nature name, referring to the great blue heavens, or a variation of the Dutch last name Schuyler. Schuyler means "scholar" in Dutch and has a patrician tinge to it: The Dutch who settled New York City ended up as some of the wealthiest residents in the place. (Recall the novels of Edith Wharton in which half the names are Dutch.) Most girls use the spelling Skylar, which can also evoke "skylark." The lark symbolizes hope and daybreak and festivity—a flitty and pretty association. Skylar jumped in popularity after the release of the Woody Allen movie *Everyone Says I Love You,* in which Drew Barrymore's debutante character was Skylar Dandridge.

Variations: *Sky, Skyla, Skylar, Skyler, Schuyler*
Alternatives: *Meadow, Lark, Aria, Fleur, Rowan, Shea*

Sloane first appeared as an American baby name in 2008. The name has a tony quality: It is associated with Sloane Square in London, which is where young fashionistas live. (To have a "sloaney" accent is to speak veddy, veddy upper-crust English.) Parents naming their children now might have movie character Ferris Bueller's glamorous girlfriend, Sloane Peterson, in mind.

Alternatives: *London, Parker, Joan, Mona*

❦ **Sonia** is a nickname of Sophia, inspired by the Russian form of that name, Sofya. In the early 1900s, Sonia became a name itself. Sonya became more popular in the 1930s, in the wake of Norwegian figure skater Sonja Henie's career. (Although Americans embraced the name, they did not embrace the *j*, which became a *y* in English.) Fashion designer Sonia Rykiel's popularity in the 1970s might be the one to thank for Sonia with an *i* peaking in that decade. Whatever the reason for her former fame, Sonia is flying just under the radar these days, making it a unique pick for parents wanting to steer clear of the Sophia/Sophie masses.

Variation: *Sonya*
Alternatives: *Nadia, Mariah, Mona, Nora, Soraya*

Sophia Greek for "wisdom," Sophia has roared into the spotlight in the past ten years or so. It's an antique gem that proves as well as Emma and Abigail that if you wait long enough, everything comes back into fashion. The Hagia Sophia was a spectacular church built in Constantinople during the Byzantine era, meaning "holy wisdom." The building became a mosque and is now a museum. Sophia is one of the enduring, classic names, having been used by royalty, Hollywood (Sophia Loren, Sofia Coppola), and many others. Its huge increase in popularity now, however, may lead to a backlash later. Sophie had long fallen off the map in the United States until Meryl Streep played the title character in *Sophie's Choice* in 1982.

Variations: *Sofia, Sophie, Sonia, Zofia*

Alternatives: *Maria, Josephine, Sidonie, Aisha, Jenna, Amelia, Augusta, Georgiana, Sylvia*

Great Names in Sports

The sports world is fertile ground for names that have power, triumph, and grace.

- **ALTHEA** *(Gibson, tennis player)*
- **BILLIE JEAN** *(King, tennis player)*
- **FRAZIER** *(boxer Smokin' Joe)*
- **GABRIELLA** *(Sabatini, tennis player)*
- **KATARINA** *(Witt, figure skater)*
- **MARTINA** *(Navratilova, tennis player)*

- **MARY LOU** *(Retton, gymnast)*
- **MIA** *(Hamm, soccer player)*
- **NADIA** *(Comanici, gymnast)*
- **PICABO** *(Street, skier)*
- **SILKEN** *(Laumann, rower)*
- **SONJA** *(Henie, figure skater)*
- **TENLEY** *(Albright, figure skater)*
- **WILMA** *(Rudolph, runner)*

Stacy Look for Stacy with Amy and Kim. The bumper crop of these girls was born in the late 1960s, early 1970s. Stacy appeared in the United States in 1950. The name comes from several places: from the boy's name Eustace, which means either "good grapes" or "standing," and possibly also from Anastasia, which means "resurrection." And it may have gotten a shot in the arm from the *Spiderman* comic, which introduced the hero's first girlfriend, Gwen Stacy, in 1965.

Variations: *Stacey, Anastasia*
Alternatives: *Nancy, Maisie, Sadie, Lacy, Aimee*

Stella "Stelllllaaaa!" How'd you get so popular? A few years ago, you would only think of this name for grandmothers, or for Marlon Brando's tormented wife in *A Streetcar Named Desire*. Well, this literal "star" has stepped into the spotlight and is rising fast. In company with Isabella, Lucy, Sophia, and Emma, Stella is a comeback kid. Her reappearance on the scene in 1998 may be thanks in part to the career rise of Stella McCartney, who started grabbing headlines after she graduated from fashion school in 1995 and quickly became a star designer. The Elizabethan poet Sir Philip Sidney is credited with first using the word as a name in *Astrophel and Stella*. *Stella Maris* is another way of saying "the Virgin Mary" in case you're looking for a religious connection.

Alternatives: *Astrid, Asta, Luna, Starling, Esther, Celia, Tara, Venus*

Stephanie comes from Stephen, which means "crown" in Greek. Saint Stephen was the first Christian martyr; he was stoned to death for his beliefs, as recorded in the Bible's book of Acts. Stephanie has been around for a long time, but the name doesn't sound common in the way that some other traditional ones, say Katherine or Margaret or Jane, do. Perhaps it's because the name was so intensely trendy in the 1980s; it sounds like it could've stepped out of that bangles and leg warmers era.

Variations: *Stephany, Stefania*
Nicknames: *Steph, Steffi, Stevie, Fanny, Annie*
Alternatives: *Josephine, Michelle, Miranda, Tiffany, Penelope*

Summer She's warm and breezy, outdoorsy and sunny. Summer is a nature name that is impossible not to like. Appearing on charts in 1970, Summer was perfect for the Age of Aquarius, but not so flaky that it doesn't work now. Its appeal has only grown over the years. As the name becomes more mainstream, look for it to bloom even more.

Alternatives: *Skye, Meadow, Poppy, River, Sabrina*

Susan comes from Susannah, which comes from Shoshana, a biblical name meaning "lily." Although the name Susan was sure and steady for many years, it became extremely popular from the mid-1940s through mid-1960s—a peak that probably brought

on its precipitous decline. It's hard to believe that
this stalwart is now down to being in the top 700s
(and Suzanne has not even hit the list since 1999!).
Poor Susie Q. Look to Susannah and Shoshana for
variations that feel more current.

Variations: *Suzanne, Susannah, Shoshana*
Nicknames: *Suzie, Susie, Susy, Suzy, Sukie*
Alternatives: *Karen, Lauren, Julie, Nancy, Donna, Cindy*

Sydney Sidney is a last name from England meaning
"wide meadow"; it can also be French in origin, an
anglicized contraction of Saint-Denis. And Sydney is
the capital of Australia, which was named for English
politician Lord Sydney. The name also has Jewish
connections: A whole generation of Jewish men
was given names like Sidney, Morris, and Milton to
facilitate their assimilation into American society.
Now it's their granddaughters (and many others;
Sydney is in the top fifty) who are enjoying the name.
Most parents choose Sydney with a *y* because the
exotic letter makes it seem more feminine.

Variations: *Sidney, Sydny, Sydnee*
Alternatives: *Sidonie, Riley, Avery, Marlow*

Sylvia This name has strong roots—literally. Sylvia
means "forest," and is Roman in origin. The name is a
classic that has been weeded out of late, but seemingly
for no good reason. It's a natural choice for parents

who like Sophia but don't want to pick an overly
popular name. And it's sure to appeal to lovers of
Italy and Shakespeare as well—Silvia was the heroine
of *The Two Gentlemen of Verona*.

Variations: *Sylvie, Silvia*
Alternatives: *Lydia, Arden, Salome, Vivian*

T

Tabitha is an Aramaic name meaning "gazelle" or
"doe"; its Greek equivalent is decidedly less elegant:
Dorcas. It goes without saying that there's a world
of difference between the two. Tabitha sounds girlish
and spritely, helped along by the little girl witch in
the 1960s sitcom *Bewitched*. Dorcas, alas, sounds
uncomfortably close to "dork." (*Bewitched* first aired
in 1964; the name hit the United States charts in 1966.)
Author Stephen King's beloved writer wife is Tabitha.
And Tabitha Soren reported for MTV. Tabitha was
the name of a kind woman who was resuscitated by
St. Peter.

Nicknames: *Tabby, Tab, Tibby, Tib*
Alternatives: *Meredith, Samantha, Amanda, Matilda*

Tamara comes from Tamar, a biblical name meaning
"date palm." The *a* on the end of the name makes it
more feminine. The name is widely used in Russia,
Arabia, and the Balkans. There was a Queen Tamar

who ruled in Georgia during the twelfth century who was later canonized. And there is an Armenian folk tale about a Princess Tamar and her doomed lover who cries for her as he's swept out to sea. Tamar is in the top ten in Israel. In America, Tamara is much preferred.

Variations: *Tamra, Tamar*
Nicknames: *Tammy, Mara, Tama, Tam, Tara*
Alternatives: *Tamsin, Tara, Tamia, Samara, Lina*

🖉 **Tamsin** is the feminine form of Thomas. It's rare outside of England, where it is widely used, but it holds a girlish allure similar to Bronwyn and Gwyneth. The name has thrived in the Cornwall region for centuries. Perhaps it has star potential like that other unlikely Cornish name that hit it big, Jennifer.

Nicknames: *Tam, Tammy*
Alternatives: *Poppy, Imogen, Philippa, Maisie*

I'd love it if she sounded . . .
Israeli

~ Adi	~ Nili	~ Talia
~ Hila	~ Noa	~ Tamar
~ Irit	~ Shira	~ Yael

Tansy If you're hoping for a flower child in more ways than one, consider Tansy. This plant with cheery yellow blossoms was believed by the ancients to increase longevity. So if she has immortal charms, this might be just the name. Is the name too close to potential schoolyard taunt "pansy"? You decide. The alternate spelling Tansie or Tansey might help somewhat.

Alternatives: *Pansy, Maisie, Nancy, Marni, Willow*

Tanya is a nickname for Tatiana and is now widely used as a first name itself. Tanya is far removed from its Russian origins, and thanks to country singer Tanya Tucker, it sounds much more down home than overseas.

Variations: *Tania, Taniya, Taniyah*
Alternatives: *Sonia, Natasha, Katya, Anya*

Tara Happy little Tara skipped up the hill in the '70s and now is skipping back down. (Tara is an Irish name meaning "hill.") She first came on the scene following the 1939 release of the movie *Gone with the Wind,* in which Scarlett O'Hara's beloved plantation was called Tara. This girly, nickname-proof name also means "star" in Sanskrit, explaining its popularity among Indian families—maybe she deserves to shine again.

Alternatives: *Erin, Kelly, Kerry, Adira, Clara, Cara, Amara, Taryn*

> ### I'd love it if she sounded . . .
> #### Hindu
>
> ~ **ANITA** *("guileless")*
>
> ~ **APARNA** *("goddess," "leafless")*
>
> ~ **BIMALA** *("pure")*
>
> ~ **BINA** *("harmony")*
>
> ~ **GITA** *("song," "poem")*
>
> ~ **INDIRA** *("powerful," "prosperous")*
>
> ~ **KAMINI** *("beautiful")*
>
> ~ **LAKSHMI** *("prosperity")*
>
> ~ **LALIMA** *("beautiful")*
>
> ~ **MAYA** *("wealth")*
>
> ~ **MIRA** *("ocean")*
>
> ~ **PADMA** *("lotus")*
>
> ~ **SAVITA** *("sun")*
>
> ~ **SHIRINA** *("night")*
>
> ~ **SOMILA** *("serene")*
>
> ~ **TARA** *("star")*
>
> ~ **USHA** *("dawn")*
>
> ~ **VANDANA** *("adoration")*
>
> ~ **VARA** *("blessing")*

Tatiana is Russian all the way. Saint Tatiana is the Russian patron saint of students. And Tatiana is the heroine of Pushkin's famous poem *Eugene Onegin*. Two Tatianas were Russian royalty, a princess and a duchess. The name itself comes from an ancient Sabine king, Titus Tatius, who ended up ruling Rome alongside Romulus.

Variation: *Tatyana*
Nicknames: *Tania, Tanya, Tiana*
Alternatives: *Natalia, Natasha, Katerina, Sabina, Alexandra, Sasha, Liliana*

Tatum Last name turned first name, Tatum would not be on the charts if it weren't for actress Tatum O'Neal. It's a tomboy name, bucking the vowel-ending fashion for girls. Tate is believed to mean "pleasure," and Tatum is a derivation of the name.
Alternatives: *Taylor, Autumn, Neely, Parker, Sutton*

Taylor means, no surprise, one who cuts and fits clothing. It has been a boy's name for hundreds of years, but only since 1979 has it been a girl's name, too. This little seamstress shot from obscurity to the top ten in the mid-1990s and is now sliding back down. Taylor has a pretty ring to it, thanks to the *tay* sound up front, and its muted ending gives it a tomboyish quality that appeals to many as well. Be forewarned that the name is unisex: Your girl Taylor may end up dating a boy Taylor as happened with singer Taylor Swift (f.) and actor Taylor Lautner (m.).
Alternatives: *Sailor, Hailey, Bailey, Piper, Parker*

Teagan This last name turned first name appeared seemingly out of nowhere in 1999 and has since smoldered up the charts. It's a variation on the Gaelic word for "poet," and is often used by families who want a quirky-cool Irish name that stands apart from the more common Megan.
Alternatives: *Megan, Regan, Keely, Shea, Caitlin, Siobhan*

Teresa is the name of two enormously popular saints: Teresa d'Avila, seventeenth-century Spanish mystic and nun, and Therese de Lisieux, twentieth-century French nun known as the Little Flower of Jesus. Not to mention Mother Theresa, the famous missionary nun. Although the name is believed to have originated in Greece, and may be a reference to the Greek island of Thera or the word for summer, the two saints and one saint-in-waiting have dominated the name so completely that Teresa (or Theresa, Therese) sounds as Catholic as Bernadette. The nickname Tess, on the other hand, has a frisky cast to it, thanks to Thomas Hardy's fallen woman in *Tess of the d'Urbervilles*.

Variations: *Teresa, Theresa, Therese*
Nicknames: *Tess, Tessa, Terri, Tracy, Tracey, Resi, Reese, Tisa*
Alternatives: *Cecilia, Maria, Veronica, Monica*

Thalia was the Greek muse of comedy and poetry as well as one of the Graces. The word means "to flourish." Name your girl Thalia if you have artistic or theatrical hopes for her. A similar name, Talia, comes from one of two sources: It is a Hebrew name as well as a nickname for Natalia. Nowadays, there are more Talias than Thalias, maybe in part to simplify pronunciation.

Variations: *Talia, Taliyah*
Nicknames: *Tally, Alia*
Alternatives: *Grace, Aglaia, Calliope, Dahlia, Tallulah, Galia*

Tia means "aunt" in Spanish and it is a nickname for a variety of other names: Lucretia, Cynthia, Patricia, Tanya, Titania, and others. The name was used for one of the children in the 1968 novel and 1975 film *Escape to Witch Mountain,* which may have boosted its profile. The name has been on the decline since the 1990s. (Note: Actress Tia Carrere was born Althea.)

Variations: *Tea, Thea, Tiana, Tiara*
Alternatives: *Mia, Rita, Tina, Anita*

Tiana Say "Tiana" and lush orchid leis spring to mind. Tiana isn't Hawaiian—it used to be a nickname for names like Christiana and Tatiana—but it has tones reminiscent of Leilani and Keanu. The name has been popular since the 1970s, and may make another splash thanks to the Disney movie *The Princess and the Frog,* which features the company's first African American princess, named Tiana.

Variations: *Tianna, Diana (pronounced dee-AH-nah)*
Nicknames: *Tia, Ana*
Alternatives: *Ayana, Anita, Rihanna, Iman, Liana*

Tiffany comes from the Greek for "epiphany." In America, Tiffany usually has no ties to religion or spiritual enlightenment. Instead it relates to the famous jeweler on Fifth Avenue in New York City that was celebrated in the 1961 movie *Breakfast at*

Tiffany's. Tiffany hit the baby name list a year after the release of the film, and reached its glittering heights in the 1980s. It is declining rapidly now. Tiffany may sound very ritzy at first glance, but here's the epiphany—it's more sparkle than substance.

Variations: *Tiffani, Fanny*
Nickname: *Tiff*
Alternatives: *Crystal, Audrey, Stephanie, Epiphany, Ashley, Tiara*

Tori Since 1959, some Americans have been naming their baby girls Tori. Not Victoria. Just Tori. Why? Tori is a great name. It's sporty, Anglophile (sounds like the conservative political party as well as Queen Victoria), and pretty, too. But it's still a nickname. Do her a favor, name her Victoria (see page 264), Victory, or even Astor (or Astoria), and then call her Tori. Tori means "bird" in Japanese.

Alternatives: *Antonia (Toni), Aurora (Rory), Cornelia (Corry)*

Trinity is a religious name masquerading as an edgy one. It refers to the Holy Trinity of the Christian church: Father, Son, and Holy Spirit. It will also evoke for many people one of the lead characters of the *Matrix* movie series. So you can have it both ways with this one: gun-toting babe or the soul of piety.

Nicknames: *Trina, Trini, Niti*
Alternatives: *Imaculada, Emmanuelle, Katrina*

Ulrika Ulric, a boy's name, is believed to come from the Old English name Wulfric, meaning "wolf power." Ulrika is the feminine form. It's a common name in Scandinavia, and could be unexpected and unique here.

Variation: *Ulrica*
Nicknames: *Rica, Ricky, Ullie, Ulla*
Alternatives: *Erika, Freya, Ingrid, Astrid, Dagmar, Sigrid*

As U Like It

U is a popular letter when it comes to texting friends ("where r u?"). Not so much when it comes to naming babies. Yet many unsung *U* names have the felicitous vowelly sounds that have made names like Anna and Ava stars. Consider these:

~ **ULLA**
(Danish name. Also nickname for Ulrika.)

~ **UMA**
(Hindu name. And now Hollywood name. Thank you, Uma Thurman.)

~ **UNA**
(Irish name. See Oona, pages 209–210.)

~ **UNDINE**
(famous Edith Wharton character. Means "little wave.")

~ **UNIQUE**
(I'm sure you think she is, but there are better ways to appreciate her gifts.)

~ **UNITY**
(A values name, see page 214.)

~ **URSULA**
(popular in Scandinavia and Latin America)

~ **UTA** *(German name. Famous acting coach Uta Hagen.)*

ℓ **Ursula** means "bearlike" and is popular in Scandinavia and Latin America. Saint Ursula was a princess who became the patron saint of young girls. It is a strong name that a little girl will proudly grow into. It's also in the so-out-it's-in category along with fellow sleepers Matilda, Mabel, and Cornelia. A fine choice for a real but quite unusual name.

Nicknames: *Ursie, Sula*
Alternatives: *Tabitha, Matilda, Priscilla, Magdalena*

Valentina From St. Valentine, Valentina is associated with love and the famous feast day on February 14. The name, like Valerie, relates to strength and valor. A melodious name that works in all languages, Valentina is gaining in popularity. It's a great alternative to Victoria and similar long, girly names that are becoming overused.

Nicknames: *Val, Tina*
Alternatives: *Adelaide, Constantina, Matilda, Valeria, Cosima, Delphine, Seraphina*

Valerie started life as a last name in Roman times (Valerius), then became a boy's name (Valéry is still popular in France for boys), and is now a common first name for girls. The name means "strength." Can't you hear the "valor" in it? It has a girl-next-door quality to it for many Americans because of sitcom actresses Valerie Bertinelli and Valerie Harper. If you like the sound of Valerie but want something more contemporary, consider Mallory, which has a whiff of the knights of the round table (as well as the TV show *Family Ties*) about it.

Variations: *Valeria, Valery*
Nicknames: *Val, Aerie, Lee, Lia*
Alternatives: *Victory, Veronica, Mallory, Marjorie*

Vanessa is a code name created by Jonathan Swift for his student and lover Esther Vanhomrigh. (He took the Van from her last name and added Essa, which is a nickname for Esther.) The name appeared in print in Swift's poem "Cadenus and Vanessa" in 1726. It has since received legitimacy from actresses like Vanessa Redgrave, Vanessa Paradis (Johnny Depp's paramour), and Vanessa Williams. With her lilting *-essa* ending, Vanessa would fit in very well with Ella, Tessa, and Bella.

Nicknames: *Vanna, Nessie, Essa*
Alternatives: *Amanda, Cressida, Estella, Melisande*

🖋 **Veronica** Ornate, beautiful, and traditionally very Catholic, the name means "true image" and comes from the story of St. Veronica, who gave Jesus a cloth with which to mop his brow as he was carrying the cross. When he gave it back to her, the image of his face appeared on it. Veronica is closely related to the name Bernice (believe it or not), which is the Greek version. The name was immortalized in song by Elvis Costello, in film by 1940s bombshell Veronica Lake, and in comic strips by Archie's dark-haired love interest. It's a great alternative to the immensely popular Victoria.

Variations: *Veronique (French), Veronika (Eastern Europe)*
Nicknames: *Vera, Nico, Ronnie, Rhona, Rana*
Alternatives: *Monica, Frederica, Domenica, Annika, Beatrice*

Victoria means "victory," and is an expansive, upbeat, but still very graceful and girlish name. No wonder it has burst to the top of the charts. Victoria was one of the most beloved and influential monarchs in British history, and the name has a regal bearing by association, suggesting high teas, sumptuous velvets, and delicate lace. With a variety of nicknames, it's extremely versatile.

Variations: *Victory (modern twist), Victoire or Victorine (French), Vittoria (Italian), Viktoria (Eastern European)*
Nicknames: *Vicki (young and gamine), Tori (young but sophisticated), Ria (cool), Vic (tomboy), Vita (to life!)*
Alternatives: *Eugenia, Edwina, Veronica, Clementine, Arabella*

Viola The heroine of Shakespeare's *Twelfth Night* and consequently of the film *Shakespeare in Love,* Viola is a name filled with music and poetry. It's a stringed instrument similar to the violin. And it

Babes of the Bard

The ladies of Shakespeare's plays boast names ranging from the exotic to the classic, some evoking the mystical and mythical, others suggesting regal bearing and noble birth. The playwright himself is credited with making up several names that strike us as ages old now, like Jessica and Miranda. If you seek a literary pedigree, you can't do better than one of Will's picks.

- **BEATRICE**
  (Much Ado About Nothing)

- **CALPURNIA**
  (Julius Caesar)

- **CELIA** (As You Like It)

- **CLEOPATRA**
  (Antony and Cleopatra)

- **CORDELIA** (King Lear)

- **DESDEMONA** (Othello)

- **HERMIONE**
  (The Winter's Tale)

- **HERO**
  (Much Ado About Nothing)

- **JULIET** (Romeo and Juliet)

- **MIRANDA** (The Tempest)

- **NERISSA**
  (The Merchant of Venice)

- **OPHELIA** (Hamlet)

- **PERDITA**
  (The Winter's Tale)

- **PORTIA**
  (The Merchant of Venice)

- **ROSALIND** (As You Like It)

- **SILVIA**
  (The Two Gentlemen of Verona)

- **TITANIA**
  (A Midsummer Night's Dream)

- **VIOLA** (Twelfth Night)

smacks of royalty as well as moodiness, coming as it does from the word *violet* or purple. Viola would play nicely with Ruby and Rose.

Alternatives: *Celia, Lavinia, Lola, Miranda*

Violet is the color of royalty and mystery, creativity and moodiness. Violets are flowers that signify modesty. This one has Hollywood appeal: Gwyneth Paltrow won her Oscar for portraying Viola De Lesseps in *Shakespeare in Love* (Viola is the heroine of Shakespeare's *Twelfth Night*). And Ben Affleck and Jennifer Garner named their eldest daughter Violet.

Variations: *Viola (shades of Shakespeare there, see previous page), Violette (French), Violetta (Italian), Yolanda (Spanish), Jolanda (Eastern Europe)*
Nicknames: *Letty, Vie*
Alternatives: *Ruby, Scarlett, Jacaranda, Lillian, Dahlia, Jacinta*

Virginia comes from Virgin, meaning "pure." The name has a regal quality to it because of its associations with Queen Elizabeth I, the Virgin Queen, for whom the state of Virginia was named. It brims with independence, not only thanks to Queen Elizabeth but also to maverick writer Virginia Woolf, and even to the 1970s cigarettes Virginia Slims, whose marketing campaigns were about women's lib.

Nicknames: *Gina, Geena (actress Geena Davis is a Virginia), Gigi, Ginger, Ginny*
Alternatives: *Victoria, Carolina, Georgia, Bettina, Giovanna*

Vivienne You can hear the life in Vivienne, which means "alive." It's an enthusiastic name, vibrating with energy, but still ladylike. This vivacious choice was said to be one of the names for the heroine of Arthurian legend in "The Lady of the Lake," giving it a misty air of mysticism.

Variations: *Vivian, Viviana*
Nicknames: *Vivi, Viva*
Alternatives: *Fabienne, Josephine, Bastienne, Christiane, Genevieve*

Wanda comes from the same root as the word *vandal*. The Vandals were a tribe from Eastern Europe that moved west to ravage the Roman Empire in the fifth century. We get the word "vandalism" from the destruction they wrought, as well as "wander" from the great distances they strayed from their home base. That's a strange foundation for a girl's name, but the associations may make it an interesting choice for parents who live to travel, or who hail from the post-punk generation. The wacky movie *A Fish Called Wanda* boosted recognition of the name but also cast it in a comic light. Wanda was popular in the mid-twentieth century—but don't look for it to come roaring, or even wandering, back.

Alternatives: *Willa, Winifred, Miranda (Randa), Kendra*

Wendy J. M. Barrie's creation Wendy Darling was born in 1904 with the release of the play *Peter Pan*.

There are a few examples of Wendy existing before then, but Barrie unquestionably put her on the map. Legend suggests that Barrie got the name from a little girl who was a friend of his who called him "my friendy" and whose lisp translated the endearment to "my fwendy." There is an undeniable similarity between Wendy and Welsh names like Gwendolyn, so Wendy may actually derive from them. Wendy, please note, was very trendy. She surged to popularity in the early- to mid-twentieth century and then sharply declined after the 1970s. Her trajectory follows that of Lisa or Heather—a rush followed by a retreat.

Alternatives: *Gwendolyn, Gwyneth, Brenda, Cynthia*

Whitney This last name turned first name feels distinctly American and securely upper crust. It's a name you can imagine hearing at an exclusive yacht club in Newport, Rhode Island. Whitney has an aristocratic bearing to it because of heiress art patron Gertrude Vanderbilt Whitney, who founded New York City's Whitney Museum of American Art. Singer Whitney Houston caused the name to skyrocket into the top one hundred in 1985 with the release of her debut album, which set sales records. The name stayed on top for ten years and then sunk precipitously, like the singer's own career.

Alternatives: *Ashley, Peyton, Parker, Kenley, Finley*

Wilhelmina comes from the Old German for "helmet." The name is quite pretty when you remember that the second *l* is silent. It is a great pairing for short, blunt last names. Queen Wilhelmina was the longest-reigning Dutch monarch in history. And Wilhelmina has fashion connections: It's the name of a famous modeling agency (from founder Wilhelmina Cooper), and it was the name of a scheming fashion magazine editor on the TV show *Ugly Betty*. Lots of nickname possibilities for this one.

Nicknames: *Wilma (though of course you'll think of Mrs. Flintstone), Billie, Willa, Willie, Wills, Velma, Mina, Minnie*
Alternatives: *Tabitha, Geraldine, Clementine, Matilda, Millicent*

Willow Like the tree that bears the same name, Willow sounds like a tall, slender, gentle soul. The

---

The Wind in the Willows

Trees give us shade, fruit, and gorgeous scenery. All are strong. Many are supple. It's no wonder these beloved features of the natural world have inspired so many baby names. The hardiest specimens follow.

~ APPLE	~ HOLLY	~ OLIVE
~ ASH	~ LAUREL	~ PLUM
~ ASPEN	~ LILAC	~ ROWAN
~ FRASER	~ MAGNOLIA	~ WILLOW

---

name bestows gracefulness with an airy, New Agey, outdoorsy quality. Willow was a sorceress on the TV show *Buffy the Vampire Slayer,* which made its debut in 1997. By 1998, Willow was in the top 1,000 baby names, and it's been rising ever since.

Nicknames: *Willa, Willie, Wills*
Alternatives: *Aspen, Rowan, Haley, Darla, Summer, Lake*

 Winifred was a popular name once upon a time in the 1800s and early 1900s; it was all but gone by the 1970s. A Welsh name meaning "reconciled" or "blessed," an adult Winifred would exude confidence and substance, while a little Winnie or Freddie would be awfully cute.

Nicknames: *Wynne, Freddie, Freda, Winnie*
Alternatives: *Frederique, Gwyneth, Wilhelmina*

X

Ximena (pronounced hee-MEH-nah) or Jimena is believed to be a Spanish-language variation of Simone, which means "hearing." The name appeared in the top 1,000 American names in 2001, and it climbs every year. A lovely choice for families seeking to celebrate Spanish or Latin American roots and/or hipsters looking for a coveted "cool" letter in the name, like *x*.

Alternatives: *Yesenia, Simone, Yasmina*

Xiomara The Spanish-language name Xiomara (pronounced see-oh-MAH-rah) first attracted notice in America in 2004. The meaning of the name is uncertain. Some believe it means "ready for battle"; others say that it means "foreigner," a relative of Xenia. Given its similarity to Xenia, the name certainly sounds exotic. In the United States, it's used primarily by Latin American families.

Alternatives: *Mara, Tamara, Samara, Xena*

Yadira Popular with Spanish-speaking families in the United States, Yadira was a character on a Mexican telenovela in the 1970s. The name is warm and comforting, having the sound of the word *dear* in it.

Nicknames: *Yadi, Dira, Yaya*
Alternatives: *Indira, Darina, Nadia*

Yamilet A Spanish-language variation of Jamila, Yamilet means "beautiful" in Arabic. Yamilet is gaining ground for American babies, especially those born into Muslim and Latin American families. This alluring name is also reminiscent of the graceful Hebrew Ayelet, which means "gazelle."

Alternatives: *Bella, Camilla, Juliette, Shakira, Yasmin*

Yasmeen is Arabic for Jasmine (see page 131).
Jasmine spelled with a *J* is usually considered more
Western; Yasmeen with a *Y* and its variations are
considered more authentically Middle Eastern.
Playwright Yasmina Reza is a Frenchwoman of Iranian
descent. Yasmin Le Bon, also with Iranian roots, is the
model wife of 1980s rocker Simon Le Bon.

Variations: *Jasmine, Jessamine, Yasmin, Yazmin, Yasmine,
Jazzmine, Yasminia*

Nicknames: *Yaz, Meena*

Alternatives: *Layla, Miriam, Sonia, Jenna, Carine, Shakira*

Yesenia A common Latin American name, Yesenia
can be pronounced Jessinia or Yeh-sinia. It's light and
lively, and certainly scans positively (how can anyone
say no to someone whose name says yes?). Yesenia was
the title character of a Mexican TV show in 1970.

Variations: *Jessenia, Llesenia*

Nickname: *Jessie*

Alternatives: *Jessica, Melissa, Erminia*

Yolanda is the Spanish-language version of Violet.
It experienced a heyday in the late 1960s and early
1970s, and then declined steadily until it fell out of the
top 1,000 in 2003. While Violet is inching back from
obscurity, today her sister Yolanda feels dated.

Nicknames: *Yoli, Lonnie*

Alternatives: *Violet, Ramona, Rosalinda*

Yvette is a French name relating to the yew tree, which is an evergreen tree with poisonous leaves. The branches were used to make archery bows, giving the name a sense of strength—and danger. Yvette is a powerful lady, one with a hint of mystery. The name has declined in popularity since the 1960s, but this temptress may be worth a second look.

Variations: *Yvonne, Ivette, Evonne, Yvetta, Yvonna*
Alternatives: *Yvonne, Evie, Willow, Simone, Violette*

Z

Zahava Meaning "golden" in Hebrew, Zahava scans like Savannah, but has a more exotic ring to it. This beautiful name is strongly ethnic (it is typically used by Jewish families), but travels easily.

Alternatives: *Hava, Chava, Evie, Savannah, Shoshanna*

 Zara is a twist on Sarah (Hebrew for "princess"), as well as Zahrah ("blossom" in Arabic). The most famous Zara is Zara Phillips, Queen Elizabeth II's granddaughter via Princess Anne, whose unorthodox name surprised the nation. The name is also that of a Spain-based clothing chain. Zara may become more popular thanks to its similarity to Zahara, another word for Sahara, which is the name of one of Brad and Angelina Jolie-Pitt's children. The name is perfectly

on-trend: cute, two syllables, containing an exotic
letter, ending with an *ah* sound.

Variations: *Zaria, Zariah, Zahrah*

Alternatives: *Fleur, Rose, Sarah, Lily, Mara*

✐ **Zelda** She's a movie star. A dancer. A video game
princess. An international woman of mystery. There
is something undeniably glamorous and artistic
about this name, which is believed to have started out
life as a nickname for the nearly forgotten Griselda.
The Zelda that gave the name a lot of its flair was,
of course, F. Scott Fitzgerald's racy flapper wife and
sparring partner, Zelda Fitzgerald. A bold, creative
choice.

Nickname: *Zell*

Alternatives: *Selma, Helga, Philippa, Josephine, Gypsy, Daisy*

Zion is another word for Israel, the traditional land of
the Jews. The word also means "heaven" or "utopia."
This unisex name has been popular since the early
2000s. The word itself has a cool, edgy sound to it, but
realize that it has strong religious ties for both Jews
and some Christians. This name is a statement.

Alternatives: *Jordan, Shiloh, Heaven*

Zoe (pronounced ZOH-ee) comes from the Greek
and means "life." Zoe is a name that sounds too cool
to be real, but it is traditional, in use since at least

Literary Lions

I f you are looking for a name with literary
provenance, consider choosing the name of
a beloved author.

- **BEATRIX** (Potter)
- **CHARLOTTE** (Brontë)
- **DJUNA** (Barnes)
- **DODIE** (Smith)
- **DORIS** (Lessing)
- **DOROTHY** (Parker)
- **EDITH** (Wharton)
- **FANNIE** (Flagg)
- **FLANNERY** (O'Connor)
- **GEORGE** (Eliot)
- **GWENDOLYN** (Brooks)

- **HARPER** (Lee)
- **ISAK** (Dinesen)
- **JANE** (Austen)
- **LOUISA** (May Alcott)
- **MADELEINE** (L'Engle)
- **MAYA** (Angelou)
- **VIRGINIA** (Woolf)
- **WILLA** (Cather)
- **ZADIE** (Smith)
- **ZELDA** (Fitzgerald)
- **ZORA** (Neale Hurston)

the A.D. third century. Saint Zoe died in Rome in the
200s; Byzantine Empress Zoe lived during the 400s
and is commemorated in gorgeous gold mosaics in
Istanbul's Hagia Sophia. Zoe was considered exotic
until the 1980s, when it was rediscovered and shot way
up in popularity. Actresses Zoe Caldwell (venerable)
and Zooey Deschanel (hipster) prove that it works
at any age. Zoe is a lively and meaningful choice for
any fan of J. D. Salinger: his novel *Franny and Zooey*

was published in 1961, though the titular Zooey is
a boy.

Variations: *Zoey, Zooey*

Alternatives: *Phoebe, Chloe, Penelope, Zelda*

✒ **Zora** is a Slavic name that means "dawn," but it
reminds most Americans of Zora Neale Hurston.
Hurston was one of the stars of the Harlem Renaissance
and a prolific author. But her work fell into obscurity
and it wasn't until after her death, with the help of
Alice Walker, that her books attained their greatest
successes. She is best remembered for *Their Eyes Were
Watching God*. As a name, Zora travels well, working in
all languages, and sporting a fashionable exotic letter
as well as ending in an *ah* sound. This name is one to
look out for.

Alternatives: *Nora, Aurora, Rory, Nella, Georgia*

Boys

 A

Aarav A Sanskrit name meaning "lotus," Aarav has been popular in the United States only since 2008. It is the name of the son of Akshay Kumar, Bollywood superstar, as well as the name of his character in the 2009 film *Blue*. Kumar has the name tattooed on his back.

Alternatives: *Kumar, Pranav, Rishi, Rahul*

Aaron was the brother of Moses, who became the first high priest of Israel according to the Old Testament. Like Moses, Aaron is believed to be an Egyptian name. The name was a classic that held steady popularity until the late 1950s and early 1960s, when it started soaring. Hank Aaron was busy then becoming one of the greatest baseball players of all time and Elvis Aaron Presley was rocking his way to stardom. The name used to be predominant in the Jewish community but it is used by many people now.

Variation: *Aron*
Alternatives: *Ethan, Alden, Moses, Solomon*

Abdullah means "servant of God" (you can see "Allah" in the alternative spelling of the name, Abdallah). It is one of the most widely used names in the Arabic world. The name was that of the prophet Muhammad's father and is a celebration of humility. It is the name of the King of Jordan as well as other royalty and statesmen of the Middle East, including Turkey, Lebanon, and Saudi Arabia. It has been widely used in the United States since 1996.

Variations: *Abdallah, Abdiel (Jewish), Obadiah (Old Testament; Christian)*
Nickname: *Abdul*
Alternatives: *Muhammad, Bashir, Habib, Sharif*

✑ **Abel** was the shepherd son of Adam and Eve who was murdered by his brother Cain in the book of Genesis in the Bible. Abel means "breath," which may allude to the ephemeral nature of life. The name has been consistently popular, mostly among Jewish families, throughout the ages. (Cain, on the other hand, not so much.) The name is appealing for its strong sound and for its aural associations with the word *able*, which suggests competence and reliability.

Alternatives: *Ariel, Caleb, Ezra, Eli, Levi*

✑ **Abraham** is a patriarch, a leader. Biblical Abraham was the father of the Jews and is considered the father

Mad Men

I f you love all things 1950s and 1960s, from midday martinis to your Wormley sofa, you might like mid-twentieth-century modern names. These favorites from the *Mad Men* era have retro appeal for future hipsters of America.

- ALAN
- BERT
- DONALD
- DOUGLAS
- DWIGHT
- FRED
- GARY
- GENE
- HAROLD
- HERB
- KENNETH
- LEONARD
- MARTIN
- NORMAN
- RANDALL
- ROGER
- RUSSELL
- STANLEY
- VERNON
- WALLY
- WALTER

of Islam as well: His son with the servant Hagar, Ishmael, became the ancestor of the Arabs. In modern times, we think of Abraham Lincoln, one of the most esteemed presidents in United States history. So though the name's literal meaning is "father of many nations," it has come to embody honesty and integrity as well. The name dipped in popularity in the mid-twentieth century and is now coming back with oldies-but-goodies like Henry and Samuel.

Variations: *Avram, Abram, Ibrahim (Arabic)*
Nicknames: *Abe, Abie, Bram*
Alternatives: *Solomon, Isaac, Jonah, Ruben*

Old Testament Names for Boys

The Old Testament is a classic source of strong, unique names for babies. These are choices with colorful histories and rich meanings. Some are well known (Daniel), others deserve to be rediscovered (Abner).

- **AARON** (Hebrew or Egyptian, "high mountain" or "exalted")

- **ABEL** (Hebrew, "breath")

- **ABNER** (Hebrew, "father of light")

- **ABRAHAM** (Hebrew, "father of the multitudes"; originally Abram)

- **ABSALOM** (Hebrew, "father is peace")

- **ADAM** (Hebrew, "man" or "earth")

- **AHAB** (Hebrew, "uncle")

- **ASHER** (Hebrew, "happy" or "blessed")

- **BALTHAZAR** (Hebrew, "Lord or God protect the king")

- **BARUCH** (Hebrew, "blessed")

- **BENJAMIN** (Hebrew, "son of the right hand" or "son of the south")

- **BOAZ** (Hebrew, "swiftness"; one of the few unambiguously good guys in the Old Testament)

- **CAIN** (Hebrew, "acquired"; Cain was the first murderer—there are few if any positive associations with this name)

- **CALEB** (Hebrew, "dog," "faith," or "heart")

- **CANAAN** (Hebrew meaning unknown; a son of Ham and a grandson of Noah)

- **DANIEL** (Hebrew, "God is my judge")

- **DAVID** (Hebrew, "beloved")

Ace As in a deck of cards, Ace is the tops. This sporty, confident name was popular in the late 1800s, and then disappeared. But now it is making a comeback. Do we have online poker to thank for this? Or perhaps *American Idol* finalist Ace Young (né Asa)?

- **ELAM** *(Hebrew, a variant of Eilam, meaning "forever" or "eternal")*

- **ELEAZAR** *(Hebrew, "my God has helped")*

- **ELI** *(Hebrew, "high" or "ascension")*

- **ELIJAH** *(Hebrew, "Yahweh is God"; Elias (Greek) is a variant)*

- **ELISHA** *(Hebrew, "God is my salvation"; lately a popular variant on "Alicia" for girls)*

- **ENOCH** *(Hebrew, "dedicated")*

- **ENOS** *(Hebrew, "man"; this grandson of Adam lived for 905 years!)*

- **EPHRAIM** *(Hebrew, "fruitful")*

- **ESAU** *(Hebrew, "hairy")*

- **EZRA** *(Hebrew, "help")*

- **GIDEON** *(Hebrew, "feller of trees," "mighty warrior")*

- **GOLIATH** *(Hebrew, possibly "tall," "exile," "uncovered")*

- **HARAN** *(Hebrew, "hill")*

- **HEZEKIAH** *(Hebrew, "God strengthens")*

- **HIRAM** *(Hebrew or Phoenician, "exalted brother")*

- **ISAAC** *(Hebrew, "laughter")*

- **ISHMAEL** *(Hebrew, "God listens"; considered the ancestor of the Arabs)*

- **JACOB** *(Hebrew, "he who supplants")*

- **JEREMIAH** *(Hebrew, "raised up by God")*

- **LEVI** *(Hebrew, "joining together")*

- **MICAIAH** *(Hebrew, "who looks like God")*

- **MORDECAI** *(Hebrew, "little man")*

- **MOSES** *(probably Egyptian)*

- **NOAH** *(Hebrew, "at rest")*

- **RUBEN** *(Hebrew, "a son")*

- **SAUL** *(Hebrew, "to ask")*

- **SOLOMON** *(Hebrew, "peace")*

Traditionalists could name the boy something else (how about Chase or Pace?) and just nickname him Ace. It's a bold name, but some might say that it's tempting fate.

Alternatives: *Jock, Chase, Asa, Skip*

Adam is a classic. After all, he was the first man, according to the Bible. In fact, his name means "man," and comes from the Hebrew word for "earth" (*adama*). Adam was in the top twenty in the early 1980s and remains in the top one hundred, though it's waning some. Famous Adams include early punk rocker Adam Ant, U2 band member Adam Clayton, goofy comedian Adam Sandler, and early Batman portrayer Adam West. Needless to say, it's a traditional, manly choice.

Variations: *Adan, Aden*
Alternatives: *Ruben, Noah, Seth*

Addison ("son of Adam") is a patrician-sounding last name turned first name. Its use for boys goes way back, but look for it to fall out of favor quickly. The reason? The girls discovered it as an alternative to Madison and the name has skyrocketed. When a name gets taken over by girls, the boys stop using it. Nice knowing you, Addison. Parents looking for a similar feel might try Lincoln, Truman, Atwood, or other last names with meaningful provenance.

Alternatives: *Ellis, Buckley, Carlyle, Davison, Jameson*

Aditya Think of this name as the sun. Aditya is a reference to a heavenly body in Sanskrit and a group of gods. It is also an alternative name for Vishnu, the Zeus of Hinduism. Aditya as a name has been used by Indian families in the United States since 1999. They are not deterred by the name's feminine (to Western eyes) appearance.

Alternatives: *Pranav, Aarav, Rishi, Advait*

Adlai A modern contraction of an obscure biblical name, Adaliah ("God is just"), Adlai rose to prominence alongside 1950s presidential candidate Adlai Stevenson. To some, the name sounds too close to Adelaide and rings feminine; to others, it's a cool, unique, gentrified choice. Will Adlai play lacrosse or soccer at Andover?

Variation: *Adaliah*
Alternatives: *Adrian, Alden, Addison, Stevenson, Brooks*

Adolfo This German name has a very cool meaning: "noble wolf." But it has a very uncool association: Adolf Hitler. Adolfo, happily, does not sound so similar, thanks to the third syllable and the Latin sing-songiness of it (everything sounds better in Italian or Spanish, no?). It also helps that the *a* in Adolfo is soft, while in Adolf it is hard. The name was borne by royalty in Germany and Sweden. Still, use it with caution.

Variation: *Adolphus*
Nicknames: *Dolf, Dolph, Ado*
Alternatives: *Wolf, Ulrick, Rudolph, Lowell*

Adonis A hard name for the little guy to live up to. Adonis was a youth in Greek mythology loved by goddess Aphrodite. He was killed by a wild boar sent by one of Aphrodite's jealous lovers. His name has become a generic term for an extremely handsome man. Do you want to tempt the gods with this one? Parents in the United States have been doing so since 1993.

Nickname: *Donny*
Alternatives: *Athens, Troy, Ulysses, Thor*

Adrian is a "man from Hadria," the area around the Adriatic coast from Italy to Dalmatia. Roman Emperor Hadrian was responsible for the creation of a gigantic fortified wall running across the width of England, which secured one border of his empire. Hadrian was considered one of the best, wisest, and kindest of all the Roman emperors. That the name is close to its female counterpart Adrienne hasn't hindered its popularity at all. Actors Adrian Brody and Adrian Grenier prove that the name works well for boys.

Variation: *Adrien*
Alternatives: *Hadrian, Darius, Alden, Cameron*

Adriel This once obscure Old Testament name has been rediscovered. It means "God helps me" in Hebrew. The name sounds fresh and contemporary, like a mix of Ariel and Adrian. But to people of a certain age (who grew up on Saturday morning cartoons), it might be reminiscent of Azriel, the snickering feline sidekick of the Smurfs' nemesis, Gargamel.

Variations: *Adriell, Azriel*
Alternatives: *Ariel, Axel, Adrian, Aidan*

Ahmad means "highly praised" in Arabic. It is one of the names that the prophet Muhammad was known by. Ahmad and its variation Ahmed are common names in the Arabic world, having been used for centuries by famous people, leaders, and everyone else. Prince Ahmed is one of the characters from *One Thousand and One Nights*.

Variation: *Ahmed*
Alternatives: *Bilal, Habib, Azam*

Aidan A traditional Irish name, Aidan has careened into the spotlight, going from barely known in the 1980s to the top hundred by 2001. The name means "fire," and a variation of it was the name of a Celtic sun god. Saint Aidan is believed to have been born in Ireland and eventually moved to the small English isle of Lindisfarne in the 600s, where he worked to build a powerful monastery and convert many locals to Christianity. Actor Aidan Quinn may have boosted the name's profile in recent years, and Carrie's hunky boyfriend on the TV show *Sex and the City* probably didn't hurt either.

Variations: *Aaden, Aiden, Aedan, Aydan, Ayden, Aydin*
Alternatives: *Keegan, Caleb, Liam, Finnegan, Kieran, Quinn, Hayden*

Aidric If you are searching for a name with medieval cred, with a strong meaning but melodious sound and a Celtic whiff about it, then Aidric might be just the thing. Aidric ("fire power") was a bishop in the court of Charlemagne who became a saint. The name is an unusual alternative to Aidan and Adrian.

Alternatives: *Alaric, Alberic, Hugh, Theodoric, Cedric*

Alan is a Celtic name that traveled from France to England with William the Conqueror. The meaning is lost, though some experts wonder if it comes from "rock" and others "sun." Variations Allan and Allen are more likely to be last names turned first names. The name was very popular in the 1940s through 1960s, and suggests an easygoing, good-guy nature (thanks, Alan Alda!).

Variations: *Allan, Allen, Alain, Alun*
Alternatives: *Alden, Landon, Damian, Harold (Hal), Roger*

✎ **Albert**, believe it or not, was an extremely popular name until the 1930s. Unlike the girls who were popular with him—Sophie, Lucy, Hannah, Emma, et al.—who are now back in style, poor Albert is fading more every year. The name comes from the German and means "bright and noble," which people have taken to mean "famous." Not too shabby. The name was popularized in nineteenth-century England by Queen Victoria's husband, Prince Albert, and came to suggest brilliance of another sort by Albert Einstein. Prince Albert of Monaco proves that Alberts can even be playboys.

Variations: *Alberto, Albrecht, Alberic*
Nicknames: *Al, Bert, Bertie, Albi*
Alternatives: *Robert, Albion, Edmund, Philip*

Alden A last name turned first name, Alden is believed to mean "old one" or "old friend." The name sounds upper-crusty, with shades of Holden Caufield, but it's not without warmth. It's close to Arden ("love"), and it sounds similar enough to Alan to suggest strength and reliability.

Alternatives: *Holden, Alan, Madden, Declan, Adlai*

I'd love it if he sounded . . .
Greek

- AENEAS
- APOSTOLOS
- ARISTOTLE
- COSMAS
- FILIPOS
- GREGORIOS
- KONSTANTINOS
- LEONIDAS
- NIKOLAS
- PAVLOS
- SOKRATES
- SPIROS
- STAVROS
- STEPHANOS
- VASSILIS
- YIANNI

Aldo From the medieval name Aldous ("old" in German) comes the Italian name Aldo. Aldo Moro was the Prime Minister of Italy in the 1960s and 1970s. Aldo Bensadoun established the shoe company that bears his first name. This traditional name has a cute factor going for it, thanks to the two syllables and the vowel finish. It also goes well with last names that could use softening.

Variations: *Aldous, Aldus*
Nickname: *Al*
Alternatives: *Waldo, Otto, Milo*

Alexander The name of a warrior, Alexander exudes strength and leadership and vitality. Thank you, Alexander the Great. The Macedonian King who grew up to take over much of the known world in the years before the Christian era is credited with popularizing this name. He became such a legend throughout the world that he remains the first Alexander to leap to people's minds. The name did exist before him: Some speculate that it may have been a title for the goddess Hera, meaning as it does "defender of man." Alexander has never been more popular than it is now. And Alexandra is all the rage for girls.

Variations: *Alexzander, Aleksander, Alessandro, Alejandro, Alexis, Alexandre, Alistair, Iskander*
Nicknames: *Al, Alex, Alec, Alexi, Sandy, Sasha, Xan, Xander, Zander, Sandro, Lex*
Alternatives: *Axel, Felix, Maxfield, Oscar*

Alfonso Stand back—Alfonso is "battle-ready."
This dignified name is a Latin translation of the
German Alphonse. It is common in the royal families
of Spain and Portugal, as well as in the Hispanic
community in the United States. If you want a cute
nickname or you like doo-wop and leather jackets,
you could call him Fonzie. *Ayyyy.*

Variations: *Alonzo, Alonso*
Nicknames: *Al, Zo, Fonzie, Fonz, Alfi*
Alternatives: *Alberto, Cosmo, Federico*

Alfred, like his cousin Albert, is on a long slow
slide to oblivion. Alfredo, on the other hand, is
holding steady. The names both mean "elf council"
in Old English. Which makes you wonder if some
supernatural beings from fiction with similar
names—Hobbit Frodo Baggins from Tolkein's
The Fellowship of the Ring, and Alf, the furry alien
from the eponymous sitcom—were carefully named.
It's hard to find hip Alfreds: Alfred E. Newman,
the mascot of *MAD* magazine, and director Alfred
Hitchcock don't fit the bill. But famous Alfredos
are more appealing, including the creamy fettucine
dish and actor Al Pacino, whose full name is Alfredo.

Variations: *Alfredo, Avery*
Nicknames: *Al, Fred, Fredo, Alfie, Avery, Freddie,
Freddy*
Alternatives: *Frederick, Albert, Calvin, Herbert*

Think Inca

Some families of Latin American extraction are turning to indigenous civilizations for naming inspiration. If you want your boy to have a real one-of-a-kind name, try the Inca civilization for ideas.

- **ATAHUALPA:** *the last king of the unified Inca Empire*

- **CONIRAYA:** *god of the moon*

- **HUÁSCAR:** *fought his brother, Atahualpa, for control of the empire*

- **HUAYNA:** *a great general*

- **INTI:** *god of the sun*

- **KON:** *god of the southern rain and wind*

- **LLOQUE** (*Yupanqui*): *a wise ruler, though not much of a looker*

- **SAYRI:** *the king of the crumbled empire who made peace with the Spanish*

- **VIRACOCHA:** *the creator god and a king named for him*

- **YÁHUAR:** *a king whose name means "blood-crying Inca"*

Ali, which means "exalted" in Arabic, is a very popular name with Muslims around the world. Muhammad's first cousin was Ali, and al-Ali is one of the ninety-nine names of God. (According to the Koran, there are ninety-nine names that are associated with Allah.) There are two Alis that first jump to American minds: Ali Baba, from *One Thousand and One Nights*, who foiled the revenge plot of forty thieves and gave us the phrase "open sesame"; and Muhammad Ali, the boxing legend who changed his name from Cassius Clay when he converted to Islam. Ali is also a popular nickname for many other names beginning with Al for both boys and girls.

Alternatives: *Muhammad, Tariq, Salim*

Alvaro is a fashionable name in Spanish- and Portuguese-speaking nations, and has a vaguely Italian sound to it as well. It has Germanic origins and is believed to mean "guardian." Many South American sports figures and politicians bear the name.

Alternatives: *Valerio, Alvin, Romeo*

Alvin means "elf friend," so it's an appropriate name for a singing chipmunk. Is it right for your child? Dance legend Alvin Ailey made it work, so maybe your guy will, too. The name is believed to be a variation of Calvin (literal meaning, "bald"), which was given to children in honor of John Calvin, the French Protestant reformer of the sixteenth century. Alvin was popular in the 1920s, but don't bet on a big comeback.

Nickname: *Alvy*
Alternatives: *Calvin, Melvin, Valentine*

Amar'e Amar'e Stoudemire is the forward-center for the Phoenix Suns. The popularity of Amar'e as a name, which first appeared in the United States in 2005, coincides with the rise of Stoudemire's basketball career. It may also have been helped by

Gloria Estefan's song "Te Amaré," which was released in 2004. Amare is "to love" in Latin. The name Amari may be a variation of Amar'e, or it might be a variation of Omar (page 472).

Variation: *Amari, Amato*
Alternatives: *Amadeus, Armand, Roman*

Amir means "prince" in Arabic. The name is a title for a ruler as well as a name, more commonly seen as the variation Emir. The female form is the lively Ameera.

Variations: *Ameer, Emir*
Alternatives: *Rashid, Ilyas, Basim*

Amos ("carried by God") was a prophet who lent his name to a book of the Old Testament. The name may remind some parents of cookie entrepreneur and literacy champion Wally "Famous" Amos. Others may think of quirky singer-songwriter Tori Amos. Still others will remember influential Israeli writer Amos Oz. But some may pause at the name: Are we far enough away from "Amos 'n' Andy," the famous radio minstrel show of the 1930s to 1950s, to revive this biblical classic?

Alternatives: *Linus, Abel, Ennis*

Anderson Son of Anders, the Scandinavian variation of Andrew, Anderson is a very common last name that has also been a first name for hundreds of years. In recent years, newsman Anderson Cooper has been a high-profile person with the name, as has Anderson Silva, a mixed martial arts fighter.

Alternatives: *Henderson, Sander, Anders, Alaric*

Andrew is one manly man—"strong man" is the meaning of his name. Andrew sounds perennially fresh, but he goes way back: In the Bible, he was one of Christ's disciples. He's also one of the most beloved saints, patron of fishermen and golfers. The name has been in the top hundred for more than a hundred years, and was boosted even further by the birth of England's Prince Andrew in 1960.

Variations: *Andreas, Anders, Andres, Andre*
Nicknames: *Andy, Drew*
Alternatives: *Edward, Malcolm, Nicholas, Timothy, Stephen*

Angel Angelo has been a consistently popular name for centuries, a classic in Italian and Spanish. Now Angel is trendier. It was barely used until the 1900s but has steadily worked its way up the charts. The word means "messenger." In Spanish-speaking families, Angel is pronounced "AHN-hell," not "AIN-jell," which increases the masculinity of it. But TV vampire Angel pronounced his name the American way, and he certainly didn't seem any less manly for it.

Variation: *Angelo*
Alternatives: *Luis, José, Santino*

Angus is a hardy Celtic name with positive associations: the meaning of the name is "one," suggesting primacy. Angus was the name of a man who lived until old age and then died peacefully, according to an ancient manuscript. And Angus was a Celtic god. The name suggests physical prowess and size (perhaps because of its similarity to Magnus), and yet comes with the adorable nickname Gus.

Alternatives: *August, Magnus, Gustave*

Anthony comes from a Roman last name. The traditional spelling is actually without an *h,* which was added later to give the name a connection to the Greek word for flower. Although Anthony hit the top ten most popular names in 2005, it arrived there slowly and steadily—there's very little risk of it seeming too trendy. For those seeking a religious connection, St. Anthony, a Franciscan, is the patron saint of Padua and the finder of lost things.

Variations: *Antony, Antonio, Anton, Antoine, Antwan*
Nickname: *Tony*
Alternatives: *Francis, Julian, Bernardo, Marcus, Vincent*

✐ **Archibald** Where's Archie? This great name meaning "true and bold" is not on the radar anymore. Comedy couple Amy Poehler and Will Arnett chose the name for their first son, calling him Archie. Look for it to make a comeback. Lest you think Archie sounds too

Hindu Gods

The Hindu religion is pantheistic, so there are a lot of gods and goddesses and other deities to choose from when you are naming your baby. The names and stories behind them are as rich and fanciful as what you find in the Ancient Greek religion. Some of the most popular:

- **GANESH:** *the elephant god of wisdom and removing barriers*

- **HANUMAN:** *the monkey god and divine aid to the hero Rama*

- **INDRA:** *a god of the sky*

- **KRISHNA:** *the dark one, an incarnation of Vishnu*

- **RAMA:** *a joy; an incarnation of Vishnu*

- **RUDRA:** *a name that means "roarer" and is associated with storms*

- **SHIVA:** *creator and destroyer of the earth*

- **SURYA:** *god of the sun with arms and hair of gold*

- **VARUNA:** *another god of the sky*

- **VISHNU:** *righter of wrongs*

much like a goofy comic book character, keep in mind that the real name of Cary Grant—perhaps the most debonair man ever—was Archibald Leach.

Alternatives: *Cornelius, Bartholomew, Casper, Oliver*

Ari is a former nickname that has been a given name since 1969. It can be short for Ariel (as in the case of Hollywood agent Ari Emanuel and the *Entourage* character based on him, Ari Gold) or Aristotle, as in

Ari Onassis. Other names it can abbreviate include
Aristides and girls' names like Ariana and Arabella.
Ari means "lion" in Hebrew.

Alternatives: *Leo, Wolf, Amos, Eli*

Ariel In Hebrew, Ariel is "the lion of God." Too bad
it's closer to "the little mermaid" in English—Ariel was
the name of the title character in that Disney movie.
Shakespeare doesn't help butch it up either: Ariel in
The Tempest is a sprite. But Ariel can be shortened to
Ari (page 295), which sounds more rambunctiously
boyish. The name is much more popular in Israel
(think former Prime Minister Ariel Sharon) than it is
in the United States.

Nickname: *Ari*
Alternatives: *Israel, Asa, Elijah*

Arjun is a hero from the Hindu epic containing the
Bhagavad Gita. The name means "shining," from the
same root as the Latin word *argentum* ("silver"). Arjun
was a warrior, a masterful archer, and a friend of Lord
Krishna to whom Krishna revealed the scriptures.

Alternatives: *Krishna, Vishnu, Pranav, Vikash*

Armando A relative of Herman, Armando means
"soldier." The name is used at a consistent, middling
level among Spanish, Portuguese, and Italian families.

Round Table Round-up

Everything was perfect in Camelot. Will you find the ideal name among the ranks of King Arthur's closest friends and associates? If you are looking for something celebrating Celtic heritage, you'll be on the right track.

~ **ARTHUR:** *the enlightened king*

~ **GALAHAD:** *the illegitimate son of Lancelot and the seductive tart Elaine; Galahad himself is pure-beyond-pure*

~ **GAWAIN:** *one of the most noble, chivalrous, and true knights; if Gawain had a fault, it was following the rules too closely*

~ **GRINGOLET:** *Gawain's horse*

~ **LANCELOT:** *a name with a lot to live up to; Lancelot, talented and tragic, was the greatest of King Arthur's knights*

~ **MERLIN:** *is it a bird? (yes!); is it a plane? (yes!); is it Arthur's magical, bearded advisor? (yes again!)*

~ **PELLEAS:** *a valiant knight and a bit of a romantic*

~ **PERCIVAL:** *one of the knights who sought the Holy Grail*

~ **TRISTAN:** *a knight who fell tragically in love with Iseult*

~ **UTHER:** *though a bit of a meathead, Uther Pendragon was fair and kind—oh, and he was Arthur's dad*

Armani is a recent variation, inspired by Italian fashion designer Giorgio Armani. Do you really want to name your child after him? Go with Armando and use Armani as a nickname if you must.

Variations: *Herman, Armand, Armani, Armin*
Alternatives: *Lorenzo, Orlando, Fernando*

✐ **Arthur** was the king of England during the fifth century and the source of some of the greatest legends of all time. The Duke of Wellington (Arthur Wellesley) contributed to the name's popularity. He was the dashing soldier who led the defeat of Napoleon at Waterloo and became England's prime minister. On his death in 1852, Wellington was given a state funeral and eulogized in a poem by Tennyson. It was Tennyson who boosted the name further in his *Idylls of the King*, which appeared in the mid- to late 1800s. The name was in the top fifteen in the United States at the opening of the twentieth century and has been on a long slow slide since then.

Variation: *Arturo*
Nicknames: *Art, Artie*
Alternatives: *Edward, Tennyson, Gawain, Laurence*

Aryan means "noble" or "of high caste" in Hindi. And it means the same thing to Westerners, but not in a good way—the word retains its Nazi associations of ethnic cleansing. Although this name is a big deal in Bollywood, it could be a big mistake for families who are living in the United States.

Alternatives: *Krishna, Vishnu, Arjun*

✐ **Asa** ("healer") was a King of Judah in the 900s B.C. This Old Testament favorite is pleasing to contemporary ears. *American Idol* singer Ace Young was born Brett Asa Young. Asa Buchanan, a patriarch of TV soap opera *One Life to Live*, who started appearing in 1980, may have boosted the name.

Nicknames: *Al, Ace*
Alternatives: *Amos, Enos, Jesse, Judah, Eli*

✐**Asher** Cheerful Asher isn't a trade name but would be at home among Archer, Cooper, and friends. The name is biblical in origin and means "happy"; Asher was a son of Jacob, and his people settled in a fertile land on the banks of the Mediterranean and were blessed with fruit and rich pastures. Parents are crazy for this jovial little fellow—since the name's rediscovery in 1992, it's zipped quickly to the top 200.

Nickname: *Ash*
Alternatives: *Caleb, Levi, Jacob, Dashiell*

Ashton arrived in 1982 and has quickly gained steam thanks in large part to actor Ashton Kutcher. Had Kutcher not come along, Ashton might have been swamped by parents of girls looking for a hipper alternative to Ashley. The name holds appeal because of its tony English quality (it means "the town of ash trees") and cool nickname, Ash.

Curious side note: In the epic novel *The Far Pavilions*, set in the Raj-era Himalayas, the hero is born of English parents and named Ashton. When

Ashton's parents die, he is adopted by a native servant and renamed Ashok for his safety. Ashok is Sanskrit for "happy"—the same meaning as Asher.

Nickname: *Ash*
Alternatives: *Dashiell, Martin, Alden, Barton*

Atticus Finch is the lawyer hero of *To Kill a Mockingbird*, the father of Scout. Gregory Peck played him in the film, and in 2003, the character was voted the number one greatest hero of American film by the American Film Institute. The next year, the name cropped up on birth lists for the first time since 1881. The name literally means "from Greece,"

I'd love it if he sounded . . .
Scandinavian

~ AARVO	~ GUSTAV	~ LEIF
~ ANDERS	~ HARALD	~ NILS
~ AXEL	~ HENRIK	~ OLE
~ BJORN	~ INGMAR	~ PER
~ BO	~ IVOR	~ SOREN
~ EDVARD	~ JOHAN	~ STIG
~ ERIK	~ KAJ	~ THOR
~ GUNNAR	~ LARS	~ VIGGO

but has come to mean "moral, kind, and just" because of the close connection to Finch. The name is one from antiquity. Atticus of Ancient Greece is credited with publishing the speeches of his friend Cicero. Note: Attica is a famous prison in upstate New York—maybe not the most auspicious connection.

Alternatives: *Cicero, Cassius, Silas, Augustus*

August Noble, great, magnificent. Is there a name with a grander meaning than August? Adopted by the Roman emporers as Augustus, the modern shortened version of the name was on the wane before parents realized how hip it could be. Amid the trendy Tylers, Logans, and Ryans, August will stand out.

Variations: *Augustus, Agustin, Austin*
Nicknames: *Gus, Auggie, Gusty, Gusto*
Alternatives: *Archibald, Julian, Gustav*

Austin Twang! There is an unmistakable Southwestern flavor to Austin because of the capital of Texas, which was named for "the father of Texas," Stephen Austin. Originally, the name was a contraction of Augustus (see August, above). It was doing very nicely, had just hit the top ten, when *Austin Powers: International Man of Mystery* was released in 1997. The movie boomed; the name started to dip.

Variation: *Austen (could be a nice homage to Jane)*
Alternatives: *Houston, Logan, Dustin, Travis*

Avery Don't get too attached to Avery. It's a great name, a variation of Alfred, surprisingly (see page 289), and has been used for boys for centuries. But the name has been eagerly snatched up by the parents of girls and has shot from oblivion to the top forty in the space of twenty years. When girls co-opt a name, the boys usually start opting out. Avery sounds cultured and moneyed (think Lincoln Center's Avery Fisher Hall), and it also is reminiscent of birds (it's not a far leap from aviary to Avery). Averill might be a better bet for boys.

Variation: *Alfred*
Alternatives: *Addison, Buckley, Mortimer, Averill*

Axel An excellent alternative to the popular Alexander, Axel is a classic name of Germanic origin that was rediscovered by parents with the help of rock musician Axl Rose and actor Eddie Murphy. The name appeared in the top 1,000 in 1989, one year after the release of Guns N' Roses's smash hit song "Sweet Child O' Mine." The choice to name a child Axel may have been reinforced by Eddie Murphy's title character in the *Beverly Hills Cop* franchise, Axel Foley. The name means "peace" and is popular in Scandinavia and Germany. An axle is the pin around which a wheel rotates, and that word comes from the word for "shoulder," which suggests strength.

Variations: *Absalom, Aksel*
Alternatives: *Knox, Magnus, Olaf, Thor, Viktor*

B

Bailey A bailey or bailiff is a keeper of the castle. A bailey had to be reliable and honest; the position was one of high rank. Bailey is also a place-name meaning "berry meadow." This last name turned first name was used for boys in the first part of the twentieth century; now it's used for boys and girls. The girls are claiming it in much greater numbers, which means that the boys are going to stop soon. (That "lee" sound at the end clinched the deal.) Consider other tradesman names (see pages 316–317) instead: Cooper, Archer, Fletcher, Marshall, and so on.

Variations: *Bailee, Baylee*
Nicknames: *Bay, Lee*
Alternatives: *Tucker, Porter, Marshall, Leland*

Baird is Scots for "bard." If you want a little Gaelic poet, then this is the name for you. Because Baird is not an uncommon last name, there is a whiff of WASP to it, as well as a spray of salty air and suntan oil because of the similiarity to Laird (as in Laird Hamilton, famous surfer). An altogether sunny, romantic, musical name.

Variation: *Bard*
Alternatives: *Laird, Bernard, William, Duncan*

🖋 **Balthazar** You may know Balthazar better as one of the Three Wise Men. He, along with Melchior and Caspar, were the magi who brought gifts of gold, frankincense, and myrrh to the baby Jesus. The name is believed to be Babylonian (Belshazzar was the last king of Babylon, according to the Bible). Balthazar seems ripe for rediscovery. The name has a magical aura to it because of its foreign sound and because the magi were mistaken by some for sorcerers. And the exotic letter *z* puts it on-trend. If you like names that come from *Harry Potter*, *The Chronicles of Narnia*, or *Twilight*, then give this similarly flavored choice a look.

Alternatives: *Jasper, Caspian, Augustus, Tristam, Ichabod, Vladimir*

I LOVE YOU, YOU LOVE ME

For some of us, the name Barney calls to mind Fred Flintstone's neighbor and best friend, Barney Rubble. For others, it suggests Barney, the purple dinosaur with the cloying theme song, featuring "I love you / You love me" in the lyrics. A new generation may be poised to discover a name that could be cool were it not for these unfortunate associations. Barney and its close relatives, Barnaby and Barnabas, mean "consolation." Barney is the name of Neal Patrick Harris's character on the TV sitcom *How I Met Your Mother,* which may help increase its hipster quotient.

Baron Two years after Barron Trump was born, the name Baron hit the list. Why not Prince? (Too rocker.) Or Earl? (Too trailer park.) Duke? (Too Western, sorry John Wayne.) Viscount . . . ? You get the idea. Baron is a way of giving your offspring a fancy title. The word has come to mean "titan" or "captain of industry," as in "railroad baron." Baron (or more likely Barron) can also be a transferred use of the last name.

Variation: *Barron*
Alternatives: *Prince, Duke, Earl, Count, Barry*

Barrett A last name turned first name, Barrett is believed to mean "one who argues." The name is similar to Garrett and might be chosen as an alternative. It evokes poetry, as the maiden name of poet Elizabeth Barrett Browning. And it is a hipper sounding name than the similar Barry. Still, don't blame me when Barrett hits his teen years.

Alternatives: *Tennyson, Bennett, Cabot*

✒ **Bartholomew** Nobody is using Bartholomew these days—and that's a shame. It has great nickname choices, and the name would go well with all the Hannahs and Emmas that are being born today. (Just picture the wedding announcements.) Bartholomew was one of Christ's disciples and was believed to be the same man as Nathaniel, whose name means "God has given." Bartholomew means either "son of Ptolemy"

> ### *I'd love to call him . . .*
> ### Bo
>
> S trong, manly, upbeat, but awfully short. If Bo
> seems too insubstantial, try making it a nickname
> for one of these:
>
> - **BEAUREGARD**   - **BOOKER**   - **BOYD**
> - **BOAZ**   - **BOONE**   - **BRODERICK**
> - **BODHI**   - **BOOTH**   - **BRODIE**
> - **BOLAN**   - **BOWIE**   - **ROBERT**

or "son of a farmer." The name fell out of use after the nineteenth century, whereas Nathaniel has become increasingly popular. Bartholomew would make an innovative alternative.

Variations: *Bartolomeo, Bartolome, Barthelemy*
Nicknames: *Bart, Bat*
Alternatives: *Nathaniel, Barlett, Cornelius, Archibald, Sebastian, Bartleby*

Beau The 1966 film *Beau Geste* inspired parents to name their boys Beau, which means "handsome" in French. A *beau geste* is a gracious but hollow gesture. George Bryan "Beau" Brummel was a Regency dandy who was credited with creating the modern men's suit. And Beau might seem to have a southern cast to it thanks to Beau Wilkes, a character in *Gone with the Wind*; Beauregard Jackson Pickett Burnside, who was Auntie Mame's cheerful Southern husband; and Beauregard "Bo" Duke from *The Dukes of Hazzard* TV series. (Note: Bo has been used as a given name since *The Dukes of Hazzard* appeared in the 1970s.) Great nickname. Give the kid a real name, please.

Variation: *Beauregard*
Nickname: *Bo*
Alternatives: *Roscoe, Jesse, Ty, Amos*

℘ **Beckett** has a cool sound; you can almost hear an *x* in there. And think of all the brilliant rebels the name calls to mind: Thomas à Becket, Archbishop of Canterbury, murdered for sticking to his religious guns; existential Irish playwright Samuel Beckett; and hipster rock musician Beck. You can think of the name as an alternative to Brook—a *beck* is a small stream (as well as a hand gesture, beck and call). And a *becket* is a loop and hook used in sailing, as well as a type of whitefish. So there is a touch of Ireland, genius, and rugged outdoorsiness to the name.

Nickname: *Becks*
Alternatives: *Bennett, Barrett, Abbott, Crockett, Boone*

Beckham British soccer star David Beckham, we salute you. Or at least the parents of some boys born in 2008 do. Beckham, similar to Beckett, means

It's All (Greek and Roman) to Me

Strength and power. That's what you get when you choose the name of a god from the ancient Greek or Roman traditions. You also get an automatic association with a field of interest (Neptune = water; Ares = war), which offers symbolism and meaning. Here are some of my top picks from Mount Olympus.

- **APOLLO:** *the Greek and Roman god of light and truth, Artemis's twin, and most handsome of the gods*

- **ARES** *(Mars): the god of war*

- **DIONYSUS** *(Bacchus): this god of wine likes to party. A lot. But he's also kind and fun and jovial.*

- **EROS** *(Cupid): the cherubic god of love*

- **HEPHAESTUS** *(Vulcan): a skilled craftsman, a good man, and—unfortunately—the deformed cuckolded husband of Aphrodite*

- **HERMES** *(Mercury): messenger of the gods*

- **POSEIDON** *(Neptune): not to give the little guy a power complex or anything— god of the sea, earthquakes, storms, and other big-time stuff*

- **ZEUS** *(Jupiter): lightning-throwing king of the gods*

"place near a stream." The glamorous lifestyle of David and ex–Spice Girl Victoria Beckham caused the name to hit the list the year after they moved from Europe to Los Angeles. (Their son is the cause of the name Brooklyn's popularity.)

Nickname: *Becks*
Alternatives: *Beecham, Beckwith, Kendrick*

Benjamin The youngest son of the biblical Jacob and Rachel, Benjamin's name means "son of the south," referring to his birth in Canaan, or possibly "son of older father." Once a predominantly Jewish name (with Puritan adoptions back in the day—think Ben Franklin), now everyone uses it. Here's to Mrs. Robinson for the spike in the name—her sultry drawl of recent college graduate Benjamin Braddock's name in *The Graduate* may have helped turn people on to the name. And the Benji movies of the 1970s, about a heroic mutt, didn't hurt. (Neither did comic Benny Hill, oddly.) It's a good name for distinguished statesmen: Israeli P.M. Netanyahu, inventor and statesman Franklin, British P.M. Disraeli, United States President Harrison. Note: Nickname Ben has become a name itself. Why not give him the real thing and just call him Ben for short?

Variation: *Benoni (biblical Benjamin's original name)*
Nicknames: *Ben, Benny, Benji*
Alternatives: *Nathaniel, Jonah, Samuel, Aaron*

✐ **Bennett** is the medieval form of the name Benedict, whose wonderful meaning ("blessing") was tarnished by Revolutionary War traitor Benedict Arnold. Has enough time passed for Benedict to come back? Could be. If you're on the fence, you're in luck, because in the meantime we have Bennett. Bennett is a last name, as well as a derivation of Benedict, which gives it preppy squash court cred. Bennett belongs to a yacht club. Bennett is a senator. Bennett knows how to mix a mean Manhattan. Bennett has a literary bent, too: It evokes Jane Austen, as the last name of Elizabeth, heroine of *Pride and Prejudice*.

Nicknames: *Ben, Benny*
Alternatives: *Barrett, Beckett, Abbott, Benedict*

Bentley If you plan to say your son's name with your jaw firmly clenched, this one's for you. Originally meaning "a meadow of bent grass," Bentley has become synonymous with wealth and glamour, courtesy of the ritzy, usually chauffeur-driven car of the same name. This traditional last name also sounds veddy, veddy English. Years ago it might have sounded more like a butler or dog's name, but now it is the master.

Nicknames: *Ben, Benny*
Alternatives: *Wesley, Barkley, Buckley, Trenton, Brice*

Bernard is a "strong bear." A great meaning for a once-popular name that is now in danger of disappearing in the United States. We might have the nickname Bernie to blame: It sounds schlubby and reminds this generation of parents of the slapstick comedy *Weekend at Bernie's*, and worse, of Bernie Madoff, the infamous swindler of the Great Recession. Then again, there's always Saint Bernard, who lived in the Alps and is the patron of mountaineering (hence the bearlike rescue dog named for him).

Variations: *Bjorn, Bernhard, Barnard*
Nickname: *Bernie*
Alternatives: *Hugo, Vincent, Florian, Tobias*

Blaine means "yellow," from an old Gaelic word. It's a common last name that has been turned first name for boys, and one that the girls haven't co-opted yet. Blane was the preppy hero of *Pretty in Pink* (1986) played by brat pack heartthrob Andrew McCarthy. Magician David Blaine also leaps to mind.

Alternatives: *Shane, Dale, Rain, Laird*

Blake has two meanings that are opposite: black and white. The connection to black is obvious; the connection to white is clear when you think of the French word *blanc*. Blake became popular as a boy's first name in the 1940s. Director Blake Edwards and *Dynasty*'s fictional hero Blake Carrington were prominent in the 1980s, when the name really took off. But watch out, boys! The girls tried out the name in the 1990s, and stunning young actress Blake Lively will probably spur more parents to use the name for girls.

Alternatives: *Drake, Caleb, Kane, Tyler*

Blaze Is he the hero of a romance novel or a baby boy? Blaze seems like the former. The name comes

from Blaise, a French name that means "lisping."
Saint Blaise is the patron of sore throats, having saved
a boy from choking. Blaze, however, means "fire"
and suggests he'll be strong-willed, passionate—and
possibly on the cover of *Soap Opera Digest*.

Alternatives: *Brick, Thor, Colt, Zane*

Boston, the capital of Massachusetts, got its name
from the town of Boston, England, which is an
abbreviation of St. Botolph's Town. So if you are
naming your child for the city, you can also consider
Botolph. He will be the only one in his class or your
money back! Botolph is believed to mean "messenger
wolf." Boston is also the name of a classic rock band.
Actor Kurt Russell, who is from Massachusetts, named
one of his sons Boston.

Nickname: *Boss*
Alternatives: *Logan, Houston, Cabot, Elliot*

Braden is fishy. It means "son of salmon" in Gaelic,
suggesting it was an old fishing name. This is a last
name that has been embraced as a boy's first name in
the United States since the 1970s. It is growing ever
more popular and spawning more variations than,
well, a salmon. If you like Braden, keep in mind that
not only will there be many other Bradens of various
spellings in your child's life, there will also be Jadens
and Kadens and Haydens, both boys and girls, with

312

their many spelling variations. This name sounds contemporary, but it may be one to avoid unless you have a strong reason for choosing it, like a family connection.

Variations: *Bradyn, Braeden, Braedon, Braiden, Brayden, Braydon*
Alternatives: *Fisher, Jagger, Brooks*

Bradley An English last name meaning "wide meadow," Bradley has been enthusiastically taken up as a given name. Famous Bradleys include strong, successful men like war hero General Omar Bradley, Senator Bill Bradley, legendary *Washington Post* editor Ben Bradlee, actor Bradley Whitford, and heartthrobs Bradley Cooper and Brad Pitt (who is William Bradley).

Variation: *Bradford*
Nickname: *Brad*
Alternatives: *Avery, Brodie, Leland, Hadley*

ℓ **Brady** is "large chested" in Gaelic, which suggests he's big and brawny, capable, and proud. Brady also retains a sense of warmth and familiarity for those of us who grew up watching *The Brady Bunch*. Those wholesome Bradys were the model of a loving family— they may be partly responsible for the name's gradual rise to the top one hundred. Quarterback Tom Brady probably has helped, too. The name is popular with

Irish Americans, who seem to be looking at the family tree, noting a Brady, and christening a new one.

Alternatives: *Murphy, Kennedy, Sullivan, Clancy, Grady*

Brandon is an English place-name meaning "broom-covered hill." Colonel Brandon was the strong, silent hero of Jane Austen's *Sense and Sensibility*. Marlon Brando remains a model of cool, and his name may have inspired the use of this one. After all these years—and a stint in the top ten in the 1990s thanks to *Beverly Hills 90210*—the name still feels cool but not outrageously trendy. Brandon is sturdy and dependable; he shows few signs of being swept under the rug.

Variation: *Branden*
Alternatives: *Marlon, Bennett, Darcy, Mansfield*

Branson Son of Brandon, Branson for most Americans evokes the town in Missouri that has become a popular Midwest tourist destination filled with theaters and (mostly country) music venues. Branson also calls to mind English impresario and Virgin Airlines founder Richard Branson.

Alternatives: *Lawson, Bradford, Mason*

Braxton An alternative to the popular Jackson, Braxton is a variation of Brock, which means "town of badgers." Braxton has been on the rise since 1984, and is gaining steam thanks to the similarity to Jackson, which is a very popular boy's name now. Parents looking for the cool *X* factor may be attracted to this name.

Alternatives: *Maddox, Brock, Paxton, Leighton, Jackson*

Brendan is an old Celtic name meaning "prince," and this adventurous little royal is about as Irish as they come. Saint Brendan, from the sixth century, is known as "the navigator" for his courageous sea-faring travels, which became folkloric legends in Ireland. One legend has it that he was the first Irish person to set foot in America. It's unlikely that the man really made it to the New World, but the name certainly did (it was especially trendy in the 1940s). Famous Brendans include boisterous Irish playwright Brendan Behan and actors Brendan Fraser and Gleeson.

Variations: *Brenden, Brendon*
Alternatives: *Connor, Liam, Finnegan, Ryan*

Brennan is a name for an Irish American boy. Brennan is a common last name that has become a first name, an edgier version of the traditional first name Brendan. The meaning can be "teardrop" or "raven."

Variation: *Brennen*
Alternatives: *Connolly, Sullivan, Madden, Brian*

The Butcher, the Baker, the Candlestick Maker

In ye olde days, many people took their name from their job. Picture a medieval village and the bustle of all the folks at work there: You had the butcher, the baker, the candlestick maker . . . plus the poet, the brewer, and the cloth dyer. These occupations were passed down from father to son, and the ancestral profession eventually became the family name. Well, what's medieval is now modern—today's parents are using these last names as cool first names. Here are some of the best choices.

- **ABBOTT** *(high-ranking monk)*
- **ARCHER**
- **BAILEY** *(manager of the bailey, overseer of craftsmen)*
- **BAKER**
- **BARD** *(poet)*
- **BAXTER** *(another word for baker)*
- **BISHOP**
- **BREWER** or **BREWSTER** *(beer maker)*
- **CANNON** *(church official)*
- **CARTER** *(transports things by cart)*
- **CARTWRIGHT** *(cartmaker)*
- **CARVER**
- **CHAMBERLAIN** *(bedroom attendant)*
- **CHANDLER** *(candle maker)*
- **CHAPLAIN** *(clergyman)*
- **CHAPMAN** *(traveling peddlar)*
- **CLARK** *(clerk)*
- **COOK**
- **COOPER** *(makes and repairs casks and barrels)*
- **DEXTER** *(dyer)*
- **DRAPER** *(fabric worker)*
- **DRUMMER**
- **DYER** *(dyes fabric)*
- **FARMER**
- **FISHER**

- **FLETCHER** *(maker of bows and arrows; flèche is French for arrow)*

- **FORESTER**

- **GARDNER**

- **HARPER** *(harp player)*

- **HAYWARD** *(fence keeper)*

- **HERALD** *(announces news)*

- **HUNTER**

- **JACKMAN** *(nobleman's attendant)*

- **JAGGER** *(fishmonger)*

- **JUDGE**

- **KNIGHT**

- **LAIRD** *(Scottish landowner)*

- **MARSHALL** *(officer in charge of the horses, carts, and wagons)*

- **MASON** *(bricklayer)*

- **MAYOR**

- **MERCER** *(fabric seller)*

- **MILLER** *(turns grain to flour)*

- **MINER**

- **PAGE** *(servant)*

- **PALMER** *(pilgrim to the Holy Land)*

- **PARKER** *(gamekeeper; tender of the parks)*

- **PILOT**

- **PIPER**

- **PORTER**

- **POTTER**

- **REEVE** *(administrative officer)*

- **REVEL** *(court entertainer)*

- **SAILOR**

- **SAWYER** *(one who saws)*

- **SCOUT**

- **SHEPHERD**

- **SMITH** *(blacksmith)*

- **SPENCER** *(dispenser)*

- **TANNER** *(leatherworker who tans hides)*

- **TAYLOR** *(tailor)*

- **THATCHER** *(thatches roofs)*

- **TUCKER** *(fabric worker)*

- **TURNER** *(turns wood on a lathe)*

- **WALKER** *(fabric worker)*

- **WEAVER**

- **WEBSTER** *(weaver, loom operator)*

Brent Between Brent and Brenton, there's fire on the mountain: Brent means "hill" and Brenton means "fire." Both are English place-names and last names that became popular in the 1970s and '80s. They are on the wane now.

Variation: *Brenton*
Alternatives: *Trent, Benson, Hansen, Kent*

Brett is Brittany for boys. It comes from "Breton" or "from Bretagne," which means "from Brittany." Brett even followed the trend of Brittany, peaking in the 1970s through early 1990s, though never getting near the top ten. It spiked considerably in the wake of the 1950s TV show *Maverick*, which starred James Garner as gambler Bret Maverick. The name works for sporting types like baseball player Brett Butler and football player Brett Favre.

Alternatives: *Rhett, Bart, Jett, Trey*

Brian was a king of Ireland in the 900s, so it makes sense that the Celtic name means "noble" or "exalted." Brian was in the top ten in the 1970s, during which time *Brian's Song*, a weepy football movie, and Monty Python's *Life of Brian* were released. Brian Wilson was one of the Beach Boys, Brian Jones was in the Rolling Stones, and Brian De Palma is a movie director. Bryant Gumbel was the *Today* show cohost for years.

Variations: *Bryan, Bryant*
Alternatives: *Kevin, Connor, Brendan, Ryan, Patrick*

Brice, like all names beginning with *Br*, has a strength and swagger to it. Most *Br* boys, from Brian to Bruno, have a bit of brawniness and even brutishness to them. Brice, like Brett, is a little softer than some of the others, a guy in touch with his feminine side. The name means "speckled." Bryson can mean either "son of Brice" or "strength of the sea." There's an additional connection to Mother Nature here: Bryce Canyon is a spectacular natural wonder in Utah.

Variations: *Bryce, Brycen, Bryson*
Alternatives: *Byron, Cyrus, Dyson, Simon*

Brock sounds solid, like the rock in his name. He sounds like someone who can solve problems, handle things manfully. "Don't do that; leave it for Brock to deal with." Just don't tell anyone what Brock used to mean. (It's a Celtic last name that means "he looks like a badger.")

Alternatives: *Dirk, Rocco, Brooks, Kurt, Scott*

Broderick sounds mighty or kingly; say the name and you can almost hear the armor clanging and the horse hooves pounding. Broderick sounds like he's up to any task, no matter how difficult. This surname turned first name from the British Isles tempers

The Golden Era of Film

I n Hollywood's heyday—the 1940s and 1950s— men were square-jawed and strong-willed, manly yet dreamy at the same time. If you're looking to raise a ruggedly handsome, can-do, screen idol type, consider this batch of star-kissed names.

- **BRODERICK** *(Crawford)*
- **BUSTER** *(Keaton)*
- **CARY** *(Grant)*
- **CLARK** *(Gable)*
- **ELIA** *(Kazan)*
- **ERNEST** *(Borgnine)*
- **GARY** *(Cooper)*
- **GREGORY** *(Peck)*
- **HAROLD** *(Lloyd)*
- **HUMPHREY** *(Bogart)*
- **KARL** *(Malden)*
- **LAURENCE** *(Olivier)*
- **LEE** *(J. Cobb, Marvin)*
- **LIONEL** *(Barrymore)*
- **SPENCER** *(Tracy)*
- **WALTER** *(Huston, Matthau)*

ancient glory with the familiarity and affability of actor Matthew Broderick. It's decidedly grown-up, but has some cute nickname options for when he's still wearing a onesie.

Nicknames: *Brodie, Brody, Rick, Ricky*
Alternatives: *Corbin, Roderick, Richardson, Derek, Thane*

Brodie sounds like a nickname for the friendliest guy on campus. Picture him tossing a frisbee or tapping a keg. Traditionally, the name was either Ukranian (usually Jewish) as Brody or Scottish as Brodie. Actors Adam Brody and Adrien Brody, reality TV personality Brody Jenner, as well as alpine skier Bode Miller (close enough) keep the name young and hip. He might be Grody Brodie for a while in grade school, but he'll be too cool to care.

Variation: *Brody*
Alternatives: *Bruce, Sullivan, Gordy, Jonah*

Brogan Need some wood chopped? Brogan is your guy. This is the name of a manly Celt—you can hear an Irish brogue in his name, though the meaning of the name is "shoe." And there is a bit of a rogue in there too, an aspect that may make this name appealing when Brogan grows up.

Alternatives: *Rogan, Logan, Brodie, Keegan*

Bronson You don't mess with a guy named Bronson. He means business. The association with tough-guy actor Charles Bronson is indelible; the English name itself sounds stubborn. Bronson's literal meaning is "brown son."

Alternatives: *Mason, Eastwood, Coburn, Huston*

Brooks belongs to the country club, plays a mean game of bridge, and knows his way around a sailboat. An upper-crust staple, Brooks is refined, debonair, and successful. The name calls to mind Brooks Brothers,

> *I'd love it if he sounded...*
> ## Italian
>
> | | | |
> |---|---|---|
> | ~ ALESSANDRO | ~ GIOVANNI | ~ PAOLO |
> | ~ BRUNO | ~ LORENZO | ~ PIETRO |
> | ~ EDOARDO | ~ LUCA | ~ ROCCO |
> | ~ ENZO | ~ LUDOVICO | ~ RODRIGO |
> | ~ FEDERICO | ~ LUIGI | ~ SERGIO |
> | ~ FRANCESCO | ~ MARCO | ~ SILVIO |
> | ~ GIANCARLO | ~ MASSIMO | ~ VINCENZO |
> | ~ GIORGIO | ~ ORLANDO | ~ VITTORIO |

where he might shop, and the Brooks School, where he might prep.

Alternatives: *River, Calder, Burns, Firth, Holden*

✏ **Bruce** is the name of a powerful Scottish clan, whose most famous member, Robert the Bruce, became king of Scotland in the fourteenth century. Other powerful Bruces include action-movie star Bruce Willis; decathlete Bruce Jenner; Bruce Wayne, aka Batman; and Bruce Banner, aka the Incredible Hulk. This sturdy name is strong but subtle, a sleeper but a keeper.

Alternatives: *Keith, Robert, Donald, Craig*

Bruno It's not just for Italians anymore. Everyone is realizing how cute but still masculine this name is; it is quickly migrating from Italian, South American, and German families to the mainstream. The name means "brown." Bruno Kirby was a beloved character actor who appeared frequently alongside Billy Crystal. There was a St. Bruno of Calabria. Even the silly fashion character Brüno played by Sacha Baron Cohen can't keep this good name down.

Alternatives: *Rocco, Milo, Dino, Gino*

Byron may become a poet and a heartthrob, like his namesake George Gordon, Lord Byron. Lord Byron gave his name to the term "byronic," which suggests a magnetic, mysterious rebel. The name Byron means "of the barns," and was used for cattle keepers. But this pastoral origin is overshadowed by the romantic allure of the poet.

Alternatives: *Heathcliff, Brian, Keats, James, Brice, Poe*

C

Caden Take Jaden and add some Cadence and what do you get? Caden. This name has skyrocketed from nonexistence in the 1980s to the top one hundred. The word *cade* means "like a lump," and there was a character in *Gone with the Wind* named Cade. It's the

tonal similarity to hot names like Aidan, Braden,
and Jaden that has boosted this name and its
variations.

Variations: *Cade, Caiden, Cayden, Kaden*
Alternatives: *Caleb, Aidan, Rain, Peyton*

Caleb was a biblical Israelite who left Egypt with
Moses and successfully returned to Canaan. He, along
with Joshua, believed that the Israelites could reclaim
the Promised Land. Caleb was known for his great
faith in God. The name is an old-fashioned favorite
that was rediscovered in the 1960s and is now roaring
back into style. It's an appealing alternative to just-
about-everywhere Jacob, but be warned that it's also
quite popular in its own right.

Variations: *Kaleb, Cael, Cale, Kael, Kale*
Alternatives: *Joshua, Jonah, Lucas, Jacob, Abel*

Callum is a Scottish name that comes from *columba,*
which means "dove" in Latin. Saint Columba is
credited with bringing Christianity from Ireland to
Scotland in the sixth century, and variations of his
name are still widely used in Scotland: Calum and
Malcolm ("follower of St. Columba"). The dove is
a symbol of peace and kindness. Colm is the Irish
version of the name.

Variations: *Colm, Malcolm, Calum*
Alternatives: *Colin, Malcolm, Brodie, Angus, Sean*

Calvin was coined as a first name in honor of the French religious leader who gave us Calvinism, Jean Calvin. The name actually means "bald," from the French word *chauve*. Nowadays other Calvins leap to mind: cartoon rascal Calvin from *Calvin and Hobbes*, designer Calvin Klein, president Calvin Coolidge.

Variation: *Alvin*
Alternatives: *Dennis, Ralph, Otis, Aldo*

Camden A place-name meaning "enclosed valley," the name Camden can be used to split the difference between Cameron and Caden. As a place-name, it evokes England, Maine, and New Jersey.

Variation: *Kamden*
Alternatives: *Trenton, Boston, Cameron*

Cameron A Scottish clan name, Cameron means "crooked nose." Popular with both boys (directors Cameron Crowe, James Cameron) as well as girls (actress Cameron Diaz).

Variations: *Camren, Camron, Camryn, Kameron, Kamren, Kamron*
Alternatives: *Camden, Campbell, Fraser, Graham*

Cannon An interesting choice for parents with an artistic bent: A canon is a song, a collection of literary works, a camera brand. It is also a member of the church clergy. With two *n*'s it is a gun—but don't worry, this one's not loaded. In all of its various forms, Cannon suggests dignity and strength.

Alternatives: *Channing, Colt, Madden, Logan*

Carl is related to Charles. The name means "free man" and established itself as one of the great boy's names when Charlemagne became Holy Roman Emperor in the 800s. His name in Latin, Carolus Magnus, shows the connection between Carl and Charles. Carl and Karl are popular in Scandinavia; several Swedish kings have borne the name. Famous Carls include director Carl Reiner, scientist Carl Sagan, and psychiatrist Carl Jung. If you want your Carl to be a little edgier, change the *C* to a *K*, or go with the Italian or Spanish equivalents Carlo and Carlos.

Variations: *Karl, Charles, Carlo, Carlos*
Alternatives: *Leif, Lars, Hugo, Igor, Franz*

Carmelo offers a nod to the Virgin Mary, one of whose guises is Our Lady of Carmel, a reference to the mountain in Israel called Carmel. Carmel in Hebrew means "garden." The name is popular with Italian and Spanish speakers.

Alternatives: *Mario, Angelo, Romeo*

Carson Rugged, outdoorsy, cool, Carson knows his way around a trail and keeps his wits about him when

A Little Bit Country, A Little Bit Rock 'n' Roll

The world of country music and rockabilly is rich with distinctive, colorful, endearing names. Our top picks are:

- **BUCK** (Owens)
- **BUDDY** (Holly)
- **CASH** (Johnny)
- **CLINT** (Black)
- **DWIGHT** (Yoakam)
- **EARLE** (Steve)
- **ELVIS** (Presley)
- **FOGERTY** (John and Tom)
- **GARTH** (Brooks)
- **HANK** (Williams)
- **KEITH** (Toby, Urban)
- **KENNY** (Rogers)
- **LEWIS** (Jerry Lee)
- **NEIL** (Young)
- **RASCAL** (Flatts): the band's first word is probably best used as a nickname
- **RYAN** (Adams)
- **TRAVIS** (Tritt)
- **WAYLON** (Jennings)
- **WILLIE** (Nelson)

danger appears. He gets his bravery and brawn from the association with nineteenth-century frontiersman Kit Carson and the city in Nevada named for him, Carson City. And there's a jocular note to the name from TV personality Carson Daly and comedian Johnny Carson.

Variations: *Carsen, Karson*
Alternatives: *Clark, Boone, Preston*

Carter Thank the TV show *ER* and actor Noah Wylie for this one. Wylie played Dr. John Carter, on the show from 1994 to the end in 2009, who was always referred to by his last name. Audiences watched him grow from a resident to an expert, and we all got used to the name. Carter is a trade name for someone who carts goods around (see pages 316–317).

Variation: *Karter*
Alternatives: *Chandler, Cooper, Fletcher, Turner*

Casey was a classic boy-next-door name until the girls discovered it. Now that girls are assuming the name (see page 48), boys are shying away. One clever way of using Casey is as a nickname for a boy with the initials K. C. (à la KC and the Sunshine Band).

Variations: *Kasey, Case*
Alternatives: *Callahan, Gallagher, Sullivan, Brodie*

Cash Legendary singer Johnny Cash is the inspiration for this name. The "Man in Black" died in 2003, the same year the name started hitting popularity charts. A country boy from a poor family, Cash overcame difficult circumstances to achieve enormous success. His songs celebrated struggle and redemption. It's auspicious, too, that the name suggests wealth.

Variation: *Kash*
Alternatives: *Bard, Nash, Denver, Travis*

Cason Take Casey, add one dash of Carson and one of Mason and another of Caden, and voila! Cason. This frankenname has been popular since 2002 and keeps rolling along.

Variations: *Kasen, Kason*
Alternatives: *Mason, Carson, Cass*

Cassius If you want your boy to fly like a butterfly and sting like a bee, then Cassius could be a knockout. Cassius Clay was boxer Muhammed Ali's birth name. And on a darker note, it was also the name of two high-profile assassins, the man who killed Julius Caesar and the man who killed Caligula. Cassius doesn't mess around.

Nickname: *Cass*
Alternatives: *Tobias, Titus, Julian, Bruno*

Cedric was made up by Sir Walter Scott for his 1819 novel *Ivanhoe,* and was the first name of the pampered child in *Little Lord Fauntleroy.* The first modern Cedric that leaps to most Americans' minds is movie actor Cedric the Entertainer. The name has a continental air, and indeed it's popular in France. It's on the wane in the United States.

Alternatives: *Ivan, Walter, Serden, Broderick*

Cesar Julius and Augustus Caesar influenced the world in countless ways, including naming trends. Julian, August, and Cesar are still in common use.

César (say-TSAR) is usually used by Hispanic, French, and Italian families (in Italy it appears as Cesare, CHAY-tsar-ay). The name suggests imperial power— it became a generic word for "emperor" and gave us the words *tsar* and *kaiser*.

Nickname: *Che*
Alternatives: *August, Manuel, Angel, Diego*

Chad is a child of the 1970s. The name was in the top twenty-five for a brief, shining moment. It's an obscure name from a forgotten seventh-century saint, Ceadda. Chad sounds like a strapping athlete or surfer dude. Or a country in Africa.

Alternatives: *Chet, Chas, Chase, Dag*

Chaim means "life" in Hebrew (think of the famous toast *l'chaim!*, which means "to life!"). It's the male equivalent of Chava (or Hava) or Eve. Famous Chaims include writer Chaim Potok and Kiss lead singer Gene Simmons, né Chaim Witz. It's not hard to see why Simmons switched things up: Chaim is more bespectacled bookworm than leather-clad rocker.

Variations: *Hyman, Chayyim*
Alternatives: *Ruben, Adam, Adriel, Shlomo*

Chance Luck. Good fortune. Hap. Chance suggests blessings bestowed with some randomness. The name can also be short for Chancellor, a trade name for someone of high rank in an organization. The chancellor used to be the gatekeeper for someone even more powerful than himself. Chance was the name of the simple gardener in Jerzy Kozinski's novella *Being There* (which later became a cult movie starring Peter Sellers); in it, Chance becomes an unlikely sage.

Variations: *Chancellor, Chauncey*
Alternatives: *Chase, Tucker, Parker, Cash*

Chandler is an old flame that's still burning. From the French word for "candle," the chandler was a tradesman who sold candles, soap, and sometimes other specific supplies, often for ships. The name really heated up in the 1990s, thanks to *Friends* character Chandler Bing. Though his flame burns less brightly these days, Chandler plays nicely with other now-trendy tradesmen like Cooper, Bailey, Palmer, and Fletcher.

Alternatives: *Archer, Tucker, Fuller, Porter*

Charles is one of the great traditional boy's names. A name for kings, starting most famously in the 700s with Charlemagne ("Charles the Great"), the legendary Holy Roman Emperor. The name migrated from the continent to England with Mary Queen of Scots, who chose it for her son, who then passed it down. Charles appears all over the world in nearly every language and in a variety of formats. Famous

Chucks include Prince Charles of England, former French president Charles de Gaulle, naturalist Charles Darwin, writer Charles Dickens, and of course Snoopy's pal Charlie Brown. The name becomes cute as Charlie, rugged or folksy as Chuck, collar-popping preppy as Chaz. Carlos is the Spanish variation and Carlo the Italian.

Variations: *Carlo, Carlos, Carl, Carol, Karol, Karoly, Charlton*
Nicknames: *Charlie, Chaz, Chas, Chip, Chuck*
Alternatives: *George, Henry, William, James*

Chase is a hunter, running after his prey and seizing opportunities. The name sounds preppy and affluent, thanks in part to investment bank JP Morgan Chase. Chase has many options—he could be an actor, an athlete, an outdoorsman, even a politician.

Variation: *Chace*
Alternatives: *Hunter, Tad, Chaz, Dalton*

Christian means—no surprise here—"follower of Christ." These are "the anointed" (Christ's name in Greek), and they wear their faiths (or those of their parents) on their sleeves. The name has historically been popular in Scandinavia (hello, Hans Christian Anderson); in the last thirty years it has taken off in the United States. In Hollywood, we have the famed actors Christian Bale and Christian Slater. In fashion, the famed Christian Dior and Christian Lacroix.

Variations: *Cristian, Kristian*
Nicknames: *Chris, Christy (Irish), Kit, Kris*
Alternatives: *Tristan, Crispin, Ashton, Preston*

Christopher is a popular Christian name that means "bearing Christ with me." It hit the big time after the *Winnie-the-Pooh* books, which feature a little boy named Christopher Robin, took off in the 1940s. Saint Christopher is the patron saint of travelers (his namesake Christopher Columbus seemed to enjoy his patronage). He was believed to have carried the baby Christ across a river.

Variations: *Cristopher, Cristofer, Christophe, Christoforo, Kristofer, Kristoforos*
Nicknames: *Chris, Christy (Irish), Kit, Kris, Christie (Irish), Chip, Topher*
Alternatives: *Simon, Matthew, Barnabas, Nathaniel*

Clarence This name, which comes from the River Clare in England and has been in use since the late 1800s, suggests clarity and light. And the historical and pop culture references strengthen the association: Clarence Darrow was a famous lawyer who defended John Scopes in the Scopes monkey trial and was a hero for civil libertarians. Clarence Thomas is a Supreme Court Justice. And in the film *It's a Wonderful Life*, Clarence is the guardian angel of hero George Bailey.

Alternatives: *Darcy, Lawrence, Dudley, Spencer, Gavin*

Favorite Catholic Saints

I f you name your child for a saint, he will have a patron looking out for him. Choose according to each saint's specialty as well as the beauty and meaning of his name. There are thousands of saints. My favorites include:

- **ADALBERT:** *In 1997, Pope John Paul II held a service commemorating the one-thousandth anniversary of Adalbert's martyrdom. In attendance were the heads of seven European states and about a million believers.*

- **AMBROSE:** *Patron saint of beekeepers, who was one of the most important theological figures of the fourth century*

- **ANTHONY:** *Patron saint of things that are lost. Useful for finding missing keys, wallets, etc.*

- **AUGUSTINE:** *Philosopher, theologian, and patron saint of brewers and printmakers*

- **BLAISE:** *Was attacked and martyred with iron carding combs (like dog brushes with fine metal teeth), and so became the patron saint of wool carders*

- **BONAVENTURE:** *Great man of letters, who gave his name to a number of schools and universities and whose only remaining relic is his hand and arm*

✐ **Clark** Actor Clark Gable, Superman alter ego Clark Kent, explorer William Clark (of Lewis and Clark fame)—Clark is a competent, ruggedly handsome, but understated guy. A trade name meaning "clerk," clarks were well-educated scribes and scholars of the Middle Ages. Clark Griswold, Chevy Chase's character in *National Lampoon's Vacation*, may be the only bumbling Clark around.

- **BRENDAN:** *One of the twelve apostles of Ireland, a patron saint of sailors*

- **CHRISTOPHER:** *Eighteen-foot-tall patron saint of travelers (and those with toothaches)*

- **FRANCIS** *(of Assisi): Patron saint of animals and the environment, whose famous prayer includes the phrase "where there is hatred, let me sow love"*

- **JUDE:** *One of the twelve apostles. Patron of desperate situations.*

- **MATTHEW:** *Former tax collector (and so patron saint of accountants) and author of the first Gospel in the Bible*

- **MATTHIAS:** *Replaced Judas as the twelfth apostle; the patron saint of tailors and carpenters*

- **PATRICK:** *After banishing snakes from the Emerald Isle and illustrating the Trinity with a shamrock, Patrick became the patron saint of Ireland.*

- **PETER:** *Son of John the Baptist, Peter was an early Christian leader and is patron saint of many things, including bakers, locksmiths, and the city of Las Vegas.*

- **STEPHEN:** *The Greek word stephanos means "crown." Stephen was the first martyr of the Christian Church.*

- **THOMAS** *(Aquinas): Considered by many to be the Church's greatest theologian and philosopher; patron saint of students and schools*

But he was so charming and well-meaning, we can overlook it. This one is nickname-free.

Variation: *Clarke*
Alternatives: *Blake, Boone, Laird, Palmer*

Clay is something to be molded; it is filled with potential and future greatness. It is the raw material of masterpieces, the medium of artists. A place-name and last name that have become first names, Clay is a description of the earth. It's a name that sounds solid but can appeal to New Agey tastes as well.

Variation: *Clayton*
Alternatives: *Trey, Micah, Forest, River, Trace*

Clinton An English last name and place-name, Clinton has been used as a first name since the 1800s. It was associated with politics then—George Clinton was a governor of New York—and now—Bill and Hillary Clinton have been in the spotlight since the 1990s. While Clinton is a city mouse, Clint is a country mouse—this nickname has a flinty, western feel to it (think actor-director Clint Eastwood and singer Clint Black).

Nickname: *Clint*
Alternatives: *Easton, Leighton, Leland, Clyde*

Cody All things Wild West were in vogue in the 1950s, and many little boys were named Cody as a result. "Buffalo Bill" Cody was a soldier, Pony Express rider, and finally celebrity showman. He helped found the city of Cody, Wyoming. The name suggests bravery, intrepid outdoorsiness, and cowboys.

Variation: *Kody*
Alternatives: *Carson, Brodie, Gordon, Jesse, Parker*

Cohen There are plenty of Kennedys, Finlays, Keegans, and other kids given Irish or Anglo last names as first names. Where are the Rosensweigs? The Feldmans? At last, there are Cohens. Cohen means "priest," and it is one of the most common Jewish last names. It makes a cute first name for kids of any stripe, though it may appeal most to parents with Jewish roots.

Alternatives: *Koen, Cowan, Levi, Ruben*

Colby means "charcoal place," and there are several Colby towns in England. As a name it suggests a dark, swarthy air. Colby is capable, reliable, yet the *y* on the end makes him approachable. For those parents who remember the Colby family from the 1980s soap opera *Dynasty*, there's a patrician whiff to the name as well.

Variation: *Colton*
Alternatives: *Clayton, Corbin, Barclay, Cornell*

I'd love it if he sounded . . .
Irish

~ AIDAN	~ DESMOND	~ KIERAN
~ COLM	~ DONAL	~ NIALL
~ CONNOR	~ EAMON	~ NOLAN
~ CORMAC	~ FINBAR	~ RORY
~ DECLAN	~ FINN	~ SEAMUS

Cole Traditionally the name Cole was given to boys with dark hair—not surprisingly, it means "coal." Nowadays, Cole is more likely to be suave than swarthy. The name conjures images of composer and lyricist Cole Porter and crooner Nat "King" Cole. And there's a sense he'll be a merry old soul thanks to "Old King Cole."

Variations: *Coleman, Colbert, Colson, Nicholas*
Alternatives: *Blake, Dolan, Kieran*

Colin File Colin with Reginald, Nigel, and Rupert under veddy, veddy British. Colin is an old nickname of Nicholas on the one hand, and a relation of Calum (see Callum, page 324) on the other. Actors Colin Firth and Farrell give the name heartthrob appeal. Former secretary of state Colin Powell (who pronounces it COEH-lin—unlike the more common KAW-lin) gives it authority.

Variation: *Collin*
Alternatives: *Nigel, Simon, Rupert, Elliot*

Colt is bursting with youthful vigor, brashness, and the spirit of the west. A colt is a young horse as well as a famous brand of firearm. Colton, which is closer in meaning to Colby (see page 337), sounds like the no-nonsense sheriff of a frontier town. It's like Colt, but all grown-up.

Variations: *Colten, Kolton, Kolten*
Alternatives: *Remington, Buck, Blaze, Wesson*

Connor was an ancient Irish king whose name means "lover of hounds." The name is one from the new generation of names that parents use to celebrate their Irish heritage. Famous Connors include singer Sinead O'Connor, Justice Sandra Day O'Connor, Irish writer Conor Cruise O'Brien, and Tom Cruise and Nicole Kidman's son Connor Cruise. Connor MacLeod was the name of the title character in the film *The Highlander* (1986), which helped the name rise to fame.

Variations: *Conner, Conor, Konner, Konnor*
Alternatives: *Liam, Declan, Kieran, Brendan*

Conrad is a "strong counselor," and the name sounds appropriately masculine and forceful. It is popular in northern Europe and Scandinavia, where it was the name of several saints and kings. Hotel pioneer Conrad Hilton, writer James Conrad, and fictional Elvis-like character in *Bye Bye Birdie*, Conrad Birdie, have used the name.

Variation: *Konrad*
Nicknames: *Connie, Curt*
Alternatives: *Soren, Harald, Gunnar, Jesper*

Cooper The cooper was once the barrel maker of the medieval village. Now he's more likely to be the young hipster shooting hoops than the old tradesman fitting hoops on casks. The name is a success story, appearing in 1982 and whizzing up the charts to the top one hundred in 2007. The name has a playful quality thanks to the *cooing* sound in it. It also gets sturdiness from the Gary Cooper (and even Bradley Cooper) association, and a cool, renegade factor from rocker Alice Cooper.

Nicknames: *Super Cooper, Coop*
Alternatives: *Tanner, Thatcher, Fletcher, Tucker*

Corbin Call him "the crow." Corbin is a last name that comes from the French *corbeau,* for crow. Hit TV show *L.A. Law* featured a rakish lawyer Arnie Becker played by actor Corbin Bernsen. Corbin took hold a year after the series premiere and remains popular. It feels decidedly posh and would lend a preppy note to any name.

Alternatives: *Becker, Colby, Holden*

Corey had thirty good years, the 1960s through the 1990s. Now he seems stuck in the '80s, when Corey Hart crooned "I Wear My Sunglasses at Night" and the "two Coreys," Corey Haim and Corey Feldman, ruled the Hollywood teen scene. Although the name seems youthful, it's very much of an era. If you must have Corey, consider Cornelius, opposite.

Variations: *Cory, Kori*
Alternatives: *Colby, Rudy, Terry, Marley*

✒ **Cornelius** is a serious, august name. It is Roman, like Julius, which gives it an imperial air. And it evokes the likes of railroad titan Cornelius Vanderbilt and Cornelius, the wise old elephant in the Babar series of children's books. Saint Cornelius, an early Pope, is the patron of cattle; the word Cornelius means "horn."

Nicknames: *Neil, Neely, Corey, Corney*
Alternatives: *Barnaby, Archibald, Casper, Otis*

Cortez, the Spanish family name, means "courteous" or "courtly." You can hear the heartbeat of adventure in it thanks to explorer Hernán Cortés, who helped Spain colonize the New World in the 1500s; it's also similar to the Spanish word for heart, *corazón*. Cortez is perfectly on-trend. The name features an exotic letter, *z*, its sound and meaning are both bold, and it's a last name turned first name.

Variation: *Curtis*
Alternatives: *Lopez, Rodriguez, Martinez, Cruz*

Craig is "rock" in Gaelic (think "craggy"). It's a Scottish last name that has been embraced as a first name throughout the English-speaking world. While the name hasn't risen in popularity of late, it's ubiquitous thanks to Craig Newmark, who founded the website Craigslist. No nicknames here.

Alternatives: *Peter, Rocco, Keith, Bruce*

Cruz "Cross" in Spanish, Cruz is a popular Hispanic last name turned first name. It's been a mainstay for Spanish-speaking families, and it's poised to go even more mainstream. It has two things working in its favor: the exotic letter *z*, and an association with celebrities like Penelope Cruz, Cruz Beckham (Posh and Beck's middle son), and Tom Cruise (it counts!). The name is a traditional one that is rooted in Catholicism, yet sounds edgy and alternative.

Alternatives: *Brooklyn, Santino, Ulises/Ulysses*

Cullen An NFL running back during the 1970s, Cullen Bryant is credited with helping the L.A. Rams reach the Super Bowl in 1979. Clearly he made an impression: Namesakes began appearing in numbers in the 1980s. The name is Irish and English, with a variety of meanings from "holly" to "nook." Cullen is the last name of the vampire family in the *Twilight* series. With so many fans thirsty for vampire blood, look for the name to rise in popularity even more.

Alternatives: *Sullivan, Mullen, Callahan, Colin*

Curtis Like Cortez, Curtis is "courteous." Curt can be a nickname for either Curtis or Conrad. Be very careful when pairing Curtis with a last name. The name can read as "Curt is . . ." and become a prophesy.

African American Heroes

C elebrate creativity, passion, and ingenuity with the name of one of these African American pioneers.

- **ARMSTRONG:** *trumpet legend Louis Armstrong*

- **BOOKER:** *education reformer Booker T. Washington*

- **CARVER:** *scientist renowned for his work on peanuts, George Washington Carver*

- **CLAUDE:** *writer Claude McKay*

- **CULLEN:** *poet Countee Cullen*

- **ELLINGTON:** *bandleader Duke Ellington; call him Eli or Ellis for short*

- **LANGSTON:** *poet Langston Hughes*

- **LAWRENCE:** *painter Jacob Lawrence*

- **MALCOLM:** *civil rights activist Malcolm X*

- **MARCUS:** *civil rights leader Marcus Garvey*

- **PERCY:** *chemist and inventor Percy Lavon Julian*

- **SARGENT:** *artist Sargent Johnson*

- **WALKER:** *Madam C. J. Walker was a hair care entrepreneur; novelist Alice Walker*

- **WALLER:** *musician Fats Waller*

- **WELDON:** *novelist James Weldon Johnson*

It hasn't hurt PGA golfer Curtis Strange, but it can be a grade school "kick me" sign.

Variation: *Kurt*

Alternatives: *Davis, Curran, Karl, Turk*

✏ **Cyrus** the Great was the fifth-century B.C. Persian leader who conquered Babylon to found his empire. The name is related to Cyril. Saint Cyril was a missionary who brought Christianity to the Slavic world. (The Cyrillic alphabet was named in honor of him.) The biggest Cyrus in the universe now is singer Miley who, with her father Billy Ray, gives the name country swagger with a touch of city chic.

Variation: *Cyril*
Alternatives: *Darius, Xerxes, Troy, Waylon, Roscoe*

Ancient Egypt, Contemporary Names

I f you are looking for an offbeat way to celebrate Africa, consider the names of Ancient Egypt— they're colorful, meaningful, and unique.

- **AMUN:** *the god of creation*

- **CIPPUS:** *a pointed, rectangular column, commonly depicting the exploits of Horus*

- **HEKA:** *the ancient Egyptian term for magic*

- **HORUS:** *sky god*

- **KHUFU:** *built the great pyramid of Giza*

- **NECHO:** *pharaoh from 609 to 594 B.C. who rebuilt the Egyptian fleet and conquered Syria*

- **OSIRIS:** *god of rebirth*

- **RA:** *sun god*

- **RAMSES:** *great builder, campaigner, aka Ozymandias*

- **UNAS:** *vases from Unas's rule show giraffes and other exotic animals he brought to Egypt after establishing trade with much of the surrounding area*

D

Dakota Individualistic, pioneering, remote, wild. As familiar as this Indian tribe name has become (there are two states named for it, as well as the storied Manhattan apartment building), it continues to have an allure of western exoticism and adventure. Dakota started life as a name for boys but was quickly taken up by the girls (think actress Dakota Fanning). Now the boys are losing interest. Go west, young men! Maybe Alaska will be the next big thing.

Alternatives: *Yukon, Alaska, Jackson, Apache, Hawk*

Dallas, like Dale (see Dalton, below) means "valley." But the names couldn't be farther apart in temperament. Dale is sweetly folksy, whereas Dallas is rustic, individualist, and, yes, Texan. George Dallas for whom the Texas city was named was Scottish and his name was based on a place-name in his homeland. Dallas sounds like it could be trendy like Dakota or Montana, but it is as solid and steadfast as a cowboy.

Alternatives: *Houston, Logan, Wyatt, Vernon*

Dalton From the same root as Dale, which means "valley," Dalton can have James Bond–like allure (thanks to Timothy Dalton), a country rebel edge

(Patrick Swayze's character in *Road House* was Dalton),
or an upper-class (evoking the tony Manhattan prep
school). Dale, on the other hand, has a more obvious
nature connection, but it can go too far in that
direction; for some it may be reminiscent of the Disney
chipmunks Chip 'n Dale. (If you name your boy Dale,
don't name his brother Charles!)

Alternatives: *Brooks, Dell, Val, Hale, Alton, Taft, Andover*

Damian and Cosmas were Greek brothers and
martyrs from the fourth century. The name Damian is
believed to be related to Damon ("to subdue"), which
was the name of a mythical hero who saved his friend
Pythias from death by loyally supporting him. Damon
was popularized by the early twentieth-century writer
Damon Runyan, and actor Matt Damon's celebrity
keeps it in people's minds. Damien was the name of
the Antichrist son in *The Omen* series of movies; that
connection may tip some parents in favor of Damon.

Variations: *Damien, Damion, Damon*
Alternatives: *Dalton, Adrian, Dante, Tristan*

Dane is "from Denmark." The name was popularized
by actor Dane Clark (né Bernard Zanville) who played
soldiers and other heroes in movies of the 1940s and
'50s. The name is strong and forthright like a good
Norseman should be.

Alternatives: *Zane, Søren, Dag, Blaine*

Daniel is a perennial, and it's no wonder. The biblical Daniel ("God is my judge") was revered by all: He was an Israelite who ended up in Babylon, where his talents as a dream interpreter led him to assume ever higher offices throughout the reigns of Babylonian kings and then the courts of their Persian conquerors. Through his long stay in exile, he never wavered from his faith. Daniel famously spent the night in a lion's den and emerged unscathed, proof of God's love. The name Daniel sounds distinguished. Danny sounds playful and approachable. Dan is even more of a regular guy.

Variation: *Danyal*
Nicknames: *Dan, Danny*
Alternatives: *Samuel, Gabriel, Micah, Jonah*

Dante is a name with poetry in it: Durante "Dante" Alighieri is one of the greatest poets of all time. A Florentine who lived during the thirteenth and fourteenth centuries, he wrote *The Divine Comedy* as well as love poetry that was inspired by his muse Beatrice. Pre-Raphelite poet and painter Dante Gabriel Rossetti continued the artistic lineage of the name, which means "enduring" or "sturdy" (think "durable"). Italian Americans have been using the name since the 1950s. An alternate spelling, Donte, is popular with African Americans, including NFL star Donté Stallworth.

Variations: *Donte, Durante, Durand*
Alternatives: *Ludovico, Leonardo, Michaelangelo, Palladio*

Short and Sweet

Sometimes a one-syllable name is ideal. These brief, to-the-point names go well with long, complicated last names. And they make it difficult for your child to be saddled with a strange nickname. Here's a long list of short names to choose from:

~ ACE	~ CLARK	~ EARL
~ BAIRD	~ CLAY	~ FINN
~ BARD	~ COLE	~ GAGE
~ BEAU	~ COLT	~ GEORGE
~ BLAKE	~ CRUZ	~ GLENN
~ BRENT	~ CURT	~ GRANT
~ BRETT	~ DAG	~ HANK
~ BRICE	~ DALE	~ HEATH
~ BROCK	~ DANE	~ HUGH
~ BRUCE	~ DAX	~ JACK
~ CARL	~ DEAN	~ JAKE
~ CASH	~ DEV	~ JAMES
~ CHAD	~ DRAKE	~ JAY
~ CHASE	~ DUKE	~ JETT

Darius the Great was an ancient Persian king whose name means "wealthy." Darius was a visionary leader, launching ambitious construction projects and expanding his empire. The name has been popular

- JOEL
- JOHN
- JUDE
- JUDGE
- KAI
- KANE
- KEITH
- KING
- KRISH
- KYLE
- LAIRD
- LANCE
- LANE
- LARS
- LEE
- LEIF
- LLOYD
- LUKE
- MARK

- MAX
- MILES
- NASH
- NEIL
- NOEL
  (pronounced Knoll)
- PAUL
- PIERCE
- PRINCE
- QUINN
- RAJ
- RALPH
- REX
- RHETT
- RHYS
- ROSS
- ROY
- SAGE
- SAUL

- SCOTT
- SCOUT
- SEAN
- SETH
- SHANE
- TAD
- TATE
- THOR
- TODD
- TRACE
- TRENT
- TREY
- TROY
- TY
- VANCE
- VAUGHN
- WADE
- WAYNE
- ZANE

in the United States since the 1950s, especially with African American families.

Variations: *Dario, Darian, Darien, Darion, Dariush*
Alternatives: *Cyrus, Darcy, Tobias, Silas, Xerxes, Darrell*

Darrell is a last name turned unisex first name whose popularity is on the wane. Baseball player Darryl Strawberry, producer Daryl Zanuck, rocker Daryl Hall, and actor Darrell Hammond have made the name work. But actress Daryl Hannah's popularity may have spoiled the party for boys. Darnell is a variation inspired by Darrell that is common in the African American community.

Variations: *Darnell, Darrel, Darryl, Daryl*
Alternatives: *Terrell, Cornell*

Darren appeared on the radar suddenly in the United States in the 1950s. Having come out of nowhere, it seems to be a mash-up of Darrell and Warren. Now Darren feels well established to us in the wake of Darrin, the befuddled husband on the TV show *Bewitched*, crooner Bobby Darin, and actors like James Darren, the heartthrob on *Gidget*.

Alternatives: *Warren, Madden, Hayden, Landon*

Darwin Celebrate science! Darwin gives your offspring impressive creds. Charles Darwin, of course, was the author of *On the Origin of Species* and the father of the theory of evolution. If that sounds too weighty, take heart—the name's Old English meaning is warm and cuddly: "dear friend."

Alternatives: *Huxley, Emerson, Raleigh, Newton*

David is one of the heavyweight heroes of the Bible, and his story is filled with derring-do. In childhood, he slayed the giant Goliath, wrote poetry and music (some of the Psalms are said to be his), and tended sheep. In adulthood, he fought for Israel, was exiled, denounced as a traitor, and finally became a mighty, respected king of Israel. His name is believed to mean "darling." There have been kings and celebrities of every kind named David, yet the name retains an approachable every-guy quality that some other regal names like Edward and George lack. The name is timeless, trend-resistant, travels well, and has lots of nickname possibilities.

Variations: *Davin, Davon, Davian, Davion, Daud, Dewey*
Nicknames: *Dave, Davey, Davy, Daw, Dov*
Alternatives: *Michael, Edward, Thomas, Richard*

Davis is a last name derived from David. As a first name, it can be a variation of David or, in some cases, a nod to Confederate leader Jefferson Davis.

Alternatives: *Curtis, Roberts, Jacobs, Brooks*

Dawson Like Davis, Dawson is a derivation of David and started as a last name. The hit teen drama *Dawson's Creek* (1998–2003) reminded parents of the sturdy, rustic, masculine appeal of the name, causing a run on Dawsons.

Alternatives: *Logan, Brandon, Lawson, Watson*

Dax Comic actor Dax Shepard inspired the recent rediscovery of this name. The name is that of a town in southwestern France. It sounds like the hot names Jack and Jackson as well as Pax, meaning "peace," which is the name of one of the sons of Angelina and Brad Jolie-Pitt. Dax is a high-scoring Scrabble name (see page xxv), so you know it's hip.

Alternatives: *Pax, Knox, Maddox, Felix, Dixon, Max*

Dayton sounds like a corn-fed boy from the Midwest—the first Dayton that leaps to mind is the city of Dayton, Ohio. Next might be Daytona Beach, Florida, home of the Daytona 500. If you like the sound of the name but worry it looks too hayseed, try Deighton, a place-name from England.

Alternatives: *Deighton, Peyton, Layton, Pacey*

Deacon Reese Witherspoon and Ryan Phillippe named their son Deacon in 2003, and in 2004 many other Americans followed suit. A deacon works in the church assisting the priest; you can file him under "tradesman," along with Cooper, Thatcher, Jagger, and the like (see pages 316–317).

Alternatives: *Palmer, Abbott, Fuller, Priestly, Vicar*

Dean Trade name, place-name, homage—Dean can be a church or university official, an English valley, or a tribute to bad-boy screen idol James Dean. This last name turned first name popped up during Dean's career and in the years immediately following his death. It can also be an anglicization of the Italian name Dino, as in the case of Dean Martin.

Nickname: *Dino*
Alternatives: *Abbott, Deacon, Earl, Ned, Kane*

Deangelo "Of the angels," Deangelo is an Italian last name (think actress Beverly D'Angelo) that is being used as a first name; it is most popular with African American families. Deangelo Hall is a football player with the Washington Redskins. D'Angelo is the name of an R&B singer.

Variation: *D'Angelo*
Alternatives: *Angelo, Deshawn, Terrell*

Declan Declan's parents have some Irish in them and are looking for a distinctive way to celebrate their roots. They want to push the boundaries beyond Finn, beyond Liam. And maybe they want a harder edge to the name, which the *k* sound in Declan provides. Saint Declan was a bishop from Waterford in the fifth century.

Alternatives: *Kieran, Brendan, Liam, Finn*

Demetrius is a gladiator. The name came into use in the United States in the wake of the 1954 Victor Mature movie *Demetrius and the Gladiators*. The name relates to the Greek goddess of the harvest, Demeter, and is very popular in Russia and other Slavic countries (it appears there as Dimitri). Intellectual comedian Demetri Martin may give the name a hipster vibe in the years to come.

Variations: *Dimitri, Dmitry, Demetri*
Alternatives: *Feodor, Ivan, Igor, Silas*

Dennis is a descendant of the Greek god Dionysius, the God of wine and revelry. Did the name make cartoon character Dennis Mitchell the menace that he was? Probably it was the rhyme that did it. We're not so sure in the case of basketball rebel Dennis Rodman. But many Dennises have been upstanding fellows, like actors Hopper, Quaid, and Haysbert. The name is very popular in France; the country's patron saint is St. Denis (pronounced de-KNEE).

Variations: *Denis, Denys, Deon, Dion, Dennison*
Nicknames: *Den, Denny*
Alternatives: *Leonard, Ferris, Harris, Mitchell*

Denzel Accomplished actor Denzel Washington inspired the recent interest in this name. Denzel is a last name that's adapted from the town Denzell in Cornwall, England. It's also the name of an old brand of Austrian luxury car. Denzel has a luxe, foreign air.

Variations: *Denzil, Denzell*
Alternatives: *Zennor, Kernow, Trevelyan*

Derek started life as a nickname for Theodoric. Theodoric is believed to come from German and mean "ruler," whereas Theodore is Greek in origin and means "God's gift." Derek has been a name in its own right for hundreds of years, and was most popular in the 1970s through 1990s. Famous Dereks include actor Derek "Dirk" Bogarde, fictional spy Derek Flint, baseball player Derek Jeter, and sexy actress Bo Derek. An alternate spelling, Derrick, is also popular.

Variations: *Derrick, Derick*
Nicknames: *Rick, Dirk*
Alternatives: *Terrell, Roderick, Kendrick*

✐ **Desmond** is an Irish last name meaning "from Munster." It's been a first name overseas for many years. Actor Desmond Llewelyn portrayed the gadget master in nearly all the James Bond movies. Desmond Tutu is a South African Nobel Peace Prize winner and Anglican archbishop. Since the 1950s, Americans have gotten wise to its charms—a formal salute to Ireland in one form, or a playful little boy in the short forms of Des and Desi is another.

Nicknames: *Des, Dez, Desi*
Alternatives: *Brendan, Sullivan, Murphy, Declan*

Devin is a last name that became a first name in the 1950s around the time Kevin was becoming popular. The name, like Kevin, is Irish. It is used for girls as well

Celestial Celts

The Celtic gods bestow an ancient, earthy vibe on your little one, and sound subtly (or overtly) New Agey in many cases.

~ **ABELLIO:** *the god of apple trees*

~ **AONGHUS** *(pronounced like Angus): the Celtic Cupid, god of love*

~ **ARAUSIO:** *water god and former name of the city of Orange, France*

~ **ARAWN:** *the Celtic version of the Grim Reaper, but a cool name nonetheless*

~ **BELENUS:** *god of the sun, associated with heat and healing*

~ **DAGDA:** *a good-time god of banquets and magic, but also a mighty warrior whose club is so large, it has to be carried on a wagon*

~ **FINEGAS:** *wise old man who caught and prepared the Salmon of Knowledge for the hero Finn-Macool*

~ **GWYDDION:** *exactly what you think of when you picture a druid*

~ **IRUSAN:** *a giant cat god*

~ **OSSIAN:** *wise poet and musician who fell in love with a god's daughter*

~ **WOGAN:** *god of wit and talk*

as boys. The variation Devon might evoke the county in southern England.

Variations: *Deven, Devan, Devon, Devyn*
Alternatives: *Kevin, Gavin, Melvin, Vincent*

Dexter is the geeky teenager who grows into a computer billionaire or hot grunge rocker. The name means "fortunate," "talented," and "able."

(Think about "dexterity.") The name has that Scrabble *X* factor everyone is looking for these days (see page xxv).

Nickname: *Dex*
Alternatives: *Baxter, Maddox, Dixon, Paxton*

Diego is James in Spanish. The name has long been popular in Hispanic countries, especially Spain, where Diego is a patron saint. It came to attention in America in the late 1950s because of the outsize life and work of Mexican painter Diego Rivera. The animated children's character from *Go, Diego, Go!* has helped the name stay on parents' minds and actor Diego Luna may have helped, too.

Variations: *James, Jacob, Santiago*
Alternatives: *Cruz, Angel, Pedro, Santino*

Dominic means "Lord" (think *anno domini*). Saint Dominic is the patron saint of astronomers and founded the Dominican Order of monks. Not surprisingly, the name is very closely associated with Catholicism: Many Dominics are Italian, Hispanic, or Irish. The French use Dominique, which is not recommended for predominantly English-speaking countries, where Dominique is a girl's name.

Variations: *Dominick, Dominik, Dominique*
Nicknames: *Dom, Nick*
Alternatives: *Carmine, Salvatore, Francis, Victor*

Second-String Gods and Sprites

There's no reason to limit yourself to the mightiest and best-known gods of Greece. There are minor gods and sprites with equally alluring and meaningful names.

~ **DELPHIN:** *the leader of Poseidon's dolphins*

~ **EPIMETHUS:** *god of excuses . . . oh, and afterthoughts*

~ **HELIOS:** *the god of the sun and of oaths—you might swear on Helios*

~ **HYPNOS:** *the god of sleep (wishful thinking or a jinx?)*

~ **MORPHEUS:** *literally "he who shapes dreams"*

~ **NEREUS:** *the old man of the sea, who morphed into Poseidon*

~ **PAN:** *the goat-legged cavorter in forested glens, Pan started as a rustic good-time guy and only later was saddled with the cross-cultural mantle of trickster*

~ **ZEPHYRUS:** *god of the spring-bringing west wind*

Donald What a perfect name for Mr. Trump. Donald means "rule the world" in Gaelic. So The Donald's parents couldn't have chosen better. It worked out well for Ray Croc as well, the man who turned McDonalds into a worldwide empire. If you like the idea of the name but aren't keen on the associations of Trump, Duck, Ronald Mc, and others, consider the Irish version, Donal. In the 1930s, Donald was in the top ten. Now he's much less popular.

Variations: *Donal, Donnell*
Nicknames: *Don, Donny*
Alternatives: *Ronald, Graham, Campbell, Douglas*

Donovan "Little dark one," Donovan was a nickname that has been used as a first name since the early 1900s. It's a common Irish family name whose similarity to Donald made it a good first name choice. Donovan, the Scottish singer popular in the 1960s, gave the name further legitimacy.

Variation: *Donavan*
Nicknames: *Don, Van*
Alternatives: *Giovanni, Valentine, Donal, Orlando*

Dorian Oscar Wilde coined this name for *The Picture of Dorian Gray* (1881), about a handsome man who never ages, except in a portrait. Although things end very badly for Mr. Gray, parents have embraced the name without trepidation. The name is associated with Greek culture: The Dorians were Greeks.

Alternatives: *Adrian, Damian, Troy, Theodore*

Douglas The Scottish last name Douglas is well established as a first name. It used to have some glamour to it because of the poetic meaning, "black stream," and the Hollywood connections. (Never mind that Kirk Douglas was born Issur Demsky.) But the Brigadoonlike charm of the name has worn off; these days, Doug seems like a run-of-the-mill American pick.

Nickname: *Doug*
Alternatives: *Angus, Magnus, Keith, Duncan*

Drake Call him "the dragon." Yes, Drake has that intense, fiery meaning. He's one letter away from being a rake, so watch out for this one—he'll be a ladykiller. The name used to be given in honor of explorer Sir Francis Drake, but more recently probably Rick Springfield. The heartthrob rocker played Dr. Noah Drake on the TV series *General Hospital* in the early 1980s, and suddenly Drake was back in play.

Variations: *Dragon, Draco, Drago*
Alternatives: *Griffin, Blake, Hudson, Jake*

Drew Oh, come on, just name him Andrew (see page 293) and use Drew as a nickname. If you absolutely insist on Drew and Drew alone, realize that you are in good company. Drew has been used as a name itself in the United States since about 1939. But no matter how you slice it, it's still a short form of Andrew.

Alternatives: *Trey, Wren, Dewey*

✑ **Duncan** The dark chieftain, Duncan is resolutely Scottish, the name of kings, saints, and clergy. Duncan is the king in Shakespeare's *Macbeth*. Duncan Sheik is an indy rocker. The name has an understated strength

---

I'd love it if he sounded ...
Scottish

~ **ANGUS**	~ **EWAN**	~ **LACHLAN**
~ **ARCHIBALD**	~ **FERGUS**	~ **LAIRD**
~ **CAMPBELL**	~ **FRASER**	~ **MAGNUS**
~ **DENHOLM**	~ **HAMISH**	~ **MALCOLM**
~ **DUNCAN**	~ **IAN**	~ **RAMSAY**

---

to it (countryman Malcolm is flashier) and has substance and appeal without being too popular.

Alternatives: *Hugh, Magnus, Angus, Malcolm*

Dustin is a cowboy. You can picture the tumbleweeds rolling across the—yes, dusty—plains when you say his name. You can also almost hear the word "destiny," which gives the name an immortal quality. Actor Dustin Hoffman, whose name was inspired by western film star Dustin Farnum, lends a note of urbanity to the name. Dustin was hot in the 1980s, but interest has dropped off considerably.

Nickname: *Dusty*
Alternatives: *Austin, Dillon, Cody, Justin*

Dwayne ("dark one") has wandered a ways from its Gaelic roots. These days the name seems less Irish than country and western (as in the late Duane Allman of the Allman Brothers) or African American (perhaps due to the *D* prefix that is a common African American naming convention). The name has slumped in recent decades, but Dwayne "The Rock" Johnson's rising fame may help it come back into fashion.

Variations: *Duane, Dwane*
Alternatives: *Vernon, Waylon, Amos, Dane*

Dylan Bohemian to the max, Dylan is a poet, a songwriter. He's effortlessly cool, goes barefoot as often as possible, plays the guitar. Obvious connections are Welsh poet Dylan Thomas and singer Bob Dylan (who named himself after Thomas) as well as his son Jacob. Less obvious is the louche hero of the original *Beverly Hills, 90210*, Dylan McKay. The name is that of a Welsh hero of legend and means "from the sea." Warning: It is used for girls as well.

Variations: *Dillon, Dillan*
Alternatives: *Riley, Marley, Ewan, Owen*

Eamon is a proudly Irish name that calls to mind Eamon de Valera, a republican revolutionary who became one of the early presidents of modern Ireland. The name is the Gaelic equivalent of Edmund ("wealthy protector"). An excellent alternative to the extremely popular Aidan.

Variation: *Edmund*
Alternatives: *Nolan, Aidan, Shane, Patrick, Killian*

Easton is a celebration of baseball. The name is an English last name meaning "east town," but parents most often adopt it from the baseball sports gear manufacturer Easton. For some, it may be strange to name your child after a brand; for others it's a way of nodding to the sport without referring to a player who, great as he is now, may someday embarrass your little ballplayer.

Alternatives: *Weston, Martin, Wilson, Spalding*

Eden has been a girl's name in the United States since the 1980s. Now the boys are, uncharacteristically, picking it up. Eden evokes the paradisical garden in the Bible. It is also a variation of Aidan, the popular Irish boy's name, and means "rich young bear." Edun, a variation, evokes the socially conscious clothing line that U2 frontman Bono and his wife created, which is itself a nod to the Garden of Eden.

Variations: *Edun, Edan, Edon, Aidan*
Alternatives: *Adam, Dean, Ethan, Arden, Alden*

✐ **Edgar** Powerful, ancient Edgar, meaning "rich spear holder," is an Old English royal name. Now that Edward is tending toward overuse, it's time to reexamine this choice. There is a dark edge to its associations, if not its sound: macabre writer Edgar Allan Poe, science fiction writer (and Tarzan creator) Edgar Rice Burroughs. Edgar is also a character in *King Lear*.

Nicknames: *Ed, Eddie*
Alternatives: *Edmund, Gareth, Alfred, Edwin, Harold*

✎ **Edmund** is a kissing cousin of Edward and an excellent alternative to that more popular name. It too comes from the English, and it too means "wealthy protector." Edmund suggests nobility: He is the hero of Jane Austen's *Mansfield Park,* and Sir Edmund Hillary was the first westerner to climb Mount Everest. On the downside, Edmund is the angry illegitimate son in Shakespeare's *King Lear*.

Variations: *Edmond, Edmondo, Eamon*
Nicknames: *Ed, Eddie, Ned, Ted, Teddy*
Alternatives: *Frederick, Percival, Gavin, Arthur, Julian*

Edward is a mighty and enduring English name. Edwards have ruled England for centuries, so the meaning of the word makes perfect sense: "wealthy protector." King Edward the Confessor, who was the last English king before the Norman Conquest in 1066, was so successful and pious a ruler that he was eventually canonized. Edward shares much in

Noble Names of England

To bestow an air of aristocratic authority, consider crowning your baby boy with the name of an English king. Some of these choices are classics, while others have been forgotten and deserve a second look. All are distinguished, suggesting dignity and power.

- ALBERT
- ALFRED
- ALGERNON
- ANDREW
- ATHELSTAN
- CHARLES
- EDGAR
- EDMUND
- EDWARD
- FREDERICK
- HAROLD
- HENRY
- JAMES
- OLIVER
- OSWALD
- PHILIP
- PIERS
- RICHARD
- RUPERT
- SIMON
- STEPHEN
- TIMOTHY
- WALTER
- WILLIAM

common with Emma and Sophie: It's a name that was extremely popular in the early 1900s, then declined, and is now roaring back into fashion. There have been Edwards at the top of every field, and the name will only rise in the wake of the megawatt *Twilight* series of books and films: Edward is the hottie vampire who romances heroine Bella.

Variations: *Eduardo, Edouard, Eduard*
Nicknames: *Ed, Eddie, Ned, Ted, Teddy*
Alternatives: *Edgar, Charles, William, Richard, John*

✐ **Edwin**, like all the *Ed-* names, bestows a wish for prosperity upon the bearer. Edwin means "rich friend"—who wouldn't want to hang around a guy like that? The name of an old English king turned saint, Edwin has lately followed the popularity pattern of Edward but has always lagged behind it. Look for the popular Edward to continue outpacing Edwin in the years to come, making Edwin (and other *Ed-* names) an ideal pick for a similar but different choice that packs a punch without following the pack. Astronaut Edwin "Buzz" Aldrin gives the name hero appeal (and a natural nickname option).

Nicknames: *Ed, Eddie, Ned, Ted, Teddy, Buzz*
Alternatives: *Winston, Dennis, Merlin, Albert, Spencer*

I'd love to call him . . .
Eli

E li can be a happy-go-lucky nickname for a whole range of more serious-sounding monikers:

- **ELIAN**
- **ELIAS**
- **ELIEZER** *(Elie Weisel's name)*
- **ELIJAH**
- **ELISHA**
- **ELLERY**

- **ELLIOT**
- **ELLIS**
- **ELTON**
- **ELWOOD** *(stop snickering, Elwood can be cool—he was the Dan Aykroyd half of the Blues Brothers)*

Efrain is the Spanish variation of Ephraim. Ephraim ("fruitful") was a son of Joseph and a founder of one of the Old Testament's twelve tribes of Israel. While Ephraim is typically used by Jewish families, Efrain is most often used by Hispanic ones. Armenian-Argentinian soccer star Efrain Chacurian emigrated to the United States in the 1940s, and his career success shortly thereafter may have helped boost the name. Will teen idol Zac Efron, whose last name sounds similar, continue to give it luster?

Variation: *Ephraim*
Alternatives: *Ruben, Ezra, Elijah*

⌀ **Eli** has stature. Biblical Eli was a judge from the Old Testament, and the name means "height." Despite the gravitas of the provenance and meaning, Eli sounds perky, bright, and cheerful.

Alternatives: *Levi, Ezra, Lucas, Kai*

Elian The name Elian gained recognition when Elian Gonzalez made headlines in 2000. He was a seven-year-old boy whose mother died while fleeing Cuba with him. His relatives in Miami fought to keep him in the United States; his father in Cuba fought for his return there. Namesakes started popping up immediately in the Hispanic community, but the furor has since died down. Elian is a Celtic last name believed to be related to Elvis.

Alternatives: *Elias, Ellis, William, Alvaro, Ulysses*

📎 **Elijah** One of the greatest prophets of the Bible,
Elijah ("Yahweh is my God") is all about drama. He
raises the dead; ends famines; battles evildoers;
withstands winds, fires, and earthquakes. He ascends
to heaven alongside a chariot of fire, letting his mantle
fall to his disciple Elisha. It is said that his return will
presage that of the Messiah. Actor Elijah Wood has
boosted the name, as did Elijah Muhammad, leader
of the Nation of Islam, before him. Elias is a variation
that sounds less overtly religious but has the same
meaning.

Variations: *Alijah, Elias, Ellis*
Nickname: *Eli*
Alternatives: *Ephraim, Gabriel, Israel, Abraham*

Elisha ("God is salvation") was Elijah's assistant
and inheritor of his position; he became prophet
upon Elijah's ascension to heaven. Elisha serves as
a variation of Elijah both in the provenance of the
name and the sound of it. But be warned: This one
looks more like a girl's name (it's one letter away from
Elissa), so it can cause confusion.

Nickname: *Eli*
Alternatives: *Shiloh, Raphael, Ariel, Ezra*

Elliot is a last name that comes from Elias, a variation
of Elijah. The name has a so-nerdy-it's-cool appeal:
Think Eliot Ness of *The Untouchables* fame, actor

Go West, Young Man

For rugged, outdoorsy names, you need to look to the horizon. Can you see the Rockies off in the distance? Well, imagine you can. And think back on the cowboys you have known. The names of the Wild West are reliably manly and atmospheric.

~ AUSTIN	~ DUSTIN	~ REMINGTON
~ CARSON	~ FLINT	~ ROY
~ CHEYENNE	~ HOUSTON	~ RYDER
~ CLINT	~ JACKSON	~ SAGE
~ CODY	~ JESSE	~ SHANE
~ COLT	~ LAWSON	~ TEX
~ DAKOTA	~ LOGAN	~ WAYNE
~ DALLAS	~ MARSHALL	~ WESTON
~ DAWSON	~ MONTANA	~ WYATT
~ DUKE	~ RED	~ ZANE

Elliot Gould, and New York governor Eliot Spitzer (he was nerdy-cool before he was dirty-disgraced). And it has a literary quality with patrician overtones: George Eliot and T. S. Eliot. But note: This one might become a girl's name, thanks to the popularity of a female character in the long-running TV show *Scrubs*.

Variations: *Elliott, Eliot*

Nickname: *Eli*

Alternatives: *Emerson, Ezra, Garrett, Lewis, Harry*

Ellis The biblical name Elijah spawned many variations, including this last name, which migrated via Elias. Ellis can also be an anglicized version of the Welsh name Elisud, which means "benevolent." Emily Brontë used Ellis as her pseudonym because it sounded so squarely masculine. No more. Ellis sounds like Wallis, Maris, Doris and other now-girlish names, so enterprising parents of girls might look here for the edgy next-big-thing.

Nickname: *Eli*
Alternatives: *Morris, Dennis, Elias*

Elvis lives! If you want to prove it, you can choose this name for your son. But it goes without saying that Elvis Presley broke the mold with this one, and the long shadow of the rock icon will always be there. The name has a hillbilly as well as an elfin quality to it. Proceed with caution.

Alternatives: *Presley, Levi, Virgil, Enos, Roscoe*

Emerson The name Emerson is almost as strongly linked to transcendentalist writer Ralph Waldo as Dickens is to Charles. Emerson advocated a close connection to nature and self-reliance in the mid-nineteenth century. He was enormously influential, and through his publications and speeches became known as the Sage of Concord. The name literally means "son of Emery," but is more associated with liberal thinking, individualism, and a love of nature. The name is being enthusiastically taken up by girls now.

Variation: *Emery*
Alternatives: *Whitman, Alcott, Darwin, Bronson, Dixon*

Emilio is popular with Italian and Hispanic families, but it has crossover potential. It comes from the same ancient Roman root as Emily. The most famous Emilio in the United States may be actor Emilio Estevez.

Variations: *Emiliano, Emile*
Alternatives: *Antonio, Carlos, Martinez*

Emmanuel means "God is with us"; it is another name for the Messiah. It is a joyful, triumphant name to Christians. Famous Emmanuels include Vittorio Emanuele II, first leader of unified Italy; fashion designer Emanuel Ungaro; philosopher Immanuel Kant; and diminutive actor Emmanuel Lewis.

Variations: *Emanuel, Immanuel*
Nicknames: *Manuel, Manny, Manu*
Alternatives: *Christian, Santino, Cruz, Elihu*

Emmett is a rare example of a boy's name that migrated from a female root, in this case, Emma. It has a strong Irishness about it because of its connection to seventeenth-century Irish patriot

Robert Emmet. Parents nowadays may think about football hero Emmitt Smith and the vampire character from *Twilight* Emmett Cullen. Both Emmett and Kellan, the first name of the actor who plays him, may rise in the flood tide of the *Twilight* series' success.

Alternatives: *Owen, Garrett, Cullen, Declan*

Enrique This evocative name, which is Henry ("powerful ruler") in Spanish, has slowly and steadily increased in popularity since 1900. Singer Enrique Iglesias has raised the profile—and sex appeal—of the name.

Variations: *Henry, Enrico*
Nicknames: *Rick, Rico, Quique (pronounced KEE-keh)*
Alternatives: *Mateo, Jorge, Eduardo*

Enzo is a traditional Italian name that was rediscovered in 2003. The name, which can be an Italian variation of Henry or a nickname for names like Vincenzo (Vincent), is perfect for the times. It's short, traditional, contains the exotic letter *z*, and can be understood by everyone. Use it in lieu of names like Ezra and Milo. It's also sure to appeal to fans of fast cars: Enzo Ferrari was a racecar driver who founded the luxury car brand.

Variations: *Enrico, Heinz*
Alternatives: *Ezra, Aldo, Eli, Milo*

Eric A name with Scandinavian flavor, Eric comes from the Norse for "eternal ruler." Erik the Red was a legendary Norse explorer, who gave his name to several Scandinavian kings. Musician Eric Clapton uses the name, as does the fictional prince-hero of Disney's *The Little Mermaid*.

Variations: *Erik, Erick, Eriq, Erich*
Nickname: *Rico*
Alternatives: *Soren, Gustav, Olaf, Conrad, Ole*

Ernest sounds like such a docile name. Consider the name's homonym, "earnest," which means "sincere." And Oscar Wilde's comedic masterpiece *The Importance of Being Earnest*. Or the hokey and harmless redneck character Ernest P. Worrell from movies like *Ernest Saves Christmas*. Surprising, then, that Ernest means "battle to the death." Despite its bravado, it seems like Ernest is losing the fight—his popularity has been waning for a while. (Ernests Hemingway and Borgnine were born during the heyday of the name.) Ernesto, on the other hand, the vigorous Hispanic version of the name, is doing well.

Variation: *Ernesto*
Nickname: *Ernie*
Alternatives: *Henry, Stephen, Eugene, Stanley*

Esteban The Spanish version of Stephen ("crown"), this name became popular in the United States in the 1950s, possibly thanks to the big wave of Cuban refugees then fleeing Fidel Castro's new regime. The name has music in it—it's the stage name of a Pennsylvania-born Flamenco guitarist and guitar producer. And the moniker has athletic ties as well: The Cuban ballplayer Estevan Bellan was the first Latin American to play major league baseball in the United States.

Variations: *Estevan, Estefan*
Alternatives: *Enrique, Felipe, Guillermo, Pablo*

Ethan was a minor character in the Bible whose name means, auspiciously, "long life." And it's had a long life, indeed. This stalwart was well liked in early America and took on legendary status through the heroics of Ethan Allen, a Revolutionary War patriot instrumental in the founding of Vermont. Centuries later, Gen X actor-writer Ethan Hawke helped to give the name the contemporary hipness that elevated it to the top ten and then the top five.

Variation: *Ethen*
Alternatives: *Aidan, Heath, Ephraim, Nathan*

Eugene is the quintessential geek name, despite its dignified roots (it means "noble"). Eugene was the nerd in *Grease*. Comic actor Eugene Levy usually plays dorky characters. Some other famous (and non-nerdy) Eugenes are from the 1800s: Ionesco, O'Neill, and Delacroix. Most recent Eugenes resolutely call themselves Gene: Gene Hackman, Gene Roddenberry, Gene Kelly. But the name is so out that it could become cool in the right hands. Call him Gino and it's even more unexpected.

Nicknames: *Gene, Gino*
Alternatives: *Stanley, Milton, Harold, Dexter*

Evan A relative of John, Evan is the Welsh version of the name. John means "God is gracious." As people have cooled on John, which for a hundred years (until 1973) was in the top five most popular names for boys in the United States, they have turned to alternatives like Ian and Evan. Evan has the added benefit of sounding like "heaven" and being close in form to Eva and Ava, which are wildly popular now. Some families choose to rock Evan because it sounds close to the Hebrew Eben, which means "rock."

Variations: *Euan, Ewan*
Alternatives: *Owen, Nathan, Vaughn, Kevin, Eben*

✐ **Everett** A last name meaning "brave boar," Everett sounds distinguished and worldly. The name Ever is coming into fashion, but Everett has been in use for hundreds of years as a first name; why not choose the longer, more established version? Hollywood connections to the name include 1930s comic star Edward Everett Horton, and contemporary actors Tom Everett Scott and Rupert Everett.

Variation: *Everard*
Nicknames: *Ever, Rett*
Alternatives: *Bennett, Avery, Barrett, Rhett, Emmett*

Ezekiel ("God's strength") was one of the important prophets of the Bible to whom a book of the Old Testament is devoted. Ezekiel gives you a traditional name with a trendy nickname, Zeke. Fans of the 1994 film *Pulp Fiction* might leap to credit that film, which features a quote from Ezekiel, for the name's rise, but it was already on its way when Quentin Tarantino came along.

Variation: *Ezequiel*
Nickname: *Zeke*
Alternatives: *Lazarus, Barnaby, Elijah, Ilyas, Joaquin*

Ezra If you wait long enough, anything comes back into style, as Ezra proves. A nineteenth-century favorite, and biblical mainstay, Ezra ("help") was a prophet and author of a book in the Old Testament. The name is a perfect complement to the now nearly ubiquitous Noah and Jacob, and other old-fashioned up-and-comers like Eli and Caleb. It certainly passes our test: Ezra contains the cool letter *z*, has real creds, and ends in a vowel, which is becoming trendy for boys. Influential, controversial poet Ezra Pound is the most famous representative of the name.

Alternatives: *Noah, Eli, Amos, Jonah*

F

Fabian Teen singer and heartthrob of the 1960s, Fabian brought his name into common use in the United States. The name is believed to come from the same root that gives us fava beans. Flaxen-locked romance novel cover model Fabio as well as Baltimore Ravens star Fabian Washington have kept the name in the public eye.

Variations: *Fabiano, Fabio*
Alternatives: *Adrian, Damian, Fabrizio*

Felipe The Spanish-language version of Philip, Felipe is a "horse lover." Philip was the name of Alexander the Great's father as well as one of Christ's apostles. The handsome crown prince of Spain goes by the name, as do several Brazilian soccer players. Look for the moniker to rise in popularity because of the 2010 film *Eat, Pray, Love*, in which Javier Bardem plays a central love interest who bears the name.

Variations: *Philip, Philippe, Filipe*
Nicknames: *Flip, Phil, Eli*
Alternatives: *Pedro, Juan, José, Fernando*

Felix means "lucky" and "happy" in Latin. The name has been used since antiquity by anyone wanting to bestow blessings on their baby. Cartoon character Felix the Cat and fastidious Felix Ungar of

Neil Simon's *The Odd Couple* may come to mind, but neither has had much effect on the recent popularity of the name. Felix is a classic that's long been in use—it hangs out in the middle of the baby name pack. If you like the sound of Alex but want something with a little more distinction, you'll find this a happy choice.

Alternatives: *Alex, Dexter, Maddox, Oscar*

Fernando Spanish for Ferdinand, Fernando means "ready for journey." The name of a popular ABBA song from 1976 as well as a wacky lothario played by Billy Crystal ("you look *mah*velous"), Fernando has had a rocky ride on the waves of pop culture. No matter, Nando is loved by Latin American families. Celebrities with the name include many professional baseball players and the late stereotypical Latin lover, actor Fernando Lamas (the basis for Billy Crystal's character).

Nicknames: *Nando, Fred*
Alternatives: *Lorenzo, Armando, Diego*

Finley ("fair warrior") is a Scottish last name that has been used intermittently as a boy's first name. Lately, girls have picked it up—it has an ending that sounds like the decidedly girlish Lee or Leigh—so look for the boys to cut back on it, sticking to Irish alternatives like Finn and Finnegan instead.

Variation: *Finlay*
Nickname: *Finn*
Alternatives: *Finnegan, Finbar, Riley, Devin*

THE IMDb NAMING TOOL

There are many places to deepen and widen your search for the perfect name. Baby-naming resources abound online, but one of the most entertaining, creative, and unexpected is the website IMDb (Internet movie database). Using it, you can make connections to names that you may not have thought of otherwise. For instance, if you love Walter Matthau, but don't like the name Walter, you could pull up the actor's filmography and find a list of the characters he played, which include names like Oscar, Max, Albert, Miles, Harmon, and Boris. If you adore the swingy films of Doris Day but think Doris is too fusty, consider the characters she played: Josie, Judy, Beverly, Kitty, Marjorie, Nanette, Georgia. And if you admire Catherine Deneuve but feel her name just isn't French enough, try one of her roles: Martine, Solange, Vivianne, Cecile, Delfina, Odette, or Liliane.

Searching IMDb is a fun way to find lists of names that may have enough in common to appeal to you (and you just might find some exciting additions to your Netflix queue in the process).

To Infinity and Beyond

Buzz Lightyear, the intrepid rocket explorer of the movie *Toy Story,* may not be the best example of a true trailblazer, but his name is. It's a nod to astronaut Edwin "Buzz" Aldrin. There are many other explorers to choose from whose names suggest great possibilities, thrilling adventures, and new worlds.

- ~ **AMERIGO** (Vespucci): gave his name to America

- ~ **ARMSTRONG** (Neil): astronaut

- ~ **BUZZ** (Aldrin): astronaut

- ~ **CABOT** (John): claimed Canada for England

- ~ **CORTÉS** (Hernán): claimed Mexico for Spain

- ~ **COUSTEAU** (Jacques): undersea explorer and scuba-diving pioneer

- ~ **DRAKE** (Sir Francis): second to circumnavigate the world

- ~ **EDMUND** (Hilary): first westerner to summit Mount Everest

- ~ **HENSON** (Matthew): one of the first to reach the North Pole; unlike most polar explorers, Henson was black

Finn Short and plucky Finn has boyish charm thanks to the association with Mark Twain's Huck Finn. It also has an Irish brogue: The name Finn comes from Fionn mac Cumhail, the hero of an old Irish legend, part of the Fenian Cycle. Stories of Finn's band of warrior poets, the Fianna, have existed since the third century and were finally written down in the twelfth. The eighteenth-century poet James Macpherson wrote an epic poem about Finn, furthering interest. Finn (and Fiona, its feminine derivative) means "fair." (It is

- **HUDSON** (Henry): explorer of the Hudson River area

- **KIT** (Carson): explorer and trapper of the American West, Kit is short for Christopher

- **LEIF** (Erikson): Viking explorer from Iceland

- **LIVINGSTONE** (David): explorer of the African interior (he was famously greeted by Henry Stanley with "Dr. Livingstone, I presume?")

- **MAGELLAN** (Ferdinand): first circumnavigator of the globe

- **MERIWETHER** (Lewis): explored the American West with William Clark

- **PIKE** (Zebulon): explored the Rocky Mountains; Pike's Peak was named for him

- **POLO** (Marco): one of the first Europeans to travel throughout Asia

- **RALEIGH** (Walter): established an English settlement on Roanoke Island

- **ROALD** (Amundsen): first person to reach the South Pole

- **THOR** (Heyerdahl): sailed the Pacific in a primitive raft, "Kon-Tiki," to prove ancient contact between South America and Polynesia

- **VASCO** (da Gama): found an ocean route from Europe to Asia

from Finn that we get Sinn Fein, the Irish nationalist organization.) No nicknames necessary here.

Alternatives: *Donal, Ronan, Callum*

Finnegan can be a salute to James Joyce's masterpiece *Finnegan's Wake,* or perhaps a nod to your grandmother's maiden name or your favorite Irish bar. Whatever your reasons for using it, Finnegan is a cheerful, upbeat name. And it's a way of giving little Finn a slightly longer, more traditional-sounding

moniker without resorting to Finbar. Warning:
The girls are starting to use it, too.

Nickname: *Finn*
Alternatives: *Finbar, Moneghan, Callahan, Sullivan*

Francis and its variations—the major ones are
Francisco and Frank—all mean "French." The Franks
were a Germanic tribe that moved into ancient Gaul
(present-day France), thereby giving their name to the
region. Francis and its variations were popularized
by St. Francis of Assisi, whose name was actually
a nickname, a nod to the saint's father's frequent
business dealings in France. Saint Francis is associated
with kindness, generosity of spirit, and communion
with animals. Francis was extremely popular in the
early 1900s; now Francisco, the Spanish version,
is more frequently used. But this little choirboy
may make a comeback along with other old-school
favorites like Owen and Henry.

Variations: *Francisco, Francesco, Frank, France, Franco, Francois*
Nicknames: *Fran, Frank, Frankie*
Alternatives: *Lawrence, Ralph, Howard, Richard*

Franklin means "freeman." The name has a patriotic
bent to it, calling to mind founding father Benjamin
Franklin and New Deal president Franklin D. Roosevelt.

Nicknames: *Fran, Frank, Frankie*
Alternatives: *Truman, Harrison, Jefferson, Quincy*

Frederick ("peaceful ruler") sounds like a statesman (abolitionist Frederick Douglass; various kings from northern Europe); Fred sounds like your middle-aged next-door neighbor (actor Fred MacMurray, caveman Fred Flintstone, astronaut Fred Haise); Freddy is young and frisky (rocker Freddie Mercury; actor Freddie Prinze Jr.). The name is deeply traditional, extremely versatile, and, although it is slipping in popularity, deserves a second look. This classic name goes well with all the old-fashioned names the girls are using: Sadie, Emma, Lucy, Abigail, and friends.

Variations: *Frederic, Frederik, Friedrich, Federico*
Nicknames: *Fritz, Fred, Freddy, Freddie, Fredo, Rick, Rico*
Alternatives: *Alfred, Russell, Leonard, Theodore*

G

Gabriel ("God's hero") was one of the archangels, with Michael, Uriel, and Raphael. To Jews, he is the messenger of God; to Christians, he made the annunciation to Mary; to Muslims, he revealed the Koran to Mohammed. It is believed that Gabriel will blow his horn to reveal the Judgment Day. With this kind of résumé, you would expect the name to be as big as Michael, but glory has been long in arriving for Gabriel; the name didn't crack the top twenty-five until 2008.

Variation: *Jibrail (Arabic)*
Nickname: *Gabe*
Alternatives: *Raphael, Ariel, Ezekiel, Elijah*

Gael ("Gaelic") roared to stardom in the United
States alongside the career of handsome Mexican
actor Gael Garcia Bernal. The name can be
problematic for English speakers, who may want
to pronounce it "Gail," in the vein of the girl's name
it's related to; it should be pronounced GUY-el. The
friends on the sitcom *How I Met Your Mother* summed
up the problem when they routinely referred to a
character named Gael as "male Gail."

Alternatives: *Diego, Raul, Pablo, Joaquin, Javier*

Gage is the name of the son in Stephen King's horror
novel *Pet Sematary*. The film was released in 1988; the
name started appearing on United States charts the
following year. Like other manly one-syllable names—
Cole and Dane leap to mind—Gage is a vocabulary
word, too. A gage is an old way of saying "challenge."
Gauge means "to measure."

Variations: *Gauge, Gaige*
Alternatives: *Finn, Gary, Dane, Gabe*

Garrett is a variation of the Irish first name Gerald
("rules with a spear"). While Gerald has waned in
popularity even among the Irish Catholic families that

loved it most, Garrett has done well. And while Gerald sounds serious, Garrett sounds fun-loving—picture him catching a wave or tossing a Frisbee around—but still grown-up.

Alternatives: *Emmett, Liam, Wyatt, Garrison*

Gary Have you heard of Elbert Gary? He's to thank for the popularity of this name. He was the industrialist for whom Gary, Indiana, was named. That city in turn inspired the stage name of Gary Cooper, whose career led the name to hit the top ten during the 1950s. Garry is a Scottish place-name (think Glengarry). Gary can also be used as a nickname for names like Gareth (an Arthurian name) and Garrett.

Variations: *Garry, Gareth, Garrett, Garth*
Alternatives: *Barry, Larry, Rory, Douglas, Scott*

Gavin is the modern version of Gawain, a Knight of the Round Table and hero of *Sir Gawain and the Green Knight*, a medieval romance in which Gawain shows courage and honor. The Scottish name is familiar to contemporary parents as the name of *Love Boat* actor Gavin MacLeod and rocker Gavin Rossdale.

Variations: *Gaven, Gavyn*
Alternatives: *Evan, Ivan, Galen*

𝒫 **George** means "farm work," which is ironic because it's one of the most royal, proud names around. Saint George slayed the dragon in legend and became the patron saint of England in the 1300s. There have been several King Georges throughout Europe, and in the United States, George Washington remains a hero. Former president George W. Bush and schlumpy *Seinfeld* character George Costanza may have turned some people off to the name lately.

Variations: *Jorgen (Denmark), Georges (France), Giorgio (Italy), Jorge (Spain), Georg (Germany), Yuri (Russia)*

Nicknames: *Geordie, Georgie*

Alternatives: *Henry, William, Charles, Joseph*

Significant Statesmen

G iving your boy a name from the political arena may set him up for a life of leadership and service. There are many distinguished and unusual names to choose from—take a look and then vote for your favorite.

- **ABRAHAM** *(Lincoln)*
- **ADLAI** *(Stevenson)*
- **BARACK** *(Obama)*
- **CHE** *(Guevara)*
- **CLEMENT** *(Attlee)*
- **CORDELL** *(Hull)*
- **HELMUT** *(Kohl)*
- **KOFI** *(Annan)*

- **MENZIES** *(Campbell)*
- **NEVILLE** *(Chamberlain)*
- **NEWT** *(Gingrich)*
- **SPIRO** *(Agnew)*
- **WINSTON** *(Churchill)*
- **WOODROW** *(Wilson)*
- **ZELL** *(Miller)*
- **ZENAS** *(Ferry Moody)*

Gerald Picture Gerald ("rules with a spear") doing the Charleston, his hair slicked with Brylcreem and parted in the middle. The 1930s were the heyday of this old Germanic name. It was enthusiastically taken up by the Irish, so it remains a solid choice for parents with Irish backgrounds looking for alternatives to trendy Finn and Liam.

Nicknames: *Gerry, Geraldo*
Alternatives: *Gerard, Albert, Oswald, Desmond*

Gerardo "Strong spearbearer," Gerardo is the Hispanic version of the Celtic name Gerard. Ecuadoran rapper and musician Gerardo was big in the 1990s (remember "Rico Suave"?). Gerard itself might be poised for a comeback, thanks to the popularity of strapping Scottish actor Gerard Butler.

Nickname: *Gerry*
Alternatives: *Fernando, Geronimo, Reynaldo*

German No head-scratcher here, German means "from Germany" as well as "brotherhood." It's a way of bestowing a bit of your ethnic background to your child without picking a classic German name. The name has been in use since 1973; could singer Jermaine Jackson have influenced its popularity? Maybe, maybe not.

Variation: *Jermaine*
Nickname: *Gerry*
Alternatives: *Roman, Jeremy, Herman*

Giancarlo The combination of John and Charles is a popular one in Italy (Giancarlo) and Spain (Juan-Carlos). Giancarlo has been in intermittent use in America since 1986. The career of actor Giancarlo Giannini has surely helped. He is one of Italy's top actors and famous for dubbing the voices of many American actors for Italian-language versions of their films. African and Italian American actor Giancarlo Esposito is another high-profile user of the name. Distinctly continental-sounding, Giancarlo is a name that smolders with intrigue and the elegant romance of the Riviera. Giancarlo is a guy who would look at

Bold and Brazen

I f you want your little boy to be the embodiment of derring-do, dare to give him a name that suggests strength and courage. The following choices differ in specific meaning and origin, but all evoke confidence and power.

~ AARON	~ COLT	~ GUNNAR
~ AJAX	~ DEVLIN	~ HALE
~ ARJUNA	~ ENZO	~ LUTHER
~ ARSENIO	(short for Vincenzo)	~ THANE
	~ FARRELL	
~ BEVAN	~ GIDEON	~ THOR
~ CHASON	~ GRIFFIN	~ VICTOR
~ CHESTER		~ WALTER

home in a tuxedo at a Monte Carlo roulette table. Call him Johnny until his voice changes.

Alternatives: *Alonzo, Cosmo, Fabrizio, Galileo*

🖋 **Gideon** ("hewer of trees") was a biblical hero who won the freedom of his people with cunning and guile instead of strength. For most Americans, Gideon's association with the Bible is more pedestrian—it's the brand name of the Bibles that were once found in nearly every hotel and motel room in America. *Gideon's Crossing* was a short-lived medical TV drama that aired the same year (2000) that Gideon was rediscovered by American parents.

Alternatives: *Simeon, Silas, Abner, Jericho*

Gilbert ("bright pledge") is sweet and approachable, but a warning to those who are goofy for Gilbert: He's also certifiably nerdy. Squeaky-voice Gilbert Gottfried and *Revenge of the Nerds* character Gilbert Lowe personify the name for this generation of parents. We are far away from the days when the name had upper-crust associations, as it did in the time of distinguished early American painter Gilbert Stuart. Gilberto, the Spanish-language version of the name, is slightly more popular than the Anglo version now.

Variation: *Gilberto*
Nicknames: *Gil, Gib, Gibby*
Alternatives: *Lewis, Eugene, Robert, Ernest*

Giovanni is John (see pages 419–420) in Italian. Actor Giovanni Ribisi helped Americans get used to this ethnic name. And Brazilian soccer star Geovanni inspired some parents to tweak the traditional spelling. The name goes way back, with illustrious predecessors like the main character in Mozart's opera *Don Giovanni*, writer Giovanni Boccaccio, and Fiat company owner Giovanni Agnelli. The short version of the name, Gianni, came to prominence in the wake of the death of couture fashion designer Gianni Versace. Parents seeking an edgy (and concise) way to honor a beloved Giovanni should try the nicknames Von or Gio.

Variations: *Giovani, Giovanny, Geovanni, Gianni, Johannes, Jovan, Jovani, Jovanni, Jovanny, Jovany*
Nicknames: *Van, Vanni, Von, Gio*
Alternatives: *Giancarlo, Eduardo, Stefano, Battista*

Glenn means "valley" in Gaelic. This Scottish name was popular in the 1920s through the '50s. It calls to mind the swinging sounds of Glenn Miller and his orchestra, pianist Glenn Gould, astronaut John Glenn, and leading man Glenn Ford.

Variation: *Glen*
Alternatives: *Firth, Gary, Leonard, Allen, Dale*

Gordon A Scottish place-name turned last name, Gordon was popular in the 1920s and '30s. It has been so well used as a first name it has lost its luster.

Most Americans think of Watergate mastermind
G. Gordon Liddy; cranky chef Gordon Ramsay;
Gordon Robinson, the patriarch of *Sesame Street*;
and *Wall Street* meanie Gordon Gekko.

Nickname: *Gordie*
Alternatives: *Bruce, London, Duncan, Donald*

Grady An Irish last name meaning "noble," Grady
is an excellent alternative to the increasingly common
Brady. Like Brady, it is masculine yet cheerful, and
has an air of the outdoors to it. Grady is a strapping
guy next door.

Alternatives: *Brady, Brodie, Rory*

Graham Old English for "gravelly place," Graham is
a Scottish place-name and last name. The name sounds
distinguished and storied—it would be hard to stick
a nickname to this one. Playground bullies might try
"Graham cracker" (Sylvester Graham gave his name
to the food he invented), but that won't last. Notable
bearers of the name include inventor Alexander
Graham Bell and acclaimed author Graham Greene.

Variations: *Grahame, Graeme*
Alternatives: *Duncan, Ewan, Fergus, Ronan, Murdoch*

Grant comes from the French "grand"—it means
"big." A grant is something that is given, so there
is a generosity and largesse to the name. This last

name turned first name comes from Scotland, but it's become so common it's no longer kilt-clad. Famous Grants include President Ulysses S. and dashing actors Cary and Hugh.

Alternatives: *Hugh, Brent, Trent, Kirk*

Grayson sounds like such an old, blue-blooded British name that you can almost hear Dame Maggie Smith warbling, "Grayson, we'll take tea in the conservatory now." (Maybe it's the similarity to Hobson—John Gielgud's butler role in *Arthur*—that rings in the ears.) The name has been popular since 1984, the same year *Greystoke* hit the big screens. The name has a dash of Grace in it, but a "son" in order to make it masculine. Say it quickly and you can hear an alternative to Jason shaping up. This last name ("son of Gray") shows every sign of sticking around.

Variation: *Greyson*
Nicknames: *Gray, Grady, Grey*
Alternatives: *Graydon, Leighton, Hamish, Mason*

✐ **Gregory** Leading man Gregory Peck sent his first name soaring in the 1950s and '60s, when he was at the peak of his career. The name, meaning "vigilant," is Latin in origin and is associated with shepherds keeping watch over their flocks. The name was held by several saints and popes and has a Scottish flavor. Think of the movie *Gregory's Girl* (1981) and actor Ewan MacGregor.

Variations: *Gregor, Grigoris*
Nicknames: *Greg, Gregg*
Alternatives: *Greer, Wallace, Alastair, Angus*

Griffin A mythological beast, the griffin (or gryphon) is half eagle, half lion. Griffins were frequently used in heraldry and represented strength and valor. In 1983, parents decided that the name was too good to keep as a last name and promoted it. Actor Griffin Dunne, whose mother's maiden name was Griffin, helped pave the way.

Nickname: *Griff*
Alternatives: *Sullivan, Murphy, Desmond*

Guillermo William in Spanish, Guillermo started appearing regularly on United States naming charts in the 1920s. The name has risen to pop culture prominence lately thanks to comedian Jimmy Kimmel's sidekick Guillermo Diaz Rodriguez and film director Guillermo del Toro.

Variations: *William, Guillaume (French)*
Nicknames: *Memo, Will, Willie*
Alternatives: *Felipe, Eduardo, Alberto*

Gunnar is an ancient Norse name that means what it sounds like: It's a name for a warrior. Could the name's discovery in the United States in 1991 have to do with Gunnar Nelson, Ricky Nelson's son, who with his twin brother had a hit album in 1990? Stranger things have happened.

Variations: *Gunner, Gunther*
Alternatives: *Remington, Colt, Lars, Axel*

 Gustavo comes from Gustav, which may be the most popular royal name in Sweden's history. Gustav and its variations have some of the seriousness of Augustus but with an artistic, belle epoque flavor: Gustave Eiffel designed the Eiffel Tower; Gustav Mahler was an Austrian composer; Gustav Klimt, an Austrian painter; Gustave Flaubert, a French writer. Gustavo is the Latin version, which is popular in Mexico and South America. It only adds spice and verve to an already cool choice.

Variations: *Gustav, Gustaf*
Nicknames: *Gus, Guga, Tavo*
Alternatives: *Barnabas, Vincent, Theodore*

H

Hamza was the name of an uncle of the prophet Muhammad. The name has been popular with Arabic families in the United States since 1998. It is used by the eldest son of the late King Hussein of Jordan and Queen Noor.

Alternatives: *Hussein, Nazir, Azim*

Harley means "motorcycle." If you want to split hairs, it also means "meadow," but the name was made so famous by the Harley-Davidson motorcycle company that its pastoral past is long forgotten. The name is now used more frequently by girls than by boys.

Nicknames: *Lee, Hog (Why not? It's the Harley-Davidson stock symbol.)*
Alternatives: *Farley, Marley, Riley, Benz*

Harold This Old English name once evoked English and Scandinavian royalty; the name means "ruler of the army." Now it has a sweetly dorky cast to it. Think about the Harold from *Harold and Maude*. Or *Harold and the Purple Crayon*. Or *Harold and Kumar Go to White Castle*. Other famous Harolds are from another generation: playwright Harold Pinter, British Prime Minister Harold Macmillan. Harold may benefit from the revival of interest in the name Henry, as they both share a common (and adorable) nickname, Harry.

Variation: *Harald*
Nicknames: *Hal, Harry*
Alternatives: *Dexter, Eugene, Albert, Richard*

Harrison "Son of Harry," Harrison is a last name turned first. It's a good way to offer little Harry a more formal version of his name. Musician George Harrison and actor Harrison Ford give the name, which could sound a bit snooty, an artistic, down-to-earth vibe. This is one of the few -*son* names that hasn't been co-opted by the girls; it still sounds resolutely masculine in a way that Madison and Addison no longer do.

Nickname: *Harry*
Alternatives: *Edison, Franklin, Addison*

Harry is the traditional nickname for Henry. More recently it has come to represent Harold and Harrison, as well as appearing as a name in its own right. Most parents still choose to use it as a nickname. Even the blockbuster wizard Harry Potter hasn't magically transformed that.

Variations: *Henry, Harold, Harrison*
Alternatives: *Sam, Max, Larry, Joe*

Hassan An Arabic name meaning "handsome," and a Hebrew name meaning "cantor," Hassan appears as a first name and last name throughout the Levant. As a first name, it usually signifies an Arabic background. Hassan is the name of the brother of the former King of Jordan and the late father of the current King of Morocco.

Alternatives: *Hussein, Muhammad, Salam*

Hayden A nature-loving, artistic-sounding name, Hayden means "valley of hay" and also can be a nod to

Austrian composer Josef Haydn (although the names are pronounced differently). Boys and girls are using the name in almost equal measure. Look for the boys to cool on it because of the girls' use and because of its similarity to Haley, which is taking off.

Variation: *Haiden*
Alternatives: *Grady, Bradon, Caden*

Heath is poetic yet tormented. The name defines a place where heather grows, and evokes the rugged landscape of the Yorkshire Moors, home of Emily Bronte's famous character, the brooding and passionate Heathcliff. The name was popularized in the United States by Lee Majors, who portrayed Heath on TV's *Big Valley*. It is associated most recently with the late actor Heath Ledger.

Alternatives: *Ethan, River, Firth, Clay*

Hector was a heroic prince who fought the Greeks in the Trojan War. He was celebrated in *The Iliad* for his courage and honor. His name in Greek means "restraint," which could refer to his resilience or the fact that he was defending his beloved city when he was killed by Achilles. Hector was also the name of the knight who raised King Arthur as his own son. The name is a mainstay of the Hispanic American community.

Alternatives: *Nestor, Ajax, Ulysses*

Henry is the name of kings, appropriate considering it means "home ruler." Henry and Harry were closely entwined throughout history, Harry being the spoken form of the name for most English King Henrys. Harry is not the only nickname; other Henrys have been Hals and Hanks. There have been Henrys in every walk of life, from the arts to the ballfield, from the throne room to the stage. It's an evergreen like John, James, and William.

Variations: *Enrique, Henri, Heinrich, Enrico, Kendrick*
Nicknames: *Harry, Hal, Hank*
Alternatives: *John, Edward, William, Samuel*

Holden The perfect name for a preppy, Holden ("deep valley") cannot help but call to mind Holden Caulfield, the antihero of J. D. Salinger's coming-of-age novel *The Catcher in the Rye*. It's more masculine and grounded than, say, Hayden, but maybe there is too much disaffection in it. Before you settle on it, reread your Salinger.

Alternatives: *Nolden, Salinger, Baxter, Brooks*

Houston The Longhorn State looms large over this name. Houston means "Hugh's town," but to American ears it evokes Sam Houston, the man who helped establish Texas and lent his name to one of the major cities there. The name can also call to mind the space program, since NASA's mission control is headquartered

Fictional Favorites

Reading inspires and changes us. The characters we meet in books become a part of our lives like family. Now's your chance to make family part of your books. Consider choosing a name from your library. Here are some fictional favorites:

- **ALEC** (The Spy Who Came in from the Cold)
- **ASLAN** (The Chronicles of Narnia)
- **ATTICUS** (To Kill a Mockingbird)
- **AUGUSTUS** (Lonesome Dove)
- **BUCK** (The Call of the Wild)
- **CHARLIE** (Charlie and the Chocolate Factory)
- **FRITZ** (The Swiss Family Robinson)
- **GANDALF** (The Lord of the Rings)
- **HAYDUKE** (The Monkey Wrench Gang)
- **HOLDEN** (The Catcher in the Rye)
- **HORATIO** (Horatio Hornblower)
- **HUCK** (The Adventures of Huckleberry Finn)
- **JAY** (The Great Gatsby)
- **LEOPOLD** (Ulysses)
- **MAX** (Where the Wild Things Are)
- **MILO** (The Phantom Tollbooth)
- **PHINEAS** (A Separate Peace)
- **PILGRIM** (Slaughterhouse-Five)
- **PIP** (Great Expectations)
- **RABBIT** (Rabbit, Run)
- **RHETT** (Gone with the Wind)
- **SAL** (On the Road)
- **STARK** (All the King's Men)

in Houston. ("Houston, we have a problem.") This name is bold and evocative—it should be problem-free.

Alternatives: *Dallas, Hugh, Hudson*

Howard A last name that no longer sounds like one, Howard ("noble guardian") is so well established that it's lost whatever edge it may have had. Now Howard sounds like the name of a dentist or long-retired insurance salesman. Howards that leap to mind include motel chain Howard Johnson, late broadcaster Howard Cosell, and entertainers Howard Stern and Howie Mandel. To give this name some interest, consider the nickname Ward. It's a bit edgier than Howard, but still steadfast and true (it suggests the wholesome dad in *Leave It to Beaver*).

Nicknames: *Howie, Ward*
Alternatives: *Hayward, Leland, Douglas, Raymond*

Hudson is closely related to Houston—both names mean "son of Hugh"—but has a very different vibe. Houston sounds like the tough, clean-cut Texan; Hudson, the Greenwich Village hipster. Houston has a Stetson; Hudson, a tattoo. Not that Hudson isn't a straight shooter, too. He can be just as upstanding and influential: The name calls to mind explorer Henry Hudson and the great river that honors him.

Nickname: *Hud*
Alternatives: *Mercer, Drake, Cabot, Parker*

✐ **Hugh** is ripe for rediscovery. Europe is already onto it, where Hugos frolic in numbers in the playgrounds of many nations, including France, Spain, Belgium, and

Sweden. (The name is in the top ten in those countries.)
Hugh (and his variations) means "spirit," and it has
been a favorite with royalty in France and England
since the Middle Ages. Heartthrob Hugh Jackman may
help the name make a comeback in the United States.

Variations: *Hughes, Hugo*
Nickname: *Hugo*
Alternatives: *Oscar, Otto, Milo, Luke*

Humberto means "bright spirit." Hispanic families
are using this name, but its popularity is slipping.
For English speakers it brings to mind the pedophile
antihero of *Lolita*, Humbert Humbert. On a broader
scale, it suggests bestselling Italian author Umberto
Eco (if you wish to evoke him, drop the H from the
name). Saint Hubert (the French version of the name)
is the patron of hunters.

Variations: *Hubert, Umberto, Humbert*
Nickname: *Beto*
Alternatives: *Eustace, Ignacio, Alberto, Federico*

Hunter The girls have been taking all the hip
occupational names lately, but Hunter is one that
has remained squarely male and has been gaining in
popularity. Macho and industrious, Hunter is also
iconoclastic and cool, thanks to an association with
gonzo writer Hunter S. Thompson.

Alternatives: *Jagger, Ranger, Cooper, Tanner, Carter*

I

Ian The Scottish version of John (pages 419–420), Ian crossed the pond in 1934 and became a hit. The name once sounded decidedly British, probably because it was so closely associated with English actors Ian Richardson and Ian McKellen, as well as the writer Ian Fleming, whose James Bond series of books and movies surely made American audiences take notice. These days, Ian is more mainstream.

Variations: *Ean, Iain, Euan, Jan*
Alternatives: *Rhys, Ivor, Lewis, Keith, Owen*

Ibrahim The Arabic version of Abraham (pages 278–279), Ibrahim was the father of prophets Ismail (considered the father of the Arab people) and Ishaq.

Variation: *Abraham*
Nickname: *Ibro*
Alternatives: *Ismail, Ishaq, Ilyas*

I'd love it if he sounded . . .
Russian

~ DMITRI	~ KONSTANTIN	~ PAVEL
~ FEODOR	~ MAXIM	~ SERGEI
~ IGOR	~ MIKHAIL	~ VLADIMIR
~ IVAN	~ OLEG	~ YURI

Ignacio is hot: Ignatius in Spanish, the name means "fire." The most famous saint with the name was Ignatius Loyola, founder of the Jesuits. Cate Blanchett recently named one of her sons Ignatius, so maybe more Iggies will follow. (Rocker Iggy Pop, by the way, was born James.)

Variation: *Ignatius*
Nicknames: *Nacho, Nate, Iggy, Iggie*
Alternatives: *Inigo, Cornelius, Dimitri, Valerio*

Irvin Irvine ("green water") is a Scottish place-name that became a last name. Yet most Irvins or Irvings in the United States have been Jewish, with Irving being an anglicized substitute for the traditional Hebrew name Israel. (Consider composer Irving Berlin.) The name has sporty connotations, too: Think NBA star Julius ("Dr. J") Erving Jr., and NFL player Michael Irvin.

Variations: *Irving, Irvine, Irwin*
Nickname: *Irv*
Alternatives: *Orville, Sidney, Darwin, Melvin*

Isaac ("laughter") was the son of Abraham, who escaped sacrifice by his dutiful father's hand to become a patriarch of the Jews and a prophet of Islam. Some Christians have used the name (Sir Isaac Newton), including African Americans (soul singer Isaac Hayes), but the name has been most popular with Jewish families (writers Isaac Bashevis Singer and Isaac

Asimov; fashion designer Isaac Mizrahi; musicians
Isaac Stern and Itzhak Perlman).

Variations: *Itzhak, Issac, Ishaq, Yitzhak*
Nickname: *Ike*
Alternatives: *Aaron, Noah, Esau, Akiva*

Isaiah is a major prophet and author of a book in
the Bible. His name means "God is salvation." In
the United States, the name is popular with African
American families.

Variations: *Isaias, Isiah, Izaiah, Izayah, Isai*
Alternatives: *Esau, Ezekial, Jeremiah*

Ishmael Call him Ishmael . . . if you want to reference
Moby Dick, that is (Ishmael is the narrator of Herman
Melville's famous epic). In the Bible, Ishmael was the
son of Abraham who was cast out into the desert and
became the forefather of the prophet Muhammad and
the Arab peoples. The name means "God heard." The
Hispanic version of the name is Ismael; the Arabic
iteration is Ismail. The latter calls to mind the British
film producer Ismail Merchant.

Variation: *Ismail*
Alternatives: *Elian, Lazaro, Noah, Omar*

Israel Jewish patriarch Jacob changed his name to
Israel late in life, after wrestling with the angel. His
descendants became the Israelites, and the land they

occupied became Israel. Some Jewish immigrants anglicized the name as Irvin or Irving.

Nickname: *Izzy*
Alternatives: *Isidore, Jacob, Irvin, Ishmael*

 Ivan is John in Russian. This consistently popular name is gaining ground as parents realize all the great things it has going for it: solid meaning (John means "God's grace"); a popular exotic consonant (*v*); foreign origins but not so unusual that it's intimidating or hard to spell. You have a choice for pronunciation: He can be EYE-vehn (like the great or the terrible) or ee-VAHN (like tennis champ Ivan Lendl).

Variations: *John, Ian*
Nickname: *Van*
Alternatives: *Igor, Anton, Maxim, Roman*

J

Jabari Swahili for "brave," this lyrical name has been popular with African American families since 1974. It is similar in sound to the Arabic names Jabbar and Jabir, which mean "powerful" and "comforter," respectively.

Alternatives: *Jamari, Jabir, Jamal*

Jack is a guy who can be relied on to do anything. The suffix *-jack* means a worker (jack of all trades). The name is decisive, to-the-point, fiercely masculine, and without pretentions. Jack can work hard and party hard. Jack is a nickname for John: John is the president; Jack is the playboy. The name is at the tippity top of the charts in the U.K., so maybe there is still room for growth in the United States.

Variations: *John, Jacques (the French version of James but a homonym of Jack), Jackson, Jock*
Nickname: *Jackie*
Alternatives: *Sam, Chuck, Jake, Luke, Mac*

Jackson can be a cowboy (Jackson Hole, Wyoming), a musician (Michael Jackson, Jackson Browne), a renegade artist (Jackson Pollock), a rebel (Stonewall Jackson). There is something for everyone here, so no wonder the name gets more popular every year. Some families are using creative spellings to give their Jacksons (or Jaxons) distinction.

Variations: *Jaxon, Jaxson, Jax*
Nicknames: *Jack, Sonny, Jax*
Alternatives: *Stetson, Wilson, Weston, Duke, Dustin*

Jacob, the Bible tells us, is the supplanter—the crafty younger twin who tricked his older brother Esau into giving him his birthright. Jacob has successfully supplanted all other names to become number one in the United States since 1999. How did he do it? By having an important history—Jacob is a towering patriarch of Judaism; by appealing to Jews and

The Art of the Name

Distinctive names from art history offer as much color as a paintbox and more atmosphere than you'll find in a windswept Turner seascape. Favorites include:

~ **AMADEO** *(Modigliani)*

~ **ANSEL** *(Adams)*

~ **CLAUDE** *(Monet)*

~ **DIEGO** *(Rivera)*

~ **HIERONYMUS** *(Bosch)*

~ **HOPPER** *(Edward)*

~ **JACKSON** *(Pollock)*

~ **JASPER** *(Johns)*

~ **LEONARDO** *(da Vinci)*

~ **MATTHAIS** *(Grünewald)*

~ **PABLO** *(Picasso)*

~ **PIET** *(Mondrian)*

~ **SALVADOR** *(Dalí)*

~ **SANDRO** *(Botticelli)*

~ **SARGENT** *(John Singer)*

~ **VINCENT** *(van Gogh)*

~ **WALKER** *(Evans)*

~ **WASSILY** *(Kandinsky)*

Christians alike—both groups are using the name with enthusiasm; and by having a forceful but friendly nickname: Jake.

Variations: *Jakob, Jakobe, Jacoby, Jake, Coby, Giacomo, Jacques, Seamus, James*
Nicknames: *Jake, Jay, Coby*
Alternatives: *Zachary, Luke, Ezra, Caleb*

Jaden Fad alert! Jaden came out of nowhere in 1994 and shot to the number eleven slot for boys in

2008. The name and its seemingly infinite variations are only slightly less popular for girls. The lesson here: Never underestimate the power of the celebrity baby. Will and Jada Smith gave birth to a Jaden in 1998, which got the ball rolling (young Jaden is now something of a celeb in his own right). And Britney Spears naming her son Jayden in 2006 had a thunderous impact. Jaden comes in every spelling you can imagine—variations include swapping out the *J* for every other letter (Raiden, anyone?). And all of the Jaylans can be considered family members. Jadon is an obscure biblical name thought to mean "God listens," but the name now would seem to mean "I read *US Weekly*."

Variations: *Jade, Jadon, Jadyn, Jaeden, Jaiden, Jaidyn, Jaydan, Jayden, Jaydin, Jaydon, Jaylan, Jaylen, Jaylin, Jaylon, Jalen*
Nicknames: *Jay, Jade*
Alternatives: *Grady, Marlon, Brady, Brandon, Carson*

Jadiel ("known by God") is a name that has just started appearing in the United States, probably in the wake of the success of the Latin music star Jadiel (né Ramon Gonzalez). It is typically used by Hispanic families, despite its origins as an obscure biblical name.

Variation: *Yadiel*
Alternatives: *Yandel, Javier, Azriel*

Jagger An occupational name for someone who works with fish, this is more often a way of saluting rock music by invoking the name of Rolling Stones frontman Mick Jagger.

Alternatives: *Cooper, Archer, Tucker, Mick*

Jairo (HI-roe) is the Hispanic equivalent of Jair, the name of a minor character of the Bible, a judge, whose name means "shining."

Variation: *Jair*

Alternatives: *Gilead, Simeon, Jamie*

Jamal means "handsome" in Arabic. It brings to mind acclaimed jazz pianist Ahmad Jamal and *Cosby Show* actor Malcolm-Jamal Warner (who was named for the musician). Jamal is the name of the lead character in the blockbuster movie *Slumdog Millionaire*, so maybe it will break away from the pack.

Variations: *Jamar, Jamarcu, Jamari, Jamarion, Jamir*

Alternatives: *Jalal, Malik, Kamil, Latif*

James "Oh, James. . . ." You can almost hear the breathy purr of any one of 007's lovers. Ian Fleming's superspy James Bond exemplifies the supreme Britishness of this name as well as its suave, somewhat formal sound. That tone is supported by the many centuries worth of Scottish and British monarchs named James. Funny then that one of the most

> *I'd love it if he sounded . . .*
> **British**
>
> | | | |
> |---|---|---|
> | ⁃ ALGERNON | ⁃ HUGH | ⁃ SEBASTIAN |
> | ⁃ ALISTAIR | ⁃ JAMES | ⁃ SIMON |
> | ⁃ BASIL | ⁃ NIGEL | ⁃ THEO |
> | ⁃ COLIN | ⁃ REGINALD | ⁃ TOBY |
> | ⁃ HORATIO | ⁃ RUPERT | ⁃ WINSTON |

English-sounding of English names is a close relative of the Old Testament name Jacob (pages 406–407). Jacob became Iakobos, which became Iacomus, which became James. (Two Jameses were important disciples of Christ in the New Testament.) At the time of this writing, the name James is at an all-time low of number seventeen. For the 130 or so years prior to 1992, it was always in the top ten. James is nothing if not reliable, and there are plenty of nicknames to set him apart. (James spelled backwards, Semaj, has been used as a name since 1999.)

Variations: *Jacob, Giacomo, Jacques, Seamus*
Nicknames: *Jimmy, Jim, Jaime, Jamie*
Alternatives: *Stephen, John, William, Simon, Mark*

Jameson is an Irish whiskey, an English butler ("Ring the bell for Jameson, darling"), and a porn

star (Jenna Jameson). It might also be the name
of a smart, preppy collegiate if you can get past the
other associations (maybe try the alternate spelling,
Jamison).

Variation: *Jamison*
Nicknames: *Jim, Jimmy, Jamie, Sonny*
Alternatives: *Harrison, Addison, Richardson*

Jared appears as a minor character in the book
of Genesis in the Bible. He is the father of Enoch,
grandfather of Methuselah. The name has been
used since the 1950s, probably thanks to the classic
TV show *Big Valley*, which featured a Jarrod. Jared
is familiar to Americans as the name of the Subway
sandwich chain spokesperson, which may be
contributing to recent decline in its use.

Variation: *Jarrod*
Alternatives: *Judd, Jude, Derek, Garrett*

Jaron Take the Israeli name Yaron ("joy"), add a
pinch of Jared, Jason, and Darren, and you end up
with the patchworked name Jaron.

Variations: *Yaron, Jared*
Alternatives: *Aaron, Darrell, Marlon, Galen*

Jarrett is a variation of the name Garrett (page 384),
itself a variation of Gerald ("rules with a spear"),
with a touch of Jared thrown in. Jarrett can be a

nod to NASCAR star Ned Jarrett or musician Keith Jarrett.

Variations: *Garrett, Gerald*
Nickname: *Rett*
Alternatives: *Barrett, Bennett, Corbett*

Jason was a sailor from Greek mythology who assembled a band of heroes to help him search for the Golden Fleece. Although Jason's quest ended tragically, his name shot to the top five in the 1970s. It is on the way back down now. As a result, Jason sounds like it's past its prime, despite its classical underpinnings. Nowadays, families are choosing Mason or Jackson instead.

Variations: *Jayson, Jace, Jase, Jayce*
Nickname: *Jay*
Alternatives: *Mason, Jackson, Casey, Gregory*

Jasper is a variation of Caspar, the name of one of the biblical Three Wise Men (with Melchior and Balthazar), who visited baby Jesus and brought him gifts. The name comes from Persia and means "treasurer." Jasper is also a gem name (one of few for boys); it's a hard red stone. Look for Jasper to pop. It's the name of one of the sexy vampires from the *Twilight* series of books and films. Painter Jasper Johns gives the name an arty edge.

Variations: *Caspar, Gaspard*
Alternatives: *Melchior, Balthazar, Barnabas, Jude, Jackson*

Javier Francis Xavier (Xavier means "new house") was a Basque missionary, an early Jesuit who became a saint. Javier is pronounced HAH-vee-air and is considered by some a more accessible version of Xavier. The name is increasingly popular among Spanish speakers.

Variations: *Javion, Javon, Jayvion, Jayvon, Savion*
Nickname: *Javi (HAH-vee)*
Alternatives: *Felipe, Gustavo, Pedro, Joaquin*

Jay started life as a nickname. It works for any name that starts with the letter *J*. But for more than a hundred years now, Jay has been a given name, and one that does not sound as flaky as many other nickname-to-real-name transfers. Jay Gatsby was the protagonist of Fitzgerald's haunting novel *The Great Gatsby*, J. P. Morgan was the robber baron banker, Jay McInerney writes novels about the preppy set. All in all, this is a name that conveys a good-old-boy quality. Jay is being used by Hindu families as well, because the word means "victorious" in Sanskrit.

Alternatives: *Clay, Trey, James*

Jefferson calls to mind statesman, president, architect, and all-around renaissance man Thomas Jefferson. To people who came of age in the 1970s and '80s, it may also evoke sitcom character George Jefferson, the dry-cleaning entrepreneur and erstwhile neighbor of

I'd love it if he sounded . . .
Indian

~ DEV	~ MAHESH	~ UDAY
~ DINESH	~ PRAKASH	~ VIJAY
~ ISHAAN	~ RAJ	~ VIKASH
~ KIRAN	~ SANJAY	~ VISHNU
~ KRISHNA	~ SIDDHARTHA	~ VIVEK

Archie Bunker. A hero of the Confederacy, Jefferson Davis, also leaps to mind. The name means "son of Jeffrey," but it is so loaded with other associations that its original meaning may get lost.

Variations: *Jeffrey, Jeffers*
Nicknames: *Jeff, Sonny*
Alternatives: *Truman, Quincy, Harrison*

Jeffrey is a trendy name. That is, it appeared on the charts—seemingly out of nowhere—in 1934, shot to the top ten in the early 1960s, and now is sliding away again. Cary Grant may be to thank for its early success. He played the role of Jeffrey in 1933's *The Woman Accused*. It's an old name that seems to have come from several sources, including Godfrey ("God's peace"). The British use the form Geoffrey (Chaucer anyone?), but in the United States Jeffrey remains the norm. Actors Jeff

Daniels and Jeffrey Tambor, writers Jeffrey Archer and Jeffrey Eugenides, and racecar driver Jeff Gordon all use the name.

Variations: *Jeffery, Geoffrey, Jeffers, Jefferson*
Nicknames: *Jeff, Geoff*
Alternatives: *Jeremy, Rodney, Freddie, Gregory, Stephen*

Jeremiah Times change: You couldn't give away the name Jeremiah a few decades ago, whereas Jeremy was all the rage (in the top twenty in the mid-1970s). Now we are over Jeremy, and Jeremiah is on top. Jeremiah ("exaltation") was a major biblical prophet. Jeremiahs from pop culture include "Jeremiah was a bullfrog," the first line from the 1970 song "Joy to the World," and Leonard Bernstein's *Jeremiah Symphony*. Famous Jeremys include actors Jeremy Irons, Jeremy Northam, and Jeremy Piven. Note that on the playground, Jeremy may be known as "germy."

Variations: *Jeramiah, Jerimiah, Jeremy*
Nickname: *Jerry*
Alternatives: *Zachariah, Nehemiah, Obadiah, Ezra, Jedidiah*

Jermaine This name has been popular since 1970, thanks largely to Jermaine Jackson. Rapper/producer Jermaine Dupri and basketball player Jermaine O'Neal also use the name, which means "brotherhood." The name is most common with African American families.

It's a Word, It's a Name

I f you go way back into the etymology, you can usually determine the meaning of a name. But there are plenty of names that you don't need to look up—they are vocabulary words that remain in circulation and that we use all the time. If you'd like the meaning of your son's name to be front and center, consider a pick from this list, from the list of trade names (pages 316–317), or the list of animals (page 460). Note that some of these names are homonyms and the proper vocabulary word is spelled differently.

~ ABEL	~ BLAZE	~ CLAY
~ ACE	~ BROOKS	~ CLIFF
~ ANGEL	~ CASH	~ COLT
~ AUGUST	~ CHAD	~ CURT
~ AXEL	~ CHANCE	~ DREW
~ BEAU	~ CHASE	~ DUKE

Variations: *Germain, German*
Nickname: *Jerry*
Alternatives: *Terence, Jared, Dwayne, Kane, German*

Jerome Saint Jerome is one of the most important saints in the Catholic Church. He translated the Bible into Latin, wrote extensively, and lived a hermit's life. He is associated with lions for removing a thorn from a lion's paw, and is known as a doctor of the Catholic

~ Ernest	~ John	~ Rex
~ Finn	~ Josh	~ River
~ Flint	~ Kane	~ Rusty
~ Frank	~ Lance	~ Ryder
~ Gage	~ Lane	~ Sage
~ Garrett	~ Lee	~ Sandy
~ Gene	~ Mark	~ Sincere
~ Glenn	~ Maverick	~ Sonny
~ Grant	~ Max	~ Sterling
~ Heath	~ Miles	~ Tony
~ Hector	~ Moss	~ Trace
~ Herb	~ Nick	~ Trey
~ Jack	~ Pat	~ Ty
~ Jay	~ Phoenix	~ Victor
~ Jett	~ Pierce	~ Wade
~ Joe	~ Reed	~ Will

Church. Jerome comes from the Greek Hieronymos, which means "sacred name." Famous Jeromes include composer Jerome Kern, choreographer Jerome Robbins, and writer Jerome Salinger, better known as the reclusive J. D.

Variations: *Hieronymos, Jeremy, Geronimo*
Nickname: *Jerry*
Alternatives: *Ambrose, Gregory, Augustine, Gerald, Gerard*

Jesse Tough, renegade Jesse makes his own rules and lives by them. The name sounds utterly contemporary, but is from the Bible: Jesse ("gift") was David's father. Jesse is an ancestor of Jesus, and the relationship is often depicted in art as the Tree of Jesse. The Jesses that leap to mind are individualists: preacher Jesse Jackson, outlaw Jesse James, Olympian Jesse Owens, *The Dukes of Hazzard* patriarch Uncle Jesse. For some of us, the Rick Springfield song "Jesse's Girl" may leap to mind.
Variation: *Jessie*
Alternatives: *Waylon, Vernon, Amos, Enos*

Jesus When used, Christ's first name is almost exclusively given to Hispanic babies and is pronounced hay-SEUSS. Obviously, the name is a celebration of Christ and all he represents: forgiveness, love, salvation.
Variation: *Joshua*
Nickname: *Jesse*
Alternatives: *Messiah, Christian, Javier, Manuel*

Jett appeared in 1999, the year after the Disney TV show *The Famous Jett Jackson* aired. John Travolta paved the way earlier in the decade by naming his son after his passion for aviation. The name is brisk and suggests speed—it is decidedly modern (which also means it may seem dated in a few years). There's really no way to shorten this one; it's nickname-free.
Alternatives: *Jed, Brett, Chet, Chad*

Joaquin The Spanish-language version of the name Joachim is famous to Americans thanks to actor Joaquin Phoenix and California's San Joaquin Valley. Saint Joachim ("elevated by God") was biblical Mary's father. The name was obscure until the 1990s, when it started working its way to popularity.

Alternatives: *Joachim, Yakim*
Nicknames: *Quin (pronounced keen), Keen*
Alternatives: *Javier, Sebastian, Diego, Gael*

Joel is a traditionally Jewish name that has enjoyed some crossover appeal. Its heyday was the early 1980s, but it remains well liked. It's a down-to-earth everyguy name with a bit of a nebbishy edge. Think of entertainers Billy Joel and Joel Grey. The name is a combination of an abbreviated form of Yahweh, the name of the Lord, and El, which means "God"; in full, it means "God is supreme."

Nickname: *Joe*
Alternatives: *Jael, Gael, Nolan*

✐ **John** Until 1980, John was one of the top five names for hundreds of years. As of this writing, he's at number twenty and slipping fast. But no matter how fashion's favor ebbs or flows, John's authority will never be diminished. John ("God is gracious") is one of the most sturdy, stalwart, reliable names in history. And that's not to say it's boring. John evokes a handsome, capable leader. Think John Kennedy, John Adams, John Wayne. Johns can even be artistic: John Lennon and Johnny Depp. When Mr. Big's name was revealed in *Sex and the City*, it turned out to be the iconic John.

Variations: *Juan, Johnny, Jean, Johan, Jan, Ewan, Ian, Ivan, Giovanni, Sean*
Nicknames: *Johnny, Jon*
Alternatives: *James, William, Edward, Michael, Thomas*

🕊 **Jonah** means "dove" in Hebrew. The name comes from the biblical prophet who was tossed from his ship by his crew and ended up in the belly of a whale. The name had been forgotten in the United States until the 1969 movie *80 Steps to Jonah*, which starred Wayne Newton, Slim Pickens, and Mickey Rooney. Though the film has slipped into obscurity, the name has climbed since then. Now people think of comedian Jonah Hill and the musical Jonas Brothers.

Variation: *Jonas*
Nickname: *Joe*
Alternatives: *Noah, Micah, Judah, Lucas*

Jonathan has more in common with Matthew and Nathan than it does with John. The name means "God has given," same as Matthew, but with the Hebrew syllables reversed. And Nathan is an abbreviation of the name. John, curiously, is an entirely different name. Jonathan signifies loyalty because biblical Jonathan stood by David in the face of Saul's anger. Famous Jonathans include writers Jonathan Swift and Jonathan Franzen, comedian Jon Stewart, and actor Jon Voight.

Variations: *Jonathon, Johnathan, Johnathon, Jon*
Nicknames: *Jon, Nathan*
Alternatives: *Nathaniel, Matthew, Sebastian, Benjamin*

Jordan A unisex salute to the river that Christ was baptized in, one of Christianity's holiest sites. Basketball superstar Michael Jordan helped the name shoot to stardom in the 1990s. New Kids on the Block singer Jordan Knight and fictional hottie Jordan Catalano from TV's *My So-Called Life* may have influenced the zeitgeist as well.

Variations: *Jorden, Jordon, Jordyn*
Nickname: *Jordie*
Alternatives: *Shiloh, Israel, Abel, Warren*

Jorge As the Spanish for George (see pages 385–386), the name Jorge is very popular with Hispanic families. Once foreign sounding, it doesn't seem so unusual now that so many luminaries—baseball player Jorge Posada, health guru Jorge Cruise, and the writer Jorge Luis Borges—carry the name.

Variations: *George, Jorje*
Alternatives: *José, Juan, Felipe, Carlos*

José, a variant of Joseph, is one of the most
enduringly popular Hispanic names. Famous Josés
include singers José Feliciano and José Carreras and
baseball player José Canseco.

Variation: *Joseph*
Nickname: *Joe, Pepe, Pepito*
Alternatives: *Jorge, Javier, Eduardo, Moses*

Joseph means "God adds." Joseph was Jacob's
favorite son in the Bible. He was enslaved in Egypt,
where his work for the pharaoh enabled him to
save his brothers. Joseph was also the name of the
carpenter husband of Mary, stepfather of Jesus. And
Joseph of Arimathea buried Jesus. This name, with
top-notch biblical creds, is extremely versatile: the
formal Joseph, the buddy Joe, the cute little boy Joey.

Variations: *Joe, Joey, Josue, José, Giuseppe, Yusuf, Yosef*
Nicknames: *Joe, Joey, Beppe, Pepe, Josie, Jody*
Alternatives: *Jacob, John, Philip, Thomas*

Joshua is a biblical classic ("God is my salvation")
that caught fire in the late 1960s. The blaze is still
burning bright: Joshua has been in the top ten since
1979 and the top five since 1983. Joshua is up to the
job: biblical Joshua led the Israelites to the Promised
Land after Moses's death. While Joshua sounds
serious and responsible (and mystical to some ears,
thanks to Joshua Tree National Park), Josh is the

> ### I'd love to call him...
> #### Joe
>
> ---
>
> Not all Joes have to be average—there are a number of options beyond Joseph:
>
> | | | |
> |---|---|---|
> | ~ GIOVANNI | ~ JONAH | ~ JOSIAH |
> | ~ JOACHIM | ~ JONAS | ~ JOSS |
> | ~ JOAQUIN | ~ JONES | ~ JOVAN |
> | ~ JOFI | ~ JOSÉ | ~ JOVE |

easygoing boy next door. Josh could lighten up even the most dour last name and is being used as a first name, not just a nickname, now.

Variation: *Josh*
Nickname: *Josh*
Alternatives: *Jacob, Nathan, Ezra, Levi*

✒ **Josiah** has "Puritan" written all over it. It's the name of a king from the Old Testament and means "God heals." Josiah Wedgwood was the famous creator of the distinctive blue-and-white English pottery. Josiah Quincy was a patriot related to John Adams. And Josiah Bartlett was a signer of the Declaration of Independence. (The president on the TV show *The West Wing* was named for him.) The name was rediscovered in the 1970s and is coming back into fashion.

Variation: *Jasiah*
Nicknames: *Jed, Joe*
Alternatives: *Jeremiah, Isaiah, Joshua*

Jovani can be an unorthodox spelling of the name Giovanni, which is John in Italian (see pages 419–420). Or it can have pagan undertones as a celebration of Jove, who was the equivalent of Zeus, the king of the gods, in Roman mythology. And if you want to honor rocker Jon Bon Jovi, you can drop the *an* for his nickname.

Variations: *Jovan, Jovanni, Jovanny, Jovany, Giovanni*
Nicknames: *Joe, Van*
Alternatives: *Joel, Vittorio, Ivan*

Juan is John (pages 419–420) in Spanish. There have been countless celebrated Juans throughout history. Perhaps the most famous Juan is the fictional Don Juan, the libertine lover who ends up in hell for his exploits.

Variation: *John*
Alternatives: *José, Carlos, Manuel, Gael*

Judah ("praised") was one of Jacob's sons in the Bible. The name is related to Judas, which nobody uses because it is synonymous with "traitor." While this name is mostly used by Jewish families, it may appeal to lovers of reggae as well: Judah the Lion is a common

trope in reggae music and is a reference to Emperor
Haile Selassie I of Ethiopia, whom Rastas revere as the
second coming of Christ.

Variations: *Jude, Judas, Yehuda*
Nickname: *Jude*
Alternatives: *Dov, Jonah, Julius, Noah*

Jude is a dude. Although the name is a variation
on Judah and Judas, Jude sounds less religious and
more leather jacket hipster. It evokes Thomas Hardy's
novel *Jude the Obscure*, the Beatles's song "Hey Jude,"
and actor Jude Law. Saint Jude is the patron saint of
lost causes, which gives the name emotional depth
as well.

Variations: *Judah, Judas*
Alternatives: *Judd, Thaddeus, Bartholomew, Simon*

Julian is a staunchly Roman name—it comes from the
name Julius. In addition to being used by Emperor
Caesar, the name was used by early Christian saints
and a pope. What's very old is new again: The name
is coming back into fashion. Famous Julians include
actor Julian Sands, musician Julian Lennon, and King
Julian of the movie *Madagascar*. Jerry Seinfeld named
a son Julian. Julien is the French version. Jules is used
in French and English (as for author Jules Verne and
cartoonist Jules Feiffer). Julio (WHO-lee-oh) is the
Hispanic version.

Variations: *Julien, Jules, Julio*
Nickname: *Jules*
Alternatives: *Augustus, Cornelius, Martin, Vincent*

Junior There is something charming and retro (and yes, a little Mafia-esque—think Uncle Junior from TV's *The Sopranos*) about the name Junior. But this name is one to consider carefully. Junior rides a scooter. Junior gets a haircut. Junior visits the office and spins in the desk chair. But does Junior perform surgery? Argue major lawsuits? Fly a 747? Why not give him a grown-up name—something that won't limit him; something that inspires confidence—and just call him Junior for short?

Alternatives: *Scooter, Sport, Skip*

Justice is a name that expresses a virtue, which you are more likely to see for girls. Strong and righteous, Justice is unisex, but slightly more popular for boys. It goes well with nearly every last name. And the name promises fairness and truth. It's similar in meaning to the name Judge (as in actor Judge Reinhold), which is rarely used. The variation Justus may look more masculine to some parents and is as traditional or more so. It's Latin for "fair," and has a more classic, Roman look to it than Justice which might appear more New Agey.

Variations: *Justus, Justin*
Alternatives: *Eustace, Chance, Sincere, Merritt*

Kaden Take Jaden, add a little Cadence, and what do you get? Caden. Now replace the *C* with an easy *K,* and you get Kaden. This name has skyrocketed from nonexistence in the 1980s to the top one hundred. Caden took off recently, following the trail blazed by other cool boys Aidan, Braden, and Jaden. (Incidentally, the word *cade* means "like a lump.")

Variations: *Kadin, Kadyn, Kaeden, Kaiden, Kayden, Kade, Cade, Caden, Cayden*

Alternatives: *Caleb, Aidan, Rain, Layton*

Kai is all things to all people. It appears as a name or word in many languages, and in every case it usually has a hippie feel to it. In Hawaiian and Japanese, it's said to mean "the sea"; in Scandinavian languages, "keeper of the keys"; in Navajo, "willow"; in Welsh, it relates to Arthurian legend. And so on. The name is growing in popularity in Hollywood: Jennifer Connolly, Parminder Nagra, and Naomi Watts and Liev Schreiber all named their sons Kai (it's a middle name in the last case). For unorthodox names, it's a good choice: easy to pronounce and nickname-free.

Alternatives: *Ray, Trey, Milo, Silas*

Kamari is a globetrotter: It's the name of a beach in Santorini, Greece, a district in Afghanistan

(Ab Kamari), it's said to mean "moonlight" in Swahili. This unorthodox name sounds Arabic but also seems familiar (Camaro, Armani, Atari), which may boost its popularity. Warning: The name is starting to be used by girls and does have a feminine ring to it (like Imani).

Alternatives: *Kymani, Tariq, Raqib*

Kameron A Scottish clan name, Cameron (page 325) means "crooked nose." Kameron with a *K* is an offbeat spelling. The name is popular with boys (directors Cameron Crowe, James Cameron) and girls (actress Cameron Diaz).

Variations: *Cameron, Camren, Camron, Camryn, Kamren, Kamron*
Nicknames: *Cam, Kam*
Alternatives: *Kennedy, Campbell, Duncan*

Kane Cain is not a good choice for a child; Cain became the first murderer of the Bible when he killed his brother, Abel. But if you like the sound of the name, Kane is a good alternative. With a *K*, Kane looks like the Gaelic last name it is, which offers even further separation from the biblical Cain. The meaning, however, is "one who battles." So if he's a handful, you've been warned.

Variation: *Keane*
Alternatives: *Lane, Blaine, Zane*

Kareem Arabic for "generosity," Kareem became popular thanks to basketball legend Kareem Abdul-Jabbar. Nowadays, it also brings to mind industrial designer Karim Rashid. The name is extremely popular in Arab countries, but less so in the United

AIN'T NOTHING LIKE THE REAL THING, BABY . . .

Most kids love a good nickname, but that doesn't mean your son shouldn't have a real name, too. A nickname offers the chance for a child to have it both ways, to goof around and also hit the books. It increases the possibilities in his life. Despite this reality, many parents forego formal names in favor of pet names. These shortcuts may be cute and snappy, but they may not hold up in the long run. So please, name him Robert, not Bobby. That way, if he wants

to become president, he has a respectable, commanding name for his letterhead. And if he wants to become a racecar driver or ballplayer, he can use his nickname.

All of the following names are in the top 1,000 in the United States. They are all short forms of longer names: Ben, Billy, Bo, Bobby, Frank, Frankie, Harry, Jack, Jerry, Joe, Joey, Johnny, Jon, Josh, Larry, Max, Mike, Ray, Ricky, Rudy, Sam, Sammy, Steve, Tommy, Will.

States, possibly because it sounds too close to some girls names like Carine and scans a bit like Karen.

Variation: *Karim*
Alternatives: *Ahmed, Rashid, Abdul, Muhammed*

Karson is an unorthodox (read: made up) spelling of Carson (see pages 326–327).

Variations: *Carson, Carsen*
Alternatives: *Clark, Boone, Preston*

Keaton has the spotlight of Hollywood in his eyes. Think of actors Buster, Diane, and Michael, as well as Michael J. Fox's famous character on *Family Ties*, Alex P. Keaton. The name is bright but grounded, gentrified but with a whiff of blarney to it thanks to the similar sound to Keegan and Keenan.

Alternatives: *Wheaton, Beeton, Easton*

Keegan Kiss Keegan, he's Irish. This is a resolutely ethnic choice, in use as a first name since 1979. It's a last name that means "son of Aidan," so if you like Aidan (page 285) but it's a bit too trendy for you, take a look at Keegan instead.

Variation: *Keagan*
Alternatives: *Deegan, Teagan, Reagan, Regan, Keenan*

Keenan is an Irish last name meaning "son of the ancient one." The word *keen* suggests sharp wits and eagerness. A character actor in the 1960s, Keenan Wynn, used the name. Nowadays, we think of comedian Keenan Ivory Wayans and football player Keenan McCardell.

Alternatives: *Keane, Keene, Kane*

Keith ("forest") was once so closely associated with Scotland you could hear bagpipes and see heather waving in the background as you said it. Now the name is firmly entrenched as a first name, making it hard to remember that it started out as a Scottish last name. Famous Keiths include musician Keith Urban, baseball player Keith Hernandez, actor Keith Carradine, and artist Keith Haring. No nicknames here.

Alternatives: *Heath, Campbell, Graham*

Kellen This evocative name can be Scottish, and related to Alan or Colin (McKellen means "son of Alan"), or it can come from the Gaelic word for "slender." Kellen Winslow, a famous NFL tight end, raised awareness of the name in the 1980s, and it will surely rise due to actor Kellan Lutz's portrayal of vampire Emmett Cullen in the *Twlight* series of movies.

Variation: *Kelton*
Nicknames: *Kell, Kelly*
Alternatives: *Emmett, Colin, Kendrick*

Kelvin Calvin meets Kevin in this mash-up. Yes, it's a Scottish last name with a whiff of science to it: Lord William Thomson Kelvin was a pioneer of thermodynamics who gave us the Kelvin scale. But it evokes Calvin, Kevin, and Melvin more than the highlands or the science lab.

Alternatives: *Campbell, Calvin, Malcolm*

Kendall is a last name referring to the Kent region in England. The girls started using Kendall in the 1980s, and now the usage for boys is falling fast. Kendrick may be a better choice for an unexpected alternative to Kenneth.

Nicknames: *Ken, Kenny*
Alternatives: *Kendrick, Kenneth, Campbell*

✐ **Kendrick** can be Scottish, where it is a variation on Henry (page 398), from the last name MacKendrick, meaning "son of Henry." It can be British, meaning "powerful royal." Or it can be Welsh, meaning "royal hill." In any case, Kendrick is a squarely masculine name, unlikely to be usurped by the girls. It has a pleasingly hard *k* at the beginning and end, which puts it on-trend.

Variations: *Henry, MacKendrick*
Nicknames: *Ken, Kenny*
Alternatives: *Kennedy, Roderick, Rory, Henrik, Kent, Cedric, Richard*

Kenneth can mean either "born of fire" or "handsome." The name is a Scottish heavyweight that caught fire in the United States in the 1930s and has been a mainstay since then. Famous Kenneths include actor Kenneth Branagh, economist John Kenneth Galbraith, and theater critic Kenneth Tynan. Pop culture reference: The REM song "What's the Frequency, Kenneth?" came out in 1994.

Variation: *Kenny*
Nicknames: *Ken, Kenny*
Alternatives: *Douglas, Graham, Campbell, Keith*

Kenyon is a last name that means "wolf" in Gaelic and is a place-name in England. It's also the name of a college in Ohio that may leap to many minds, home of *The Kenyon Review*, a respected literary journal. To some ears, the word may sound like the masculine equivalent of Kenya.

Nickname: *Ken*
Alternatives: *Kenneth, Canyon, Landon*

Kevin A Gaelic success story, Kevin ("handsome") went from being an unknown, highly ethnic name in 1920 to the top twenty by the late 1950s. The name used to say "I'm Irish" as surely as a shamrock (St. Kevin is one of the patron saints of Dublin), but now it's used by everyone.

Alternatives: *Ryan, Brian, Declan, Brendan, Patrick*

Khalil Arabic for "friend," Khalil carries some
poetry with it. The first association to Western ears
is Khalil Gibran, the Lebanese-born poet and author
of *The Prophet*.
Variation: *Khaleel*
Alternatives: *Bashir, Kareem, Habib*

Kieran rode into town on the latest wave of Irish
names, arriving in the 1990s. The name means "black"
and communicates that mom and dad want to get in
touch with their Emerald Isle ancestry. As other -*an*
and -*en* names like Aidan and Jaden flood the charts,
look for this one to rise with the tide.
Variations: *Kyran, Ciaran, Kian*
Nickname: *Kier*
Alternatives: *Declan, Finn, Ronan, Pierce*

Killian is an Irish name that means "conflict," "church,"
or "beer." The latter meaning is not etymological;
Killian's Irish Red is a popular brew. The name sounds
hip and outdoorsy (those from the northeast might be
reminded of Vermont ski resort Killington).
Alternatives: *William, Dillon, Mulligan*

King, Prince, Duke, Marquess, Earl, Viscount, Baron.
That's the order of the peerage in Britian. King is, of
course, the highest rank, and some families believe
that naming a child King will bestow the power and

glory of that position. All of these names except Viscount (or even Count) have caught on. King, Prince, and Marquess (or Marquis) are most often used by African American families. The others are a mixed bag. King may also be given as a family name. It disappeared from 1965 to 2005 and is only now making a comeback.

Alternatives: *Duke, Baron, Kingston, Leroy, Rex, Pharaoh*

Kingston Rocker Gwen Stefani's son Kingston (born in 2006) has spawned a run on the name, which means "king's town." Kingston is now as hot as the capital of Jamaica.

Alternatives: *Marley, Dunstan, Weston*

Kobe NBA legend Kobe Bryant has inspired many namesakes since 1997. Bryant was named for the Japanese delicacy Kobe beef, which is considered the cream of the crop (or herd) as far as meat is concerned. Coby is a variation that can either be a nod to Bryant or a variation of Jacob.

Variation: *Coby*
Alternatives: *Rory, Colby, Brodie*

Krish Krishna is a traditional Hindu boy's name that refers to a god. His name means "dark," and depictions in art often give him blue skin. Krish is a variation— and a nickname—of the more traditional long form,

The Sporting Life

To find a name that hits it out of the park, try the world of sports—the names you'll find there range from brawny to sweet. To err on the safe side, you may want to choose from among the late greats (so you won't regret your choice if your hero disappoints). But if you are dauntless about scandals, you'll have that many more cute, distinctive names to choose from.

- **BABE** *(Ruth, the Bambino, the Sultan of Swat)*

- **BECKHAM** *(as in David, the English soccer star who married a Spice Girl)*

- **BRONKO** *(Nagurski, football player)*

- **CY** *(Young, baseball player)*

- **ELGIN** *(Baylor, basketball player)*

- **HONUS** *(Wagner, baseball player)*

- **JACKIE** *(Robinson, the first African American Major League baseball player)*

- **JORDAN** *(Michael, last name's first for the basketball legend)*

- **KNUTE** *(Rockne, college football coach)*

- **KOBE** *(Bryant, basketball player)*

- **LEBRON** *(James, basketball player)*

- **LLEYTON** *(Hewitt, tennis player)*

- **MOOKIE** *(Wilson, baseball player)*

- **NOLAN** *(Ryan, baseball player)*

- **RAFER** *(Johnson, Olympic decathlete)*

- **ROLLIE** *(Fingers, baseball player)*

- **SANDY** *(Koufax, baseball player)*

- **TROY** *(Aikman, football player)*

- **TY** *(Cobb, baseball player)*

- **WAYNE** *(Gretzky, the Great One, hockey player)*

- **WILT** *(Chamberlain, basketball player)*

and may help people forget the connection to the Hare Krishnas, who use the god's full name.

Variation: *Krishna*
Alternatives: *Vishnu, Prakash, Rajit*

Kristian is a variation of Christian (pages 332–333). The *K* makes the name sound more northern European and a little edgier. But does it look more feminine this way, too?

Variation: *Christian*
Nickname: *Kris*
Alternatives: *Christer, Tristan, Sebastian*

Kristopher Christopher (page 333) with a *K*, this spelling calls to mind singer Kris Kristofferson and TV's *American Idol* winner Kris Allen. It's the Scandinavian way to spell the name.

Variation: *Christopher*
Nickname: *Kris*
Alternatives: *Crispin, Tristan, Kasper*

Kyle is a trendy name with solid foundations. A *kyle* is a "narrow channel of water" and a last name in Scotland. As a first name, it zipped to the top of the charts in the mid-1980s to 1990s and is now starting to decline. The girls discovered it in the 1970s and started using it, and then switched it from Kyle to Kylie. Kyle may be hurting as a result—or maybe there were just too many Kyles in the sandbox. Actor Kyle MacLachlan leaps to mind, as does *South Park* rascal Kyle Broflovski. Some families are playing with the name and ending up with Kyler (a Danish name meaning "archer" or a mash-up: Kyle meets Tyler) or Kylan (Kyle meets Ryan).

Variations: *Kylan, Kyler*
Alternatives: *Firth, Brook, Kai, Ryder*

Lamar has the sound of the ocean in it; it literally means "from the sea" (*la mer* in French). Lamars that leap to mind include actress Hedy Lamarr, the fey character in the movie *Revenge of the Nerds*, comedian Phil LaMarr, AFL founder Lamar Hunt, and basketball player Lamar Odom. The name is popular with African American families.

Alternatives: *Terrell, Shamar, Marlon, Lawrence*

Lance Despite its battleground associations—a lance is a long sword used by knights—Lance sounds easy-going, even debonair. It seems harmless, having more to do with glances and dances than sharp, pointy things. (The word's original meaning is "territory.") Maybe we have Sir Lancelot (no relation to the name, by the way) to thank for that, as well as cyclist Lance Armstrong and singer Lance Bass.

Variation: *Lanzo*
Alternatives: *Chance, Lawrence, Lorenzo, Vance*

Landon Amiable TV actor Michael Landon (né Eugene Orowitz) is responsible in large part for the popularity of this name. Landon started appearing on *Bonanza* in 1959, and by 1962 parents were using his name as a first name. The actor went on to become the beloved patriarch of *Little House on the Prairie,* and by the end of his run on that show in the early 1980s, the name was firmly established. *Bonanza* and *Little House* were both westerns, so it's no surprise that Landon ("long hill") has a sturdy, manly, confident feel to it. Thanks, Pa!

Variations: *Landen, Landin, Landyn*
Alternatives: *Bradon, Martin, Carter, Dalton*

Lane is a last name for people living near the local— you guessed it!—lane. Think of it as the boy's version of the popular girl's name Laney. It has the masculine sound of Shane without the wilderness edge. It's more city Lane than country Shane.

Variation: *Layne*
Alternatives: *Layton, Dane, Nate, Kane*

 Langston The Harlem Renaissance poet Langston Hughes popularized this Old English name, which was his mother's maiden name. From its pastoral origins (the meaning is "long town"), Hughes gives the pick a sense of jazz and vibrant city streets. The name is an excellent alternative to Landon and Jackson, one that can be a celebration of African American letters or American urban history, or simply a dignified but slightly offbeat choice.

Variations: *Langley, Langford, Langdon*
Nickname: *Lang*
Alternatives: *Bradford, Cameron, Lawton, Leighton, Thurston*

𝓁 **Lars** seems custom-made for a Nordic hero. The Scandinavian version of Lawrence sounds as though it ends with a *z*, which gives the name contemporary flair. There are no nicknames here, just one brawny, clear syllable. To spice things up, consider Larson, which means, not surprisingly, son of Lars.

Variation: *Larson*
Alternatives: *Lazarus, Anders, Magnus, Igor, Thor*

𝓁 **Lawrence**, or Laurence, comes from the Roman town of Laurentum. The name of the town relates to "laurel," the aromatic plant associated with victory. (Roman emperors wore crowns of laurel leaves.) Lawrence is a name that suggests dignity and levity at once. Laurence Olivier and Laurence Fishburne are serious actors. Larry Sanders and Larry David are clowns. Both names are on the slide but deserve another look. They'd go well with those Samuels (or Sams) and Maximillians (or Maxes) on the swing set today.

Variations: *Laurence, Laurent, Lorne, Lorenzo*
Nickname: *Larry*
Alternatives: *Clarence, Frederick, Maynard, Russell*

Lawson sounds like the sheriff: He's got the law in his name and with the similarity to Dawson, a bit of a cowboy twang. The name derives from Lawrence (see opposite). Don't mess with him.

Alternatives: *Lawrence, Dawson, Carson, Mason*

Layton ("meadow town") could go either way: Is it from the trailer park? (Layton is a manufacturer of trailers.) Or is it hoity-toity? (Leighton, the name from which it comes, sounds like Olde English fare.)

Variation: *Leighton*
Alternatives: *Peyton, Raymond, Clayton*

✐ **Lazarus** Let's raise Lazarus from the dead, shall we? This name, from a man in the Bible whom Jesus resurrected, is ripe for rediscovery. It's got a solid foundation, an exotic letter, and a cool nickname (Laz). Yours will be the only Lazarus in the class.

Nickname: *Laz*
Alternatives: *Ezra, Enzo, Barnabas*

Leandro is the Hispanic form of Leander, the mythic Greek boy who drowned while swimming to visit his lover Hero. Families have been using the name in numbers since 2005.

Variation: *Leander*
Nickname: *Lee*
Alternatives: *Anders, Aldo, Sandro*

Lee comes from "leah," which means "meadow." It sounds New Agey until you recall that Lee is also the name of a jeans manufacturer and the last name of Confederate General Robert E. Lee. It also reminds some of us of TV action hero Lee Majors. So Lee actually comes off more like a rough-and-tumble kid than a flower child. Warning: The name and some variations are used by girls, too.

Alternatives: *Leadon, Leland, Riley, Leo*

Leland is a proper gentleman. As a last name, it used to refer to someone who lived near a fallow field; nowadays, Leland sounds like he's living in the manor house. That association is strengthened by Hollywood producer Leland Hayward and former California governor and Stanford University founder Leland Stanford.

Nickname: *Lee*
Alternatives: *Leighton, Clayton, Anderson*

Lennon "All we are saying…" is that this name squarely and firmly evokes Beatles band member John Lennon, and there's really no way around it. This Lennon ("give peace a chance") is not to be confused with Communist revolutionary Vladimir Lenin ("give us the child for eight years and it will be a Bolshevik forever").

Nickname: *Len*
Alternatives: *Ringo, Madden, Jagger, Hendrix*

O, to Be in England!

There is a long history of using place-names as personal names. If you're an Anglophile, why not choose a name that will remind you of Merry Olde England? Here are some British place-names that may inspire:

~ **ALBANY**	~ **HASTINGS**	~ **PADDINGTON**
~ **ALBEMARLE**	~ **HUXLEY**	~ **PEMBROKE**
~ **BELGRAVIA**	~ **KENSINGTON**	~ **REGENT**
~ **BENNETT**	~ **LAMBETH**	~ **SCARBOROUGH**
~ **CHESHIRE**	~ **LANGDON**	~ **STANHOPE**
~ **DEVON**	~ **LISMORE**	~ **TEMPLE**
~ **GRAFTON**	~ **MAYFAIR**	~ **WELLINGTON**
~ **HANOVER**	~ **OXFORD**	~ **WESTMINSTER**

✒ **Leo** is a lion—and a fierce, proud, valiant name with Christian underpinnings. (Saint Leo, a pope, saved Rome from Attila the Hun.) It's especially fitting for boys with manes of red or sandy hair, or for boys born in late July, early August (when the astrological sign of Leo is dominant). It also works for anyone who likes a name with power that is also irresistibly cute.

Variations: *Leon, Leonel, Lionel*
Alternatives: *Milo, Theo, Ariel, Russell, Griffin*

Literary Luminaries

S ome authors inspire us so much that we can even imagine naming a child after them. Others have cool names that are worth borrowing.

- ~ **AESOP** (of fables fame)
- ~ **ALDOUS** (Huxley)
- ~ **BERTRAND** (Russell)
- ~ **BRAM** (Stoker)
- ~ **CARVER** (Raymond)
- ~ **DANTE** (Alighieri)
- ~ **HORATIO** (Alger)
- ~ **KEATS** (John)
- ~ **LANGSTON** (Hughes)
- ~ **LARKIN** (Philip)
- ~ **LEO** (Tolstoy)
- ~ **LEWIS** (Carroll)
- ~ **NORMAN** (Mailer)
- ~ **OSCAR** (Wilde)
- ~ **RUDYARD** (Kipling)
- ~ **SHEL** (Silverstein)
- ~ **THEODOR** (Geisel)
- ~ **TOBIAS** (Wolff)
- ~ **UPTON** (Sinclair)
- ~ **WALT** (Whitman)

Leonardo ("brave lion") had a very Italian or Spanish sound to it until Leonardo DiCaprio became famous. Families started falling in love with the poetic, artistic, ornate, but still masculine name. The other Leonardo it evokes is, of course, Da Vinci, the ultimate Renaissance man. While Leonardo's fortunes have risen, Leonard's have fallen. Go with the *-o*.

Variations: *Leonard, Leonidas*
Nicknames: *Len, Leo, Nardo, Lenny*
Alternatives: *Raphael, Giancarlo, Federico, Alessandro*

Leroy was once "the king"—the name comes from the French *le roi*. Now people are more likely to associate him with "the baddest man in the whole damn town" from the Jim Croce song "Bad, Bad Leroy Brown." File Leroy under dated. Like Elmer, Herbert, and Virgil, he sounds like he is working at a dry goods store in the 1920s.

Nicknames: *Lee, Roy*
Alternatives: *Tyrone, Maurice, Antwane*

Levi ("joining together") was a son of Leah and Jacob in the Old Testament. This Hebrew name is enjoying a resurgence. It's got that fashionable exotic letter (*v*), and it's short, cute, and long on tradition. Levi sounds sturdy thanks to the American denim company Levi Strauss. Expect this one to wear well.

Nickname: *Lev*
Alternatives: *Ezra, Eli, Jonah*

Lewis When Louis (pages 448–449) crosses the English Channel, this is what happens to his name. Instead of loo-EE you get LOO-is. Like Louis, Lewis's fortunes have been falling for some time. In the Anglo Lewis, you also have references to authors Lewis Carroll, C. S. Lewis, and explorer Meriwether Lewis. But for something with a fresher feel, Ferris or Lucas might be a better choice.

Variations: *Louis, Luis*
Nickname: *Lew*
Alternatives: *Morris, Ferris, Willis*

Liam is William with a Gaelic brogue. Along with names like Finn, Kieran, and Declan, Liam is on the crest of the latest wave of Irish names crashing down on third- and fourth-generation parents who want to seize their ancestry. Actor Liam Neeson has helped pave the way to the mainstream.

Variation: *William*
Alternatives: *Declan, Owen, Finn, Garrett*

✐ **Lincoln** A salute to freedom, dignity, and noble character, Lincoln evokes Honest Abe. There are many Lincoln place-names throughout the country (Lincoln Park, Chicago neighborhood) as well as schools and other institutions (Lincoln Center for the Performing Arts in New York City). Lincoln is a big, serious name for a little guy, but he'll grow into it and make you proud.

Nicknames: *Link, Linc*
Alternatives: *Truman, Roosevelt, Kennedy*

✐ **Lloyd** is a Welsh name for a wise, venerable man. Think actor Lloyd Bridges, composer Andrew Lloyd Webber, and architect Frank Lloyd Wright. Lloyd isn't used much anymore. Yours will be the only one.

Variation: *Floyd*
Alternatives: *Boyd, Rhys, Sawyer*

Logan is a brawny, outdoorsy name. It evokes the city in Utah, the mountain in Canada. It's a kind of rock and a kind of bog. Logan is hotter than ever. It's been intermittently popular for a long time, but two 1970s pop culture moments took it to new heights: TV show *Travis Logan, D.A.*, and sci-fi movie *Logan's Run*. Even the inevitable connection to Boston's Logan Airport can't dull the piney, western feel of this name. Families may be using the name more in lieu of Morgan, which has been taken over by girls.

Alternatives: *Boston, Hogan, Gordon*

London It's the capital of England and a famous tower and bridge there. Use it for a girl and you get that city sophistication; use it for a boy, however, and there is a rustic, outdoorsy, self-sufficient edge. It's the call of the wild offered by the connection to Jack London, the author of adventure books like *White Fang* and *The Sea Wolf*. If you are looking for a literary connection to England, try Albion, which is the ancient poetic name for England (named for the white cliffs of Dover). Warning: More girls than boys are using London now.

Alternatives: *Albion, Buck, Wolf, Landon*

Lorenzo is the Italian and Spanish version of Lawrence (page 440). Unlike Lawrence, whose fortunes have waxed and waned, Lorenzo has remained constant. Lorenzo may be a heartbreaker if he turns out like suave actor Lorenzo Lamas. Or he may have an

> ### I'd love it if he sounded . . .
> **French**
>
> | | | |
> |---|---|---|
> | ~ **ALAIN** | ~ **HONORÉ** | ~ **PIERRE** |
> | ~ **ANDRÉ** | ~ **JACQUES** | ~ **RÉMY** |
> | ~ **CLÉMENT** | ~ **JULES** | ~ **SERGE** |
> | ~ **DIDIER** | ~ **LOUIS** | ~ **YVES** |
> | ~ **ÉTIENNE** | ~ **OLIVIER** | |
> | ~ **GASTON** | ~ **PASCAL** | |

interest in the arts if he takes after Italian Renaissance patron Lorenzo de Medici or architect Renzo Piano.

Variations: *Lawrence, Lorenz, Loren, Lorne*
Nicknames: *Renzo, Enzo*
Alternatives: *Fernando, Armando, Vincenzo*

Louis ("famous warrior") is the name of kings in France, sixteen of them. The name is pronounced loo-EE, which in French has a pert, chirping sound, and in American English (LOO-ee) can end with a whine. (Try remembering the TV show *Taxi* in which Danny DeVito played Louie De Palma.) Some families solve this by going with the Anglicized Lewis (page 445) instead. The most popular version of the name is Spanish, Luis (loo-EESE). While Louis (and Lewis) have been sliding, Luis has been climbing.

Variations: *Luis, Louie, Lewis*
Nicknames: *Lou, Louie*
Alternatives: *Henry, Richard, Charles, Dennis*

Lucian Think of Lucian as the male equivalent of Lucy. The name means "light" and has a wonderful, mysterious, ancient Roman quality to it. You can almost hear the word "elusive" in it (LOO-shun). The name is an oldie but goodie that is being revived after a long dormancy, as is its Italian variation, Luciano (loo-CHA-no). Lucian calls to mind painter Lucian Freud; Luciano, opera tenor Pavarotti.

Variation: *Luciano*
Nicknames: *Lou, Luc*
Alternatives: *Martin, Cassius, Julian, August*

Luke is the name of one of Christ's apostles and an evangelist. He was a doctor and the author of one of the gospels in the Bible. Luke and Lucas refer to the same person and are equally popular names; Lucas is the more formal form, which also became a last name. Luke calls to mind *Star Wars* hero Luke Skywalker and actors Luke Perry and Luke Wilson. Lucas has a softer, more romantic sound to it. Actors Lucas Grabeel and Lukas Haas use the first name.

Variations: *Luc, Luca, Luka, Lukas*
Nicknames: *Luca, Luka*
Alternatives: *Jake, Mark, Marcus, Jonas, Micah*

Lyric is a celebration of music and poetry and meaningful feelings. It is much more popular as a girl's name, but boys are staring to pick it up, too. It sounds a little bit Greek mythology (makes you think of Erato, muse of lyric poetry) and a little bit rock 'n' roll.

Alternatives: *Eric, Caden, Harper, Apollo*

Madden John Madden is a sports icon. He has been an NFL player, coach, and commentator, and has lent his name to a popular football video game. Madden is also the last name of rocker and Nicole Richie beau, Joel Madden. The name comes from the Gaelic for "dog," making Mad Dog a great nickname.

Nicknames: *Mad, Mad Dog*
Alternatives: *Lennon, Alden, Patton*

Maddox X marks the spot of a hip name. Angelina Jolie-Pitt adopted her first child from Cambodia in 2002 and named him Maddox ("fortunate"). In 2003, other families in the United States began using the name. It's a clever alternative to Madison, which has become a girl's name.

Alternatives: *Lennox, Bendix, Paxton, Hendrix, Knox*

Malachi is a Hebrew name meaning "messenger"; it was used for the prophet of the Old Testament

who fortells the coming of Christ. Change the *i* to a
y and you have an Irish name of a kind with Kieran
and Fionn.

Variations: *Malaki, Malakai, Malachy*
Nicknames: *Mal, Mack*
Alternatives: *Solomon, Abraham, Ishmael*

✏ **Malcolm** is a man of consequence. A king (made
famous by *Macbeth*). A civil rights activist (Malcolm X).
A multimillionaire publishing scion (Malcolm Forbes).
A bestselling author (Malcolm Gladwell). The name
was once heavily Scots (it means "follower of Colm"
and Colm means "dove") but is now used by everyone.

Nicknames: *Mal, Colm*
Alternatives: *Graham, Keith, Gregory, Trevor, Fergus*

Malik is mighty: It comes from Arabic and means
"king." It is one of the names of God in the Koran.
It was taken up eagerly by African Americans in the
1970s, when there was a vogue for Arabic names.
Malik was one of the names that has stuck most firmly.
Black pride leader Malcolm X used Malik as part of his
Nation of Islam name.

Alternatives: *Aziz, Tariq, Karim*

Manuel, from Emmanuel, means "God is with us"
and is another name for the Messiah. This joyful,
triumphant name has clear Christian ties; it is also

451

very popular with Hispanic Americans. The name is a smart alternative if you feel Emmanuel is too strong.

Variations: *Emanuel, Immanuel, Manolo*
Nicknames: *Manny, Manie*
Alternatives: *Jesus, Cruz, Santos*

Marcel is from the Latin Marcellus, and a close relative of Mark. Marcel was popular in France, and used by artist Marcel Duchamp, writer Marcel Proust, and mime Marcel Marceau (who used it very, very quietly). Marcello, the Italian version, was used by actor Marcello Mastroianni. Marcellus Wallace was the baddie bigwig played by Ving Rhames in Quentin Tarantino's *Pulp Fiction*. Marsellus Wiley was an NFL player.

Variations: *Marcelo, Marcello*
Nicknames: *Marc, Marco*
Alternatives: *Julius, Augustus, Horace, Oscar*

Mario The male version of Mary may come to us from the Roman god of war, Mars. The name is enormously popular with Hispanic and Italian families. Famous Marios include chef Mario Batali, TV presenter Mario Lopez, photographer Mario Testino, actor Mario Van Peebles, and perhaps most colorfully, the Super Mario Brothers.

Alternatives: *Mars, Carlos, Pedro, Orlando*

Friends, Romans, Namesakes

The names of the great Roman Empire convey power, beauty, and dignity. If anything will stand the test of time, it's a name that dates back nearly two thousand years.

~ ANTONIUS	~ DOMITIAN	~ ROMULUS
~ AUGUSTUS	~ GALLIENUS	~ TARQUIN
~ AURELIUS	~ GORDIAN	~ TIBERIUS
~ CLAUDIUS	~ HADRIAN	~ TITUS
~ CONSTANTINE	~ MARCUS	~ TRAJAN
~ DIOCLETIAN	~ REMUS	~ VESPASIAN

Mark the Evangelist was one of Jesus's apostles. He wrote a gospel of the New Testament and ended up in Alexandria where he founded the Coptic Church. Saint Mark's remains were carried to Venice upon his death, and he became the patron saint of that city (think Piazza San Marco). He, like St. Jerome, is associated with the lion. The name itself may come from Mars, the Roman god of war. Marcus is the Latin version of the name. This name is no-nonsense, direct—and on the mark.

Variations: *Marc, Marco, Marcos, Marcus, Markus*
Alternatives: *Luke, Jake, Parker, Mac*

Marley With any name ending in a -*lee* sound, you run the risk of the girls grabbing it up. Marley was discovered by the girls in 1994 and has grown extremely popular. It brings to mind music legend Bob Marley and his son Ziggy, the naughty dog from the bestselling book *Marley & Me*, and actress Marlee Matlin. Some parents are undaunted—Marley is now in use for boys, too.

Alternatives: *Kingston, Hendrix, Coltrane, Parker*

Marlon Brando was the inspiration for this name. Tough but sensitive, magnetic, and rigorous with his craft, Brando electrified audiences in films from *A Streetcar Named Desire* and *On the Waterfront* to *Apocalypse Now* and *The Godfather*. He's an original. The name is believed to be a diminutive of Mark.

Nicknames: *Lon, Lonnie*
Alternatives: *Bogart, Cooper, Roland, Eastwood*

Marquis is a noble rank in England and France. It was taken up as a first name, primarily by African Americans, in the 1970s. Several athletes are using the name including NBA player Marquis Daniels. Before the '70s, the first Marquis you might have thought of was the notorious Marquis de Sade.

Variations: *Marquise, Marques (Spanish)*
Nicknames: *Marq, Mark*
Alternatives: *Earl, Baron, Duke, King, Marcus*

Marshall This name has authority. The marshall, or marshal, is the lawman. Traditionally a marshall (the name derives from "horse") was the king's man who oversaw large gatherings, hence the term "marshalling of forces." Marshall is competent and reliable.

Alternatives: *Cooper, Parker, Thatcher, Fletcher*

Martin The Roman god of war, Mars grew up to become Martin. Saint Martin was a soldier who gave half his cloak to a beggar, which prompted his conversion. Famous Martins include Protestant reformer Martin Luther, civil rights leader Martin Luther King Jr., actors Martin Sheen and Martin Lawrence, and director Martin Scorsese.

Variations: *Martinez, Maartens, Martyn*
Nickname: *Marty*
Alternatives: *Miles, Parker, Darwin, Tarquin, Homer*

Marvin is the modern variation of the Welsh name Mervyn. With an *e*, the name sounds suspiciously similar to Merlin, King Arthur's wizard-tutor. Marvin has a mid-century sound to most ears. Think musicians Marvin Gaye and Marvin Hamlisch; sportscaster Marv Alpert; and cute and quirky cartoon alien Marvin the Martian.

Variation: *Mervyn*
Nickname: *Marv*
Alternatives: *Harvey, Kermit, Calvin, Kelvin*

Mason A "stoneworker," Mason is an occupational name that is enjoying a huge resurgence. What could be more sturdy and manly than someone who builds houses and walls and things meant to last? Mason is a logical alternative to the overused but much-loved Jason.

Alternatives: *Asa, Peter, Dixon, Grant, Easton*

Matthew was an apostle, Evangelist, and author of a gospel in the Bible. The name means "gift of God" and is almost the same as Jonathan: The names have the same meaning ("God has given") and are composed of the same Hebrew syllables presented in reverse order. Matthew has spawned many variations throughout the ages and has been beloved by Jews and Christians throughout the world. It was at the tippity top of the charts a few years ago.

Variations: *Mathew, Mateo, Matteo, Mathias, Matias, Matthias, Mathieu, Mats*
Nicknames: *Matt, Matty, Teo*
Alternatives: *Mark, Luke, John, Emmett*

Maurice means "Moorish," suggesting someone dark-complexioned or Arab. The name sounds French, à la chanteur Maurice Chevalier. Other famous Maurices include children's author/illustrator Maurice Sendak and the titular character of a novel by E. M. Forester. The name is pronounced Morris in England, but if you live in North America, it'll be mawr-EESE.

Variations: *Mauricio, Maurizio, Mauro, Morris, Moritz*
Nicknames: *Maury, Mo*
Alternatives: *Mercer, Cyril, Horace, Julius*

Maverick A maverick is a rebel, a lone wolf, a trend-setter. Families used this name for a couple of years in the 1950s in the wake of the James Garner TV series about a renegade gambler, Bret Maverick, in the Old West. The name attracted renewed interest after a *Maverick* movie starring Mel Gibson was released in 1993. This time Maverick is hanging around and gaining steam, helped by the NBA team the Dallas Mavericks and by the 2008 presidential campaign, in which John McCain was lauded repeatedly as a maverick. (Tom Cruise's role as Maverick in *Top Gun* doesn't seem to have had much effect.)

Nicknames: *Mav, Rick*
Alternatives: *Freeman, Logan, Rookie, Buck, Mustang*

I'd love to call him . . .
Max

M aximize your full-name options with one of the following choices:

~ **LOMAX**	~ **MAXENCE**	~ **MAXIMILLIAN**
~ **MACKENZIE**	~ **MAXFIELD**	~ **MAXIMUS**
~ **MADDOX**	~ **MAXIME**	~ **MAXWELL**

Max is the greatest. Literally. Maximus, the origin of most Maxes, means "greatest" in Latin. You can't go wrong with a name this packed with bravado. Maximilian is a medieval mash-up of Maximus and Aemilianus, two Roman generals. It has a grand, belle epoque aura. Plain Max sounds more accessible. It's short and sweet, but the *x* gives it some bite. Max can have an old-mannish sound that is in vogue now. This bold little one will be right at home with Sam, Nat, and Ben.

Variations: *Maximilian, Maximillian, Maxim, Maximo, Maximus, Massimo*
Alternatives: *Alex, Mac, Sam, Harry, Jack*

Maxwell Pert, straight-laced, clever, Maxwell is a Scottish last name meaning "by Mack's river." Famous Maxwells: *Get Smart*'s earnest, lovable spy Maxwell Smart; the Beatles song "Maxwell's Silver Hammer"; Maxwell Perkins, F. Scott Fitzgerald's legendary book editor.

Variation: *Magnus*
Nicknames: *Max, Mack*
Alternatives: *Baxter, Paxton, Huxley, Rockwell*

Melvin Why is Melvin popular when Milton is not? Melvin sounds a bit nerdy and dusty. Yet it thrives, when Milton, which *could* sound posh and gentried, is about to disappear. Melvin is similar enough to other names that its shortcomings—which include its meaning ("bad place")—can be overlooked. It's riding on the coattails of Kevin, Calvin, Kelvin, and Marvin. (Whereas Milton may sound too old-fashioned and nebbishy to some.) The Scottish name originally comes from Melville, as in *Moby Dick* author Herman Melville. Mel Brooks is a Melvin.

Variation: *Melville*
Nickname: *Mel*
Alternatives: *Milton, Elvis, Elton, Grover*

Memphis If you want to celebrate southern roots, the blues, Elvis, or ties to Africa, this may be the name for you. Memphis, Tennessee, which lies on the Mississippi River, was named for the city in Egypt on the banks of the Nile. The Egyptian Memphis was the burial site of many pharaohs, and Memphis, Tennessee, has been host to a few kings as well, including blues legend B. B. King, King of Rock 'n' Roll Elvis Presley, and Martin Luther King Jr., who was assassinated there. It's also the hometown of Al Green, Muddy Waters, and Justin Timberlake. The city is celebrated in numerous songs, and for some southerners and music lovers, it has an almost Mecca quality to it. Call your kid Memphis, and people may flock to him.

Alternatives: *Nash (short for Nashville), Virgil, Presley, Mason, Sawyer*

Animal House

Names from the animal kingdom are well loved by parents. Girls usually get "soft" names like Fawn and Doe, while boys end up with the names of raptors and horses. Some options to sniff out:

~ **BUCK:** *a male deer*

~ **COLT:** *a spirited young horse*

~ **DOV:** *Hebrew name meaning "bear"*

~ **EAGLE:** *more popular are names that mean eagle, including Aquila, Arundel, and Arne*

~ **FALCON:** *a name that pops up in movies after Maltese and Millenium, but is an uncommon baby name*

~ **FOX:** *not your typical first name, but a great way to give him a wily edge in the world. Extra fun for redheads.*

~ **GRIFFIN:** *mythological beast, half eagle, half lion*

~ **HAWK:** *a common last name and not-so-common first name that's come to mean any bird of prey except owls*

~ **KESTREL:** *a beautiful and adaptive raptor that can be founding nesting on buildings;*

also the name of a short-lived X-Men character

~ **LEO:** *the lion*

~ **MERLIN:** *a beautiful and fierce little falcon; will almost certainly not be the first thing people think of when they meet your little boy*

~ **ORSON:** *a bear*

~ **PETREL:** *a sea bird named for St. Peter because it seems to walk on water*

~ **PHOENIX:** *mythological beast, a bird that rises from the ashes*

~ **ROAN:** *a horse with a speckled coat*

~ **SEAL:** *the rock musician Seal makes this a nearly mainstream choice*

~ **TIBURON:** *"shark" in Spanish*

~ **WOLF:** *usually short for "Wolfgang" but can also reference the animal*

Messiah There are more subtle ways to communicate your faith. Nevertheless, the name Messiah has been attracting converts since 2005.

Alternatives: *Christian, Jesus, Manuel, Isaiah*

✎ **Micah** was a prophet and author of a book of the Old Testament. The name means the same as Michael, "who is like God." But Micah offers an alternative to that very popular name that sounds more Hebrew, contemporary, and easy-going.

Variation: *Michael*
Nickname: *Mike*
Alternatives: *Luca, Jonah, Ezra, Noah, Micaiah*

Michael Who is like God? Michael. That's what the name of the archangel and patron saint of soldiers means. Michael has always been popular but now more than ever. The name was number one in the 1950s through 1990s and since has slid only slightly. The name is one that is truly all-purpose: It has strong roots; it is meaningful to Jews, Christians, and Muslims (Michael appears in the Koran as an angel); the name is serious but with nicknames that are playful (Mick, Micky) and down to earth (Mike). Some families skip Michael and go straight to Mike.

Variations: *Micheal, Mike, Miguel, Misael, Mikhail*
Nicknames: *Mike, Mikey, Mick, Mickey, Misha*
Alternatives: *Mitchell, Gabriel, Matthew, Raphael, Daniel, David*

461

I'd love to call him . . .
Mike

"**L**ike Mike, I'd like to be like Mike . . . " If that jingle echoes your feeling about the nickname Mike, you have some options beyond Michael:

- MEYER
- MICAH
- MICAIAH
- MIGUEL
- MIKHAIL
- MIKLOS
- MILO
- MITCHELL
- MYRON

🖋 **Miles** sounds patrician; he's a leader. The name goes back past the Middle Ages, but its origins are lost. It might relate to Michael or Emile. It might have something to do with grace. It might have something to do with magnitude. Today it calls to mind distance, which suggests endurance and longevity. (And it almost sounds like the male version of the girl's name Miley.) It's a strong choice for history buffs and music lovers: It could pay homage to notable *Mayflower* passenger Myles Standish or jazz pioneer Miles Davis.

Variations: *Myles, Milo*
Nickname: *Milo*
Alternatives: *Otto, Giles, Ivor*

🖋 **Milo** is a variation of Miles (or even Emile) that sounds like a totally different beast—a cute and cuddly one. It sounds friendly and upbeat to contemporary ears: With two syllables and a vowel ending, it has a charming, diminutive appeal. Actors Milo Ventimiglia and Milo O'Shea use the name. Milo was the main character of the classic children's book *The Phantom Tollbooth*. Actress Liv Tyler named her son Milo in 2004.

Variation: *Miles*
Alternatives: *Arlo, Hugo, Bruno, Clyde*

Milton To some ears, Milton ("mill town") is an old man playing bridge at home in Boca with Sidney, Irving, and Leonard. (Beloved comedian Milton Berle is the prototype for that guy.) To others, the name evokes John Milton and Milton Academy and sounds a bit preppy. Looking at Milton's sliding fortunes suggests the first scenario is more common. Bye, Uncle Milty. Nice knowing you.

Nicknames: *Milt, Milty*
Alternatives: *Walter, Howard, Sidney, Leonard*

Mitchell Michael by another name, Mitchell has a preppy, white-bread sound to it, as most last names turned first names do. The nickname Mitch is just as accessible as Mike. Mitch is a guy you can have a beer with at the neighborhood barbecue.

Variation: *Michael*
Nickname: *Mitch*
Alternatives: *Harlan, Douglas, Richard, Herschel*

> *I'd love it if he sounded . . .*
> ## Islamic
>
> - **BARAK** *("blessings")*
> - **BASHIR** *("messenger of happy news"; call him Bash)*
> - **BILAL** *("moist")*
> - **FAISAL** *("judge")*
> - **FARHAN** *("happy")*
>
> - **MUNIR** *("radiant")*
> - **NASIR** *("protector")*
> - **NOOR** *("light")*
> - **SALAM** *("peace")*
> - **SHARIF** *("noble")*
> - **ZAFIR** *("victor")*

Mohamed is the most significant name in Islam. Mohamed ("praised") is the prophet of Allah who communicated Allah's teachings in the Koran. Mohamed was an orphan and later a merchant; he experienced a revelation from God on his fortieth birthday, and then devoted his life to spreading the word of God and securing Mecca as Islam's holy city. Famous Mohameds include boxer Muhammad Ali; TV doctor Mehmet Oz; King of Morocco, Mohammed VI; and Mohamed al-Fayed, Egyptian billionaire.

Variations: *Mohammad, Mohammed, Muhammad, Muhammed, Mehmet (Turkish)*
Nickname: *Mo*
Alternatives: *Ahmed, Hamid, Abdul, Hassan*

Morgan is losing its luster as a boy's name as the girls take it over. Famous male Morgans include banker

J. P. Morgan, actor Morgan Freeman, and documentary filmmaker Morgan Spurlock. Female Morgans leap as easily to mind: actress Morgan Fairchild and Arthurian witch Morgan Le Fay. The name has a boldness to it that may be irresistible, especially to families in which it appears as a last name.

Alternatives: *Logan, Ronan, Spencer, Sterling, Maynard*

Moses is one of the Bible's heavy hitters as well as a prophet in Islam. The root of the name, like that of Moses's brother Aaron, is Egyptian. Gwyneth Paltrow named her son Moses. Moises is the Spanish form and Moshe the Hebrew. Thrill your baby Moses with the ditty from *Singin' in the Rain*: "Moses supposes his toeses are roses . . ."

Variations: *Moises, Moishe, Moshe, Moss*
Nicknames: *Mos, Mose*
Alternatives: *Aaron, Solomon, Eli, Abel*

Nash Don Johnson played the title character in the TV series *Nash Bridges*, which aired in 1996. A year later the name Nash hit the mainstream. Johnson was assisted by NBA player Steve Nash, as well as the city of Nashville, capital of Tennessee, which is famous for its music scene. No nicknames here.

Alternatives: *Memphis, Crockett, Dashiell*

Nasir Arabic name meaning "protector," Nasir is used by American rapper Nasir Jones and Indian actor Nasir Khan. It's a common last name and also a city in Sudan.

Variations: *Naasir, Nasser, Naseer*
Nicknames: *Nas, Naz*
Alternatives: *Bashir, Kareem, Samir*

Nathaniel and the shorter Nathan both mean "God has given." And both follow the same trends of popularity—they are at all-time highs right now. Nathan is the Jewish version, referring to the prophet of the Old Testament and the name of one of David's sons. Nathaniel is the New Testament version, which was used by an apostle (who was also known as Bartholomew). Nathaniel has a puritanical flavor, reinforced by author Nathaniel Hawthorne, whose novel *The Scarlet Letter* was set in colonial New England. Nat "King" Cole was a Nathaniel. Famous Nathans include Revolutionary War patriot Nathan Hale; actor Nathan Lane; and *Guys and Dolls* gambler with a heart of gold, Nathan Detroit.

Variations: *Nathanael, Nathanial*
Nicknames: *Nat, Nate, Nathan, Than*
Alternatives: *Jonathan, Bartholomew, Ethan, Caleb, Newton*

Nehemiah ("consoler") is the prophet who rebuilt Jerusalem. The name was used by Puritans and had disappeared throughout most of the twentieth century. It came back in 1998 and is now quite popular.

Alternatives: *Jeremiah, Obadiah, Zachariah*

Neil comes from the Irish name Niall, which was held by an ancient king. Famous Neils include singers Neil Diamond and Neil Young, astronaut Neil Armstrong, actor Neil Patrick Harris, and playwright Neil Simon. The name can be short for Cornelius as well.

Variations: *Neal, Nigel*
Alternatives: *Glenn, Finn, Ross, Dale*

Nelson (son of Neil) is a leader—there have been a number of notable Nelsons in history. Lord Horatio Nelson was the British admiral who was killed winning the Battle of Trafalgar during the Napoleonic Wars. Another leader with the name is former South African president and Nobel Peace Prize recipient Nelson Mandela. And Nelson Rockefeller was a United States vice president. If you're a music lover for whom "lead" suggests "lead singer," note that glam rocker Prince's last name is Nelson. There's also the 1990s band Nelson, which was formed by the sons of 1950s screen idol Ricky Nelson.

Variations: *Neilson, Nilsson, Niles*
Nicknames: *Nels, Neil, Sonny*
Alternatives: *Emerson, Horatio, Desmond, Emmett*

I'd love it if he sounded . . .
Israeli

~ Amir	~ Itai	~ Ram
~ Avner	~ Matan	~ Reuven
~ Dov	~ Moshe	~ Yair
~ Eitan	~ Namir	~ Yonatan
~ Gavriel	~ Nitzan	~ Yosef
~ Idan	~ Noam	~ Zohar

✒ **Nicholas** ("victory of the people") comes from Greece, where St. Nicholas is the patron. Of course, this saint is revered by children well beyond Greece (and Russia, where he is also patron)—he is also known as Santa Claus. Famous Nicholases include actors Nicholas Cage and Nick Nolte; Dickens's Nicholas Nickelby; scientist Nicolaus Copernicus; and Italian political philosopher Niccolò Machiavelli. The name is a timeless classic, one sure to make any little boy jolly.

Variations: *Nickolas, Nicolas, Nikolai, Nikolas, Nick, Nico, Niko, Claus, Klaus*
Nicknames: *Nick, Nico, Niko*
Alternatives: *Colin, Nicholson, Vincent, Lazarus*

Nigel arrived in the United States during the 1970s. The name, from the Latin *niger*, meaning "black," sounds unequivocally British. Sir Walter Scott is credited with reviving the name in 1822, when he published his romance *The Fortunes of Nigel*. Duran Duran's bass guitarist John Taylor's real first name is Nigel; Nigel Tufnel is the lead guitarist in the fictional band Spinal Tap; Nigel Hawthorne is an actor; Nigel Lawson was the chancellor of the exchequer of the U.K. and the father of TV cook Nigella Lawson. Nigel is terribly British, indeed.

Alternatives: *Basil, Simon, Niall, Winston*

Nikhil In 1996, Nikhil Chinapa became a VJ at MTV India. In 1997, storks began delivering little Nikhils in the United States. This classical Hindu name means "complete" in Sanskrit. Other Nikhils include sitar player Nikhil Banerjee, Bollywood director Nikhil Advani, and the title character from the Bollywood movie *My Brother . . . Nikhil*.

Alternatives: *Akhil, Pranav, Vikash*

Noah ("at rest," "peaceful") has hit the big time. Once a squarely Jewish name (and adopted by Puritans), Noah is now in the top twenty and widely used by everyone. Noah's story is well known: He saved his family and the animals of earth from the great flood by following God's instructions and building an ark, allowing those he rescued to repopulate the world.

Famous Noahs include lexicographer Noah Webster; Dr. Noah Drake, dreamy character on *General Hospital* in the 1980s; and *ER* actor Noah Wyle. The Hispanic and French version is Noë (know-EH).

Variation: *Noë*

Alternatives: *Jonah, Abel, Judah, Ezra*

Noel is French for "Christmas." The name is a good choice for babies due in late December. The girl's version is pronounced in the French way (NO-elle) and is sometimes spelled Noelle. The boy's version is pronounced like knoll, which gives it a hint of a nature name (think grassy knoll). This name seems poised to bring glad tidings. Parents have a choice with Noel: to add an umlaut over the e or not. The accent suggests the pronunciation NO-elle, not knoll. Noël Coward used it, but some others don't.

Alternatives: *Nicholas, Stephen, Joel, Cole, Nolan, Yul*

Nolan is rolling along and gathering steam. This Irish name, which means "champion," sounds clearly masculine but without the western tinge of say, Logan, and with less pretension than Holden. Baseball pitcher Nolan Ryan helped boost the name in the 1980s and 1990s.

Alternatives: *Lawrence, Corbin, Eamon*

O

Octavio Roman emperor Augustus Caesar spent most of his life as Octavian ("eight"), becoming known as Augustus—an honorific meaning "exalted"—later in his career. His reign ushered in an era of stability and peace in which the arts flourished. Octavio is a popular name in the Hispanic community (think Mexican writer Octavio Paz), and with its cute opening *O* and cool-guy middle *v*, it has great crossover potential. Octavio is an on-trend but ahead-of-the-curve choice.

Nicknames: *Tavio, Tavi*
Alternatives: *Julius, Augustus, Quentin*

Oliver In the early French epic poem *La Chanson de Roland*, Oliver is the hero's friend and represents wisdom. Olivier (the French version) was a confidant of Charlemagne. Olive trees, from which the name derives, represent peace and life. The name may also be connected to a Norse word meaning "ancestor." Oliver has a sturdy, hefty feel to it, unlike its French counterpart, Olivier, which has a lighter touch. Famous Olivers include Dickens's orphan Oliver Twist; director Oliver Stone; and actors Oliver Platt, Laurence Olivier, and Oliver Hardy of Laurel and Hardy fame.

Variation: *Olivier*
Nickname: *Ollie*
Alternatives: *Orlando, Charles, Lawrence*

Omar is an Arabic name that is quite familiar to Americans thanks to actors Omar Sharif and Omar Epps. In Arabic, the name means "full of life," "flourishing"; in Hebrew it means "talkative." It was the name of one of Esau's sons in the Old Testament. Other famous Omars include Persian poet Omar Khayyam and United States general Omar Bradley. Omari is a similar-sounding Swahili name used to praise God.

Variation: *Umar*
Alternatives: *Homer, Omari, Habib, Samir*

Orion could be rising. It is the name of one of the brightest constellations in the night sky. Greek myth has it that Zeus placed the hunter Orion, son of Poseidon, in the heavens after Orion's death. His celestial image has lived on, and it may be time for his name to make a comeback. It's easy to spell and distinctive, but sounds enough like Ryan that it feels familiar.

Nickname: *Orrey*
Alternatives: *Orson, Phoenix, Mars*

Orlando spills off the tongue with the promise of adventure and romance. Orlando is the Spanish and Italian version of Roland. He was a friend of Charlemagne and Olivier, and his exploits were heralded in the twelfth-century French poem *La Chanson de Roland* and in the sixteenth-century

O Where, O Where, Have Oswald, Otto, and Otis Gone?

Exotic letters are important to parents these days. Names with *v*'s and *x*'s and other letters that hold high values on the Scrabble board are in demand. While *O* won't win you many points in the board game, it should be considered an exotic letter for boys. After all, Oliver and Owen are making comebacks—there is no reason for other long-overlooked *O* names not to be revived. Consider these three prime choices for your boy and you will be ahead of your time:

- **OSWALD:** *The Spanish-language variations Oswaldo and Osvaldo are well loved—it's time Oswald had a revival. This strong, stately name has adorable nicknames, too: Ozzie (Ozzie Nelson was an Oswald), Oz, or Waldo.*

- **OTIS:** *Beverly Cleary hero Otis Spofford, singer Otis Redding.*

Otis has a cute factor that other -is ending names (like Dennis) don't have. Fans of Milo and Leo, take note.

- **OTTO:** *It's a palindrome. It's sweet (see Milo and Rocco). And it's forceful: statesman Otto von Bismarck.*

Italian poem *Orlando Furioso*. *Orlando* is a novel by Virginia Woolf about a man who travels through time and finally becomes a woman. Orlando Bloom is a heartthrob actor. Orlando Pace is a football player. Orlandos seem destined to go far.

Variation: *Roland*
Alternatives: *Oliviero, Domingo, Reynaldo*

✏ **Oscar** is working his way back into our hearts, shades of Oscar the Grouch and sloppy Oscar Madison be damned. The name, of Irish origin, means "deer lover," and dates way back to the ancient Fenian Cycle, a mythological writing. Famous Oscars include Irish playwright Oscar Wilde, lyricist Oscar Hammerstein, pianist Oscar Levant, designer Oscar de la Renta, boxer Oscar de la Hoya, Holocaust hero Oskar Schindler, and the Academy Award statuette. Look for this cool sleeper to rise in the rankings, due in part to its cool nickname choices: Oz and Ozzie.

Variation: *Oskar*
Nicknames: *Ossie, Ozzie, Oz*
Alternatives: *Eamon, Leo, Oliver, Ronan*

Owen, thought to be a Welsh relative of Eugene (pages 374–375), is quickly becoming the big name on campus. The name is darling on a little boy, like many short names are. But it also sounds utterly masculine and competent, with an undercurrent of sensitivity, on a man. Owen might be the lumberjack who plays the guitar. Guy-next-door actor Owen Wilson has certainly helped boost the name's appeal as has suave British actor Clive Owen.

Variations: *Ewan, Eugene*
Nicknames: *O, Wen*
Alternatives: *Otis, Ethan, Liam, Gavin*

P

Parker This preppy name, which has roots in the Middle Ages, is unisex but still more popular for boys. Famous Parkers include *Hardy Boys* actor Parker Stevenson (Parker was originally his last name), musician Charlie Parker, and wine guru Robert Parker.

Nickname: *Parks*
Alternatives: *Brooks, Holden, Turner, Marshall, Hayward*

𝒫 **Patrick** Saint Patrick is the patron saint of Ireland, credited with converting the island to Christianity in the fifth century. He was a Roman citizen and his name means "patrician," which suggests a noble birth. The name is so closely associated with Ireland that "Paddy" has become a rude way of referring to an Irish person. Noteworthy Patricks include actors Neil Patrick Harris, Patrick Dempsey, Patrick Stewart, and Patrick Swayze; basketball player Patrick Ewing; golfer Padraig Harrington; and American patriot Patrick Henry (who famously said, "Give me liberty or give me death"). Many Patricks masquerade as Pat: Pat Sajak, jazz musician Pat Metheny, writer Pat Conroy.

Variations: *Padraig (Ireland), Patrizio (Italy), Patrice (France)*
Nicknames: *Pat, Paddy, Rick*
Alternatives: *Eamon, Dominic, Desmond, Richard*

Paul is a Christian heavyweight. He converted from
Judaism (he was born Saul), became one of Christ's
most important apostles, authored much of the
New Testament, cofounded the Christian Church
with St. Peter, was beheaded, and finally was sainted.
The name Paul means "small," but the effects of
Paul are large. Notable Pauls include great men in
many fields. Patriotism: Paul Revere. Music: Paul
McCartney, Paul Simon. Acting: Paul Newman,
Paul Rudd. Arts: Paul Cezanne, Paul Gauguin, Pablo
Picasso, Pablo Neruda. Business: Paul Allen. Fashion:
Paul Smith. Religion: There have been seven Popes
Paul and two Popes John Paul.

IT'S PAT!: UNISEX NAMES

Noel, Robin, Pat,
Dana, Chris . . .
these names and others
like them do not reveal
the gender of their bearers.
And it's not just these
traditional names that
are tough to place. Most
fashionable names that
come from place-names or
last names are impossible
to decode. Look at the
cast of TV's *Gossip Girl*. In
five-sixths of these cases
you can't determine gender
at a glance: Leighton
Meester, Chase Crawford,
Blake Lively, Penn Badgely,
Taylor Momsen, and Ed
Westwick. If you decide to
give your child a unisex
name, consider throwing
in a middle name that is a
marker for his or her sex.

Variations: *Pablo, Paolo, Pavel*
Nicknames: *Pauli, Pablito, Paolino*
Alternatives: *Peter, Hugh, Karl, John*

Paxton X marks the spot. Paxton's *x* gives the name exotic-letter appeal that is all the rage now. It's an English place-name that calls to mind amiable character actor Bill Paxton. It also suggests peacefulness: *pax* is "peace" in Latin. (Pax is also the name of one of the Jolie-Pitt boys.)

Nicknames: *Pax, Tony*
Alternatives: *Maddox, Hendrix, Baxter, Dixon*

✏ **Peter** This name rocks. Literally—Peter means "stone." Christ famously told his apostle Peter that he was the rock upon which Jesus would build his church. Saint Peter is (with Paul) considered to have established the Christian Church. He was the first bishop of Rome and is regarded as the first pope, and he later became the patron saint of fishermen, having been one himself. Yet this solid classic (what is more solid than rock?) has been losing ground lately, which makes it a great choice for enterprising parents who are looking for an accessible, not-too-popular name with a distinguished history.

Variations: *Pedro (Spanish), Pierre (French), Boutros (Arabic)*
Nickname: *Pete*
Alternatives: *Simon, Lazarus, Paul, Thaddeus*

The Aristocrats

H ere are some names that sound to the manor born. You can find others by Googling philanthropists, the dormitories and classroom buildings of Ivy League universities, passenger lists from famous ships *(Titanic, Mayflower),* founders of old New England towns (choose specific towns), families from New York's gilded age, and so on—anyplace where you find old money.

~ ASTOR	~ ELIOT	~ PEABODY
~ AVERELL	~ FENWICK	~ SARGENT
~ BARCLAY	~ FORBES	~ SPALDING
~ BUCHANAN	~ HOPKINS	~ TATE
~ CABOT	~ LOWELL	~ THAYER
~ COPLEY	~ OSGOOD	~ VANDERBILT
~ CUSHING	~ PAGET	~ WHARTON

Peyton The title of the novel *Peyton Place* hints at the origins of this seemingly pedigreed name—it is a place-name. It has a sportiness to it thanks to NFL quarterback Peyton Manning, NFL halfback Walter Payton, and basketball player Gary Payton. But despite the name's athletic associations, be warned: Peyton has very quickly become very fashionable for girls.

Variation: *Payton*
Alternatives: *Paxton, Hayward, Leighton*

✐ **Philip** sounds noble and a bit regal. And it is. Alexander the Great's father was Philip, Queen Elizabeth II is married to Prince Philip, and Prince Felipe is the crown prince of Spain. The name comes from the Greek and means "horse lover." Philip was one of Christ's apostles and is depicted with a long staff with a cross atop it. Philip, like Peter, is another classic name with ties to the New Testament and with a long, venerable history. The name is not used nearly as much as it could be. Your Phil might be the only one in his kindergarten class.

Variations: *Phillip, Felipe, Philippe, Filippo*
Nicknames: *Phil, Pip, Flip*
Alternatives: *Stephen, Phineas, Simon, Theodore*

Phoenix is invincible. The gorgeous bird of myth dies in flames and rises from the ashes to live again. The name symbolizes hope, perseverance, and rebirth. In Greek mythology, Phoenix was the founder of the Phoenician civilization. And the word means "violet-red" in Greek. The name calls to mind actors River and Joaquin Phoenix, as well as the city in Arizona. Girls are using the name, too.

Alternatives: *River, Skyler, Hendrix, Maddox*

✐ **Pierce** Sharp, straight, resilient, Pierce relates to Peter ("rock"). The name is as strong, but rather than evoking stone, it suggests steel. It is popular in Ireland as Piers and Pearce. Patrick Henry Pearce was an Irish patriot. Franklin Pierce was a United States president. Today the name is used by actor Pierce Brosnan and TV personality Piers Morgan.

Variations: *Piers, Pearce, Pearse*
Alternatives: *Eamon, Miles, Flynn, Rhys*

Porter was an occupational name for the guy who carried things or opened doors. And it still is: Think about a hotel porter. Composer Cole Porter leaps to mind. It's perhaps a more resolutely masculine alternative to Parker.

Nickname: *Port*
Alternatives: *Carter, Parker, Horace, Corbin*

Pranav Om, the sacred syllable of Hinduism, is called Pranav in Sanskrit. Om is an expression of the mysteries and powers of God; of Hindu gods Brahma, Vishnu, Mahesh; and of creation, life, and death. Pranav would give your boy an air of mystery and strength.

Alternatives: *Aarav, Rishi, Vishnu, Mahesh*

Preston Like many family names (this one means "priest's town"), Preston sounds aristocratic. Famous Prestons include film director Preston Sturges, car designer Preston Tucker, and Dr. Preston Burke on the TV show *Grey's Anatomy*.

Variations: *Presley, Priestly*
Nicknames: *Pres, Prez, Tony*
Alternatives: *Alton, Holden, Wesley*

Prince File this one with King and Marquis. Prince is next in line to the throne, the golden child waiting to rule. While Duke and Earl have a western ring to them, Prince sounds more like a city bloke. The name is most popular with African American families. Princes that leap to mind: the musician formerly and currently known as Prince, Michael Jackson's son Prince Michael, the Fresh Prince of Bel-Air (Will Smith), and Freddy Prinze Jr.

Alternatives: *Kingston, Regis, Rex, Vincent*

Quentin means "fifth." The name sounds new and edgy thanks to that opening *Q*, but its origins are old and Roman. It evokes writer/director Quentin Tarantino, humorist Quentin Crisp, and illustrator Quentin Blake (he illustrated Roald Dahl's books). Even the prison San Quentin can't make this name sound anything other than smart, civilized, and free-spirited.

Variations: *Quinten, Quintin, Quinton*
Nicknames: *Quent, Tin Tin (after the comic strip character)*
Alternatives: *Oliver, Milton, Karsten, Augustus*

Quincy is a last name that derives from the same root as Quentin. The name has a patriotic, old New England sound to it. Quincy is the town in Massachusetts named for first lady Abigail Adams's grandfather. President and Mrs. Adams lived there and raised their family there, including son and future president John Quincy Adams. The name also has a musical ring to it thanks to impresario Quincy Jones, and it may suggest medical acuity to those who remember the TV show *Quincy, M.E.*, starring Jack Klugman as a crime-solving coroner.

Nicknames: *Quince, Quin*
Alternatives: *Barnaby, Cabot, Osgood, Windsor*

Quinn is shaping up to be a leader. Fitting, since that's the meaning of this Gaelic name. The name began life as a surname but has slowly and steadily risen in popularity as a first name. The prefix *quin* means "fifth," so it can also be used to denote a fifth child. It can also be short for Quincy and Joachin, even Quentin. Alert: The girls have discovered this name and are starting to use it in numbers. In a few years, they may have taken it over completely. (It does sound a bit like Gwen.) The 1970s child actress Quinn Cummings may have helped shift it to the girls column, and a cheerleader character on the hit TV show *Glee* may be keeping it there.

Alternatives: *August, Flint, Corbin*

R

🖊 **Ralph** One of the heavy hitters of the early 1900s is at risk of extinction. Ralph has a cool meaning, "wolf council," and several appealing namesakes: designer Ralph Lauren, actors Ralph Macchio and Ralph Fiennes. Let's bring Ralph back, shall we? Pronounce it "rafe" if you think that will help, as Fiennes and other upper crust Brits do.

Variations: *Rolf, Ralf, Raoul, Raul*
Alternatives: *Stanley, Ernest, Eugene, Philip*

Ramiro From the Latin name Ramirus, Ramiro ("famous advisor") is typically used by Hispanic families. The name is related to the popular last name Ramirez, so it's a way of honoring relatives with that name. Ramiro was the King of Aragon in the eleventh century. Baseball stars Manny Ramirez and Ramiro Peña may inspire some crossover among fans.

Variation: *Ramirez*
Nickname: *Miro*
Alternatives: *Domingo, Orlando, Angelo, Javier*

Ramon is the Spanish-language version of Raymond ("advisor and protector"). Ramon does not have a light sound to it—compared to Alejandro or Javier, Ramon lands with a thud. This may in part contribute to its waning popularity. One unorthodox way around the clunkiness is to spell the name backwards, as baseball player Nomar Garciaparra does.

Variation: *Raymond*
Nickname: *Ray*
Alternatives: *Roman, Norman, Juan*

Randall is an upstanding citizen. The genteel appeal of a last name turned first name is tempered by a wild side: Randall comes from Randolf, which means "wolf shield." When Randall relaxes after work, he becomes Randy. Actor Tony Randall leaps to mind, as do football players Randall Cunningham and Randall Godfrey, and the old tycoon Randolf Duke from the movie *Trading Places*.

Variation: *Randolph*
Nickname: *Randy*
Alternatives: *Parnell, Brewster, Elliot, Hawthorne*

Randy Why not name him Randall or Randolph and just call him Randy? Randy was a very popular stand-alone name in the 1950s and '60s. But it really is a nickname. As a vocab word it has adult connotations—more reason to give him a real first name.

Variations: *Randolf, Randall, Andrew*
Alternatives: *Kirby, Brandon, Billy, Tony*

Raphael is angelic, artistic; he has a creative soul and a pure heart. The name is biblical in origin: Raphael

Hellenic Heroes

The warriors of Greek myth and history will offer your boy a vigorous start. These are larger-than-life names that suggest boldness, bravery, and valor.

~ **ACHILLES:** *Handsome hero of the Trojan War, Achilles was the ultimate warrior—except for a weak spot on his heel. He was slow to anger, but once he got going, it was best to stay out of his way.*

~ **ADONIS:** *This most handsome of men was Aphrodite's lover.*

~ **AENEAS:** *Aphrodite's son and the Greek hero who, after returning from the Trojan War, founded the city of Rome.*

~ **HERCULES:** *Also known as Heracles, he trotted about the ancient world in a lion skin doing great things. Though not a complete meathead, he wasn't the craftiest hero—more Superman than Batman.*

~ **JASON:** *To gain the throne of Thessaly, Jason assembled a hero dream-team and carted them around the Aegean on the Argo in search of the Golden Fleece. Jason was honorable and kind.*

~ **ODYSSEUS:** *You think your commute is bad? It took Odysseus ten years to get back to Ithaca from the Trojan War. And it might've taken longer had Odysseus not been wise and cunning.*

~ **PERSEUS:** *Being the son of Zeus is a mixed blessing—your dad's on your side, but not so Hera, who's likely not your mother. Such was the case with Perseus, who had to sidestep the vindictive Hera in his quest for Medusa's head.*

~ **PROMETHEUS:** *Prometheus stole fire from Zeus and suffered horribly for it, but came out all right in the end.*

~ **THESEUS:** *At age sixteen, Theseus proved his budding heroism by picking up a boulder and then went off to slay the Minotaur. He returned to Athens as king of heroes.*

("God heals") was one of the archangels, along with Gabriel and Michael. Raffaello, known as Raphael, was one of the great Renaissance painters; he painted several rooms in the Vatican. When Raphael is shortened to Raph, it sounds cool, edgy . . . maybe even raffish. Spanish tennis player Rafael Nadal uses the name.

Variations: *Rafael, Raffaello*
Nicknames: *Raph, Rafa, Raffi*
Alternatives: *Ralph, Gabriel, Leonardo*

Rashad NFL player and commentator Ahmad Rashad has sparked interest in this Arabic name, which means "good judgment." *Cosby Show* actress Phylicia Rashad boosted its profile even more.

Alternatives: *Ahmad, Tariq, Bashir*

Raul While Ralph is disappearing, Raul (Ralph in Spanish) is going strong. The name practically sounds like "cool," which helps it avoid the nerdy stigma of Ralph. Actor Raul Julia introduced the name to wider audiences. Rahul ("capable") is a Sanskrit name that sounds similar.

Variations: *Raoul, Ralph*
Alternatives: *Ramon, Julio, Juan, Pablo*

Raymond Not everybody loves Raymond anymore, despite the popular sitcom that ran in the 1990s and early 2000s. The name Raymond (meaning "advisor and protector") has been on the slide since its heyday—it was in the top twenty in the 1910s. Raymond more often calls to mind the likes of author Raymond Chandler and actor Raymond Burr than contemporary comedian Ray Romano. Some families give their boys the nickname Ray to ensure he'll be called that (Ray Charles is not a Raymond). The name Rayan, which sounds similar, is growing in popularity in the Arab world, Persia, and India.

Variations: *Ramon, Ray*
Nickname: *Ray*
Alternatives: *Redmond, Roman, Rayan*

Reagan If you're a Democrat, name him Kennedy. If you're a Republican, choose Reagan. Or mix it up if you like. Both are Irish last names that have migrated stateside; both are used by boys and girls (Reagan is *much* more popular for girls). Reagan is believed to mean "rash" or "impetuous."

Variation: *Regan*
Nickname: *Ray*
Alternatives: *Rogan, Truman, Sullivan, Duffy, Keagan, Riordan, Finnegan*

✏ **Reed** came from England and Scotland, where folks with red hair or windswept complexions received the name. It evokes nature: Moses was found among the reeds on the Nile. And it evokes music: woodwind instruments are known as "reeds" (and don't forget rock musician Lou Reed).

Variation: *Reid*
Alternatives: *Brooks, Rhys, Kieran, Eden*

Reginald is a proper British gentleman. Reynaldo is a dashing Latin lover. Ray (or Rey) is your buddy. Reynolds is a guy whose yacht is in the next slip. The name Reginald ("to advise the king"), from which all these names descend, comes in many packages. Reynaldo is the most popular of the bunch.

Variations: *Reynaldo, Rey, Reynolds, Reinhold*
Nicknames: *Reg, Reggie, Rey*
Alternatives: *Raymond, Gerald, Oswald*

Remington can be a debonair gentleman if you think about TV detective Remington Steele, played by Pierce Brosnan, who inspired use of the name in 1983. The character was named for the old-fashioned typewriter brand. (It's also a brand of razor.) Adding to the proper, British sound of the name is the similarity to names like Wellington and Paddington. But Remington can also be a cowboy, if you think about the firearms manufacturer and the painter of the Old West.

Nicknames: *Remy, Tony*
Alternatives: *Pierce, Fleming, Colt, Weston, Flint*

René Walk away from René unless you have very strong connections to France. The name, which means "reborn," is better known in the United States as a girl's name and has been on the wane for both genders. Mathematician/philosopher René Descartes and actor René Auberjonois from *MASH, Benson,* and *Star Trek: Deep Space Nine* are Renés of note.

Alternatives: *Renault, Remy, Didier*

Rex Actor Rex Harrison. Singer Rex Smith. Film critic Rex Reed. *Nero Wolfe* creator Rex Stout. Oedipus Rex. And of course, Tyrannosaurus rex. Rex means "king" in Latin. The name has an old-fashioned appeal with a hint of the West about it, thanks to the similarity to Tex. It's not very fashionable now, but don't count it out yet: It has that *X*-factor exotic letter that modern parents love.

Alternatives: *Tex, King, Mac*

Rhett is an old southern name made famous by Margaret Mitchell in her novel *Gone with the Wind*. Rhett Butler was the rogue hero who won Scarlett O'Hara's love and then walked away from her. The name has potential as a moniker for girls— something to keep in mind when naming your little heartbreaker.

Alternatives: *Beauregard, Judd, Cody*

Rhys A hot new import from Wales, Rhys (pronounced Rees) means "love." Actors Rhys Ifans and Jonathan Rhys-Meyers use the name. Reece, Reese, and Rees are anglicizations, all of which have a warm whiff of the South to them. Alert: Reese Witherspoon has sparked attention from parents of girls.

Variations: *Reece, Reese, Rees*
Alternatives: *Owen, Hugh, Wren, Pierce*

✏ **Richard** Pick Rick! Richard the Lionhearted, the king of England in the waning years of the 1100s, was aptly named, because Richard means "strong king." This noble name of enduring popularity had its heyday in the 1940s. It's slipped out of the top one hundred now, meaning that it's a brilliant pick for families looking for an evergreen classic with myriad nicknames. Ricky is a cute nickname with Latino references: Ricky Ricardo, Ricky Martin. Rich has an air of luxury. Dick is not much used anymore (no need to explain why).

Variation: *Ricardo*
Nicknames: *Rich, Rick, Ric, Dick, Ricky, Dickie, Richie, Rico*
Alternatives: *Edward, John, Charles, Robert*

Riley sounds smiley, and it's no coincidence: As the old saying goes, to lead "the life of Riley" is to have an easy go of things, to be trouble-free. The name, which in this spelling is English in origin, comes from a place "where rye is grown." The Irish family name Reilly is unrelated. It has a singsong quality and does sound squarely Irish—and lucky to boot. The girls discovered this one in 1990 and have overtaken the boys. Look for the name to decline for boys.

Variations: *Reilly, Rylee*
Nicknames: *Lee, Riles*
Alternatives: *Kieran, Desmond, Murphy, Leland, Bradley*

Rishi This modern-sounding Hindu name (meaning "sage," "singer") is actually very, very old. The Vedas were revealed by rishis, who were similar to biblical prophets, communicating God's wisdom to man. The famous Bollywood actor Rishi Kapoor keeps the name current and helps give it a nonreligious edge.

Alternatives: *Raj, Arnav, Krishna, Rahul*

River Rising star River Phoenix inspired the use of this nature name. Rivers can be a symbol of freedom, the passage of time, purification, harmony, and new beginnings.

Alternatives: *Brooks, Reed, Ash, Rain*

Robert ("famous") is an Old German name that migrated to France and then over to England in the Norman Conquest. William the Conqueror's father was Robert. The name is beloved in Scotland for the poet Robert Burns, and especially Robert Bruce, who liberated the country from England in the 1300s. Robert is one of the only *-bert* names that has remained consistently popular, is used by many ethnic groups, and has a bountiful variety of nicknames. The name Roderick, while not a strict variation of the name, means the same thing and is very similar in sound (it's Rod Stewart's real name). The Spanish version of the name, Rodrigo, is well liked, and a clever way to pass on the last name Rodriguez.

Variations: *Roberto, Rupert, Roberts, Robertson, Robin, Rigoberto, Roderick, Rodrigo*

Nicknames: *Bob, Rob, Bobby, Robby, Bert, Bertie*

Alternatives: *Albert, Edward, Bruce, Douglas*

Rocco means "rest," but let's face it: It sounds so much like "rock" that that's how most of us think of it. Boxer Rocky Marciano was born Rocco, which inspired Sylvester Stallone to name his boxer character Rocky. Meanwhile Madonna's son Rocco Ritchie and TV chef Rocco DiSpirito keep interest in the name solid.

Nickname: *Rocky*

Alternatives: *Rico, Bruno, Paolo, Nicolo*

Rodney was the last name of a British naval hero from the American Revolution. The name used to be that of old codgers like comic Rodney Dangerfield and actor

Whatever Happened to Baby Bert?

Names containing Bert used to be all the rage. Not so much anymore. (Is it Ernie's friend's fault?) They have held up in one place, however: the Hispanic community. And it's not hard to see why: Albert = fusty, Alberto = cool. Here's a roundup of Bert names in case you want to bring one back.

- **ALBERT** *(Queen Victoria's beloved husband; Albi is a cute nickname)*
- **COLBERT** *(yes, please! Thanks comic Steven Colbert)*
- **DAGOBERT** *(the name of Frankish kings)*
- **DILBERT** *(no thanks—think of the comic strip)*
- **ENGLEBERT** *(word association: Humperdink)*
- **GILBERT** *(is it dorky or sweet? your call)*
- **HERBERT** *(Rigoberto in Spanish)*
- **NORBERT** *(not likely to make a comeback)*
- **ROBERT** *(this classic has stuck)*
- **SCHUBERT** *(for music lovers)*

Rod Steiger. Now there are many athletes keeping the name afloat, including basketball player Rodney Carney, baseball player Fernando Rodney, and football player Rodney Peete.

Nickname: *Rod*
Alternatives: *Roderick, Barnaby, Nero, Randall, Dabney, Lawrence*

Noble Names of France

While the aristocracy lost their heads in the Revolution of the late 1700s, their names have lived on. The French may live for liberty, equality, and fraternity, but everybody likes a name that sounds distinguished. These are the most popular names from the great kings of France.

- **CHARLES**
- **CLOVIS**
- **DAGOBERT**
- **FRANÇOIS** (Francis)
- **HENRI** (Henry)
- **JEAN** (John usually hyphenated: Jean-Paul, Jean-Christophe, etc.)
- **LOUIS**
- **NAPOLEON**
- **PÉPIN**
- **PHILIPPE** (Philip)
- **ROBERT**

Roger ("famous spear") crossed the channel with the Normans to become popular in England. In the 1940s, the letter *r* was expressed as "Roger" by military personnel using the phonetic radio alphabet (Romeo has since supplanted it). *Roger* meant "received," as in "message received." A Jolly Roger is the skull and crossbones flag flown by pirates. "Old Roger" was another way of referring to the devil. And to "roger" someone had a bawdy meaning. All in all, it's a name with a colorful past. It has been used with success by tennis great Roger Federer, musician Roger Daltry, James Bond portrayer Roger Moore, and baseball players Roger Clemens and Roger Maris. The Spanish version of the name, Rogelio, is an intriguing variation.

Variations: *Rodger, Rogelio, Rutger*
Nickname: *Roge*
Alternatives: *Robert, Richard, Gordon, Palmer*

Roman means the same as Romeo (below): man from Rome. While the Italian version sounds fiery and impetuous, the anglicized version sounds dignified and upstanding. Rome was the center of the world for much of history, and its empire covered nearly all of Europe and into North Africa. Rome was a place of law and organization, and the name reflects that. As the Christian era arrived, Rome remained the focus of the world, this time as the seat of power of the Catholic Church. Although disgraced director Roman Polanski is the most famous example of the name, parents aren't letting that negative association cloud their vision. The name is on the rise, and several celebrities, including Debra Messing, Cate Blanchett, Molly Ringwald, and Harvey Keitel, have used it for their kids.

Variation: *Romeo*
Alternatives: *Nolan, London, Rufus, Victor*

Romeo ("from Rome") is a heartbreaker. The name is Italian, used by Shakespeare's tragic hero, Romeo Montague, fashion designer Romeo Gigli, and one of the sons of Victoria and David Beckham. Romeo comes and goes over the years, but lately it's on the rise.

Variation: *Roman*
Alternatives: *Benvolio, Oberon, Claudius, Prospero, Tristan*

Ronald Former president Ronald Reagan and fast-food mascot Ronald McDonald loom large over this name. The name means "to advise the ruler," making it similar to Reginald. Ronald was a big deal in the 1940s but its star has fallen lately. Some parents are skipping Ronald and going straight to Ronnie.

Nicknames: *Ron, Ronnie*
Alternatives: *Donald, Reynolds, Roald, Randall*

Ronan means "little seal" in Gaelic. It's a popular last name in Ireland and rapidly becoming a favorite first name in the United States. It sounds distinctly Irish, but is not as traditional as Declan, Liam, and Finn. Look for Ronan to run up the ranks. Ronin has become a variation, one that suggests Japan as well (in Japan, a *ronin* was a rogue samurai).

Variation: *Ronin*
Alternatives: *Conan, Rogan, Rowan, Nolan*

Rory started as a nickname for Roderick and means "red." It is energetic and can-do. (Can you hear the "roar" in there?) There have been many famous Rorys throughout Irish history, among them kings, rebels, artists, and sportsmen. Rory is a manly name, but one that sounds disarmingly sweet.

Variation: *Roderick*
Alternatives: *Corey, Gregory, Redford, Leo*

Ross is another redhead, like Rory, Reed, Rowan, and Roy. The name is Scottish, a common last name. Ross Perot and *Friends* character Ross Geller leap to mind. Ross is about as hip as either of them.

Alternatives: *Moss, Reese, Reed, Duncan*

Rowan is the "red one" as well as a tree with red berries. Girls use the name in almost equal numbers as boys, which may make it a less appealing choice for boys. But the variation Rohan looks more masculine to some eyes. The most notable male example of the name is British comedian Rowan Atkinson, of *Mr. Bean* fame.

Variation: *Rohan*
Alternatives: *Rogan, Jasper, Owen, Ash*

Roy is one of several "red" names of Gaelic origins, this one from Scotland. It also exists as a nickname for Leroy, which means "the king" in French. Roy has a Wild West feel to it, thanks to cowboy entertainer Roy Rogers and rockabilly musician Roy Orbison, and just a wild feel to it when you consider the outlaw hero of Scotland, Rob Roy.

Variation: *Royce*
Alternatives: *Elroy, Brice, Red*

Ruben A consistently popular—but never *too* popular—name, Ruben is resistant to trends. The biblical Ruben ("a son") was born to Jacob and Leah and was ultimately cursed by his father. The name was a Jewish favorite as Reuben. Ruben is the Spanish spelling. The most famous Reuben is the corned-beef sandwich, which may make some parents lose their appetite for the name.

Variation: *Reuben*
Nicknames: *Rue, Rube*
Alternatives: *Manuel, Noah, Abel*

Rudy Why name him stodgy Rudolph when you can cut to the chase and name him Rudy? That was the sentiment of many pioneering parents in the late 1800s. Now Rudolph is all but gone, but Rudy remains. Since Rudolph means "wolf," you can consider Rudy a "little wolf." While most Americans aren't using Rudolph anymore, Rodolfo is still prevalent in Hispanic American families.

Variation: *Rudolph*
Alternatives: *Roddy, Bruce, Colby, Randy, Truman*

Russell ("red") was a very trendy choice around the turn of the twentieth century, and up until the 1980s when it really started to wane. Could the sound of "rustling" in there have helped keep it alive during the 1950s while America's fascination with the Old West was running high? Maybe. Versatile Russell can easily wear a pinstripe suit or a ten-gallon hat. You might want to call him Rusty in the latter case. Inspirations include philosopher Bertrand Russell, journalist Russell Baker, actor Russell Crowe, and comedian Russell Brand.

Nicknames: *Rust, Russ, Rusty*
Alternatives: *Leo, Clifford, Frederick, Bernard*

Ryan In the 1940s, the children of Irish immigrants, nostalgic for their ancestral home, started naming children distinctly Irish names. Ryan was one of the big ones from that era. The name means "king" and was helped in its rise to popularity by handsome actor Ryan O'Neal. O'Neal's star turn in *Love Story* and David Lean's film *Ryan's Daughter*, both released in 1970, sent the name into the top twenty in just a few years. Soap opera *Ryan's Hope* (1975) bolstered its position. Its popularity holds all these years later, and now even girls are using the name, often with variations like Ryanne.

Alternatives: *Kevin, Sean, Eamon, Trevor, Niall*

Ryder This English last name became a first name in 1994, around the time actress Winona Ryder's career was hot. It's only gained favor since then, no doubt helped by actress Kate Hudson's son Ryder Robinson, born in 2004; as well as perhaps a character in the video game *Grand Theft Auto: San Andreas*. The name means "horseman."

Variation: *Rider*
Alternatives: *Randall, Philip, Colt, Marshall*

Ryker sounds like "striker" and carries as much of a sense of dangerous strength as you would expect of a name that evokes an infamously treacherous prison (New York City's Riker's Island). Ryker is a Dutch name meaning "rich and powerful." Captain Riker sat in the cockpit of the Starship *Enterprise* in *Star Trek: The Next Generation*.

Variation: *Riker*
Alternatives: *Atticus, Ryland, Torsten*

A POCKETFUL OF RYE

Ryan became popular in the wake of Ryan O'Neal's rise to stardom, the movie *Ryan's Daughter,* and waves of Irish immigrants who were looking to remember the homeland in their sons' names. Eventually Ryan hit its tipping point and parents grew tired of it, but not of that magical *Ry* beginning. If you like Ryan, you can take the first two letters and tack on a new suffix to make Ryder, Ryker, Rycroft, Rylance, and many others. Bye-bye Jaden, hello Ryden?

S

Sage Sage Stallone, son of Sylvester, starred in *Rocky V* in 1990. The following year parents were naming their baby boys Sage. The name suggests not so much "wisdom" as "western." Sage is up there with Shane and Zane as one of the cowboy standards. Note that it is more often used for girls than boys.

Alternatives: *Shane, Zane, Gage, Chance, Phoenix*

Salvador means "savior" in Spanish, and the name is a reference to Christ. (And it could be a clever way of referring to El Salvador, if one's family is from there.) Surrealist painter Salvador Dalí and Paraguayan soccer player Salvador Cabañas are famous examples of the name. Salvatore is the Italian version, as in shoe designer Salvatore Ferragamo. Savion is an up-and-coming variation inspired by tap dancer Savion Glover.

Variation: *Salvatore*
Nicknames: *Sal, Sally, Sonny*
Alternatives: *Emmanuel, Santos, Messiah, Cristobal*

Samir is a popular name in Muslim countries, from India to the Arab world, and among Muslim families in the United States. It means "evening entertainer" or "conversationalist."

Variation: *Sameer*

Nicknames: *Sam, Sammy*
Alternatives: *Namir ("leopard"), Salim ("whole"),*
Latif ("kind"), Munir ("brilliant")

Samson was the strongman from the Bible who
was sapped of his power by the temptress Delilah.
His tragic story has inspired artists, poets, composers,
and occasionally parents throughout the ages. Despite
Samson's tumultuous tale, the meaning of his name
("sun") is happy.
Variation: *Sampson*
Nicknames: *Sam, Sammy*
Alternatives: *Mason, Sanford, Apollo*

Samuel ("God has heard") is a perennial whose
popularity dims occasionally but always brightens
again. Right now Samuel is flourishing. This old-
fashioned name was considered stodgy in the 1960s,
but we love it now for its biblical tradition (Samuel
was a prophet and judge), its historical precedents
(from literature: Samuel Coleridge, Samuel Beckett,
Samuel Johnson), and its humble, happy-go-lucky
nickname, Sam.
Nicknames: *Sam, Sammy*
Alternatives: *Maximillian, Eli, Nathaniel, Benjamin*

Santiago means St. James in Spanish. How did
James become Iago? James comes from Jacob, or

Yacob or Yacov, which became Iacomo or Iaco or Iago in Latin-based languages like Italian and Spanish (in Spanish it ended up as Diego, see page 357). Santiago is the patron saint of Spain and the name of the capital of Chile. The hero of Hemingway's *The Old Man and the Sea* was Santiago, making this an interesting choice for literature lovers and Spanish speakers alike.

Alternatives: *Santos, Diego, Domenico, Emmanuel*

Santos is Spanish for "saints." The name is typically used by Hispanic Catholics. It's a common last name as well as first name. Santino ("little saint") is a nickname or variation, with a lighter, more playful touch.

Variation: *Santino*
Nickname: *Sonny*
Alternatives: *Salvador, Cristobal, Joachim*

Saul ("to ask") was one of the kings of Israel. Saint Paul was called Saul before he converted from Judaism to Christianity. The name has been used by Jewish families with consistency throughout the years. Saul is not a trendy choice, perhaps because of its great heft. The name sounds weighty and serious, qualities not in fashion now. Author Saul Bellow is one of the most famous users of the name. Note that some other bearers of the name are actually not Saul but Sol, short for Solomon, which sounds exactly the same.

Alternatives: *Moses, Solomon, Ruben, Noah*

✐ **Sawyer** In the top 1,000 since 1991, Sawyer is an occupational nickname for someone who saws wood. The rustic quality of the name is bolstered by Mark Twain's creation, Tom Sawyer, whose misadventures on the Mississippi with Huck Finn have become a symbol of carefree childhood. Sawyer is an excellent alternative to overused occupational names like Tanner.

Alternatives: *Archer, Fletcher, Tucker, Turner*

Scott Great Scott! The name that means—can you guess?—"Scottish" soared to popularity in the 1960s and then settled back down. The name is amiable, thanks to its familiarity, and decisive, thanks to its brevity. Distinguished Scotts include writers Sir Walter Scott and F. Scott Fitzgerald. "Beam me up, Scotty!" is a catchphrase from *Star Trek*, something Captain Kirk would say to engineer Montgomery Scott. The downward trend of the name can be a blessing for those who like it. It's particularly useful for long and complicated last names.

Alternatives: *Todd, Mark, Pierce, Rhys, Robert*

Seamus Irish poet Seamus Heany was awarded the Nobel Prize in Literature in 1995, the same year his first name started being used widely in the United States. Seamus is the Irish form of James (pages 409–410). (The similar Hamish is the Scottish form.)

The Boys of the Bard

Shakespeare is a go-to guy for many creative questions, and names are no exception. For distinction, poetry, and literary cred, try a name from the Bard's varied cast of characters.

- **BALTHASAR** *(a name that recurs in at least four plays)*

- **BENEDICK** (Much Ado About Nothing)

- **BERTRAM** (All's Well That Ends Well)

- **CLAUDIO** *(Measure for Measure and* Much Ado About Nothing)

- **DUNCAN** (Macbeth)

- **FERDINAND** (The Tempest)

- **FORD** (The Merry Wives of Windsor)

- **JACQUES** *(pronounced JAY-kwees in* As You Like It)

- **JULIUS** (Julius Caesar)

- **LORENZO** (The Merchant of Venice)

- **LYSANDER** (A Midsummer Night's Dream)

- **ORLANDO** (As You Like It)

- **SAMPSON** (Romeo and Juliet)

- **SEBASTIAN** *(Twelfth Night, as a good guy; and* The Tempest, *as not such a good guy)*

Variations: *James, Hamish*
Alternatives: *Declan, Finbar, Sullivan*

Sean is John to the Irish. Sean was imported to America in the 1940s in the same case as Kevin and Ryan. James Bond actor Sean Connery boosted the profile of the name and Sean Penn keeps it fresh in our minds, as does music impresario Sean Combs (aka P. Diddy). Sean has also been used as a jumping-off point for more creative mash-ups like Keshawn and Deshawn.

Variations: *Shawn, Shaun, Keshawn*
Alternatives: *Shane, Owen, Seamus, Ryan*

Sebastian You can easily recognize Saint Sebastian in an art museum: He's the guy shot through with many arrows and looking gloomy. He quickly became a patron saint of soldiers. Johann Sebastian Bach leaps to mind, as do Viola's twin brother in *Twelfth Night* and the fey playboy in *Brideshead Revisited*, Sebastian Flyte. This is an ornate but masculine name with history and meaning ("august"). It's already on the rise; look for more Sebastians soon.

Variation: *Sebastien*
Nicknames: *Seb, Sebby*
Alternatives: *Orion, Bartholomew, Thaddeus, Archibald, Nicholas*

Sergio, an Italian and Spanish name, means "servant." Musician Sergio Mendes leaps to mind as does spaghetti western director Sergio Leone. In foreign forms, we have French singer Serge Gainsbourg and Russian composer Sergei Prokofiev. There were several popes named Sergius—which is a much more serious variation.

Variations: *Serge, Sergei*
Nickname: *Serge*
Alternatives: *Fabrizio, Giorgio, Giancarlo*

Seth was the third son of Adam, whom Eve said had been appointed to take Abel's place; the name means "appointed." It is used mostly by Jewish families and has become quite popular since the 1970s. Famous Seths include actors Seth Green and Seth Rogan, TV writer Seth MacFarlane, and one of the werewolves in the *Twilight* franchise.

Alternatives: *Noah, Jesse, Boaz*

Shane is the pronounciation of Sean in some parts of Ireland. Eventually, the spelling changed to match the sound. Shane still has an Irish vibe (think of Shane MacGowan from The Pogues), but the rollicking western one endures thanks to the book and movie *Shane*, which prompted parents of the 1950s to start choosing the name for their boys. British actor Ian McShane brought Shane's two sides together when he starred in the western series *Deadwood*.

Variations: *Sean, John*
Alternatives: *Dane, Emmett, Pierce, Logan*

Sheldon is an English place-name that sounds like an old Jewish man—because it usually is. Like Sidney and Milton and other monikers with English roots, Sheldon is a name that was enthusiastically taken up by Jewish immigrants in the New World looking to assimilate. Sheldon brings to mind pulp novelist Sidney Sheldon and artist and poet Shel Silverstein.

Nicknames: *Shel, Shelly*
Alternatives: *Elton, Milton, Madden, Landon*

Sidney Once Sidney was a tony English last name
(English majors will remember Sir Philip Sidney),
then it was a first name, then it was a first name for
American Jewish men looking to assimilate, and now
it is more likely to be a girl's name (see page 252).
Writer Sidney Sheldon, director Sidney Lumet, and
actor Sidney Poitier are famous male bearers of
the name.
Variation: *Sydney*
Nicknames: *Sid, Syd*
Alternatives: *Milton, Irving, Morris*

Silas is a Puritan favorite that is so dated and dust-
covered it's becoming all the rage. It's a pastoral name,
coming from *Silvanus,* which means "of the woods"
in Latin. Silas was a friend of St. Paul's in the New
Testament. George Eliot's novel *Silas Marner* leaps
instantly to mind, as does the albino killer in Dan
Brown's *The Da Vinci Code.*
Nickname: *Sy*
Alternatives: *Titus, Paul, Timothy, Peter*

Simon ("to hear") is a New Testament name—two
of Christ's apostles were Simon—that sounds of the
old English country manor born. Famous Simons

include Duran Duran frontman Simon Le Bon, actors
Simon Baker and Simon Callow, and Venezuelan
revolutionary Simón Bolívar.

Variation: *Simeon*
Alternatives: *Rupert, Gideon, Nigel, Peter*

Sincere It's usually girls who end up with quality
names: Prudence, Hope, Faith, and so on. Sincere is
a rare example of a virtue name being used for boys.
It is one of the few male virtue names in use today,
and it is most popular in the African American
community.

Nickame: *Sin*
Alternatives: *Ernest, Cyrus, Virgil*

Skyler, which looks like Tyler, is more likely to be
a boy; but Skylar, which looks like skylark, is more
often a girl. Both names have an old New York quality
to them, originating as they do from the Dutch last
name Schuyler ("scholar"). Schuyler Colfax was vice
president under Ulysses Grant.

Variation: *Skylar*
Nickname: *Skye*
Alternatives: *Brock, Claus, Hanson, Rutger, Felix*

📖 **Solomon** ("peace") is serious and substantial.
This Old Testament heavy hitter evokes justice
("the judgment of Solomon"), wisdom, leadership,

and power (Solomon's long reign brought great wealth to Israel). And it sounds like "solemn." Solomon was a son of David, king of Israel, and author of the biblical book of Proverbs, Ecclesiastes, and the Song of Solomon. A big mantle for your little guy, but one that is infinitely dignified and meaningful.

Variations: *Shlomo, Shalom, Sulayman*
Nicknames: *Sol, Solly*
Alternatives: *Moses, Saul, David, Nathan*

Sonny An all-purpose nickname meaning "son," Sonny calls to mind singer and politician Sonny Bono, saxophonist Sonny Rollins, and rockabilly star Sonny Burgess, as well as Sonny Crockett, Don Johnson's character in the TV series *Miami Vice*. The name can be a bit too sweet and may work better as a nickname. In fact, in every example given here, the men have "real" first names. They are, respectively, Salvatore, Theodore, Albert, and James. Consider choosing a more formal name and using Sonny as a nickname.

Alternatives: *Buddy, Skip, Sport, Junior*

Soren This Danish name is suddenly making its way into American hearts. Is it related to Thor, Norse god of thunder? Is it related to the Latin *severus*? Nobody knows. Philosopher Søren Kierkegaard, former MTV VJ Tabitha Soren, child actor Soren Fulton, and golfer Søren Hansen all use the name. The name almost sounds like it starts with a *Z*, giving it some exotic letter appeal.

Alternatives: *Axel, Christer, Dag, Gustav, Erik*

Spencer is a noble English name made world famous by Diana Spencer, Prince Charles's first wife. Venerable actor Spencer Tracy perpetuated the name's classy, formal-sounding charm. The name has a preppy edge, especially when you consider the nickname Spence, which is the name of a tony private school in New York City. Despite its fancy sound, Spencer is an occupational name that comes from the word "dispenser."

Variation: *Spenser*
Nickname: *Spence*
Alternatives: *Randall, Windsor, Emerson, Elliot*

✐ **Stanley** Colorful meaning: "field of stones." Fashionable sounds, like Finley, Bailey, Riley. Masculine through and through. So why does Stanley seem so nerdy? Stanley was Blanche DuBois's aggressive lug of a brother-in-law in *A Streetcar Named Desire*, played by Marlon Brando. The Stanley Cup is the big hockey trophy. Stanley is a major power-tool manufacturer. Director Stanley Kubrick. Actor Stanley Tucci. There is no good reason why Stanley should be slumping. Stan could become the man.

Nicknames: *Stan, Lee*
Alternatives: *Ernest, Eugene, Bradley, Martin*

✏ **Stephen** means "crown." Saint Stephen was the first saint, thus an important figure in Christianity. Stephen is the patron saint of Hungary, where many kings were given the name. Other famous Stephens include writer Stephen King, actor Steve McQueen, computer guru Steve Jobs, physicist Steven Hawking, and comedian Stephen Colbert. The name is going through an unfashionable phase right now, making it a smart choice for families who want tradition without overpopularity.

Variations: *Steven, Stephanos, Steffan, Stephane, Esteban*
Nicknames: *Steve, Stevie, Steph*
Alternatives: *Joseph, Richard, Thomas, Crispin*

Sterling sits on the board of directors. He donates to high-profile charities. He wears cufflinks. Sterling means "little star" but is associated more with money (sterling is the currency in the U.K.), and silver (which is how the currency got its name). Football players Sterling Hitchcock and Sterling Sharpe use the name.

Variation: *Stirling*
Alternatives: *Augustus, Felix, Hayden, Jasper*

Sullivan Sully! Sullivan is a classic Irish last name and lately a first name, too. Why not? It's easy to spell, easy to say, familiar but unusual as a first name. And it isn't being used by girls (yet). Sullivan sounds distinguished and formal. He could be a lawyer or

Earth, Wind, and Fire (and Water)

Parents have always been attracted to names that come from nature. There is nothing like having a baby to make you feel at one with the cycle of life. While some nature names feel a little too Age of Aquarius, others have become downright mainstream. Here are some favorite, and uncommon, picks.

- ~ **EARTH:** Cliff, Dell, Forest, Heath, Leaf, Moss, Rock, Stone, Vale

- ~ **WIND:** Cirrus, Gale, Zephyr

- ~ **FIRE:** Ash, Blaze, Ember, Flint

- ~ **WATER:** Ford, Lake, Marin, Nile, Ocean, Rain, Rio, River, Wade

a banker. But Sully is the guy who'll play stickball with you. Sully will bring the keg. Sully is a rollicking nickname.

Nicknames: *Sully, Ivan, Van*
Alternatives: *Murphy, Walsh, Gallagher, Doyle, Mac*

Talan Parents fell in love with this name in 2005, after an actor named Talan Torriero appeared on the MTV reality series *Laguna Beach*. Talon with an O has been in use even longer—it is the word for a raptor's claw.

Variation: *Talon*
Nickname: *Tal*
Alternatives: *Alan, Damon, Buck, Hawk*

Tanner is a Hollywood success story. This occupational last name—a tanner is a leatherworker—became an American first name upon the success of the 1976 movie *The Bad News Bears*, which featured a character with the name. Further bolstering the name are baseball manager Chuck Tanner and the fictional Tanner family on the syndicated sitcom *Full House*. The name has gotten very popular in a relatively short time, which makes it a trendy choice that risks becoming low rent in a decade or so.

Alternatives: *Turner, Porter, Fletcher*

Tate Roy Tate was a character played by Lee Majors on TV's *The Virginian* in 1970. In 1971 Tate hit the top 1,000 for the first time. It stayed there a few years, and then dropped off. Then Jodie Foster's movie *Little Man Tate* appeared in 1991, and Tate reappeared on the list. Tate has an upscale feel to it—think of the Tate Gallery in London. The name means "delight" in Gaelic, and it has a chirpy, upbeat sound. It does for boys what Kate does for girls.

Nicknames: *Taye, Tater*
Alternatives: *Tad, Trey, Scott, Bates, Wade*

Taylor was a typical boy's name for decades, coming from the occupational name for a cloth worker. That all changed in the 1980s when the girls fell in love with it. It became one of the fastest rising girl's names ever, zipping from oblivion to top ten in less than fifteen years. It's no longer an ideal choice for boys without a compelling reason like a family connection. (Check pages 316–317 for a list of other occupational names that might suit.)

Nicknames: *Tate, Taye*
Alternatives: *Turner, Porter, Carter, Saylor*

Teagan is a variation on the Irish word for "poet." The name is of a kind with similar Irish last names like Reagan, Keegan, and Deegan. The girls are using it at twice the rate as the boys (sounds like Meegan), so look for it to quickly fade from the boys' column and move firmly to the girls'.

Alternatives: *Donal, Sullivan, Murphy, Gallagher, Walsh*

Terrell is an Irish last name that may be related to the French verb "to pull," suggesting someone as stubborn as a mule tugging against his reins. In the United States, the name is most popular with African Americans. There are several famous athletes with the name, including football player Terrell Owens.

Variation: *Tyrell*
Alternatives: *Merrill, Darrell, Daniel*

Terrence originally comes from an old Roman name; it rode the same wave that helped revive Terry (page 516). Some parents decided they'd like a more formal version of Terry, so they worked backward to Terrence. Famous Terrences include English actor Terence Stamp, playwright Terence McNally, and singer Terence Trent D'Arby. Terrence is a common choice in the African American community, perhaps as a more traditional alternative to Terrell (see page 515).

Variations: *Terrance, Terence*
Nickname: *Terry*
Alternatives: *Lawrence, Trevor, Cassius, Titus*

Terry is a relative of Theodore that means "ruler of the people." The French version, Thierry, is quite popular abroad (actor Thierry L'Hermitte is well known to francophones). Here we think of football player and commentator Terry Bradshaw, film director Terry Gilliam, and fantasy writers Terry Brooks and Terry Pratchett. Terry may be slumping in the United States because it is a squarely unisex name. Actresses Teri Garr and Teri Hatcher leap as easily to mind as these men do.

Alternatives: *Theo, Tad, Jerry, Barry*

✐ **Thaddeus** was one of Christ's apostles in the Bible. His name is closely related to Theodore, also meaning "gift of God." The name is also related to Jude (the apostle was sometimes called Jude Thaddeus) and Bartholomew (both are patrons of the Armenian church). Thaddeus is not well known, making it a smart choice for parents who want to be different but not outlandish. Nicknames are darling and preppy: Tad and Taddy. You can even call him your little Tadpole for a while.

Nicknames: *Tad, Taddy, Tadpole*
Alternatives: *Theodore, Jude, Bartholomew*

✐ **Theodore** is "God's gift." A lovely sentiment for a name that is old fashioned in all the right ways. Think of how fitting Theo is alongside his girlfriends, the Abigails, Lucys, Emmas, and Charlottes of the world. And among well-educated parents, it's a favorite; the name feels very upper-crust. Theodore Roosevelt boosted the name and gave the world the teddy bear, which was named in his honor.

Variations: *Feodor, Fyodor (both Russian)*
Nicknames: *Theo, Teo, Ted, Teddy*
Alternatives: *Thaddeus, Nathaniel, Bartholomew, Edmund*

✐ **Thomas** was Christ's apostle who did not believe in the resurrection until he put his finger in Christ's wounds. Hence the expression "doubting Thomas." Curiously, the name means "twin." Thomas has historically been in the top ten most popular names for boys. In the 1960s, it started a very slow decline. Famous Thomases throughout history include religious figures Thomas à Becket and Thomas More; president Thomas Jefferson; inventor Thomas Edison;

Old Names, New Testament

Some of the names of the New Testament are still among the most familiar to us today: Think of Jesus's apostles like Matthew, Mark, Luke, and John. But the good book is full of other more unexpected picks. See if any of them works for your guy.

- **ANANIAS** (Hebrew via Greek, "Yahweh is gracious")

- **AQUILA** (Latin, "eagle")

- **BARNABAS** (Aramaic, "son of consolation")

- **BARTHOLOMEW** (Aramaic via Greek, "son of Talmai." The name of an apostle who was also known as Nathaniel. The nickname "Bart," is now inextricably linked with The Simpsons.)

- **CORNELIUS** (Latin, "horn")

- **FELIX** (Latin, "lucky," "successful")

- **FESTUS** (Latin, "festival," "holiday")

- **GAIUS** (Latin, possibly "rejoice")

- **JESUS** (Aramaic via Greek, form of Joshua, "Yahweh is salvation." Risk: giving your kid a Christ complex.)

newsman Tom Brokaw; actors Tom Hanks, Tom Cruise, and Tommy Lee Jones; football player Tom Brady; singer Tom Jones; big-band leader Tommy Dorsey; fashion designers Tom Ford and Tommy Hilfiger; writers Tom Clancy, Tom Wolfe, and Thomas Pynchon; poet T. S. Eliot. Don't doubt the strength of this name for a minute.

Variations: *Tomas, Thompson*
Nicknames: *Tom, Tommy, Thom*
Alternatives: *Richard, Simon, Paul, Silas*

~ **JUDAS** (Hebrew, "praised." Not a popular choice; if you like the sound of the name, consider Jude or Judah.)

~ **LAZARUS** (Greek via the Hebrew name Eleazar, "my God has helped")

~ **LINUS** (Greek, "flax")

~ **MATTHIAS** (Greek via Hebrew, variant of Matthew, "gift of Yahweh")

~ **NATHANIEL** (Hebrew, "God has given")

~ **PHILEMON** (Greek, "affectionate" or "loving," patron saint of hatters and pastry chefs)

~ **RUFUS** (Latin, "red-haired")

~ **SILAS/SILVANUS** (Latin, "wood," "forest")

~ **SIMEON/SIMON** (Hebrew, "he has heard")

~ **TERTULLUS** (Latin, "third")

~ **THADDEUS** (Greek via Aramaic, possibly meaning "heart")

~ **THEOPHILUS** (Greek, "friend of God"; it is the same name as the Latin Amadeus, or "lover of God")

~ **TIMOTHY** (Greek, "honoring God")

~ **TITUS** (Latin, unknown)

~ **ZACHARIAS** (Greek form of the Hebrew Zecheriah, "the Lord remembers")

Tiburon means "shark" in Spanish. If you live in California, you already know this name because the state boasts one town and many streets with the name. As a boy's name, it suggests sleekness, strength, and stealth, as well as a love of the water. He might grow up to be a surfer dude, or he could become a shark in the boardroom.

Nicknames: *Tib, Tibby*
Alternatives: *Oberon, Balthazar, Sebastian, Griffin, Hawk*

✒ **Timothy** ("honoring God") was a companion of St. Paul. Although the name is a traditional, familiar biblical one, it is not as popular now as it might be. Famous Timothys include James Bond actor Timothy Dalton, comedic actor Tim Allen, director Tim Burton, country singer Tim McGraw, and Charles Dickens's iconic character Tiny Tim. Why the hesitation to choose Timothy? Is it the soft sound of the *th*? Does it sound too similar to some girls' names like Tiffany and Brittany? Timothy deserves another look, alongside names like Nathaniel (whose *th* bothers nobody) and Samuel (Tim is an excellent alternative to the nearly ubiquitous Sam).

Nicknames: *Tim, Timmy*
Alternatives: *Theodore, Matthew, Ethan, Nathaniel*

Titus is an old Roman name experiencing a revival. Comedian Christopher Titus, who had a sitcom called *Titus* in 2000, boosted the name considerably, and it's more popular in America than ever before. The name sounds regal and imposing, and rightly so: Noteworthy Tituses include Shakespeare's *Titus Andronicus*; the friend of St. Paul who appears in the Bible (and is believed by some to be the same man as Timothy); and Roman emperor Titus whose triumphal arch still stands in Rome. The name's similarity to the word "titan" doesn't hurt.

Alternatives: *Silas, Cassius, Micah*

✐ **Tobias** was rediscovered in the 1960s. It's an Old Testament name meaning "God is good." Tobias enjoyed the protection and blessings of the angel Raphael. The name has a cool Puritan air, one that's warmed considerably by the playful nickname Toby. Author Tobias Wolff and actor Tobey Maguire are both named Tobias. Sir Toby was a Shakespearean clown in *Twelfth Night,* and Toby was the hangdog communications director on *The West Wing.*

Variations: *Toby, Tobey, Tobit*
Nicknames: *Toby, Tobey*
Alternatives: *Silas, Tobin, Barton, Elias*

✐ **Todd** is on a rollercoaster. The name was unusual until the 1930s, then it zipped to the top thirty in the 1960s, and now it is on the verge of disappearing again. Although it doesn't have the weight of the Bible or ancient history behind it, it has a sassy meaning from the English—"fox," suggesting cunning and cleverness—and is a popular last name. Todd sounds more serious than, say, Ty, and more substantial than one-syllable Hollywood darling Kai. There isn't even a huge raft of incredibly famous users of the name, making this an even more appealing choice.

Alternatives: *Scott, Tad, Trent, Brett*

Tony The nickname for Anthony (page 294) is also used as a name itself. Tony used to seem very Italian

American (Tony was the hero of *West Side Story* and the don of TV's Soprano clan), but now he's every guy. As a vocabulary word, *tony* means "rich" or "fancy." Famous Tonys that leap to mind include former British prime minister Tony Blair, inspirational speaker Tony Robbins, actor Tony Curtis, singer Tony Bennett, and cereal mascot Tony the Tiger. Of those, only Tony the Tiger and Tony Curtis (né Bernard Schwartz) are not really "Anthony."

Variations: *Anthony, Antony, Antonio*
Alternatives: *Gary, Rudy, Andy, Mario*

Trace is similar to Trey. While Trey is how "three" is pronounced in Italian (*tre*), Trace is "three" (*tres*) in Spanish. So many Traces that we know—for example, football player Trace Armstrong—are actually just using the name as a nickname and are themselves "thirds" (Trace Armstrong is really Raymond Armstrong III). The name can also be the male version of Tracy.

Variation: *Trey*
Nicknames: *Tray, Trey*
Alternatives: *Troy, Trip, Ray*

Travis comes from "to cross" (think *traverse*) in Old French and was used by toll collectors. The name has a country-western twang to it thanks to Travis Tritt and a hint of danger thanks to *Taxi Driver*'s deranged character Travis Bickle.

Nickname: *Trav*
Alternatives: *Virgil, Amos, Cyrus*

Trent is a last name that comes from a river in England. The name of the river is probably related to the word *traverse* and is closely related to the place-name Trenton ("Trent's town"). Trent Lott, the conservative senator; golfer Robert Trent Jones; and musicians Trent Reznor and Terence Trent D'Arby leap to mind. Trenton is now more popular than Trent; some parents like the more formal sound of it and keep Trent as the nickname.

Variation: *Trenton*
Alternatives: *Benson, Wren, Kent*

Trevor is a Welsh last name meaning "large town" that has become a first name thanks to English actor Trevor Howard. His success sparked an interest in the

ONE-SIZE NICKNAME FITS ALL

Some nicknames clearly go with longer proper names: Sam comes from Samuel, Mike from Michael, Joe from Joseph. But you don't have to have a nickname that matches perfectly. These classics work for just about any name: Ace, Bubba, Buddy, Buster, Chip, Digger, Jock, Junior, Scooter, Skip, Sport, Trey, Tripp, Tucker.

name in the 1950s that has continued. Stage director Trevor Nunn, baseball player Trevor Hoffman, and basketball player Trevor Ariza all use the name. Hybrid variations like Trevin and Trevon are contemporary creations.

Variations: *Trevin, Trevon*
Nickname: *Trey*
Alternatives: *Ryder, Devon, Mason, Ever, Igor*

Trey is a nickname for a boy who is "the third." Example: William Henry Gates III can be called Trey (and sometimes Bill Gates is). The word comes from the Latin word for "three." One of Will Smith's sons uses it. It was the name of Kyle McLachlan's character on *Sex and the City*. Trey Parker is one of the cocreators of *South Park*, and Trey Anastasio, a member of the jam band Phish. Trey suggests a family legacy right up front—you don't have to wait for "the third" to get that he's one in a long and possibly storied line.

Variation: *Trace*
Alternatives: *Troy, Ray, Kai*

Tristan is the title hero of the Celtic medieval legend of Tristan and Isolde. Tristan was meant to escort princess Isolde to her wedding. Instead, he falls in love with her and she with him, and eventually they die as a result of their tragic love. The name became popular in the United States thanks in large part because of handsome soap opera actor Tristan Rogers, who played Robert Scorpio on *General Hospital* in the early 1980s. The name is chosen for the romantic but still manly sound, and is often an alternative to the less subtle Christian.

Variations: *Tristen, Tristian, Tristin, Triston, Trystan*
Nickname: *Tris*
Alternatives: *Merlin, Albion, Carlyle, Arthur, Galahad*

Troy "As for you, Troy Donahue . . ." you made this name hot. The 1950s teen screen idol caused Troy to pop to the top one hundred for a few decades. NFL athletes Troy Brown and Troy Aikman use the name. And look for this generation of teens to remember it fondly in a few years: it's the name of Zac Efron's character in *High School Musical*. Historically, Troy is the famous city in modern Turkey that was attacked by the Greeks, as recorded by Homer. A Trojan, as a citizen of Troy was called, is someone who is enduring and stalwart.

Alternatives: *Homer, Roy, Sawyer, Darius*

Tucker is an occupational name for a garment worker. A tucker is the same thing as a fuller, someone who removed the oils of wool fibers. Tucker has a patrician sound but with more froth than some others. There is a playfulness to the word that leavens it. Robin Hood's Friar Tuck leaps to mind, as do conservative pundit Tucker Carlson, guys-guy writer Tucker Max, and automobile entrepreneur Preston Tucker.

Nickname: *Tuck*
Alternatives: *Buckley, Huck, Fuller*

Ty Traditionally Ty is a nickname for Tyrus (as in the case of baseball player Ty Cobb), Tyrone (as for actor Tyrone Power), or other *Ty-* names (football player Ty Law is Tajuan; *Extreme Home Makeover* personality Ty Pennington is Tygert). However, some parents prefer the short version and use it as a name in its own right. One thing you can say for Ty: There are no nicknames.

Alternatives: *Kai, Ryland, Trey*

Tyler An occupational name—Tyler was the guy working with tiles—that became enormously popular, especially in the 1990s. Trendy Tyler is now starting its decline. Famous Tylers include film producer-actor-director Tyler Perry and TV chef Tyler Florence.

Nickname: *Ty*
Alternatives: *Taylor, Saylor, Sawyer, Thatcher*

Tyrone became popular in the 1940s, following the fame of the actor Tyrone Power. It has roots in Northern Ireland, but in recent decades it has taken on a much more American flavor; it is especially popular with African Americans. Notable bearers of

From the Halls of Valhalla

For families of Scandinavian origin and/or those who seek offbeat names with a whiff of mystery to them, Norse mythology offers some surprising and inspiring options.

- **ASBRU:** *the rainbow bridge that leads to Valhalla*

- **BALDUR:** *god of light, beauty, love, and happiness; his death is a sure sign that the end of the world is near*

- **EARENDEL:** *hero and adventurer whose frozen toes were flung into the heavens to become stars*

- **FENRIR:** *a fierce wolf monster that will join the giants in their battle against the gods during Ragnarök (the apocalypse). Also seen as Fenris*

- **FORSETI:** *the god of justice*

- **HEIMDALL:** *the watchmen of the gods who guards the gateway to Valhalla*

- **LOKI:** *a trickster god of deception and fire who causes all sorts of mischief*

- **ODIN:** *the chief god of the Norse pantheon and ruler of Asgard. Odin is associated with war, but also with magic and poetry.*

- **THOR:** *the god of lightning and thunder whose hammer, Mjöllnir, became a symbol of defiance during the Christianization of Scandinavia; his day is the fifth of each week*

- **TYR:** *Odin's right-hand man and onetime owner of the wolf Fenrir, which bit off Tyr's left hand*

the name include football players Tyrone Carter and Tyrone Wheatley.

Nickname: *Ty*
Alternatives: *Orlando, Ronald, Ronan, Titus*

Tyson The original meaning of Tyson—someone
with a temper—aligns perfectly with its strongest
association: feisty boxer Mike Tyson. Tyson Beckford,
a top male model, gives the name allure, but take note:
The name also conjures the meat-processing megalith
Tyson Foods.

Variation: *Kyson*
Nickname: *Ty*
Alternatives: *Leonard, Clay, Rocco, Robinson*

Ulysses Hero, adventurer, wanderer. Ulysses was
the star of Homer's *Odyssey*. He encountered terrible
travails on his ten-year journey home to Ithaca from
the Trojan War, but finally arrived safely to find his
patient wife and grown son still waiting. *Ulysses* is also
the title of James Joyce's masterpiece about a day in the
life of Dubliner Leopold Bloom. Ulysses S. Grant was
the United States president during the Civil War. Ulises
is the version most often used by Hispanic families.

Variations: *Ulises, Odysseus*
Alternatives: *Homer, Virgid, Aeneas, Ajax*

Uriah No English major would choose this name; it
calls to mind Charles Dickens's calculating liar Uriah
Heep from *David Copperfield*. (Fans of heavy metal
music may feel otherwise, remembering Uriah Heep,

a band from the 1970s.) The biblical Uriah was cuckolded when King David seduced his wife Bathsheba. Perhaps the related name Uriel ("angel of light") is the better bet.

Variations: *Urijah, Uriel*
Alternatives: *Elijah, Micah, Ariel*

Valentin In 2006, the New York Mets won the National League Eastern Division title. José Valentin, who had signed with the team the fall before, hit two home runs and three runs, helping the team clinch the title. The next year, the name Valentin popped from the top 900s to the 600s. Valentin means "strength" and "honor" (think valor, value), and, yes, "love." Although St. Valentine may not have originally had anything to do with love, he sure does now, and the name enjoys a glow of warmth because of the association. Valentino sounds even more romantic, thanks to legendary heartthrob Rudolph Valentino and fashion designer Valentino.

Variations: *Valentinus, Valentino*
Nicknames: *Val, Tino*
Alternatives: *Valerio, Cornelius, Augustus, Constantine*

Vance Familiar but distinctive. Your child might be the only Vance in class, but he'll have a name that is easy to spell, easy to pronounce, easy to remember. Once a last name for families living in marshy areas,

Vance has a Hollywood heyday sound to it. The name flashed on the TV screen for many years thanks to *I Love Lucy*'s Vivian Vance. Philo Vance was the name of a gentleman detective in a series of books from the 1920s. And the nickname Van brings to mind 1950s actors Van Johnson and Van Heflin, and singer-songwriter Van Morrison.

Nickname: *Van*
Alternatives: *Vince, Lance, Chance, Chase*

Vaughn is a Welsh last name that means "small." The name calls to mind comic actor Vince Vaughn, musician Stevie Ray Vaughan, and the hockey equipment manufacturer of the same name. It also has a subtly southern air. This name is a unique choice, one that may appeal to parents seeking that elusive Scrabble-letter factor.

Variations: *Vaughan, Von*
Alternatives: *Todd, Paul, Morgan, Rhys*

Victor is a winner—literally. Once the name had a religious cast to it: It referred to Christ's triumph over death. Victors that leap to mind include *Casablanca* hero Victor Laszlo, Italy unifier Vittorio Emmanuel, French author Victor Hugo. The name has never been the most popular on the playground, but it's always reliably there, assertive and positive. It also contains an exotic letter, making it a fashionable yet traditional choice.

Variations: *Vittorio, Viktor*
Nicknames: *Vic, Vick*
Alternatives: *Marcus, Arthur, Oliver, Dixon*

✒ **Vincent**, like Victor, is a winner. The name means
"to conquer." (Think of the aria from *Turandot,*
"Nessun Dorma," whose big finish is "*Vincerò!*"—
"I will win!" in Italian.) The name can have an Italian
American slant to it—*My Cousin Vinny*, anyone?—but
one of the beauties of the name is the variety of forms
and nicknames it offers. You would hardly notice that
actors Vince Vaughn, Vincent D'Onofrio, and Vin
Diesel share the same name (Vincent is Diesel's real
last name). Other famous Vincents include painter
Vincent van Gogh, football legend Vince Lombardi, and
actor Vincent Price.

Variations: *Vincente, Vicente, Vincenzo*
Nicknames: *Vin, Vinny, Vinnie, Enzo, Vince*
Alternatives: *Tristan, Sebastian, Julian, Gavin*

Wade evokes water, and not just because you wade
through it. The word is a derivation of an ancient
mythical sea monster. Former Red Sox player Wade
Boggs is a famous example of the name. This one's
short and simple—no nicknames here.

Alternatives: *Kai, Cliff, Brook, River*

✐ **Walker** A walker was a clothing worker who walked on finished cloth while it was submerged in a tub in order to remove the lanolin and any debris from the wool fibers. Famous Walkers include photographer Walker Evans, authors Walker Percy and Alice Walker, Heisman trophy winner Herschel Walker, and the fictional Texas Ranger played by Chuck Norris, Cordell Walker. Parents may run, not walk, to this one.

Alternatives: *Booker, Fuller, Tucker*

✐ **Walter** Admiral, general, commander: Walter means "ruler of the army," so he was all these things. The name has a distinguished history, especially in England (author Sir Walter Scott), and used to be one of the greats in the United States—in the early 1900s it was in the top fifteen. It's been on a long steady slide toward disuse since then. Most Walters you can think of are old or dead: Walter Cronkite, Walter Matthau, Walt Disney. But things change: Walt and Wally are sweet and unexpected. They could be so far out they come back in.

Nicknames: *Wat, Walt, Wally*
Alternatives: *Albert, Roy, Stanley, Howard*

Warren In 1921, Warren was the way to be. The name is a cousin of Parker, as it refers to French game park La Varenne. And it also means "guard." Lothario

Warren Beatty comes to mind, as do finance guru Warren Buffett and president Warren G. Harding.

Alternatives: *Parker, Darren, Reynolds*

Waylon is a hillbilly with a heart of gold. Waylon Jennings sang the theme song for and narrated *The Dukes of Hazzard* TV show. His good-old-boy shadow looms large over this name.

Nicknames: *Way, Lon, Lonnie*
Alternatives: *Beau, Billy Ray, Lloyd, Duke*

Wayne comes from "wagon" and was a name carters used. The career of steely-willed cowboy actor John Wayne (birth name: Marion Morrison) coincides with the popularity of this name, which peaked in the 1940s and 1950s. Other famous Waynes include lounge singer Wayne Newton, hockey player Wayne Gretzky, rapper Lil Wayne, Bruce Wayne (aka Batman), and Wayne Campbell, the fictional star of *Wayne's World*.

Alternatives: *Duke, Garth, Shane, Carter, Wainwright*

Wesley is a man of God. John Wesley, founder of the Methodist church, popularized this name, which means "western lea." John Wesley Hardin was an Old West outlaw; John Wesley Harding (with a *g*) is an indie folk musician who named himself after a Bob Dylan album; Wesley Snipes and Wes Bentley are actors; Westley is the hero of *The Princess Bride*.

I'll Take Manhattan

If Queens and Staten Island feel too weird to use as names (and they should!), break out of the five-borough mold with one of these unconventional New York City–centric options:

~ **BAXTER** *(Street)*

~ **BLEECKER** *(Street)*

~ **CHARLTON** *(Street)*

~ **CLARKSON** *(Street)*

~ **CLINTON** *(neighborhood)*

~ **DELANCEY** *(Street)*

~ **FULTON** *(Street)*

~ **GRAMERCY** *(Park; with Gram as a cute nickname)*

~ **HUDSON** *(River; Street)*

~ **JACKSON** *(Square)*

~ **SULLIVAN** *(Street)*

~ **WALKER** *(Street)*

~ **WEST** *(Street)*

Many family names ending in a -*lea* sound have been appropriated by girls. Wesley's not one of them.

Variation: *Westley*

Nickname: *Wes*

Alternatives: *Weston, Wells, Presley, Churchill, Goodman*

Weston The opposite of Easton, Weston is the "town toward the west." The name evokes its Old English origins much more than its Old West sound. Kim Weston recorded "It Takes Two" with Marvin Gaye in 1966, around the time boys were being named Weston. Weston is the name of one of Nicolas Cage's

sons and the name of the art photographer Edward
Weston. Fans of Jane Austen's books will remember
Mrs. Weston as Emma's former governess.

Nickname: *Wes*
Alternatives: *Easton, Wesley, Dalton*

✐ **William** If you are looking for a highbrow, classic,
regal-but-not-tacky name, your search is over.
William the Conqueror, William Shakespeare, William
Wordsworth, Bill Clinton, Prince William, Will Smith
. . . the list of great Williams goes on and on. The name
is distinguished (meaning "staunch protector") and
the variations and nicknames are numerous. You can't
go wrong with this superior choice.

Variations: *Wilhelm, Guillaume, Guillermo, Giulemo, Liam*
Nicknames: *Willie, Willy, Will, Wills, Bill, Billy, Liam*
Alternatives: *George, John, Charles, Edward*

Wilson "Son of Will," Wilson is a presidential last
name (Woodrow Wilson was the twenty-eighth
president of the United States). Other famous
Wilsons: the grumpy next-door neighbor in the
comic strip *Dennis the Menace*, Mr. Wilson; musician
Wilson Pickett; and the sporting goods manufacturer
(Tom Hanks calls the volleyball he befriends in the
film *Cast Away* "Wilson" after its brand).

Nicknames: *Will, Wil, Willie, Wills, Sonny*
Alternatives: *Truman, Reagan, Clinton, Willis*

Winston This English last name gained fame as the first name of Britain's most famous prime minister, Winston Churchill. The association with Churchill gives the name gravitas and almost removes the other connections: the cigarette brand; jeweler Harry Winston; and the doomed hero of Orwell's novel *1984*, Winston Smith. Winston means "joyous stone," making a strange connection between Churchill and Gladstone, a prime minister during Queen Victoria's reign.

Nicknames: *Win, Winnie*
Alternatives: *Spencer, Windsor, Easton, William*

Wyatt ("strong warrior") rides a horse and wears a cowboy hat and a shiny silver star. There is no escaping the Wyatt Earp association with this one. The movie starring Kevin Costner about the lawman of the Old West caused the name to soar to the top one hundred; it climbs more each year.

Alternatives: *Hyatt, Vernon, Marshall, Garrett*

Xavier Francis Xavier (Xavier means "new house") was a Basque missionary, founder of the Jesuits, and finally a saint. Latin bandleader Xavier Cugat is the best-known modern Xavier. The name is pronounced ZAY-vee-er or ex-ZAY-vee-er, as opposed to the

Spanish version Javier (see page 413), which is
pronounced HAH-vee-air.

Variations: *Xxavier, Zavier, Javier*
Nicknames: *Zavy, X*
Alternatives: *Joaquin, Savion, Ivan, Phoenix*

Yael A Hebrew name with a twist. Yael (yie-EL) comes
from Jael, which means "ibex" in Hebrew. Change the
Y to a *J* and you end up with something edgier and
with a bit of a Muslim or Spanish flavor. Since Jael is
a woman's name in the Bible's book of Judges (Jael
invited evil Sisera into her tent and then killed him),
maybe the *Y* makes it more masculine in some eyes.

Variation: *Jael*
Alternatives: *Gael, Yale, Abel*

Yahir means "enlightenment" in Hebrew. Yair
(yie-EAR) was the father of Mordecai in the Bible.
Yahir Reyes is a mixed martial arts fighter from
Mexico whose success in the ring may have inspired
American parents to begin using his name. The pop
singer Yahir, who got his start on a Mexican reality TV
show, gave the name a huge bump in 2003. In Israel,
Yair is popular.

Variations: *Yair, Jair*
Alternatives: *Xavier, Joaquin, Jabir*

Yandel is half of the Puerto Rican reggaeton duo Wisin y Yandel. Yandel was born Llandel, but anglicized his name. Since 2005, Latin American parents have been inspired to use his name for their children.

Variation: *Llandel*
Alternatives: *Randell, Wendell, Wisin*

Yusuf is the name Joseph (see page 422) in Arabic. Yusuf is one of the great prophets of Islam, and his story is told in detail in the Koran. The folk singer Cat Stevens changed his name to Yusuf in 1977.

Variations: *Yosef, Youssef, Joseph*
Alternatives: *Ibrahim, Ishaq, Ismail, Yunus*

WE DON'T NEED ANOTHER HERO

In some cultures, babies must be named after a deceased relative. There are a number of reasons why, but here's one that is especially powerful: Heroes sometimes fall from grace. If you name your child after a living person, you could end up being disappointed. That admired business partner may betray your trust, and then you'll never want to hear the person's name again. That celebrity may become embroiled in a nasty scandal that you don't want to be reminded of. Or that beloved ballplayer may (the horror!) defect to the reviled rival team. Note that the more common the name, the less of a concern this is, as there will be other nice people connected to it.

Z

Zachary A biblical superstar, Zachary rocketed from unused in 1945 to number twelve in 1994. The career of suave (forgotten) actor Zachary Scott may have helped. It may also help that the name appeals to all the three major religions, Judaism, Christianity, and Islam. There were several Zacharys in the Bible, notably the father of John the Baptist and a Hebrew prophet. The name means "God remembered." Zack is now the guy next door: Think actors Zac Efron, Zach Galifianakis, Zach Braff, Zachary Levi.

Variations: *Zachery, Zackary, Zachariah, Zack, Zechariah*
Nicknames: *Zack, Zach, Zac*
Alternatives: *Jeremiah, Ezekiel, Malachi*

Zaid An Arabic name meaning "abundance," Zaid is the name of a child Muhammad took under his wing and raised.

Variation: *Zayd*
Alternatives: *Kareem, Jabir, Munir, Imad, Hassan*

Zaire is the African country that used to be known as the Belgian Congo and is now known as the Democratic Republic of Congo. The name Zaire comes from the river Zaire, also known as the Congo River. Naming your child Zaire is a way of communicating an African heritage. This earthy and evocative name

539

is similar to the Arabic name Zahir, which means "helper."

Alternatives: *Zahir, Cairo, Zamir*

Zane has a cowboy twang to it because the name was popularized by pulp western writer Zane Grey. The similarity to Shane only adds to the effect. Zain is a separate Hindu name that means "light."

Variation: *Zayne*
Alternatives: *Dane, Wyatt, Earl, Shane, Zain*

Zayden A frankenname: Take Jaden, Caden, Aidan, Hayden, or Braden and replace the first sound with one that sounds more exotic. This name is a trendy one that will appear dated in a few years. Take it from a Jennifer.

Variation: *Zaiden*
Nickname: *Zay*
Alternatives: *Braden, Caden, Hayden*

Zion This name can sound New Agey at first listen but it has deep, and deeply religious, roots. Zion refers to the biblical Promised Land and Jerusalem. Zionism is a movement that is devoted to protecting Israel as a Jewish state, thus the name has a whiff of activism to it. Although Zionism is largely a Jewish movement, the name is more likely to be used by Christians than Jews.

Alternatives: *Shiloh, Asher, Jericho*

Index of Alternative Names

The following names are not given top billing in the main alphabetical list of names, so they are highlighted here—you will find them mentioned as alternatives and in sidebars throughout the book.

Girls' Names

Boys' Names

C

AN ASSORTMENT
OF NAME INSPIRATIONS

Girls

Boys

Acknowledgments

Thanks to my editor, Kylie "channel of water" Foxx McDonald; my agents at the Miller Literary Agency, Angela "angel" Miller and Sharon "fertile field" Bowers; contributors Garth "gardener" Sundem and Leigh "meadow" Anderson; editorial assistant Liz "promise of God" Davis, production editor Beth "promise of God" Levy, designer Jen "fair lady" Browning, cover designer David "beloved" Matt, publicist Stefanie "crown" Rosenblum, director of publicity Beth "promise of God" Wareham, typesetter Barbara "foreigner" Peragine, and production overseer Robert "famous" Vargas.